Then We Sailed Away

John, Marie Christine and Rebecca Ridgway

Margaret,

You only live Once!

Into the mist...

Rebecca Ridgway —

Elizabeth

Marie Christine Ridgway

LITTLE, BROWN AND COMPANY

A *Little, Brown* Book

First published in Great Britain
by Little, Brown and Company 1996

Copyright © John, Marie Christine
and Rebecca Ridgway 1996

Map by Alec Herzer.
Plans of *English Rose VI* by Arthur Saluz.
'Ardmore' from *Collected Poems* by Norman MacCaig.
Reproduced by permission of the Estate of the author and Chatto & Windus

A CIP catalogue record for this book
is available from the British Library.

ISBN 0 316 87709 3

Typeset in Sabon by M Rules
Printed and bound in Great Britain by
Clays Ltd, St Ives plc

Little, Brown and Company (UK)
Brettenham House
Lancaster Place
London WC2E 7EN

Then
We Sailed
Away

Contents

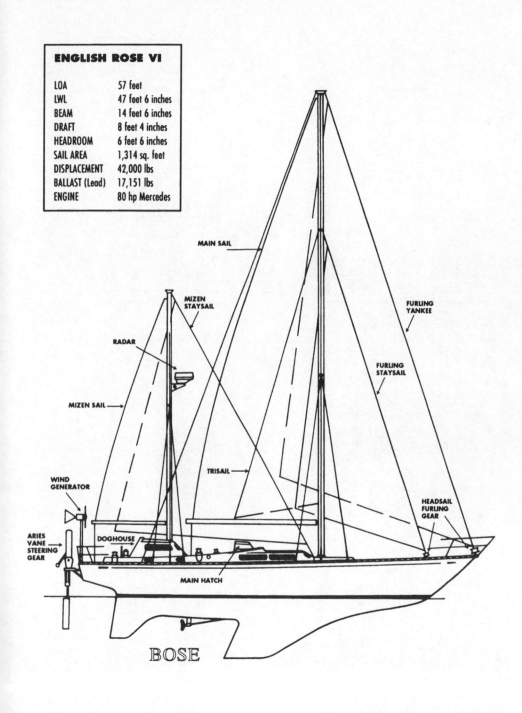

ENGLISH ROSE VI

LOA	57 feet
LWL	47 feet 6 inches
BEAM	14 feet 6 inches
DRAFT	8 feet 4 inches
HEADROOM	6 feet 6 inches
SAIL AREA	1,314 sq. feet
DISPLACEMENT	42,000 lbs
BALLAST (Lead)	17,151 lbs
ENGINE	80 hp Mercedes

MAIN SAIL

MIZEN STAYSAIL

FURLING YANKEE

RADAR

FURLING STAYSAIL

MIZEN SAIL

TRISAIL

WIND GENERATOR

HEADSAIL FURLING GEAR

ARIES VANE STEERING GEAR

DOGHOUSE

MAIN HATCH

BOSE

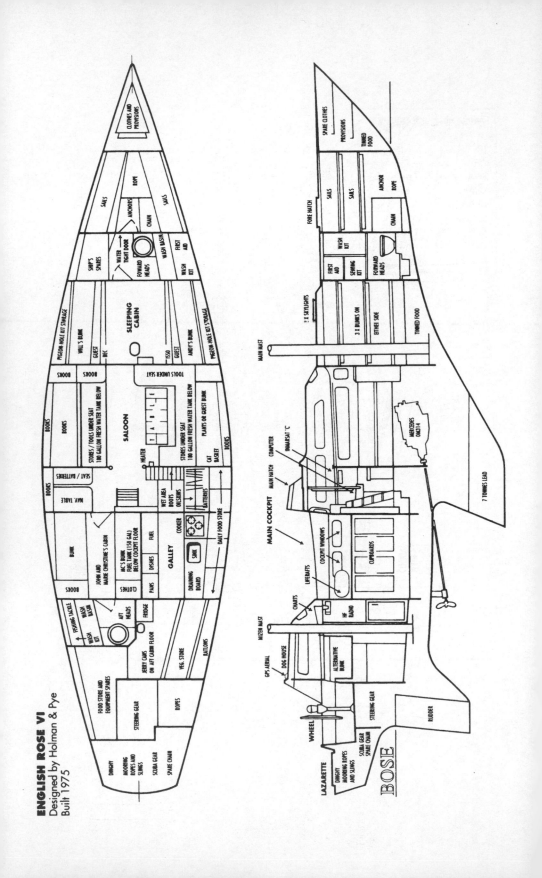

ENGLISH ROSE VI
Designed by Holman & Pye
Built 1975

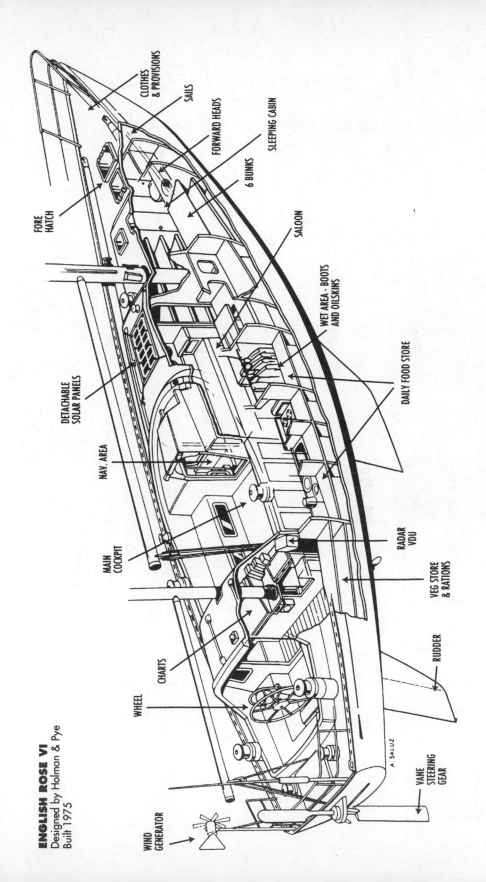

ENGLISH ROSE VI
Designed by Holman & Pye
Built 1975

WIND GENERATOR

WHEEL

CHARTS

MAIN COCKPIT

NAV. AREA

DETACHABLE SOLAR PANELS

FORE HATCH

CLOTHES & PROVISIONS

SAILS

FORWARD HEADS

SLEEPING CABIN

6 BUNKS

SALOON

WET AREA - BOOTS AND OILSKINS

DAILY FOOD STORE

RADAR VDU

VEG STORE & RATIONS

RUDDER

VANE STEERING GEAR

A. SALUZ

Voyage of English Rose VI

4th. October, 1993 – 10th. April, 1995

90°W

45°N –

North Pacific
Ocean

15°N –

Cari

Pana
Can

Perlas
Archipelag

Equator

Galapagos Is.

Santa Cruz I.
Academy Bay, Ayora
29 Jan. – 3 Feb. '94

Marquesas Is.
Hiva Oa
25 Feb. '94

Tuamotu Is.

15°S –

Bora Bora

Raroia Atoll 19 Apr. '94

Society Is.

Tahiti
Papeete, 1 May '94

Gambier Is.
Mangaréva 12 Jun. '94

Raivavaé
3 Jun. '94

Austral Is.

Pitcairn
Passed close by 18 Jun. '94

South Pacific Ocean

135°W

Area not covered by detailed
topographical information

Quillabamba

Chaullay

45°S –

Gulf

Lambras

Lucma

Pucyura

Huancacalle

Machu Picchu

Nueva
Esperanza

Vilcabamba

Chucuito Pass

R. Urubamba

Capiro

R. Toroyunca

Osambre

Choquetira

Huamus Pass

Lucmahuayco

Acobamba

Amaybamba

R. Apurímac

------- John, Marie, Christine & Isso
••••••• Rebecca
–ı–ı–ı– Impassable join-up
••••••• Truck   ←—→ Railway

–N–

0   30
Kilometres

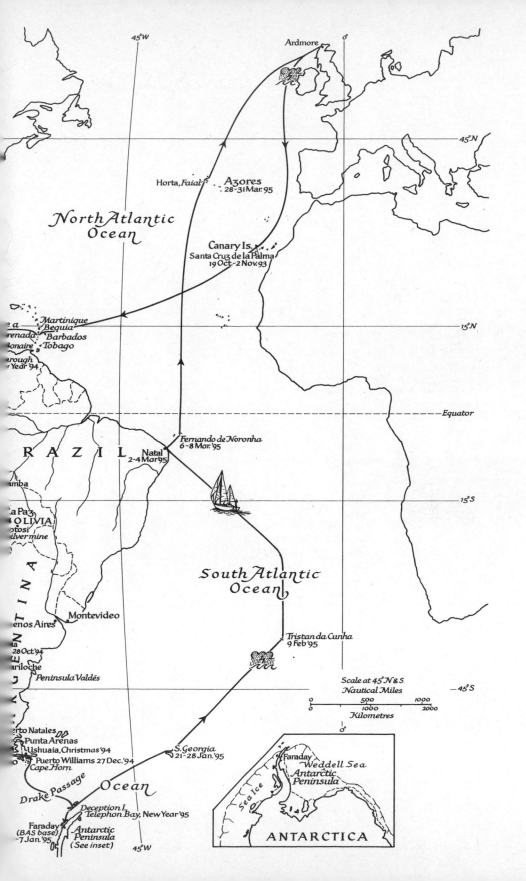

45°W

Ardmore

0°

North Atlantic
Ocean

45°N

Horta, *Faial*
Azores
28-31 Mar. '95

Canary Is.
Santa Cruz de la Palma
19 Oct-2 Nov. 93

15°N

Martinique
Bequia
Barbados
Tobago
Bonaire
enada
rough
Year '94

Equator

RAZIL

Fernando de Noronha
6-8 Mar. '95

Natal
2-4 Mar '95

15°S

mba

a Paz
OLIVIA
otosi
ilver mine

South Atlantic
Ocean

TINA

Montevideo

enos Aires

Tristan da Cunha
9 Feb '95

28 Oct'94

riloche

Peninsula Valdés

45°S

Scale at 45°N & S
Nautical Miles

0   500   1000
0   1000   2000
Kilometres

o Natales
Punta Arenas
Ushuaia, Christmas '94
Puerto Williams 27 Dec. '94
Cape Horn

S. Georgia
21-28 Jan. '95

0°

Faraday
Weddell Sea
Antarctic
Peninsula

Drake Passage

Ocean

Sea Ice

Deception I.
Telephon Bay, New Year '95

Faraday
(BAS base)
-7 Jan. '95

Antarctic
Peninsula
(See inset)

45°W

ANTARCTICA

'Strange suggestions to travel may be dancing lessons from God.'
Kurt Vonnegut

1

The Great Escape

JOHN

It was raining steadily, straight down, as only the west coast knows how. I had to almost tear Marie Christine away from her home. We walked out, leaving the door unlocked, everything in confusion, as if we would return within the hour. The grassy hillside was slippery wet.

The mounting pressure of the final days leading up to our departure, set for nine o'clock sharp on the morning of 4 October 1993, had reduced Marie Christine to a state of mute despair. Exhausted and anxious – she had been cooking for forty every day right up to the end of our twenty-fifth season at our adventure school two days before – she felt the moment of departure looming like the guillotine. She and our adopted Peruvian daughter, Isso, dragged, more than carried their final bits in black plastic bags down the steep 100ft hillside to the shore. It was an awful wrench. Ardmore had been our home for more than thirty years.

When I resigned from the Parachute Regiment in the early months of our marriage, Marie Christine and I had left the soft underbelly of southern England to live an independent life and become crofters on this rocky peninsula of some 800 acres, 15 miles south of Cape Wrath on the lonely north-west coast of Scotland. When we arrived in 1964, there had been four houses, only one of which was occupied, in the township of Ardmore (Gaelic for 'big hill'). Fierce autumn gales tear away at unattended roofs in these parts and empty houses are quickly destroyed. A narrow footpath wound for 3 miles through the hills to the single-track coast road which led to the world we had chosen to leave behind.

The depradations of two world wars marked the start of the decline of the crofting life around the loch. Few young people born there remained, and one by one our old friends died. Rebecca was born, and Marie Christine and I decided to start up the John Ridgway School of Adventure, concentrating on developing leadership qualities, using the sheltered sea loch for dinghy-sailing and canoeing and the hills for walking and climbing. Lance and Ada Bell arrived and helped us to build the school and bring up Rebecca.

Gradually we patched the roof, laid on water and put up other houses. The coming of electricity, eighteen years later in 1982, spelled the end of paraffin lamps and flinging an old wellie into the peat-fired Rayburn to increase the heat for baking.

The school occupied us all through each summer, and we worked until we dropped. We had also run a salmon farm for seventeen years. And to honour our decision to live adventurously, we made an expedition on mountain, ocean or river every other winter. I'd already rowed across the North Atlantic with Chay Blyth in 1966; I'd sailed single-handed to Brazil. We traced the Amazon from its furthest source to the sea, and spent another winter crossing an unexplored ice cap in Patagonia. When Rebecca was seven, we made a winter sailing trip to the Spanish Sahara, nearly sinking off Ireland on our return in December. We caught the running bug and twice ran in the New York Marathon, driving across America along the way. With a crew of instructors from the adventure school, we raced *English Rose* in the 1977–8 Whitbread Round the World Race. There was a climbing trip to Nepal, and numerous expeditions to Peru, where we found Isso. In 1992, Bec became the first woman to canoe around Cape Horn. Somewhere between all this I found the time to set a record for a non-stop double-handed circumnavigation of the world.

My self-esteem was at a low ebb. I felt I was leaving Ardmore in disgrace. Wounded, humiliated, worthless. Blimey. I took a last look back at the tower, my little office built on the roof because there was no room to extend the house sideways. I only hoped Hamish had bolted it down good and secure against the storms. My father, a retired civil engineer, was always saying he thought the weight of all my books was critical.

'Hurry up, Mum!' Isso called back up the hill. Numb, we walked on down to join the handful of friends at the water's edge. Some had come a long way to say goodbye, and some, knowing my frame of mind, were wondering if we would ever come back. It was as if we were going into exile.

Bec was loading the last batch of her stuff on to the assault craft that would take us out to the yacht. Her black crocheted hat was pulled tightly down over her newly cut short blonde hair, and she was grinning at Isso. The sisters would be seeing lots of each other in the months to come, sharing the same sleeping quarters.

'Will I really have to share the same room as Andy and Will?' fourteen-year-old Isso kept asking excitedly.

'Yes, and there'll be Richard and Brian, too.'

Isso couldn't believe it. She was picturing the school dorm, ghost stories after lights out and getting dressed under her dressing gown. How was she going to manage in a pitching boat? 'Don't worry, darling, you'll probably just stay in your clothes for the first bit,' her mother tried to reassure her, knowing how hard the early days were likely to be.

Already out on the boat were Andy Adamson and Will Burchnall. Andy, a wiry twenty-five-year-old Yorkshireman – who, true to the county of his birth, liked to call a spade a spade – skippered the yacht on some of the adventure-school courses. He had been chasing around these last few weeks getting the boat ready for her voyage. Even now I could see him and Will, thirty, our chief instructor and Bec's dashing boyfriend, standing at the main mast sewing the last tapes on the mainsail track slides. 'A boat that can sail in October can sail the whole world over.' I could hear the words of wise old Granny Ross, now long dead, ringing in my ears. Everything had to be extra strong.

As well as the six of us, the permanent crew, I'd asked a couple of old friends to join us for fun for the two-week first leg down to the Canary Islands. At fifty, Brian Cunningham was an experienced helmsman free of seasickness, and I felt he'd stiffen the crew a bit in the early days. A lean ultra-long-distance runner, Brian was half Ulsterman, half American. Richard Robinson, tall and full-bearded, was in his midfifties and worked with stained glass. He hadn't done much boating, but as a stalwart fellow with impeccable manners, I hoped he'd enjoy the experience.

After shaking hands all round, the stout-hearted band of well-wishers boarded our small red fishing boat and went on ahead into the misty, rain-flattened waters of Loch Laxford. We rowed out to *English Rose*, scrambled up the wooden ladder and on to the stern and dumped our sopping belongings in the saloon. Alone at the wheel, I watched as the crew fiddled with the mooring lines up on the foredeck. Miserably, I glanced back up the hill, where Lance and Ada Bell were huddled in the doorway of the old stone bothy by the gate, high up on the edge of the birch wood. The rain dripped from the brow of my old yellow sou'wester; the new red oilskins kept me dry, but they couldn't warm my spirit. Those two old friends, now retired after helping us with the adventure school, had made our dream of living at Ardmore come true. Lance was an ex-iron foundry foreman from Teesside. He'd met Ada during the war, when she was driving a crane at the foundry. The old man meant so much to me: his battered flat cap, his crooked grin and those spark-resistant moleskin trousers; the arthritis; Lance patching the byre with hessian and pitch, and making gate hinges from old wellies. I'd been his 'marrer' as we built the concrete founds for the school twenty-five winters ago. And together we'd hauled many a lobster creel. 'There's nobody indispensable, save Adam!' he'd snort.

I waved and the Bells waved back. Then Lance walked the few steps to the gate and slowly disappeared into the birch wood.

'Mooring's gone!' came the cry from the bows. I pushed the throttle into slow ahead, then Marie Christine and Isso came up into the centre cockpit and gazed numbly as home slipped astern.

Alone now, standing under the dripping stone mantle in the bothy doorway, Ada was our last tie with Ardmore. I knew she was waving to Rebecca, up with the others on the foredeck. They had been so close ever since Bec was born. It was Ada who'd taught Rebecca up at the Blue House for the crucial first years of her education; Ada who'd made all those cakes and mended all those tents and sails down the years. This was the end of a long chapter in all our lives. Now everything was about to change for ever. They were old, and I knew then something awful was going to happen and I would never see the Bells again. Blinded by tears, I looked away and headed *English Rose* into the mist.

There was just enough wind to carry us out to the long swells rolling into the mouth of Loch Laxford. Then, as our sodden friends waved forlornly from the little red fishing boat, Arun Bose turned the wheel for home.

Quite suddenly, all the rushing was over. Still only three miles from home, we were alone in the queasy grey wastes of the North Atlantic and the enormity of what we were committed to began to sink in. Below decks we were in chaos. Weeks of painstaking packing of provisions, food, clothing, equipment and spares for an eighteen-month voyage through every season and climate on the planet – each item carefully recorded in Bec's red stowage book – had filled every compartment. There was little space left for all the kit Brian and Richard had brought with them – and none for the mounds of last-minute clothing and gear just brought out by each of the six permanent crew.

The rain continued to fall as we sailed south-west all day. We were exhausted, and when not on watch, most people just jammed themselves among the heaps of kit on their bunks and fell asleep, leaving the unpacking until they overcame the nausea of seasickness.

Slipping through the Little Minch between Skye and the Outer Hebrides, we began to get to grips with our new way of life. We were falling over each other, even on smooth seas in clear moonlight. My last long trip in *English Rose* had been ten years before, a 203-day non-stop right round the world. We'd seen land just once in those seven months, but there had only been two of us, myself and Andy Briggs, aboard. Now, with eight of us and so much kit, changing watches was not easy. The oilskin locker in particular, bulging with overladen coat-hangers, was a battleground. But we managed three two-hour watches well enough until dawn; A Watch – Marie Christine and I – even found it quite exciting. With one steering and the other sat in the doghouse with Isso, Richard joined us, preferring to sit up rather than endure his bunk up in the forward sleeping compartment.

It was calm all next day and so we motored on, anxiously pressing south and still struggling with our unpacking. The glass had been rising steadily ever since we'd left Ardmore, as the low passed over the Irish Sea, moving north-east across England. We threaded our way through fleets of sturdy black seine-netters, the last reminders of home, aiming all the while to keep well out in the Atlantic, giving Aran Island off the north-west corner of Ireland, a wide berth.

By late afternoon on that second day at sea we were to the west of the low and a northerly wind began to blow. The sea picked up fast and darkness brought storm. The scourge of seasickness dogged Andy, and now he retired to his bunk, out of action for the foreseeable future, the grim prospect of eighteen months at sea stretching his imagination.

By midnight, quartering seas were raking the boat and only Brian and I could manage the wheel. We settled into a routine of two hours on and two off, with Bec and Will helping out where possible.

MARIE CHRISTINE

I think it was that icy spurt of Atlantic forcing itself through our tiny
cabin window and drenching John that jerked me out of my swamp of
misery.

Clad only in his undersuit, he wailed: 'I'm drenched. I'll freeze. I've
nothing dry to wear.' We rummaged through the bunks in our lurching
cabin, half the size of one on the Euston—Inverness night sleeper.

'My bedding's soaked. My kit is ruined.'

'Serves you right,' I muttered – he had appropriated the bigger of the
two bunks – but I handed over my new longjohns and top. The storm
had hit us on Day 2. I felt I had set off in a complete muddle, having
been cooking for the courses almost until the last minute. If I'd died
suddenly I couldn't have left everything in more disorder.

And in a sense this was like dying: leaving the green land and grey
mountains for the desert waste of a slate-grey ocean. A kind of uproot-
ing. I loved my home, which clung to the hillside above the sea loch, and
the view of the mountains from my window; the abandoned plants
which balance on every windowsill, my precious patch of garden, nur-
tured over many years; the leggy pink roses which I hadn't the heart to
cut down, the purple Michaelmas daisies just coming into late flower. I'd
been miserable about leaving our five cats, who had been taken away
from Ardmore in so many baskets and found homes.

But now it was time to be positive, and as we set off I resolved to
make a great effort, and particularly to cope with every aspect of sailing.
But once we were underway the memories of when John and I, together
with a crew of ten, had raced round the world in the 1977–8 Whitbread
yacht race had come rushing back. I'd been Britishly stoic, but frankly,
most of that nine-month voyage had been an ordeal. I'd sworn never to
step on a yacht again, and – with the exception of spending several bitter days on a sloop a few months earlier, persuaded by John that it was
necessary to help Andy gain his Yachtmaster's Certificate – I never had.
What, then, was I doing here, retching over the side? I could feel myself
being sucked into that familiar vortex of self-pity. 'Poor Mama,' Isso
crooned. She was coping really well, only occasionally complaining of
feeling 'a little pale'.

I'd done practically no sailing since, yet here I was again on the same
boat, with the same skipper. And this time it would be for twice the
duration. I kept telling myself this was going to be different: instead of

ten scratchy men, there was my family and Andy and Will. But we were still all squeezed into the same 57ft plastic tube (which is not exactly how a yachtie would describe our beautiful *English Rose*). I loved adventure, travel and challenge, but sailing made me feel sick, trapped and sometimes very frightened.

I hoped I might change. And, knowing how contrary my nature is prone to be, I probably would change. Perhaps I'd become the keenest yachtsperson ever, and regret all those missed chances: the time in 1983, when I declined John's invitation to sail round the world again, this time non-stop; all those perfect June days when I had preferred not to sail across the Minch and gaze back at the majestic backdrop of Sutherland's mountains; those trips to St Kilda and the Faroes. 'No, I'm far too busy,' I'd always offered as an excuse.

But the sneaky man had dreamed up a trip of such allure that even I, reluctant and seasick as I was, could not resist: a trip for all of us, with nobody left behind to worry about; a trip to the Caribbee, the lost Atlantis, then on to the Pacific Islands. Of course I was going, but oh! the seasickness, oh! the discomfort, the squalor, the lack of privacy. I knew that after six weeks I would feel all right and hoped that in a couple of months, when we had fewer people on board, I would adjust and it would creep over me that it was the best thing in the world to be sailing along without a care, the sun warm and the wind set fair.

On board, apart from sailing and running the boat, schooling for Isso would be part of each day. Bec was now grown up, but I had vivid memories of another winter voyage, to the Spanish Sahara – six of us in a much smaller boat without an engine – when she was seven. Memories of huddling in the cockpit, muffled up in duffle coats, struggling with the irrelevancies of the 'Peter and Jane' reading books as our boat bucked and reared over grey and lumpy Atlantic waves. This time round Isso and I had chosen the books. Isso, born high in the Andes, far from the sea, had shown no sign of suffering from seasickness, unlike the rest of the Ridgways.

'Mama, can I get a grass skirt in the South Pacific?' was her current main concern.

In the months before we sailed, John had woken often at two in the morning, worrying about the rigging, the new doghouse and whether we had enough calibrated chain. One of my anxieties had been the rations. We had the promise of half-a-hundredweight of fudge and several stone of oatcakes. I thought we'd end up taking what was left in the store at the end of the season, and just making do until we reached warmer lands where fruit would be cheap and the coconuts fell into our laps as we dozed in the sun. In the event we ended up with generous contributions from various companies and every spare square inch on board was packed with provisions. Isso had wisely managed to stuff her essentials next to her bunk: two Cabbage Patch dolls, numerous tapes for her Walkman and her Peruvian granny's *manta*.

Now, as the storm raged on, I knew I must contribute: we had had no hot food for thirty-six hours. I struggled into the pitching, damp galley. Squirting three measures of meths to heat up the paraffin in the pressurised ring, I managed to produce a hot circle of blue flame on the cooker. Soon a pan of water was steaming. It bounced alarmingly on the stove as we lurched with each rollercoaster wave. Grimly, I worked on, locating the oats in one of nine jerrycans lashed together in the aft cabin, and after a long hour of struggling, broken by several dashes to be sick, porridge and hot tea were dished out. By now my rage was equal to the storm outside. I flew at John: 'How could you do this to us?'

He looked worn down and weary. And now the wife was playing up.

JOHN

The noise of the wind was making communication difficult, but there was no mistaking my wife's frame of mind: 'That's it, John Ridgway, I'm off – thirty years is enough!' From my miserable perch by the wheel, I looked down the too-narrow hatchway from the bleakly functional new doghouse. From the galley, Marie Christine's pale oval face peered up malevolently. 'You love it, don't you?' she spat. The obedience vows had not survived three decades. I was glum. This was not a good time to knock away the supporting props of marriage. The water generator turbine was gone, the self steering wrecked. The Navstar aerial, lifebuoy, strobe light, spinnaker jockey pole and a winch handle had all been washed away. Sitting up in the doghouse with me, Richard disappeared into his greying beard, squirming with embarrassment. He was spending very long hours there, offering good cheer and chocolate to whoever was on watch.

Down below, our home for the next eighteen months had swiftly deteriorated into little more than a rolling jumble of soggy cardboard boxes. My bunk was awash, the leaking windows quite unable to repel the rollers raking the deck. It was the hard routine again. I slept for two hours on the boards in the saloon and then spent a couple of hours at the wheel.

I kept reassuring the others that the seas were 'only average for this boat', which I'd twice raced round the world. But I was no longer quite so sure myself. I'd read in the *Guinness Book of Records* that the biggest wave in the world had been recorded one autumn off the west coast of Ireland. One hundred and fifty feet was the measurement that came to mind.

'Big one, John!' Will called, looking back into the night. Out of the corner of each eye, on either side, in the glow from the stern light, I glimpsed a white curtain rearing up to overtake us. The bow dropped to seven o'clock and the stern rose to one. I misjudged it. The bow swung to the right as we broached and the boat charged across the side of the breaking wave as it rolled over us. We were on our side. The wheel was wrenched from my hands. I was swimming. The ammonia taste of salt water squirting up my nose reminded me of failed childhood surfing in Cornwall. Only the safety harness held me in the cockpit. I thought of little Isso in her bunk below.

The 25-ton boat shuddered gallantly upright, water streaming from her decks. This used to stimulate me; now I was just frightened, and my legs were shaking.

The new high-frequency radio wouldn't transmit. I thought gratefully of the slim blue box above the chart table. Newly fitted at Ardmore just hours before we left, by the ever-resourceful Roy Morley for BT, this was our INMARSAT C satellite communications system. The blue box was a radio transmitter—receiver linked to an antenna unit, a GPS (global positioning system) and our laptop PC, which contained Roy's software to drive all this. Working through earth stations at Goonhilly in Cornwall, Singapore and other sites, we could leave messages in a mailbox at the appropriate earth station. Andy was a wizard with our new GPS system. As soon as it had arrived from Glasgow in May, I'd asked him to set it up on the kitchen table in his house so he could familiarise himself with its every secret.

Although I was now feeling pretty rough myself, I felt happier doing the navigation on my own. Given the conditions, I felt we were getting too close to the Irish mainland so I altered course to take *English Rose* further out into the Atlantic.

Then a wave washed down through the main hatch and drowned the laptop. And so, unless we took the irrevocable step of tripping our emergency search-and-rescue beacon, it looked as if we could no longer communicate with the outside world. We got on with the main job in hand: keeping the boat afloat until the storm abated.

Meanwhile, back at base camp in their crofthouse on Ardmore, our friends Bruce and Rita Reynolds were watching a dot moving across a chart on the screen of their own PC. And because that dot was moving steadily in the right direction, they weren't too fussed about the lack of radio contact.

REBECCA

During that first storm, off the west coast of Ireland, when the waves became too large for my limited experience at the helm, my job was to sit facing the huge following sea and call out 'Wave!' or 'Big one!' to the helmsman. The 'big ones' came in sets, and unless we got them straight on our stern, the boat hurtled off on one side. Brian said he was glad my nerve was strong. I was not so sure.

As I shouted as best I could into the torrential rain and literally howling wind, I could not hold back the faint cries of terror as the 'big ones' began to crash in on top of us. Although we were both clipped on securely, the cockpit frequently became completely swamped and I would be swimming, aware of the cries of 'Hold on! Hold on!' from the helm.

Sometimes my legs would shake from fear. This was going to be another of those typical 'family holidays' . . .

Exhausted though I was, it was hard to sleep with all the banging and crashing below decks. Isso was thrown right across the cabin, landing on my bunk on the opposite side. Luckily, she just seemed to think it was part of the fun of being on a boat.

After one bad broach, I leaped from my bunk. Pans and plates had exploded from their cupboards in the galley and water was gushing in through the main hatch. Scooping up a tub of wet sugar from the galley floor by torchlight, I thought, 'Some sugar is better than none.'

I can laugh now about the screaming row I had with Dad. I was in tears at the wheel in 60 knots of wind, requests sent below for advice and help to reef our already tiny sails having brought the reply that Will and I should do it ourselves. It seemed impossible to me to steer, winch and tail the furling line all at the same time. We needed help – I didn't care if I seemed a wimp. Poor Will was caught in the middle. 'Go and tell Dad we are not doing *anything* until he comes! We'll damage the boat, or worse, lose our fingers,' I yelled over the shrieking wind. I was really frightened; I knew this 'good experience' stuff could end in disaster. 'Pull yourself together,' came the familiar retort, as Dad eventually appeared in his rain-soaked waterproofs to assist. At least I'd gained Brownie points for sewing the mainsail we had damaged the day before.

JOHN

After thirty-six hours of heavy weather, the bolts securing the steering gear to the rudder post buckled and the key jumped free of the keyway. Rather like a faithful old horse giving up the unequal struggle, the boat gave a sort of relaxed swing and came broadside to the wind. The thumping of the flapping rudder, which was threatening to stove in the hull, worked like a magic drum. All hands came to the rescue – even Andy tumbled out of his bunk. Quickly, we fitted the Hammerite green scaffolding pole of the emergency steering. It was like a giant socket wrench, sliding through the floor of the aft cockpit and engaging directly on to the head of the rudder post. We lashed the makeshift tiller to one side of the cockpit and silenced that death-knell drumbeat.

Wondering what damage might already be done to the hull, I called everyone to a meeting. It was past noon as we all gathered in the saloon. There was some nervousness. This sort of situation was not new to me. I faced the crew across the table and began negotiations. Marie Christine was all for selling the boat in Vigo, the nearest port, and flying home to plant her winter bulbs. Rebecca thought the cats would be missing us. To her eternal credit, fourteen-year-old Isso narrowed her Inca eyes and declared that it was better than school.

Andy was still feeling too seasick to contribute much. Will was tight-lipped with shock from his experience thus far – he had done little boating before, and was clearly wondering if this was normal ocean sailing. If so, how on earth was he going to last the full eighteen months? I thought it better not to ask his opinion. Brian was fairly stimulated, but Richard stayed silent, eyes watchful.

Luckily, by the end of the discussion, Andy was coming back to life again. With a supreme effort, he fished out a length of threaded rod brought aboard by our engineer, James Ross, just before we'd sailed. This rod, though not of hardened steel, was of just the right size to make replacement bolts for the steering. While Will held the torch, Andy jammed himself under the aft cockpit by the rudder stock, and set about fitting the new bolts. Half an hour passed. We listened to the breakers hissing spitefully as they passed, rolling us helplessly broadside to the swell. At last, Andy was done. We unfurled a scrap of Yankee headsail and we were on our way again, running south in improving weather. I was able to pencil in the log: 'And so, they sailed on, with hope in their hearts!'

But alone at the wheel my mind was a jumble. What exactly was the point of all this? At fifty-five, I'd come round to the view that at the end of the day, when all the trumpeting was done, the family was the most valuable part of my life. I'd come to realise that I was rather an anxious person, really, frightened of the dark and lots of things besides. The opposite of an expert, I had always been under-confident; indeed, I had spent my life taking advice from others and following it slavishly. 'Give me the man who has looked into himself and is frankly appalled,' summarised the kind of person with whom I was most at ease. My best chance was to envisage the voyage as a simple continuation of the non-stop circumnavigation of ten years ago. That trip had begun when Andy Briggs and I walked down the steep green slope from the crofthouse to the sea loch below, rowed out to *English Rose* and sailed away – for 203 days, right round the planet: south of Africa, New Zealand and round Cape Horn – on that magic carpet which lies, always unrolled, at the foot of the croft. Coming into Ardmore, we felt we could have sailed on, right round the world for a second time.

I'd felt the need to get in the groove again before it was too late. How I longed to return to the clean world of giant skies with their towering tradewind clouds.

'What's your ambition, now?' people asked.

'Peace of mind, I think,' I'd reply, when I remembered.

I looked forward to that soothing feeling which comes when I have time on my hands, when I can do small jobs, exactly as I want them done. Perhaps that's why some troubled grown-ups keep model trains. Then there are the inspiring people we'd meet along the way, and the frightening times. All the time I'd be working to keep the team together for eighteen months in a rolling, pitching tube.

At the end of the seven-month non-stop circumnavigation of ten years before, I'd promised myself I was done with regrets. But now I hoped I wasn't beginning to regret having brought Isso to Europe seven years earlier from the war-torn jungles of Peru. There was so much in modern Europe which was less than admirable. Maybe this voyage would make it up to her: at least she'd be where the love was. I had felt relaxed and full of enthusiasm for the adventure.

But now that the storm had sparked me up a bit, I wondered if I still felt the same way. I felt a little more combative, and perhaps this was no bad thing. 'Why do it, kid?' I asked myself so many times over the previous fifty-five years. My best answer seemed to be dissatisfaction; that fundamental, everlasting dissatisfaction with his situation that has brought man to ascendancy over all living creatures. He will never be content to sit down and chew the cud.

The year 1993 had been a very bad one for me, and this voyage was my Great Escape. If I'd had cancer, or a fatal car accident, everything would have had to have ended anyway. By leaving home, I knew I was really walking out and leaving everything, teetering on the edge of doing so for good.

Of course, it was my own fault. Foolishly taken in by a television company which had neither interest in nor knowledge of team-building, or of what I was doing at Ardmore, I'm afraid I'd shown myself to be a very soft touch indeed. I became another subject of the media's habit of building up someone only to knock him down. The film which I had hoped would celebrate twenty-five years of our school of adventure went awry. Taking the promises on trust, I'd gone ahead with the project for free. In spite of my misgivings, the film company was allowed to influence the selection of course participants by the client company, carefully choosing several candidates who were unsuited to the hardships of the particular programme the sub-sea engineering company had chosen for the film. These individuals were placed together in two of the four teams to create maximum conflict for the two camera crews. The MD gave me his personal assurance there would be no commentary – the film was to speak for itself – but particularly ill-informed commentary there was, combined with selective use of footage, exaggerated sound effects and falsified windspeeds: little tricks which lent support to a preconceived notion. The whole package of dramatised hype, enticingly full of personal conflict, made great commercial television, but team-building it was not.

The programme was transmitted four times on the British network and in countless other countries besides, from the USA to Japan. I've no doubt that it helped sell masses of consumer goods, but in my heart I knew I'd been duped into a trivial triumph of commerce over truth. Ironically, I was portrayed as representing the opposite of the three principles of the school: self-reliance, positive thinking and leaving people and things better than you find them. After twenty-five years and 10,000 students, I was going out on a steepish downbeat.

'Never explain, never complain,' I blustered in public, steadfastly refusing to comment, but I was hurting badly. I felt I'd wasted a lot of my essence. Self-doubt was eating into me. What if the conclusions drawn by the film were correct? Had I really got everything wrong from the outset? Those twenty-five years could never be relived.

I had read somewhere that a tourist never knows where he's been and a traveller never knows where he's going. We had a rough plan, but the whole idea was to be free of schedule and routine, free to go wherever we wished. Travelling offered something to do; wilderness might revive hope. I longed for a visit to the Antarctic and another sight of the albatross and the whale in the Southern Ocean where there's no trace of the human race. And I couldn't wait for those long days on foot in deep jungle and the cleanliness of the high Andes of Peru. Perhaps we might stop for a while in the Caribbean. Passing through the Panama Canal, we could turn left or right – South America or Alaska. It might be both. We'd make up our minds as we went along. It would surely kill off the worm of pointless bitterness which was eating away at my insides.

But I was big and ugly. It really was high time I took a tug at my bootlaces, stopped sulking like a spoiled child and made the most of a new kind of reputation. Leadership is not a popularity contest.

REBECCA

I lay on my belly, panting after a fast climb on wobbly sea legs. Up and up, right to the lip of this 1,000ft cliff. Pale sun warmed my back through a drizzly sky. I could feel warm damp seeping into my elbows and knees from the spagnum moss and Luing heather which covers the island of St Kilda.

I was alone.

Just to the north, I could see Boreray, standing like a giant's molar flanked by two incisors, Stac Lee and Stac an Armin, thrusting hundreds of feet up through the cold ocean from the outermost edge of the Hebridean shelf. Boreray's steep green southern flank was dotted with wild sheep, her western cliffs thick with golden-headed gannets.

Garlanded with thousands more of these screeching white birds, the grey-black cliffs of the two stacs were dusted with their snow-like guano.

Being rather wary of heights, I wriggled forward and peered over the edge of the great cliff. Way below, grey Atlantic rollers crashed on the rocks. I could just make out the shape of a seal, bottling in the washing-machine waters. A sudden movement caught my eye. Just a few inches to my right crouched a baby fulmar, still flightless. It didn't notice me for some time. Then, coiling its neck back and upward, it began to squawk alarm. Adult fulmars, gliding on the updraughts, shot up to watch the chick, whose parents, just one of 45,000 pairs, had found this ledge and hatched their little bundle of down there.

This was all in the calm after the storm. In favourable conditions, the passage here takes no more than twenty-four hours, but we had left Ardmore three days previously, battling into a gale with sails as small as can be. Six of our eight passengers – including the skipper and the other watch-leader – had been seasick, and all said they'd have left the boat if they'd been able to reach the shore. I'd been able to hold out. The boat, veteran of two circumnavigations of the world, had stood up as well as ever.

Familiar damp, unpleasant smells and discomfort had made themselves known. Really, why did I want to put myself through eighteen months of this? What was I trying to prove this time?

Oh, the relief of stepping on to dry land, here on St Kilda. I had been filled with doubts as I climbed the cliff, but for some reason they fell away as I lay looking into the eyes of that young fulmar.

I knew it would be mentally hard. Leaving home, beating into October gales on the first leg to the Canaries. It couldn't possibly be anything less than two weeks of torture. But what would I learn? I know there will be other fulmars' eyes to look into.

2

The Warming

JOHN

Ninety-three days of crossing the North Atlantic in an open rowing boat, without sleeping bags or any form of bedding, in 1966, had taught me one thing: involuntarily, the human frame adapts to appalling conditions. Held back by his imagination, man surprises himself when his back is against the wall. We had made a memorable start to our Family voyage, and now each of us was adapting to the new way of life. For Richard and Brian, it was only a matter of getting through another ten days or so until we reached the Canaries, but the main team had to adapt and accept this plastic tube, with all its confinements, as our home beyond the foreseeable future.

Lying in the top bunk of the three on the starboard side of the forward sleeping compartment, pressed against the roof, pitching and heaving in semi-darkness and drugged with oversleep, Andy was coming to terms with life beyond school and university. His Yorkshire grit was being shined and sharpened. Nobody can be cheerful all the time, and I had suffered just this sort of 'looking in the mirror' situation myself. I was hoping that Andy would win through.

It was a tighter ship which met the next gale twenty-four hours later. The steering was checked every couple of hours and Andy's repair held good. Then there followed days of headwinds, rain squalls and lumpy grey seas. October was no time for this particular passage, but would we rather have stayed at home watching others on television? Ahead of us, like the Holy Grail, lay the warming. Every mile brought us nearer to blue seas and sunshine.

Marie Christine rallied the troops by example, forcing herself to roast the chicken we had been keeping in the cold box.

With Andy still out of action, I needed to improve morale, so I rejigged the watch system back to three teams. Brian was helped by Richard; Marie Christine, Isso and I managed A Watch between us and I hoped Bec would get into the swing of running a watch with Will. My own angle on the run-in I'd had with her during the bad weather was that we should protect the team by not allowing anyone to get overtired to the point where errors of judgement began to creep in – like getting too close to the Irish coast at the start. But it was wrong to fall into the trap of relying on Brian or me at any time of day or night, and it was imperative that Rebecca settled down to being a watch leader, able to keep a good look-out, foresee possible difficulties and to react to them – reducing sail in good time, for example. While we were cruising, major sail changes were best done in advance at the change of the watch – or was I just too tired and sick to move my bum?

Marie Christine

After the storms I realised that my moods and resolve had been as up and down as the ocean. My rage with John had sprung mostly from my concern about Bec and Isso's survival. He had been the motivating force in this lifetime trip. Bec was of an age to make her own decisions, but not Isso. Our teenager's stoical Quechua background was standing her in good stead. She never complained. It wasn't until after the two storms that she'd confessed that every time *English Rose* slammed into a wave she'd thought we were hitting a rock. 'Can we touch the bottom, Mama?' she asked. And no wonder she didn't like using the lavatories – or heads, as they are called on boats. Quite logically, she thought that all our waste was emptying down below the floorboards rather than into the ocean through a valve. I had worried terribly about the wisdom of taking Isso on this first part, and even whether it was right to take her out of school for so long. John felt she should be part of the team from Day 1, and I must admit that of all of us, she seemed the most able to cope. Perhaps having lived as a half-starved refugee in Peru put Atlantic storms into perspective. Nevertheless, I fervently hoped we had made the right decision.

Us being all together as a family was what Isso loved best. She had endured three schools: the teachers were undoubtedly very kind to her, as were most of the pupils, but much of what they were trying to teach held no great significance for her. Perhaps now we could bring some relevance into her learning. Sums would be for real. The answers had to be right, or else we would miss landfall or run out of water. History and geography would be chasing Columbus over the horizon rim as we tasted the same salt spray on our lips.

Sometimes I, her teacher, would lie limply in the cabin when not on watch, while Isso rummaged in the big locker under the seats on the starboard side of the saloon, packed with a great selection of her very own books. 'One at a time,' I would call out weakly, my teaching timetable gone to pot.

A few weeks before we'd left, we had squeezed in a few moments between the cooking and office work and chosen a long list of mouth-watering books. The parcels arrived in good time, addressed to Miss Elizabeth Ridgway. Excitedly, she unwrapped brightly illustrated encyclopaedias: *How Science Works, The Great Atlas of Discovery, Explorers and Map Makers* and many more that would expand her knowledge – and ours – of the places we would be visiting. It was to be one hell of a field trip. Like most parents, I had also ordered some of my own favourite childhood books, hoping Isso would enjoy them too. There was an illustrated *Treasure Island*, with fearsome piratical faces staring out of the pages; all three volumes of *The Borrowers, Wind in the Willows, Black Beauty, Little Women*.

Isso was addicted to stories. Her imagination had had to work overtime. The victim of a terrorist war in Peru, she had been cared for by her refugee grandparents in the remote high Andes. She had never seen a wheel, a windowpane or anything powered by electricity, and there were no books in the scrabble for survival. When she came to us, aged seven, she was like a child from another century. Gradually she learned to communicate, to ask questions and to understand, but for a long while she was, in a sense, gagged, living in her own fantasy world. Stories were her element – the more dramatic, the more she identified with them: stories of escape, stories of ghosts, spirits, magic. She rather scorned our pragmatic approach. 'Do you believe in ghosts,' was much more important to her than, 'Where do you live?' or 'Do you have any brothers or sisters?'

Isso was thrilled to be on the boat with Andy and Will, and it was not long before she had fallen madly in love with Andy. Once he was back among us after the seasickness, I noticed her peeping at him archly through downcast almond eyes. It was early days, but I felt we were all going to get along well.

Will, Bec, Andy and I had already had a taste of being together on a boat that spring. We needed a new yacht skipper, and Andy was very keen to take on the job. Boats had been his passion since a small boy, and having spent many holidays on his dad's small yacht, he had no difficulty passing the shore-based theoretical exam for his yachtmaster's qualification. Then the four of us spent three freezing days aboard the 34ft sloop *Piota*, owned by yachtmaster instructor Keith Stanley. I couldn't believe I was back on a boat again.

Chased by biting February snow squalls, we hurtled from Inverness across the Moray Firth and out into the North Sea. The weather we could all just about endure, but when Andy was required to go below to study the charts and plot our route, he lasted only a moment before the colour drained fast from his already pale face and he lurched up through the tight companionway to throw up over the side.

When we got home, he came up the hill to discuss the situation. 'I can't do it, John, I know I can't,' he said, choking on his words. My heart went out to him: I knew what he had suffered during the previous week, and I knew how much he wanted to pass his yachtmaster's certificate. 'I don't want to let you down,' he croaked, his thin frame shaking, the chronic seasickness eating away at his confidence. We needed him to be the yacht skipper, all right – 'Twice-round-the-world' John couldn't be in two places at one time, and he was needed to run the hillwalking course. Will, Bec and I weren't in the running at all. Andy had to do it.

Andy, a biology student, was twenty when he first came to Ardmore in 1988 to help as an assistant instructor with the summer courses. Tall and slender, with hair that grew into a fuzzy dark bush if it wasn't trimmed regularly, he spoke only rarely. He came back again the following summer, and at the end of the day he would often come and talk to me while I whirled around the kitchen preparing meals. I heard about his family in York: about his mother, who was a primary-school head-teacher and had helped him a lot with his studies; about his dad, who worked at the university and could do anything from rebuilding a Land Rover to assembling and repairing advanced computers and complicated electrical systems. He had an elder sister, too, and they seemed a close and happy family.

Andy must have liked Ardmore, because he kept coming back each year, and when a position became vacant on our salmon farm, he swapped roles and accepted the all-year-round job. His slender frame belied his gritty Yorkshire toughness. After a couple of years of running the salmon farm, alone in the winter with plenty of practice at handling small boats in extreme conditions of wet, wind and cold, he was ready for anything – except the debilitating seasickness.

But he loved yachting. John talked him round and by the next weekend we were back on the North Sea for a second time, again fighting seasickness and the wretched cold. I was surprised to find that I didn't feel sick, and in spite of the bitter cold, I liked sailing *Piota*, which seemed gentler on us than the bigger *English Rose*, which gave me the feeling of being aboard a runaway racehorse.

Andy's examination was set for March, during another cold, blustery spell. In a highly nervous state we returned to Inverness and the Caledonian Canal. Andy performed faultlessly, springing *Piota* off the busy Inverness harbour wall, his years of practice on inland canals standing him in good stead. We didn't let him down, jumping to our stations when the examiner flung a bucket overboard, screaming out the long-awaited 'Man overboard!' It was grins all round as Andy was awarded his Yachtmaster's Certificate. We celebrated on our return with a round of Rusty Nails, Keith Stanley's favourite drink of Drambuie and whisky. So Andy became the yacht skipper, and curiously, when he was in charge of the boat, his seasickness diminished.

Bec was moderately keen on yachting, but she had never forgotten her trip to the Spanish Sahara as a seven-year-old, when we'd nearly foundered 120 miles off the west coast of Ireland at Christmas in 1974. For ultra-polite Will, strongly built and square-jawed, boating was a completely new experience which, I suspected, he was drawn into because of his developing fondness for my elder daughter that spring. Mothers have a sixth sense in these matters, and aboard a 34ft boat it was hard not to notice the lingering glances in her direction, the teasing and laughter over Bec's jokes. Will had come back early to prepare for the instructors' course. He was to be the chief instructor and would not be involved with *English Rose*, but 'a bit of yachting instruction would be useful', he said.

After seven years in the City, Will had had enough of Yuppie life. 'We must teach you how to drink champagne, Will,' they'd told him, 'for no reason at all.' At Ardmore, hard work and his natural charm and sense of fun won him friends from every quarter. Living in London he had kept fit, playing in the centre for Richmond Rugby Club. He first visited us briefly in the autumn of 1991, when there was a particularly tough course in progress. John thought he would fit in, so Will returned to join the month-long instructors' course the following spring. Although he was a few years older than the other instructors, he slipped easily into the Ardmore regime of early-morning runs, and his fierce determination soon made him the fastest. He relished the open-air life and freedom. He confided to me that he was really a farmer at heart: the happiest moments of his youth had been spent rearing game chicks and tending his ferrets at home in Gloucestershire. But he seemed more than happy to have escaped an office life as a commodities broker, even if it meant a big drop in income.

I had long since learned that it was a waste of breath asking Bec about her affections, but Isso and I couldn't help but notice how pally she and Will seemed. Purely professionally, of course. It is hard to keep anything a secret at Ardmore, but they were both very circumspect. However, when Will started going out late in the evening along the path and returning even later with a giant bunch of lilies or red roses, delivered by Interflora to Rhiconich, our nearest drop-off point, I realised that my suspicions had not been unfounded. He could do no wrong in my eyes, so as the plot thickened and John became determined that we should sail away in the autumn, Will was asked to join the crew. I felt he would be a civilising influence, with his good manners and sense of fun, his order-liness and his fondness for Bec. Of course we would all get on well. I never imagined that their friendship would become a difficulty that John and I would have to cope with.

JOHN

We were beginning to look 'something like', as Lance Bell would have said. The clumsiness was diminishing as each of us became a part of the prison ship. The North Atlantic rowing trip had instilled in me a quest for simplicity, reliability and effectiveness. In my enthusiasm to avoid sinking, I had, for many years, insisted on boats free of valves in their hulls. This meant proper sailing boats, without engines or heads: sort of prison ships. *English Rose VI* could not be called a comfortable boat, though she did have an 80hp Mercedes engine and two heads, but there was no piped fresh water and ventilation was kept to a minimum to avoid leaks from the decks.

A 57ft-long ketch, weighing some 25 tons when fully laden, *English Rose* has a 70ft main mast, 35ft mizen mast and a maximum width of 14.5ft, and she needs nearly 9ft of water to float in. Using fourteen winches, she can set up to five different sails at one time when we are sailing off the wind. Between the bows and the main mast, the Yankee and the staysail are set on the forestay and inner forestay respectively; as the wind increases, both these sails can be reduced in area by being wrapped round their stays, using furling lines which are controlled by winches right back by the doghouse on the aft deck. The mainsail, set on the main mast, is reduced by reefing it down on the main boom. The mizen staysail is a cheery red, white and blue, set between the two masts in light weather, and the mizen sail is a much smaller version of the mainsail, set on the mizen mast and reefed on the mizen boom.

Below decks the boat is laid out for long-distance cruising. Right up in the bows, behind a 4-ins-thick watertight bulkhead, lies the fore-peak, with access to the foredeck by means of the forehatch. In there we keep anchors and chain cable beneath the floor, but with new headsail furling gears wrapping their sails away on their forestays, we are able to carry many fewer sails than before, so extra space has become available for stowing all sorts of other gear.

The forward heads lie aft of the forepeak, with a lavatory, washbasin and cupboards for personal gear on the starboard side and on the port side, racks for winch handles, lines and small gear used in the everyday running of the boat. The lavatory needs to be treated with the utmost respect: we have known people to pump the evacuating handle without opening the exit valve. The subsequent burst fills the air with a ghastly emulsion, then they come tottering aft, like glistening chocolate soldiers, losing friends with every stride.

Another watertight door leads aft to the forward sleeping compartment. Only about 7ft long, this is home to six bodies, three on either side. Two small leaky hatches in the white-painted deckhead never supply quite enough light and there is insufficient ventilation for hot climates. In spite of the varnished pine lining boards, which nicely match the crofts at home, this is something of a hellhole. Personal kit, well sealed in plastic bags, is stowed in cubbyholes along the outboard side of each bunk. Suitably wrapped in their scaffolding pole frames, the tan canvas bunks can be detached for burials at sea. Andy slept on the top bunk on the starboard side, and Isso on the bottom one. A few feet away, on the starboard side, Will had the top bunk and Bec was on the bottom, directly across from her sister. The middle bunk on either side was reserved for visitors or covered with netting to house a great jumble of stores.

Adding a nautical touch, the main mast comes down through the middle of the deck at the after end of the forward sleeping compartment, passing through the non-slip brown lino on the cabin sole on its way to the step on the keel below. Along with all the crashing and banging of waves on the outside of the hull, the creaking vibrations of this large silver-grey alloy tube rather reinforce crew anxiety in stormy weather.

Next comes the saloon, the heart of *English Rose*. Teak-lined, with pilot berths serving as stores above bench seats on either side, this is entered from forward by way of an oval doorway, the curtains serving to screen those sleeping in the forward compartment. At mealtimes, the crew gathered round its functional rectangular table, raised the white-painted flaps and tucked into the grub, which was passed forward across the seaboot rack in wooden bowls from the narrow galley, set further back on the starboard side. Saloon is a rather inappropriate name, since very little drinking is ever done here, and Marie Christine and Rebecca were to spend much time softening its austerity with brightly patterned tablecloths, plants and various adornments on the bulkheads. Beneath the deck, and painted Samsonite green, the splendid 80hp Mercedes warmed the atmosphere whenever it was charging batteries or driving the boat.

The teak steps of the main companionway lead up through the leaky main hatch into the main cockpit from the after end of the saloon. At the foot of these steps, a small door leads aft into the skipper's cabin on the port side, with a bunk and cupboards on either side, and on through another door, into the aft heads.

Further to port of the main companionway, and part of the after end of the saloon, lies the navigation area. Set at the widest point of the boat, this station has been made rather redundant by the recent addition of Arun Bose's doghouse. And although charts are still stowed under it, the chart table has become the computer centre. Using all his thirty years of IBM know-how, Brian soon replaced the drowned laptop with a spare PC we were carrying. This was no mean feat since it involved a fair amount of juggling with Roy Morley's programmes to keep us on the INMARSAT.

Aft of the saloon, on the starboard side, lies the seaboot rack, and then the large open oilskin locker with hangers on a rail along the side of the boat for up to a dozen sets of gear. Leaky sliding windows set in either side of the main cockpit light the skipper's cabin to port and the narrow galley to starboard. There is storage space in the sides, floor and deckhead of the galley, which is more functional than decorative, with a paraffin cooker set next to a small sink and draining board.

Dressed up in the many layers of clothing required by a cold climate, passing through the galley into the aft cabin on the way up on watch is a delicate business. The aft cabin is a cramped sort of place: the mizen mast comes down through the doghouse above on its way to a step on the bottom of the boat, and bunks used for storage line its sides. The high-frequency (HF) radio, for long-distance communications, is set up on the bulkhead near the mast and the massive Whitlock steering gear occupies the central space below the doghouse. At sea, Lance's boarding ladder, solidly built of good Scottish larch, is lifted from the stern and slid down through the deck to serve as access to the doghouse.

Set on the deck around the mizen mast, the doghouse is the biggest advance we've made to long-distance cruising. With windows all round, bench seats, a chart table and electronic navigation gear, it adds a separate dimension to the boat. All navigation is now conducted from here, and, away from those below, the watch can sing and talk, even play music, without fear of disturbing the sleeping crew below. In foul weather the Aries self-steering gear on the stern can be controlled by two lines leading through the perspex drop boards which seal the hatch, out to the wheel in the aft cockpit. It's really neat. Winches and jammers set around the cockpit control the sails and there is further stowage in the lazarette right on the stern.

REBECCA

'Ribeeka, more water on this side,' the voice of my stoical young sister advised me as I stood, bent forward and wobbling, in the main cockpit, rinsing my hair in a bucket.

At last conditions had improved after the storms. Now I could wash my hair in a pint of warm, fresh water, and brush my teeth after over a week of being on watch and sleeping in the same damp clothes. Thank goodness I had had my hair cropped for this voyage.

My straw hat came out with the warm, gentle breezes and hot sun and after two weeks I was able to discard my thermals at last. Pulling back from the abyss, I felt we were really living at last.

What wonders we'd seen: fifty dolphins jumping in a solid mass from the same wave; two small flying fish dumped on our decks; a shark and a sunfish. Chirpy, the little yellow siskin which landed exhausted on the boat in mid-ocean, was fed and watered for four days before he recovered enough to fly on towards the dim lump of Palma on the horizon.

MARIE CHRISTINE

It took us fifteen days to reach the Canary island of Santa Cruz de la Palma. It had been every bit as tough as I had remembered from other sea trips, and I felt my reluctance had not been misplaced. Along the way, Brian had got a message through to Bruce and Rita, who were joining us for the 3,000-mile tradewind Atlantic crossing to Barbados: 'The cooker doesn't work, there's hardly any water and very little food.' It can't have cheered them much. The cooker needed coaxing. It would work, but it didn't get much use on the first leg. We had decided beforehand that the cooking would be done on a rota basis, mostly by Will, me, Bec and Andy. But none of us felt equal to it. Isso would come into my cabin when I was off watch and wishing I was anywhere but on this boat, and ask wistfully, 'What will we have for lunch, Mama?' During the first week I couldn't bear to think about food, let alone prepare it. A hot drink, an oatcake, a piece of Richard's supply of chocolate (which, in spite of his generosity, lasted the whole fifteen days) and maybe an apple were quite enough for me. John and Richard were always happy to eat muesli. Brian was permanently hungry, and quite rightly ate most of our store of tinned pilchards and mackerel fillets, which were accessible along with the oatcakes, in the main cockpit combing above the galley ceiling. I panicked, thinking he would eat our whole supply, but the poor bloke had to eat something. One night I cooked a chicken, but it nearly finished me. I felt I had hit rock bottom on another day, when all I could do was open tinned sardines, crouched over newspapers on the saloon floor. But gradually the weather warmed and the sea calmed, and the seasick began to feel human again. Cooking recommenced once we had cleared up the galley. There were sticky patches from the spilled sugar and vintage dregs of tea and coffee swilling about the sink and at the back of the cupboards. The cooker had All-Bran on and under it, along with boiled-over soup, and there were black hairs stuck to every damp surface. The fruit and vegetables had been as battered as the crew. Nearing the Canaries, with the sun warming our backs, we sorted through them, leaving a trail in our wake.

I knew my clothes stank. I'd been wearing the same things for well over a week. I flung my tights into the garbage bag when I finally peeled them off and managed the first glorious wash of the trip with a pint of warmed water balanced cautiously in the aft heads and scented soap. With cleanish hair and new clothes, I felt that maybe I would make a comeback.

Nearing the land, the old familiar excitement mounted. Seabirds and dolphins escorted us towards the small, fertile, mountainous island of La Palma. Years ago, John and I, with seven-year-old Bec, had stopped here on our way to the Spanish Sahara, and I remembered the welcoming yacht club, the swimming pool and a good bar crowded out with many other sailors waiting for the right time to cross the Atlantic. John and I struggled with our memories. It all looked so different now. Where were all the yachts? Part of the harbour appeared to have been filled in. Finally we spotted the yacht club, beside a big road which hadn't been there before. A stout Spaniard, his deep suntan interrupted only by white aertex shorts in which his generous private parts were bagged up, shouted from a nearby boat, 'Muy peligroso!' His eyes rolled dramatically. 'El viento, el muelle!' The wind, the wall. We smiled back. We felt euphoric. We had survived the perils of the North Atlantic; surely nothing else could be as bad. We had read in the pilot that 'El Caldero' blew only in December, tumbling down the mountain in hurricane-force gusts. We dropped our anchor, tied up to the shore to be safe and opened the champagne.

We planned to stay here for two weeks, to ensure that our arrival in the Caribbean would fall after the end of the hurricane season. We had a lot of sorting out to do, and John's father was coming out to join us for a few days. It would be like a holiday. Spirits were high. Sadly, Brian had to rush back to IBM headquarters in Paris. He caught a flight early the next morning. Richard stayed on, kindly bringing back to the boat bottles of delicious wine, cakes, cheeses and bunches of flowers. Soon all the jugs on board were stuffed with flowers: champagne-pink roses fought for space alongside yellow and ruby chrysanthemums and exotic strelitza, their orange plumage flying high over a bunch of blue papery everlasting flowers. Hotter at anchor than sailing, John and I preferred to sleep in the saloon. With us lying there, on either side, wrapped in our white cotton sheets, the flowers lent our quarters an air of sepulchral finality. But the strelitzas were not allowed to stay there long. Three times they toppled, spilling water over John's sleeping area. 'Haven't we had enough of this?' he snarled through clenched teeth as he thrust them out into the cockpit, where Andy had moved to sleep. 'Oh, am I to have the budgies, then?' he chuckled.

It was good to feel safe again. We aired and dried our bedding, got our washing organised and started on the big job of sorting out the stowage. On the second night, I rather bullied everyone into going to the theatre for a recital of chamber music. The handsome colonial building was packed out with smartly dressed locals. Shamefully, we all fell into a deep sleep during the first part and then again after the interval. The next night, at an old restaurant in town, we celebrated Richard's birthday with a huge paella and vast quantities of red wine. We took a bus into the mountains, where the air was sweet with the scent of Canary pines. Life seemed pretty good. How carefree we had become.

John

A couple of days later the 8,500ft mountains were wreathed in swirling black cloud and vicious downdraughts gained strength all day. What the whole team badly needed was a peaceful holiday in the sun. I was feeling fat and listless. On leg 1 my hair had turned greyer and the horizon looked blurred when I was tired. I was losing my prized long sight.

The few foreigners in the harbour were soon in trouble. Trying to escape, a trendy French sloop cut a Dutch boat's anchor line, causing it to tangle with an old Canadian schooner. I felt sick just watching. Unable to afford both the insurance premium and trip, I'd chosen the trip, so I was unwilling to just sit and wait for disaster to strike. We had to leave the anchorage. I would have preferred the open sea, but the harbour entrance was very tricky in these conditions and besides, I needed to go into town the following morning. So we dropped our moorings, lifted the stern anchor and joined several other boats motoring desperately round and round the harbour in gathering darkness. It was the beginning of a long night. The huge road signs on the roundabout were flattened, palm trees crashed down and deckchairs whirled crazily along the waterfront. Curtains of rain came swooping down from the mountains, temporarily obscuring everything. Then, shortly after midnight, a power cut killed the streetlighting and everything went black.

Over the VHF radio, from one of the circling boats, a Frenchman told us he was recording 70-knot gusts and more. 'I don't know what to do!' I wailed into the night as I weaved in and out of the other boats. More dangerous were the almost submerged rafts of debris blown into the harbour, threatening to entangle our propellor.

At last, with the dawn, the wind dropped and a watery sun struggled out to warm us. Wearily, we tied up and went ashore to continue shopping for the long haul across the Atlantic. Andy and Will stayed aboard to look after the boat. After lunch, Marie Christine and I were quick to accept my father's offer of a rest in his hotel room.

When we awoke at 5 pm the storm had returned. Restaurant chairs came bowling along the pavement to meet me as I dashed through torrential rain. What was the point in running? Utterly alone, but for the drumming of an awning, I slumped in a café chair in the lee of a wall. It was like newsreel footage of one of those hurricanes in a Florida town. I knew for certain that *English Rose*, lying broadside to the wind across the end of the quay, could not have survived. I'd lost the boat which had taken me twice round the world. So this was how the end would feel. At least the family were safe.

But after a while I could wait no longer. I ran splashing through rain-lashed streets. The empty cars were already axle-deep in water by the time I struggled across the road to enter the port. Beyond the oily-brown flood-stain sweeping across the harbour, I caught a glimpse of her white bow as I jinked between the stacks of banana containers. Impossible: she was still afloat. How many lives can a cat have? I raced on with fresh strength in my legs.

'Oh, the gusts were nothing like as strong as they were in the morning, while you were out shopping in the sun,' grinned Andy, as we secured the boat for the night, laying our third anchor and chain across the dirt road, among the deckchairs still strewn below the yacht club wall. He and Will had saved the day, and a lot of other days to come, by hauling the boat 30ft clear of the wall.

Later that night we heard that a British yachtsman had been killed when his boat was crushed against the harbour in Funchal, further to the north.

Our few days of rest passed too soon. 'I'll miss your nightly phone calls from Ardmore,' sighed my elderly father as we drank a last cup of coffee. It was time for us to sail for Barbados.

'Well, I'll fax you in Wimbledon every night,' I said, feeling a flash of guilt at sailing off for eighteen months with only part of the family. Marie Christine's mother in Brighton, the same age as my father, was also left behind. 'Switch your machine on before you go to sleep, and my message will be there when you wake up.'

When Bruce and Rita arrived from an inter-island ferry, we were ready for the Atlantic crossing. In the Reynolds' absence from Ardmore, Roy and Moira Morley were kindly relaying any messages for us over the INMARSAT C from their home in Southampton and Roy soon got us working a sensible schedule. Isso was always on the look-out for the flashing yellow light on the blue box which heralded an arriving signal, and she was now expert at setting up the replacement IBM Thinkpad PC my father had brought out with him.

We weighed anchor at 12.40 pm on 2 November and motored out of the harbour waving forlornly at the disappearing figure of Richard. Isso scattered in our wake the last of the flowers with which, to Marie Christine's delight, he had filled our saloon when the boat was in port. It was calm and sunny but we motored down the rocky coast of Santa Cruz de la Palma with heavy hearts at leaving my father and Richard.

The familiar pangs of anxiety returned with the coming of night and blinking lighthouses. Ancient mariners, making their departure from the Old World at this point, fearful lest they might fall off the edge of the flat earth, had called the Hierro Light the 'End of the World'. On the midnight watch, as Marie Christine and I watched the ancient light dip below our eastern horizon, we too wondered if we would survive all that would surely befall us.

3

Trail of Dreams

MARIE CHRISTINE

We had been away from Ardmore a month. The shocking experiences of the Atlantic storms had cauterised my misery at leaving home. The two weeks in Santa Cruz de la Palma had helped us feel human again. The old town, with its narrow cobbled streets lined with ornate stone town houses and intricately carved timber balconies, probably hadn't changed much since the early traders sailed to the New World. Our 2,500-mile journey across the Atlantic was very much in the tradition of countless others begun from this westerly island in the Canaries group.

Bec and I grimly finalised the stowage before the seasickness set in. We had to be better prepared for the storms to come than we had been on the last leg. Although we already had a vast amount of grub on board, squirrel-like, Bec and I had acquired even more. The dehydrated and canned stores put on at Ardmore were being saved for the Antarctic, still another twelve months away. But we might have to eat it sooner: we had heard rumours of high food prices in the Pacific, with cabbages selling for US$8 apiece.

Our projected journey was enormously ambitious. We had so many hurdles to jump: crossing the Atlantic, getting through the Panama Canal, negotiating uncharted coral atolls in the Pacific, taking Elizabeth to Peru . . . And then there was the Antarctic – in a plastic boat! My over-active imagination raced through every possible scenario as we pushed and shoved boxes of cheaper-than-milk wine into lockers, sorted luscious tomatoes and peppers into boxes so they wouldn't bruise, poured the best oranges in the world into nets, wrapped and listed the homes of cheeses, bread, milk, lettuces, salamis. I hoped our lovely fresh supplies would last a while.

Replacing Richard and Brian, we now had on board our good friends Bruce and Rita Reynolds from Ardmore. Bruce slightly built, dark, with a badger-like grizzled beard, had a schoolboy's sense of adventure and had jumped at our invitation. Rita, his wife of two years, did not need much more persuasion. We had known Bruce for over twenty years. With his enthusiasm, energy and integrity he had successfully moved on from selling his own cabbages and fresh eggs at sixteen to becoming company secretary to a group of light-engineering firms in Surrey. He loved the mountains and wild places and had frequently visited us at Ardmore. Bruce had cared for his parents throughout their lives. Less than a year after his father had finally died, he had fallen in love with and married Rita. Bright as a sunbeam, she transformed his life. Rita had run her own PR company, handling the British Airways account for Scotland, as well as bringing up her two sons. When we heard that croft number 79 at Ardmore was to be put on the market, we phoned them. Waterfall Cottage became their home, and Rita gave up the high-flying executive life to garden and become a housewife. They felt they could live at Ardmore and earn their living outside, so Bruce set up in business as a management consultant, and was constantly in demand. He often walked in along the rocky path to Ardmore late at night, clutching a bunch of flowers for his lovely Rita.

Before we set off, Rita, who had run her own office for many years, had generously offered to run 'Base Camp', dealing with our mail and bookings for the summer courses we planned to resume when we returned eighteen months later, as well as receiving and relaying the many messages that whizzed back and forth from *English Rose* via INMARSAT C. Rita soon discovered how keen a communicator John was, and had to put in a plea for him not to send messages during Bruce's precious sleeping time. She had also cleaned out all the Ardmore fridges and all the muddle I had left behind. When I apologised for all the extra work we had given them, particularly Rita, she turned her bluest of eyes to me and said, 'Oh, but you have given us Ardmore.' I loved her then for caring about the place we thought most precious.

Bruce and Rita, in brilliant form, joined Andy's watch. And knowing there was a good chance he would be sick as soon as the swell formed,

Andy ran through the abandon-ship procedure once again. Bruce was wearing two anti-seasickness patches behind his ears and looked a little spaced out. The Reynolds had little sailing experience and were both non-swimmers, but they were just brimming with enthusiasm and soon had the cockpits cleaned and polished to match the shiny white topsides we'd scrubbed and waxed in Santa Cruz.

The wind piped up as we left the lee of the island and we bent on the new mainsail and engaged the Aries self-steering gear. With five sails up, *English Rose*, steering herself by the wind, skimmed along on a smooth milky-blue sea, searching for the north-east tradewinds. At last, John's promise was beginning to come true: we really were running downwind on the trail of dreams, heading for the Caribbean in the New World.

The good weather helped us all, and particularly Andy, to quickly get over any initial seasickness, and we soon settled into our routine after the days of loafing around onshore. I knew John preferred this discipline – he had been trained for this life since he first went to the Nautical College in Pangbourne at the age of twelve. At his interview, the captain superintendent had jotted down his impression of the candidate: 'A rather dull and uninteresting boy.' I had to disagree with him on that, at least. Perhaps the college, and his time in the Parachute Regiment, had changed him. After all those years of turning out on parade in the smartest of uniforms, he liked everything to be orderly and precise. On land, this, and his constant sense of doom, seemed cranky and out of place; here, on a small boat in a vast ocean, where all manner of threats lurked, 'shipshape and Bristol fashion' made sense. I felt safe with him.

The days and nights passed slowly as we clocked up the mileage. Life at sea requires patience. Coping with some aspects was easier than others. I suppose we all found the night watches hard. I wondered if I would ever get used to waking up at 11.50 pm with John and Isso, running the boat for two hours, then sleeping again until we came on for our six-to-ten morning watch, which was much easier than the midnight session. But these watches at least gave us some time to ourselves, something I felt was most necessary in such a confined space.

Bec and Will shared a watch, and I felt it would certainly put their friendship to the test. They were going to see each other in every situation and mood.

Most nights it was just a question of keeping a good look-out, checking the self-steering and the set of the sails. Above all, we had to make sure nothing was chafing. This was John's nightmare: he expected things to last for ever. But sometimes the two hours between midnight and two in the morning seemed interminable. John and I usually kept up a conversation, discussing every topic imaginable. Naturally, the more controversial it was, the more engrossing it would be. We agreed on most subjects, but very often a book we were both reading would produce violently opposing opinions. One of the first I read on this leg was *The Happy Isles of Oceania* by Paul Theroux. I was greatly taken with his style of writing and was enjoying his rather downbeat approach. After I had tried rather badly to explain this, John remarked: 'Women would like that sort of book,' which I thought insulting, though maybe it wasn't meant that way.

'What do you mean by that?' I retorted. We twittered on, both feeling the other was being contrary.

'I don't want to spend all night arguing with you,' John shouted, loud enough for me to hear over the surfing waves. I fumed silently and wondered about the point at which a discussion turns into an argument and becomes personal.

If it was a quiet night, Isso would sit in a heap in the doghouse, pretending to be awake. It was hard for her, but we were a team and she had to contribute. Soon she became an important part of it. 'I'll just go and read the barometer,' she would mutter, suddenly waking just before the hour. Squeezing through the tiny hatch, hampered by her bulky red oilskins, she would beetle down the rickety wooden ladder and clump through the darkened galley and into the saloon. Flickering her torch on the main bulkhead, she would read the barometric pressure from the brass instrument she polished daily and scuttle back to fill in the logbook. Kept in the dry, on the doghouse table, our logbook was red, a Collins feint-lined one with black masking tape stiffening the spine. It was treated with even more respect than the Bible. And woe betide anyone who made a wrong entry. In the early days, we crew didn't dare write anything more than what was essential. John, however, used the logbook as a noticeboard, listing jobs, exhorting us to be watchful of chafe, or simply counselling patience: 'Reel out, reel in.' Later on, debates were carried on in these pages: differing views over time zones; did a waning moon face inward or outward? After our experience of running the boat during the nine months of the Whitbread race, John and I were wary of open discussions with opinionated individuals. We knew that the pressure-cooker atmosphere on a three-week ocean-crossing voyage could turn innocuous subjects into contentious issues in moments. We had so far to sail: we had to work at getting on together.

Mealtimes were a highlight of the day. With the exception of John and Bruce, we took it in turns to do the cooking. If it wasn't too rolly, each of us felt compelled to try to produce ever more imaginative dishes within the limitations of our ingredients, a dodgy oven and two burners in a lurching galley. We all wanted to be top chef. Will always made a great effort, spending hours poring over my tattered copy of Katie Stewart's *Times Cookery Book*, but his enthusiasm waned temporarily when he tried baked stuffed marrow.

We were running downwind, before the south-east tradewinds, making good progress, with the Yankee headsail poled out to starboard and the mainsail well out to port. But this exaggerated the rolling motion, and below in the galley, each lurch had to be anticipated. Twice the steaming silver-foil torpedo shot out of the oven and on to the floor. The marrow survived and was eaten with gusto: it was Will who exploded, with rage. Used to taking lots of exercise on land, he was finding being penned up on board a small boat very frustrating. Having spent thirty years with John, I recognised this problem early on. Long winters at Ardmore, when the ice stopped us from our daily run out to the main road, turned my husband into a wild bear, irritable and depressed. 'I'm getting off at Bermuda!' Will would fume at Bec. She giggled to herself, since of course it was Barbados we were headed for.

On the night watch, we would gaze into the velvet black sky, watching shooting stars exploding in a final annihilating flash. Often John went below to fax messages up to one of the satellites we could see spinning across the firmament, way above us, and the signals would be passed back to earth somewhere in faraway Europe.

Isso would be trying to keep awake but frequently, and thrillingly, I would be alone at the wheel, steering into the night as the boat surfed on the luminous crests. Between six and eight in the morning, the rest of the crew would be sleeping, although Rita was usually up well before her watch at ten. She'd wash and dress in the privacy of her kaftan, the wondrously voluminous blue tent she slept in – quite handy when you are sharing a cabin with five others. But usually the boat was ours alone from six until seven o'clock. John worked out an exercise plan for A Watch, as we called ourselves, and there was lots of knee-bending, running on the spot and loosening up. We sang loudly to keep up the rhythm and hung on like grim death to save ourselves from falling over the side from a sudden lurch or too much mirth. Isso and I struggled to hide our giggles from our strict PT master.

Life on board had definitely improved since Leg 1. For one thing, in the Canaries, Andy had glued up the leaks in our cabin windows with black mastic and there was no more seawater gushing in to wet my bedding. Instead we had a hot, dry airless box. And it was getting hotter by the day. John was soon sleeping naked, covered only by a sheet, on the seat on port side of the saloon. I was ambivalent at the decision to remove the partition between our heads and the aft cabin, which had become a store and a passageway to the doghouse. Now, when we washed or went to the lavatory, we were on view to anyone moving to or from the doghouse. I wondered whether our loss of privacy was worth this slight increase in airflow. I rigged up a curtain from a tea towel, but I wasn't too happy about it. I soon followed John into the saloon, taking the narrower starboard seat for my bunk and rolling up my sheets whenever I was up. It was to be the first of several moves to find somewhere cool in a boat with very little ventilation, set up primarily for the Antarctic climate.

JOHN

Stretched out on my bunk in the skipper's cabin, I was reading Alan Clark's *Diaries*. They reminded me of all I was trying to escape: Madonna pop culture, ugliness, squalor, noise, aggression, deceit, shallowness, glib superficiality and an all-embracing lack of integrity. Clearly, I was going dotty.

In my negative state of mind, the great tradewind sail across the Atlantic produced none of the balm I'd experienced on previous voyages. The place seemed like a desert, and I a stranger to it. My essential enthusiasm for life had vanished in my searing rage over that damned film, which seemed to have rubbished the central twenty-five years of my life. I didn't feel well; I had no energy. Physical strength in my arms and legs was gone. If I leaned on a winch it hurt, and the imprint remained in my flesh. Even here, deep down in the pointless abyss of self-pity, I couldn't escape the programme: faxes pursued me, wanting this and that for the version going out on the American network. I felt used, eaten up with chagrin. There's no fool like an old fool. But I suppose the truth was, having lived by the publicity sword, I was now dying by it, so to speak.

I'd lost, and I was proving a very bad loser. Not really the sort of person you'd look for as a skipper.

Marie Christine sang her heart out on the long night watches, but it was no good. I was in a terrible sulk.

REBECCA

The days were passing slowly for all of us. By day 15 of our Atlantic crossing, we were over halfway across this watery desert. Bustling along at the rate of 150 miles each day, it was hard to believe how utterly empty it was. We had seen no ships for eight days and for once we were longing for a sign of human life.

I had to confess that sadly, even though the sea must be in my blood, I found this straight-line course almost like being in suspended animation, just something we had to get through to reach the oasis of the Caribbean. I wished it was otherwise and felt terribly ungrateful that it was not. Maybe I would learn to love the ocean in time. If squeezing toothpaste from the wrong end of the tube upsets you, ocean-sailing may not be your bag. Considering that we were all used to a hectically busy and physical way of life, the eight of us thrust together in the heat and rolling confines of a 57ft fibreglass boat were getting along and coping well.

The three watch teams now consisted of Dad, Mum and Isso (A Watch); me and Will (B); and Andy, Bruce and Rita (C). Our days fitted quickly into a pattern. Our watch system formed the framework of each twenty-four hours: two hours on and four off during the night; four on and eight off in the daytime. Will and I took over from two until six each afternoon and it was always boiling hot. But often the heat was relieved by heavy showers, for which we donned light waterproof jackets over our swimming costumes.

Our foremost duty on watch was to keep a good look-out, but there was seldom anything to see. All the same, on every hour we filled in all the columns in the log: date, time, log, course steered, course required, wind speed and direction, barometer and the steering check. When the engine was running to charge our batteries (so that Isso could play her tapes of Madonna, Kylie and the like) we recorded the temperature and oil pressure and how many pumps were needed with the foot pump to fill the header tank with fuel. Then there was the number of pumps required to empty each of the bilges: forward, main and aft. Hundreds of miles from land, the Global Positioning System, or GPS, took a lot of the work out of navigation; all we had to do was look at the little screen in the doghouse and write down the latitude and longitude – it was as simple as that. It also told us how many miles we still had to go.

The wind blew steadily in the north-east trades, so with the help of the Aries self-steering gear on the stern, *English Rose* was guiding herself happily downwind. Really, we had very little to do – except for performing Dad's interminable lists of boring jobs, which appeared all over the log. There seemed to be no end to polishing and working up the boat for the challenges ahead.

We did the maintenance work during our daytime watch. The only real hitch would come in the very unlikely event of a fish taking a bite at the yellow plastic 'muppet' which Dad had rigged up to trail behind.

We were the last watch of daytime, so everyone else relaxed. Dad lay in his bunk, naked but for a scrap of sheet, reading anchoring techniques and muttering, 'Land is the most dangerous thing at sea, that's why I've always kept away from it,' while Mum read autobiographies or encouraged Isso with her geography and history books – I wish I had learned the same way – and Andy kept his nose in his *Practical Boatowner's Guide to Maintenance*.

Every 15 degrees of longitude we covered to the west – roughly every five days at the speed we were travelling – we knocked twenty minutes off our watch, as did the other two watches. This total of an hour kept the hours of light and dark correct and took us into the next time zone. Each night we stood two watches, but they were only two hours long, from ten until midnight and from four until six each morning.

As we looked up into the star-filled sky, discussing everything under the moon, we had great laughs and jokes. The conversation always reverted to food, and what we were going to do when we got home. My garden was soon replanned, the cooker would be moved and Marron hens purchased for daily eggs. We did have the very occasional midnight feast, but my meanness and obsession with conserving rations did not allow poor Will much.

Of course, as on Leg 1, there were new wonders to be seen. Bullet-nosed flying fish lifted from the waves, gliding out of control, their tails a vague rudder, escaping their hunters until they crashed into the sea again. Best of all, the green flash, which I was lucky enough to see on our first evening out from Palma. It is visible only in cloudless conditions as the last of the sun disappears below the western horizon. We have been chasing it ever since.

Marie Christine

By day, the saloon resembled a library reading room. Although none of us were seasick any more, some still felt queasy, and it was an effort to do anything, particularly if you were not the duty cook. Reading was about as much as we could manage, and you could lie down to do that. Isso never once felt sick from the sea, and it was in this rather convalescent atmosphere that she really got to grips with reading, which pleased me and John greatly. She became completely immersed in a book I had just finished – *Adrift* by Steven Callahan, the graphic account of a young American yachtsman whose boat was sunk in a collision with a whale on the very same route we were now following. With extraordinary fortitude, he managed to survive for seventy-six days in a rubber liferaft with virtually no food or water, constantly under attack by dorados and sharks. The author had illustrated the book with his own haunting pencil drawings, and it absolutely captivated Isso. Struggling with Christopher Columbus, at last she had found something which seemed really relevant.

Our days were punctuated with small events recorded in the log-book: 'Day 12, 1600 hrs, solitary white-tailed tropic bird sighted. Day 13, 0800 hrs, return of solitary white-tailed tropic bird. Day 14, 0400 hrs, only 1,000 miles to go!' On 14 November we celebrated Bruce's fiftieth birthday with champagne in plastic mugs and a stupendous cold lunch prepared by Rita, British Airways style, as we lurched along. She knew exactly what Bruce would like on this special day. A meat-and-two-veg man, he stoically chewed his way through bowls of 'string' (spaghetti), and the risottos and juicy pizzas we were managing to make in our rather erratic oven. He was beginning to look rather thin. Now Rita's corned beef, served with some of the vegetables that were still just hanging on, brought a smile to his face.

Some of us were longing for the land after so many days of this unrelieved water. The name Antilles is supposedly a corruption of the name Atlantis, the mythical lost continent that Columbus thought he had found as he searched for a new route to the Orient. And 500 years on we were following in his wake, watching the same sun rise and set; the same tropical moon rise in a jewelled night sky; tasting the same salt on our lips as the tradewind whipped up the sea. It was a giant geography and history lesson Isso and the rest of us would never forget.

'Oh Bruce, we've too much to lose! Don't let's take such a risk again!' I wasn't exactly eavesdropping, but on a small boat it is sometimes impossible not to overhear conversations. We had almost crossed the Atlantic; Barbados was just beyond the western horizon, where the big red sun was falling fast through a copper sky. But in spite of the Caribbean warmth an icy shiver went through my soul. Our own journey had hardly started.

Bruce and Rita were watching their last dazzling Atlantic sunset before returning to a late-November Ardmore – gales and lashing rain, days that end almost before they begin. Together, as always, they were busily blowing up cumbersome blue fenders in the centre cockpit, in readiness for our arrival, and musing over the past twenty days. By now the warm sun, blue skies and sea had seduced me: I didn't want to return with them, but I well understood what Rita was saying.

I knew John was worrying about the Reynolds missing their plane to London. Would we ever find Barbados? In olden times, before the magic of GPS dispelled contrary currents and winds, it could be difficult to find. 'Barbados done sunk. We was where she is, but she ain't dere no more!' was how schooner captains often used to justify their failure. Our pilot advised getting on the same latitude as this low-lying most easterly of Caribbean islands while still 100 miles out in the Atlantic. I'd read that the name Barbados comes from the Portuguese *los barbudos*, the bearded ones, after early sailors spotted wispy shoots hanging from the upper branches of the banyan trees growing near the shore. This tree-covered island, just 21 miles by 14, was claimed by England in 1625. Within a few years the trees had been cleared and almost the entire island was planted with sugarcane for the production of rum and muscovado sugar. African slaves and convicts from Britain worked the plantations and for a while the island was known as 'the brightest jewel in the English Crown'. At independence in 1966, Barbados remained part of the British commonwealth and of all the Caribbean islands it was probably the most British. Nowadays, most of the population of 260,000 are involved in tourism, but there is still a small sugarcane industry making plenty of rum. Cricket is played obsessively. Gary Sobers, Gordon Greenidge and Malcolm Marshall all came from Barbados. It would suit both John and me: I would sample the rum, and John might see a bit of cricket.

John nursed an illusion about what he considered his exceptional powers of long sight. Years of ghastly family trips on boats had established a desperate competition for the first to spot land, and the prize was always the same: a notional Penguin biscuit. On day 20, at 8.55 am on Sunday 21 November 1993, Rita and I both spotted what we thought was land. The others were sceptical, and no Penguin was awarded. Ten minutes later, I was alone at the wheel when the sea boiled just in front of *English Rose*, and a huge brown whale surfaced dead ahead. With it a strong odour of fish filled the air. I was shocked and thrilled at what I saw. In terror I gripped the wheel, knowing there was no way at these close quarters that I could avoid hitting it. The boat would be holed and we would all sink, maybe drown. My screams brought everyone rushing up on deck but the whale had gone and never reappeared. More scepticism.

Wild excitement among Isso, Will, Bec and me at the proximity of land had us hurtling around, tidying up and generally getting ready. John, who always preferred the being-at-sea bit, had hinted that he wouldn't mind carrying on. His last trip had lasted for 203 days without stopping.

'Look at my shoes,' wailed Bruce, waving his mildewed brogues. 'They look just like I feel,' he grinned, speaking for us all. Blueish-grey mould covered much of our smarter going-ashore kit which had been stowed away in plastic bags in the lockers.

A sunny West Indian voice came up on the airwaves, filling our boat with still more excitement. 'Come on in, *English Rose*. Welcome to Barbados.' It was all so different from grey Europe.

By 1.30 pm we were there, through the reefs and currents and neatly tied up in Bridgetown Harbour. Clutching his father's battered briefcase, John clambered up the iron ladder on to the wharf. Wearing rather torn duck shorts, a smart white shirt and long socks to match, and a grimly determined expression, he set off in the baking heat on the half-mile walk around the harbour to get clearance for the crew to land. A flashy Swedish yacht followed us in and immediately cracked open several bottles of champagne while we looked on, somewhat disdainfully, sipping tea from chipped mugs. We had drunk champagne on arriving in the Canaries to celebrate having survived the North Atlantic. Compared to Leg 1, this had been a doddle.

4

Shattered Illusions

JOHN

Striding across the quay to the smart new port offices, built to entice ever more cruise liners to the island, I was very much aware of the great romance of it all. My legs stretched proudly: this was not just another grey day at the office.

I had to do the rounds, sitting quietly before uniformed officials in their box-like offices: Customs first, then Immigration and, finally, Health. It all took time, and I reminded myself that I was in a foreign land and must be patient and adjust to a slower pace. The fellows were polite, taking pains to explain why they had to be so careful: just recently, an unidentified yacht had put a small group of Africans ashore by rubber dinghy, telling them they were safely in Brazil. After the yacht disappeared into the night, the unfortunate Barbadian taxpayers had had to foot the airline bill to repatriate the poor mugs.

After a few days in Barbados, we planned to sail overnight for Bequia to pick up our friends Richard and Jink Morris-Adams, who were flying out to join us for a pre-Christmas ten-day cruise south through the Grenadines. Unfamiliar with the Caribbean, we had only a hazy outline of a plan really. We hoped to visit Mustique, Mayreau and maybe Carriacou on our way to Grenada; then, after dropping off Richard and Jink, we would make a bee-line for Bonaire for Christmas. But top priority was a spell of lazing in the sunshine. 'Begone dull care . . .'

But first we had a rendezvous to keep in Carlisle Bay. 'We are

anchored in front of your hotel. Your yacht awaits you!' I beamed my
INMARSAT message up into space and down into the Grand Hotel, where
my brother Paul was just sitting down to his supper, like a latterday
James Bond. Unfortunately, we couldn't quite live up to the grandiosity
of all this high-tech stuff and our dinghy was drowned in the surf. So it
was a pair of sopping wet 'real cool dudes' who squelched out of the
night and into the hotel lobby. Still, it was good to show up on cue, after
all the hypothetical talk at home.

Next morning a beautiful racehorse came swimming round the
English Rose, black and as finely tuned as the magnificently sculpted
groom at its neck, its nostrils flared with the effort.

We spent a week in Barbados, battling with Customs and airport officials, struggling to trace and clear our fine new mizen staysail in red,
white and blue which had been flown over from Ratsey's on the Isle of
Wight, and the replacement parts for the Rutland wind generator, which
had overwound itself during the storm in faraway Palma.

This was a time for acclimatisation. With the trip coming right at the
end of a busy twenty-fifth season at home, we seemed to have been on
the move for ever. Now, anchored close in, where the shallows were
good for snorkelling and the long crescent beach in Carlisle Bay ideal for
running, I was able to relax at last. And after a few days, the years began
to slip away and I felt the old optimism seeping back through my veins.

Bruce and Rita flew home to the coldest November weather on
record, and it was some time before they opened up from Base Camp on
the INMARSAT. Storms brought down both electricity and telephone poles
along the path to Ardmore, and no sooner was this damage repaired
than an electrical storm blasted their fax machine, computer terminal
and modem.

It was stiflingly hot aboard *English Rose*, and I began a humiliating
running battle with prickly heat. From the yellowed pages of my
Traveller's Guide to Health, I extracted the following:

The prickling sensation is due to a blockage of the mouths of the
sweat glands which prevents the sweat from escaping. Back pressure is set up and the sweat tries to force its way out through the
neighbouring layers of skin cells. Fine eruptions appear, compris-
ing vesicles set in red inflamed skin, accompanied by intense
irritation. The condition is greatly aggravated by heat or exercise
which would otherwise cause an increase in sweating. Sleep is

commonly interfered with and the lack of adequate rest and sleep may cause a deterioration in general health and mental wellbeing. Infection of the unhealthy skin is likely to occur, especially if the patient has been scratching. No treatment has yet been found to be very successful although many soaps, powders, lotions and ointments have been tried. Prevention of secondary infection calls for two or three cool showers daily, with gentle but thorough drying by dabbing and the application of calamine lotion BP. If infection has supervened, wash the area with cetrimide solution (see lacerated wounds) and apply dibromopropamidine cream.

With six long months in the tropics stretching ahead of me, I would come to regret not reading these pages more carefully. In the market, a huge mama advised the medicated soap she plucked from a shelf in her stall, pushing a tin of dusting powder my way. But it didn't do much for me.

'I think I'm going to fall in love with the West Indies,' Marie Christine crooned, 'but I never dreamed we'd get you here, Johnny.' At least this was a welcome change from the recriminations of Leg 1.

Brother Paul joined us for the gentle night passage across to Bequia. We were met by the dramatic rock silhouettes and welcoming green of the North Grenadines as dawn swept in from the ocean behind us. A battered red fishing boat, no larger than the wooden dinghies we use for crossing the loch at home in Scotland, was battering its way to windward, struggling for the first chance of the day at the fish on the edge of the shelf. A solitary fisherman in the stern waved to us with that easy elan so often found among those unfettered by possessions. This image of material poverty contrasted strongly with the backdrop of manicured lawns nestling among dense scrub on the discreet super-rich and private island of Mustique.

Coming slowly into the shelter of Bequia's Admiralty Bay, we were greeted by a wall of heat and the sight of more than fifty yachts at anchor. Bequia looked as close to paradise as anything I've ever seen. We found a little space and dropped our 75lb CQR anchor in 6 metres of clear, blue water. On either side dense tropical vegetation clung to steep volcanic slopes in many shades of green. It was all so restful on the eye after the glare from the sea.

But sadly, the little black hands stretching out to greet us as we came to the shore wanted only our dollars. And while tying our trusty Avon inflatable to the dinghy dock at the foot of the town pier, I noticed that other boats were secured by padlock and wire cable. The narrow waterfront road, lined with boutiques and ice-cream parlours, was thick with brand-new taxis and bright shiny pick-ups with names like Fatman and Gideon. These symbols of progress had appeared with the opening of the airport the year before. The sub-branch of Barclays Bank was still advertising 'loans for purchasing vehicles' in their window.

But it was difficult to be sure where progress was leading. Bequians come in all shades and sizes, but mostly they are descended from the slaves freed in 1832, tall and athletic, graceful and jet-black, with proud African features. They appeared simple folk, gently laid back. The comparatively easy business of extracting pickings from tourists had swamped almost every other form of livelihood; goods were almost all imported and simply sold on to holidaymakers. The transient nature of this trade precluded long-term relationships and the mostly affluent, white visitors were held in barely disguised contempt by the locals. Any flicker of sincerity was soon extinguished by the passing of the dollar bill. But who could blame them? If anyone should bear a grudge, surely the descendant of a slave has a right to do so. Many of today's island families had relations doing menial work abroad, and letters home reporting abuse and the cold shoulder in Britain hardly fostered good relations. Perhaps it all boils down to doing as you would be done by. And the road-improvement scheme was sponsored by the People's Republic of China.

I may have been unduly pessimistic. The sun shone and as their song went, 'everythin' will be all right'. I hoped so.

While I was looking for the wild places hardly touched by modern man, I think the others aboard *English Rose* were content to find sun and fun in a British winter. The Caribbean was never going to be the best part for me. It was just somewhere I had to pass through to reach the Pacific.

Searching for something real among the dross, the fishing seemed the only natural thing. The rest was a theme park. I found an old man in a large, silent, empty shop making up traces, linking heavy nylon with thick Japanese swivels to piano wire. Patiently, he showed me how to whip soft seizing wire round the shanks of his double hooks to prevent fish from pulling them apart and straightening them. His fingers were long and misshapen and his wife had to work out the change for him. But he knew about fishing. The squid-like muppets were double-skirted in neon red and yellow plastic, and they worked.

Andy and I set up the heavy reel drum on the stern with 220m of green plaited polypropylene line leading to the old man's thick monofilament trace. When the fish took, the reel handle was braked by thick shock cord which whirred and thumped as it paid out, while we happy six were overtaken with panic. The muppet was trailed far astern, so as to allow plenty of spring in the long line, enough to take the shock of the leaping fish. Marie Christine's cooking turned them into the best marinated fish steaks I'd ever eaten. That memory was worth the three months and 6,000 miles we'd already travelled.

MARIE CHRISTINE

Bequia was the magic Caribbean hideaway island that everybody hopes to find, but as more and more people discover it, so the magic disappears. Maybe we were just not ready for it, still too wound up, too anxious. We had hardly dropped anchor in Admiralty Bay alongside the many charter boats when enterprising Bequians were out in their gaily painted boats trying to sell us everything from hair plaiting to fresh water, fruit, lobster, laundry services and fuel. It was all transacted in a lighthearted fashion, but we were in no doubt that we were the tourists to be fleeced.

Paradise took a dip and John despaired. Depression was on the verge of setting in in a big way. It was hard to hide it from the others on the boat. Knowing John, I so understood his unmitigating view. The TV bashing had already knocked his resilience and optimism, and he was sad to find this gem of an island sold out to tourism, honest values gone and materialism reigning supreme. But the rest of us were determined to enjoy ourselves: the show had to go on.

A long journey is a form of pilgrimage. The hardships reduce one to a state of uneasy grace. 'Missus, you mated with a Chinaman?' our ferryman asked me as he paddled Isso and me back to the boat. My lovely slant-eyed daughter and I laughed at his question.

We were no different from the thousands of tourists flooding in through the newly opened airport, come to enjoy a fortnight in the sun on a boat. But while they had worked hard at their office desks all year to spend freely for a week or two, we were on a tight budget. 'You shouldn't come to the west if you haven't got money. Stay home, missus!' one woman scolded, as I scoured the colourful fruit market along the frangipani-fringed beach for reasonably priced bananas. I knew after one look at us the prices doubled.

Much of my time ashore was spent shopping for food. We were a big family to feed. Just in case we were marooned at Christmas, I found and purchased a 'Piggy' – a ham smoked and cured in Virginia and sewn into an unbleached cotton bag devoid of anything resembling a sell-by date. By the look of its coating of dust, it would have been way past such a date anyway. Of course, there were exceptions. I asked if I could buy a breadfruit roasting in a fire on the beach, near where we left our dinghy. 'No, lady, you have it,' laughed a fine black man, raking it out of the embers and with easy swipes chopping off the blackened skin. He wrapped it in banana leaves and gave it to me with a dazzling grin. It was our first taste of these bright green football-sized fruits which nestled among the shiny dark green leaves on this handsomest of trees. Though better known for his mutiny, it was Captain Bligh who first brought breadfruit to the Caribbean, from Tahiti in 1793. It was delicious hot with butter. I paddled ashore later with some bars of our precious hoard of Thornton's fudge. I felt it was a good swap.

When we had got most of what we needed, we moved a mile or so out of Admiralty Bay to a more secluded spot where the water was clean and we could swim. The hot sun shone from a perfect blue sky while the south-east tradewinds cooled our tanning bodies. Life seemed pretty good. Some other yachties thought us eccentric because we didn't use an outboard on the back of our rubber dinghy preferring to row. Will had to be restrained – he soon broke two paddles overdoing the effort. At least, without an outboard, we didn't have to worry about our dinghy being stolen. It was a long haul from our new bay back to the town, but it could be managed. We took turns at going ashore to see the sights in the evening after supper. Isso definitely preferred to go with Bec, Will and Andy.

The old fogies, John and I, would boat-sit, relishing being on our own. Being of the same generation, and different from the others, John and I realised how much we agreed with each other after all. After folding away the huge white canvas awning which afforded us shade by day, we'd sit together on deck, with a glass of rum and freshly squeezed lemon, watching the sun drop into the sea, and breathing the sweet, cool air scented by many different trees and the waxen frangipani blossom. At such times life couldn't be better.

John perked up a bit when Richard and Jink Morris-Adams arrived and we sailed immediately for tiny Mustique, where we were ordered to pick up one of the buoyed moorings off the beach. Later that evening the mooring broke. Luckily, John was on deck. While we slept more easily lying to our own anchor, we understood the islanders' problem: repetitive anchoring is damaging the coral reefs.

John and Richard rushed ashore to get their scuba-diving equipment set up. It was fun for John to have a playmate. Once they were out of the way, Jink and I helped Isso into her mask, snorkel and flippers. She had never looked below the waves before, and I hoped that once she saw what was there she would be hooked. And so she was; we all were. 'You should have seen all the coloured fish: blue and red and yellow that were swimming with us, Danny!' Isso bubbled excitedly when her father returned. (She called him Danny, after the first friend she had made in Lima, Peru.) We had worried about her. While she liked the idea of swimming, when it actually came to getting into the water she would freeze in horror. We couldn't waste a year in the tropics, but what were we to do? No amount of coaxing would encourage her. I knew she was afraid of the surf, which was reasonable enough, and probably, if she thought too much about it, she would worry about what was underneath her as she swam round the boat. It was a problem we had to overcome together. She had swum at home and could easily keep afloat. Her compact, buoyant body was smooth as a seal's. Inevitably, one afternoon my patience ran out. 'Elizabeth, if you don't *try*, we're going to have to send you home and back to school,' I squawked. She knew I meant it. After a storm of tears and sulking, she plucked up the courage to give it a go. Very soon she was swimming round the boat and off the silver coral beach. Then she was jumping into the waves and calling out, 'Look at me, look at me.' It was a triumph. She was to become one of the keenest swimmers in the crew.

Bec had a new streamlined look in the water. 'Mum, will you cut my hair? I want it really short.' She was too hot. I remembered her rage when she was ten and I'd cut her fringe wrongly. Could I handle it? Blonde wisps floated away on the tide, mingling with white frangipani blossom as I snipped. It was quite the bravest thing I did on this voyage.

We planned to sail some 80 miles south to Grenada. Scattered across our route lay hundreds of tiny islands, cays, reefs and sandbars, known as the Grenadines. With a 9ft draught, we would need to proceed with great caution. We carried on board the *Admiralty Pilots* and *Don Street's Cruising Guide*, which were intriguing sources of information, covering historical and current matters as well as routes and hazards. Describing the lights and buoyage system, he wrote: 'Ranges in the

Tobago Cays will tend to put the yachtsman trying to sail into the anchorage right on the rocks.' He continued: 'The buoys at Montezuma Shoal and Grand de Coi are virtual boobytraps, likely to put yachtsmen right on top of the very dangers they are trying to avoid.' But a warm following breeze pushed us from one jewel of an island to another. All about, lush green tropical forest, fringed with blindingly pale coral sand, sloped gently into the translucent turquoise water. It was strange to take off the hair shirt I had worn for the thirty years I'd been married to John, who has never been known to do anything the easy way. Had he gone soft?

Arriving off the lovely near-deserted island of Mayreau on 8 December 1993, we found a giant white Christmas cake of a P&O liner landing its passengers on Saline Beach for a picnic. This was apparently a weekly event in the tourist season. John was appalled; the rest of us were intrigued to watch the bussing of 1,500 sun-dried pink tourists back to their ship in fast inflatables. In their wake, high-speed young staff collected the picnic paraphernalia – beach beds, umbrellas, barbecues and bars – while behind the dunes, locals from nearby islands were packing up their souvenir stalls, too. The tourists were a good cash crop for people who, until recently, had been living at barely subsistence level.

From our anchorage, the milky-blue water paling towards the golden sand of the nearby beach exactly matched the cover of John's battered copy of Eric and Susan Hiscock's *Around the World in Wanderer III*. Yet, catching up with his heroes forty-odd years on, John found these islands very different from the remote paradise so bewitchingly described by Eric in 1952. John blamed the Jumbo jets and cruise liners, disgorging their unending hordes of faceless short-term tourists, year after year, for subduing the locals into a bunch of waiters, guides and taxi drivers.

As the sky turned from blue, to rose, to gold, we ritually gazed at the setting sun dipping below the horizon, waiting for the green flash. I never saw it. And as we watched the big ship, lit over-all, disappearing into the night, the deserted half-mile-long beach of golden sand looked as if it had never been visited.

The following day we gingerly set course for the fabled Tobago Cays. Bec read out loud to us from our well-thumbed copy of the *Cadogan Guide to the Caribbean*, which I had bought in Inverness for John's birthday the previous July, hoping that we would really get here. 'Devotees of the Tobago Cays talk of them as the closest thing to heaven, and somehow it is true.'

By mid-morning we had dropped anchor. It *was* the perfect setting – even if we weren't the only boat. In fact, there were quite a number: nineteen short-term charter yachts. We had all come to see this horse-shoe lagoon of pellucid turquoise water. Within its coral rim lay a handful of tiny Bacardi islets, some just a single emerald palm above a strip of blinding silver sand. The Cays are now protected as a national park: no chucking of rubbish, no fishing for lobsters on the reefs. No spearing the brightly coloured parrot fish which the French especially love to eat, and which were rapidly being fished out.

John and I didn't have a double bed on the boat and we missed being together. I didn't want eighteen celibate months as well as all the other deprivations, so when we reached Union Island, he announced that he would buy planks of wood to make up a bed for us in the doghouse. These planks re-established marital harmony. We placed three of them across the seats in the doghouse, giving ourselves just enough space to crawl in under the low roof and lie side by side, full length across the boat. We padded the planks with the plastic-covered cushions and laid our bedding on top: a sheet in the tropics, sleeping bags and blankets when we got into cold waters. It was something like being in a tent on one of John's expeditions, and although the arrangement was only used when we were at anchor, the doghouse bedroom was a great escape.

At anchor in the tropics, Bec and Will developed their own sleeping quarters on deck, on the roof above the saloon, where they tied a small awning to the stays to provide shelter and some privacy. If a heavy squall hit, they leaped up, flinging their bedding down the hatch and racing to undo the flapping sailcloth. The rest of the permanent team, Isso and Andy, slept on the saloon seats which John and I occupied at sea.

Unused to boating in the tropics, we had had a windscoop made of blue canvas. It had the look of half a bathing tent hanging vertically over the forward hatch, catching any draughts and directing them down into the boat to ventilate the vessel and cool the air. It was worth every penny we spent on it. Apart from this, since we had blocked up the ventilation tubes to prevent leaks, *English Rose's* ventilation was almost non-existent, and lacking the electrical power of other boats, we couldn't run fans. While others admired her strong rigging and stormworthiness, *English Rose* was generally like an oven. But we would cope: it was more important to feel that we were in a strong boat designed for extreme conditions. Comfort could wait till we got home

JOHN

The old port of St George's is built on Grenada's steep slopes surrounded by tropical vegetation. They say it's the prettiest town in the Caribbean, a haunt of pirates in olden times. We sailed in late on a Sunday as the ochre-tiled roofs of the old buildings glowed in the evening light. What a magnificent setting. But there was an air of resentment and subdued violence to the town.

I hadn't noticed pictures of the rocket-shattered hotel in any of the glossy brochures I'd seen. These moonlit ruins presented a powerful reminder of the island's turbulent recent history. The following evening, Marie Christine and I went to find out more about it.

The rush-hour traffic splashed through the puddles as we waited in the darkness beside the main road at the entrance to the yacht club. At last, a powerful small black saloon braked to a halt and the driver leaned across to open the passenger door. 'John Ridgway?'

'Yes,' I nodded in the rain.

'Leslie Pierre. Hop in!' I pulled the seat forward and Marie Christine climbed into the back. Then I slid in beside the driver and slammed the door.

From the corner of my eye I studied our host, a stocky Grenadian in his mid-fifties with short, crinkly hair and a strong face. He was wearing a youthful claret turtleneck and dark trousers. In the casual manner of one who wields power, he seemed rather preoccupied and I didn't want to distract him since we appeared to be driving on the usual sort of time trial common among people under pressure.

'British resident's Christmas party,' barked Leslie at last, 'Sort of a farewell, really. He's been posted to Seville.'

Marie Christine took up the conversation, while I remained silent, feeling I'd learn more that way. Leslie admitted to owning a newspaper on the island; he was a friendly enough cove, but kept his distance. I decided he was the sort of fellow who was used to doing the talking, but in our case it was just small talk.

Turning down a dark lane in one of those island enclaves reserved for the rich, we were suddenly among parked official cars and lounging chauffeurs. Before leading us into the party, Leslie went to some trouble to ensure he would be able to make an early getaway.

Everyone was there. We were introduced to the prime minister, the chief of police, various members of government and the bishop. This was

the sort of place where it was important to be seen, and it offered people the chance to ask the odd favour in an oblique sort of way. Leslie
asked the prime minister, a solid-looking citizen from Carriacou, if he
could change the date of the forthcoming budget as it would help
reportage in his newspaper, but this request was greeted with chuntering
political prevarication.

It was not, however, our goldfish bowl and we felt out of place.
Pretty soon we found ourselves with another foreigner, a palid record-
company owner on vacation from New York with a bevy of dolly birds.
Others whispered that he'd once been Sting's drummer, so of course he
must be a multi-millionaire. He'd chosen to come dressed as Gandhi.
Our points of common interest being few, I turned to a tall distin-
guished-looking Grenadian of middle age who also appeared to be
rather out of the main flow.

I explained what we were doing on the island. He nodded across the
room towards his wife, a pretty Glasgow lawyer. 'We are retired now
and farming in the middle of the island, so we don't come into town
much any more,' he said rather sadly. 'But years ago, it was all very different. I went off to London and worked in a packaging factory to
support my legal studies. When I qualified, I applied for a job with the
Western Region of British Rail.' He smiled gently. 'They were wantin' a
fast bowler, so I got the job – as legal adviser – an' we won the regional
championships that year.'

By this time, Leslie had checked everything out and spoken to everyone who interested him. It was time to leave. Back in his car he was
noticeably more relaxed, even eager to talk. 'That tall retired chap
seemed a decent sort of fellow,' I said, recounting the fast-bowling story.

'I'm afraid I don't share your view,' Leslie replied coolly, as we
bumped along on the pot-holed road. 'We've known each other all our
lives. We were at school together. As you might have noticed, we didn't
shake hands.' I hadn't.

There was no stopping him now. He went on to explain how, when
the New Jewel Movement had come to power in the coup of 1979, my
fast-bowler friend had come home to Grenada to become attorney-
general under the communist leader Maurice Bishop.

'But didn't Bishop do rather well to begin with, in healthcare and education and so on?' I asked.

'Oh yes, they did – to begin with. But it wasn't radical enough for
some; they wanted closer ties with Cuba and the Eastern Bloc,' Leslie

went on grimly. 'I founded the *Voice*, a newspaper to voice public opinion in a dictatorship. I knew they would put me in jail, and they did. They also shot Bishop and veered sharply to the left.'

'How did you know you would ever be released?' Marie Christine asked.

'Well, I was sure the Americans must come. The Cubans came and built an international airport, ready to take the big cargo jets from Russia.' He paused. 'This was an unacceptable situation for America.'

Leslie told us he'd been psychologically tortured. His wife was allowed to visit him only once a month, and even then they'd sometimes cancel the visit to unsettle him. On other occasions they'd confiscate half the fruit she brought. 'They were rarely physically violent,' he said quietly.

'What about when you were released? Weren't you determined to bring those who'd persecuted you to justice?' Marie Christine was indignant.

'There were those who suggested that, but I didn't feel it was right. It would have done nothing to heal the wounds on the island. We needed reconciliation, not bitterness.' The black car purred downhill through the night and into the boatyard across from *English Rose*. I sensed that Leslie would have liked to have continued, but I felt we should go back to the boat.

Marie Christine

Richard and Jink flew home from Grenada on 18 December and the six of us set sail for Christmas on Bonaire, a little over 300 miles to the west. 'We'd better get there!' Bec levelled at her father. But she needn't have worried: John was keen – by mid-January he wanted to be in the Galapagos Islands, far out in the Pacific.

This was the first time we had been on our own, just Andy, Will, Bec, Isso, me and John. And while it had been great having friends on the boat, it had distracted us from the main task of actually concentrating on the overall voyage. The boat needed constant attention and maintenance if she was going to get us to all the destinations we had planned. And all the nasty jobs, like greasing the heads, checking the stowage in the bilges and the rigging and changing the engine oil, were harder to do when the atmosphere was all about having fun.

John was very good at trying to keep us up to the mark on the maintenance, but he wasn't always popular for it. Andy was our key man, and there wasn't much he couldn't fix. He would consult his thick *Practical Boatowner's Guide to Maintenance* and burrow under the port seat in the saloon, untying the line which held down the lid to the locker in case we turned over, and extracting the tools he needed.

We were soon back into the seagoing routine. Andy now ran the third watch on his own – or with Isso, if he needed help. We were all hot and queasy and with some twenty-four hours to go, Bec suddenly went quiet and spent her free time just lying in her bunk. When I asked, she admitted to having an ache in her lower back and stomach. The wind was increasing and I worried about her. Was this going to be like the time high in the Andes when she had developed otitis media, a swelling infection of the eardrum? John and I had thought she would die. Probably only a course of antibiotics had saved her then. Once again we were far from help, and my awareness of our vulnerability increased.

The wind grew stronger and it was becoming difficult to steer a course that would keep us clear of the islands just to the south of us: Los Roques and Las Aves. In the log, John wrote: 'We are in a hazardous low-lying area with poor visibility, everyone needs to be on their toes. A few hours later, in big capitals, he added: 'DO NOT GO SOUTH OF 12.20'N'. All that night he remained in the doghouse, watching our course.

Bec's condition was getting no better. She looked deathly under her tan and I could tell she was in a lot of pain. I feared it could be kidney trouble. We had to get her to a doctor. At the wheel in heavy seas that dark night, my body was rigid with concentration. A shade to the right and we would broach; a shade to the left and we would hit the low unlit islands. Our route passed through a narrow channel. There could be no error.

Three days out from Grenada, we arrived at Bonaire in the heat of the day. Over the radio, John explained our situation and the immigration police kindly arranged transport to take Bec and me to the hospital. We shared the car with a friendly but doped-up sniffer Alsatian. At the hospital, the efficient Dutch doctor decided it wasn't anything too serious and prescribed some medicine. Our hearts lighter, we walked into the town and found the chemist, which was well stocked, its chrome and glass gleaming clean. While we were there I searched for something to soothe John's prickly heat, which was still driving him mad.

Bonaire, a mixture of the Caribbean and Holland, is the second-largest island in the Netherland Antilles, low, and covered with scrub and cactus, situated just 40 miles north of Venezuela on the continent of South America. Even tempered by the tradewinds, the temperature was in the 80s. The Dutch first came to Bonaire in 1626. In 1817, Governor Kikkert, tired of the pastel shades and blinding white of other Caribbean islands, decreed that Bonaire buildings should be painted in dark colours, and in the main town of Kralendijk (rhymes with marlinspike), we found buildings still painted in distinctively solid colours: deep orange, ochre, even brown and green, with white stucco tracing their Dutch colonial outlines. A few expensive cars roared up and down the main shopping street and along the seafront, the words 'Diver's Paradise' stamped on every number plate. While not as fabulously rich as its neighbours, Curaçao and Aruba, which have benefited from Venezuelan oil, Bonaire nonetheless has an air of stolid prosperity. Income is derived from tourism, salt and the two major radio stations whose masts we had noticed sailing down the coast: the Dutch World Service and Transworld Radio, a mighty religious station.

Bec and I walked past shops stuffed with glittering goodies. The fake snow decorating the windows seemed odd, as did the sound of Christmas carols drifting out into the drilling heat. I felt a million miles from home, and Christmas just wasn't right. But I had to make it happen: we had to drum up that sense of excitement. I knew that Bec would be bitterly disappointed if we didn't make it into a really special day. She brought back to the boat the best scarlet poinsettia I'd ever seen. Here at least was a familiar Christmas plant that really flourished in this hot climate. Of course, Isso was wildly excited about how many presents she would get. We had brought lots out with us and hoped they hadn't been wrecked on Leg 1. Finding them was going to be a challenge.

'But Mum, how will Father Christmas find us out here?' Isso, in her sweet innocence, was an absolute believer. Ghosts and spirits were real to her, after all, so why not Father Christmas.

I got the feeling that Andy was pretty relaxed about Christmas. He was having such fun snorkelling, spending hours in the water and travelling great distances from the boat, duck-diving to get a closer look at a barracuda or brilliant parrot fish. I knew it was a big day for Will, who would feel let down if we didn't make an effort. With three boisterous brothers, Christmas in Gloucestershire had been a typical high-spirited family time for him. 'Chrimbo decs, Bec. We must get the Chrimbo decs up,' he called to Rebecca. John, however, was still feeling low. The enforced jollity was absolutely not his scene. We all had to cope with each other's expectations, and once again, in this small space, irritating habits and silly words jarred. We all had our share of tantrums. Bec was furious that her Dad was not making an effort; she wanted this Christmas, with us all and Will, to be special. It did not augur well.

On Christmas Eve, Andy, Will, Bec and Isso went off in a hired car to look round the island. This gave John and me some breathing space and a chance to organise the party. I tackled the mince pies, which I began to regret as the butter in the pastry went runny in moments. But I wanted Christmas to be as traditional as was possible out here, just as we would have spent it if we had been at home with our families. The radio was playing up so we couldn't even get the World Service or the Festival of Carols and Lessons from King's College, Cambridge. Instead, we wallowed in a saccharine-sweet tape of Christmas love songs, featuring seasonal favourites by Bing Crosby, Perry Como and the like.

That starry night, when all were sleeping, Father Christmas (me) crept through our sultry boat with heavy, lumpy stockings for each bunk. I just managed to stifle a scream when I disturbed a fruit bat feeding on a stick of bananas in the saloon. It clattered clumsily away, flying up through the main hatch like a Christmas vampire.

Instead of going to church, we jumped off the boat into the warmest, clearest water, teeming with brilliant fish. We might have felt maudlin about what we were missing, but look what we had in its place: the American turkey, bought at the local expensive supermarket, was delicious; and the Christmas pudding and cake given to us by friends at home was spectacular. By the end of the feast even John was cracking jokes. Mellowing out with the Carriacou wine and Andy's guitar, we chattered on into the late tropical Christmas night. And I was pleased that we had got through this particular minefield in one piece.

5

Heading for the Pacific

JOHN

Christmas was over, and we were flying. I felt a surge of excitement. Free from Caribbean claustrophobia at last. Off the north-west corner of Bonaire on Boxing Day, we freed the sails and bore away towards the Panama Canal, some 700 miles to the west, our speed jumping to 9 knots.

Immediately, the trailing muppet was hit. A flash of gold burst into the air as a big dorado danced on its tail. He was on for a few seconds and then, with one huge leap, he broke free. I felt happy for him.

We bounced along, passing Curaçao and Aruba by midnight. But we hardly appreciated the view. Except for Isso, we were all feeling groggy with seasickness. Luckily, my own foolishness helped us over this misery. I'd broken the self-steering by using it as a step to get out of the water while swimming in Bonaire, so now we had to steer by hand. This cleared our heads. At least, that's the way I saw it.

The glass fell 8 points over a couple of days and the tradewind grew to a following gale. Early on the morning of our third day at sea, we were surfing at 16 knots down thundering crests when the cloud cleared, and there, 80 miles away to the south, Isso caught her first glimpse of South America since she left her native Peru seven years before. The 17,500ft snow-covered peaks of Colombia glowed a white beacon of welcome to the little Quechua returning home. Enjoying Marie Christine's delicious marinated dorado for supper at sunset that night, I realised that, for me, this had been by far the best day of the trip so far.

But by the following night the wind was gone and we were just slopping along on the relics of the gale, slowly pulling away from Colombia and cutting north-west across the western end of the Caribbean. There was no moon, but the lights of passing ships encouraged us on: we were nearing the Panamanian coast a bit to the south of the canal.

It was very dark. At the wheel, I was trying to make the most of the failing wind. 'Sounds like a motor, Johnny – very close!' called Marie Christine anxiously from the open cave of the doghouse just in front of me.

Suddenly, it was right above us, barely clearing the main mast. Downdraught from the helicopter's clattering rotors sucked at our hair. The searchlight caught us completely by surprise. Like rabbits trapped in a pool of brilliant light, we felt naked. There was nowhere to go. 'Don't move! Just keep still!' I bellowed. 'It's drug surveillance. If we move, we'll look guilty.'

I maintained our course and speed. Breathless, we waited, praying there would be no machine-gun bullets. Bec, Will and Andy crawled out through the hatch, squinting up into the blinding light. Above me, I could see the bone-dome helmets of the military outlined at the doorway against the stars. Then, at last, the sinister machine dipped to port and slipped away, banking round ahead of us towards the menacing silhouette of a large warship, now on station only a few hundred yards off our starboard beam.

In spite of warnings about piracy, we had toyed with the idea of calling into a Colombian port. It was just as well we'd decided against it. A few days later, I met an American officer, born and educated in the Panama Canal Zone. One of his friends from high school had joined the Customs. 'Boy, you lucky you didn't go to Colombia,' he said, shaking his head. 'The Customs keep a computerised list. Once you on that list, you stay right on it. It goes worldwide, man. You get hassled every port you call in. The only way you get off that list, is if the officer put you on deeletes you! He dies, you on for life, boy!'

Half a day short of the canal, we still had a slim chance of getting through to the Pacific before the New Year festivities brought everything to a grinding halt. We were bowling north close under the wild eastern shores of Panama. Mysterious cloud-wreathed mountains, rising steeply from the surf, were clothed in a dense green. The abundance of truly

huge trees was a good measure of wilderness. A big swell rolled up the bot-
tleneck of the Caribbean and I could see little in the way of shelter for
ships. The Spaniards had used mules to bring plundered Peruvian gold
over the mountains and through the steaming jungles from the Pacific
coast. I was trying to puzzle out how on earth they'd got the treasure
aboard the galleons when I spotted an inviting bay tucked in behind a tall
headland. But we were already past it, running before the wind at 8 knots.

On impulse, I put the wheel hard to port. This was the delight of
cruising. No plane tickets or deadlines. We could do as we wished.
Exultantly, I swung the boat in a smooth curve, giving a wide berth to
the ugly reef guarding the entrance to the bay. Then we saw the other
guards. On either side and at the inner end of the bay stood grey stone
lines of what looked like roofless huts, facing out to sea.

Riding the swell into the bay, we soon realised that these 'huts' were
stone gun bays, each with its own long black cannon run out ready to
rake Franky Drake's little ships if he dared attack the mighty treasurehouse. But he never did. Instead he died waiting off the mouth of the
bay, and his casket lay beneath the waves.

The ancient port of Portobelo is a jungle-covered backwater of history, kept steaming moist by 12ft of warm rain each year. The
treasurehouse was being restored as part of the celebrations marking the
500th anniversary of Columbus's discovery of America – not exactly a
happy memory for the indigenous peoples. Of the sixty Indian tribes
inhabiting the isthmus at the time of the Conquest, only three had survived until the end of the twentieth century, but then again, left to their
own devices, perhaps they would have just gone on killing and eating
each other anyway. Would the Inca and Aztec civilisations still be in
existence today? And would it have been more fun working for them?
Would you rather be tortured by a Spaniard or cooked by a Carib?
Perhaps the unpalatable reality is that, by the natural process of evolution, the stronger side usually survives.

Our own little Indian was really excited at going ashore. She knelt and
kissed the ground. 'Same me! Same me! My people. I'm so glad I come
from here,' she cried. But it was getting dark and the open drains stank;
flies were everywhere and mangy dogs were trailing us. The children had
runny noses and wore bedraggled hand-me-down clothes. The dark little
shops, lit with smoky oil lamps, held only the barest necessities of life.
This was a very poor place, barely more civilised than the *pueblito* in the
Andes which Isso might have been remembering. Within half an hour, our

daughter was whispering, 'I don't like it here. I think I come home with you, Mama.' And Marie Christine wrinkled her nose with pleasure.

Further along the street we came to the simple tin-roofed cathedral. By the wavy light of many guttering candles, we stared up at the life-sized figure of the Black Christ. Shipped from Europe and bound for the Viceroy of Peru, this symbol was intended to encourage the country's newly pressed Catholic citizens. But it sank here in the bay, and because the natives rescued it, they were allowed to keep it.

We settled down on our plank bed in the doghouse that night, under the guns of the fort. In my dotty state, hard by the underground dungeons, I felt I could hear Francis Drake:

Take my drum to England, hang et by the shore,
Strike et when your powder's runnin' low;
If the Dons sight Devon, I'll quit the port o' Heaven,
An' drum them up the Channel as we drummed them long ago.

Morning stole softly across the mist-wreathed waters of the narrow bay. It was the sort of morning on which you might expect to hear wood pigeons cooing. Fishermen were casting nets from their dugouts as we crept gently out on to the Atlantic swell. It was New Year's Eve, and some of us were still hopeful of transitting the canal before New Year.

For the very first time, Isso clambered up on the seats flanking the aft cockpit, grasped the big wheel, and, looking forward over the doghouse roof, steered the boat towards the Panama Canal. To begin with, she had difficulty allowing for the quartering waves, which kept twisting the boat as they rolled under the hull.

'I can't do eet! I can't do eet!' came the usual cry.

I was as helpful as ever. 'Of course you can, you little rat fink! Take your time . . . take your time. Just relax!'

Perhaps the reality of conditions in her own 'South America' had stiffened something in her mind. Maybe now she really did want to join the crew of the good ship *English Rose*. Whatever the reason, this time she did stick at it. And with a rush, it came to her. She could do it! She was thrilled, and we were all pleased to have another member of the team as we prepared to cross the American continent.

Panama is an S-shaped isthmus, at its narrowest, no more than 45 nautical miles across, connecting the great land masses of North and South America. With only a quarter of the land populated, nearly half the people live in the violent cities at either end of the famous canal, which cuts a 280ft-high notch between two mountain ranges. Only five hours from Portobelo, we found ourselves very much back in the modern world. Financial control of the canal is exercised in Balboa, at the Pacific end, but it appeared that very little of the income was finding its way back to Colón and Cristobal, the twin cities at the Caribbean end.

It was already late afternoon on Friday 31 December when we slipped between two huge breakwaters, motoring past a string of ships anchored in the great harbour. Cautiously, we approached the Cristobal Yacht Club. I was not in the best of moods. From a little homework on the masses of paperwork, I knew there would be little chance of us transiting before the following Tuesday.

Colón was stinking hot, with appalling slums and a reputation for violent crime second to none. Five minutes there was quite long enough to be mugged, never mind four days. Thronging one bank of a dead-end canal cut, the flags of many nations hung limply on an array of wilting yachts of all shapes and sizes. With the tops of a couple of masts sticking above the murky waters in mid-channel, marking the presence of an old British schooner, coming in to moor stern-to generated all the nervous strain of the first tee at Sunningdale.

Once ashore, we were in the company of all sorts of long-distance sailors. But my self-esteem was still dreadfully low and I hated the stinking heat. More than anything, what I needed was to spend some time with a sparky idealist.

Now thirty-five, Jonathan Selby had been on a course at Ardmore when he was fifteen, and for the past ten years he'd been sailing the world, mostly alone. Refreshingly, Jonathan didn't confuse style with substance. His bubbling enthusiasm enabled him to earn a living as a freelance computer programmer whenever funds needed topping up. Crouched against the cooker in the cabin of his rusting 25ft *Xaxero*, listening to his yarns about rounding Cape Horn, and details of all the electronic gadgets he'd invented while sitting at his little workbench-cum-navigation table, I thought I recognised something of myself from long ago.

> *If you can hear the truth you've spoken*
> *Twisted by knaves to make a trap for fools,*
> *Or watch the things you gave your life to broken,*
> *And stoop and build 'em up with worn-out tools . . .*

It was worth sailing those 5,000 miles just to meet Jonathan. I'd got two arms and two legs like anyone else. It was high time for me to stop whingeing.

There were lots of plucky people battling away here. Like the gallant Californian lady cooking for the guests her cheery Polish husband was skippering. 'I know it's really beautiful, good for diving too,' she'd sigh, 'but I don't remember it – I was always down below cooking.' Or the elderly American who had been bashing his boat into the gale which had swept us down from Bonaire. He came limping back into port, his sails torn to shreds. Now he sat on an upturned fruit box, wondering if he had the stuffing to begin all over again, with a young Swiss boy who'd never been to sea before and was thinking only of getting to San Francisco to meet up with his girlfriend. They had different dreams.

Alongside us a young Hungarian couple and their precocious child were champing at the bit to get away. Bursting with vitality, they were sailing round the world in a small steel boat they'd built in a garage to publicise the 1996 World Trade Fair in Budapest. With fitted fawn carpet across the floors and up both walls of their boat, they were finding it a bit warm in the tropics.

Fred was a retired US navy aviator, a cool but lonely Bing Crosby lookalike. He introduced himself: 'I worked with Joint Chiefs in the Pentagon . . .' He'd sailed solo from Florida and Jonathan was helping him mend his electronics. He didn't know where he was going, but he sure hoped he'd find a girl soon. 'If you get tired of that son of a gun,' he drawled at Marie Christine after a few beers, 'just come and join me.' But he was smaller than me.

An enchanting young Venezuelan girl came up the narrow companionway on the old teak schooner. She listened, smiling patiently, as her much-older husband, a diminutive long-retired financial adviser from Seattle, boasted of his elk-hunting and his flying. It looked a perfect love match, but when we got to know her better she told us this was her last trip to sea. She was heading back to Cartagena in Colombia – she couldn't stand the seasickness.

Colón is a place of shattered dreams. Here, between the two oceans, dream voyages ended. Wives flew home and husbands hung about to sell the boats. This was definitely the place to buy a second-hand boat, and Jonathan had his eye on a particularly ugly duckling: a 50ft steel junk nobody would be rushing to buy. She lay in a quiet corner reserved for long-term moorings. As well as Jonathan, there was one other person interested in this bizarre hulk: Roxanna, a glamorous and volatile Argentinian who'd sailed with him round Cape Horn. 'Jonathan, he 'as ze body of a Greek god, I want to have eez baby . . .' she'd cry, eyes flashing with passion. Jonathan looked embarrassed, but maybe, unlike other Englishmen, his feet were not quite so cold in bed. While he especially appreciated the spacious workshop fitted beside the Saab diesel in the centre of the boat, Roxanna saw this space as just the place for the crêche.

It was hot and bureaucracy was at its most difficult over the New Year. I got fed up with it. So early one morning, Marie Christine agreed to come with me on my daily trip from the yacht club to customs, immigration, port captain and so on, 'to see what you're fussing about'. We passed through the coils of razor wire surrounding the yacht club, and by walking and running alternately, we kept clear of the muggers.

My wife is sometimes a little more soft-hearted than me and when we were accosted by a very thin local who called me 'Cap' and offered to guide us round the various offices, she took him on. This did nothing to improve my temper. Finding ourselves standing at a grassy crossroads among the seedy grey office buildings, I suggested that I waited hopefully for the officials to show up while our 'guide' took my fiery wife off to the fruit market a few hundred yards up the street. We didn't part on the best of terms, and making my way back to the measurer's office, I wished I'd come alone.

'John Ridgway?' a voice called. I whipped round, in a bit of a snarl. A pocket-battleship sort of chap, about 5ft tall with blue eyes and a badly broken nose, looked ruefully up at me. His beige trousers were torn at the pockets and buttons were missing from his shirt, and he was accompanied by a rather taller girl, with dark hair and a friendly but rather sorry smile.

'Thought I recognised you. I was in 1 Para for twenty years, I think you were in 3 Para. Now we're in yacht delivery.' He nodded at the girl. 'Taking a boat down to Peru. We just got robbed.'

I looked up the street. My wife was already out of sight, at the 'fruit market' with the guide. Blimey!

'What happened?' I asked.

'We were looking for a bakery a couple of hundred yards down the street. A couple of blokes jumped us. One held a knife to my throat while the other went through my pockets. My first thought was about her.' He nodded at the girl again, and she sort of grinned. 'Then they ran for it. I chased them, but they lost me in an alley. Luckily, I didn't have much on me.'

Looking back, I saw Marie Christine and the guide coming towards us, carrying bags of fruit. It was too risky. I hadn't done well.

MARIE CHRISTINE

Once we were safely tied up at Cristobal Yacht Club, Roxanna, a zany artist from Argentina, became a firm friend. She flamboyantly told us everything and more about her relationship with the English Jonathan. Wearing a different hat each day, always set at a jaunty angle, she would come and pick up Isso in the morning to paint her, sitting her under one of the palm trees regimentally planted along the lawn. Isso was happy to be looked at by this fellow South American.

At night the grounds were the haunt of armadillos, which dug and burrowed under the manicured grass, to the despair of the patient black groundsmen. We became the buffer in a row between the boats either side of us. The old warrior American had fished out a dead armadillo bumping about in the murky water between our boats and was on his way to the bonfire to burn it. Our precocious nine-year-old Hungarian neighbour begged to be allowed to keep it. 'Well, take it on to your boat, but don't leave it around here stinking,' the American drawled. Of course, the boy forgot about it and it started to smell. Then the armadillo corpse was carted off to the tip and the Hungarian parents took sides with their screaming child in a fierce set-to with the crotchety old Yank. Neither boat knew that it was actually Roxanna who finally got rid of it.

The heat was the culprit – we were barely 500 miles north of the equator. The days passed in a blur. There was always a multitude of jobs to do: I elected to wash the seat covers in the saloon, which were made from exotic material I had bought at a Liberty's sale, thinking I would make it into curtains some day. I'd never imagined they would be used for the yacht. The heavy, beautiful fabric was hardly suitable: an Islamic pattern in soft mauves, pinks and blues. The washing job turned into a huge struggle, since only a dribble of water could be coaxed from the freshwater hose. And of course, the covers shrunk a bit, so it took a Titanic effort to get them back on.

The place to recover was the yacht club bar, a large old room with a solid wooden counter, high stools and the usual faded photos of better times for some. Here the air was deliciously cool, and the beer sold cheaply in enormous litre jugs. Stationed just outside, a Cuna Indian lady from the San Blas Islands was selling beautiful *molas*, the colourful hand-sewn appliqués for decorating blouses. Well under 5ft tall, she wore nose- and earrings, and with her straight black hair cut in a severe fringe and an angular costume, she could have walked straight out of an ancient Egyptian scroll. She always smiled sweetly at us, and particularly Isso. There was often a rather cruel-looking older man with her, and I imagined him taking the money for the items she had made and sold. I hoped I was wrong. Over a few days, we got to know her quite well and she was most interested in Isso's background. We bought four bright green parrots embroidered on to a black background, and stuck them up in the saloon to brighten our home during the months to come.

Just before our departure, Roxanna agreed to come to the supermarket with me. I needed more supplies for the 4,000-mile trip to the Marquesas. Accompanied by Andy and Isso, Roxanna carried a long heavy tube, just in case. We took a taxi into the city, passing through a desolate slumland crossed by rickety buses with names like 'In Line of Fire'. Uniformed security men toting Uzi sub-machine-guns surrounded the busy supermarket, and more armed guards patrolled the aisles as we whizzed round with several trolleys. It wasn't much like Safeway in Inverness. Andy was particularly good at finding the best buys, having spent summers catering for himself on a tight budget while working on nature reserves. The shelves were well stocked, mostly with American merchandise at a good price. Sadly, we couldn't buy too much because *English Rose* was already very low in the water. But with hindsight I wished I had stocked up on more, because, other than quite expensive corned beef, we found we were unable to buy tinned meat anywhere else along our route.

Wheeling past the frozen-chicken section, I felt tempted to buy Will a present of a bag of yellow scaly feet, or better still, one containing a tangle of necks, heads and beaks which I noticed nestling among the more expensive bags of breasts and legs. These bargain bags were for people on an even tighter budget than mine. Will had a horror of what he called the 'iggly bits'. But instead we loaded up with some of his favourites – mustard, peanut butter and mayonnaise. On a good day, Will was grand, full of energy and humour, but I worried for him; I knew he wasn't happy on the sea. Unlike Andy, who was intrigued by the whole business of sailing and would spend all his spare time reading and trying to find out more about every aspect of boats, what held Will was still his romance with Bec. At least in that respect we didn't seem to have much cause for concern – they certainly appeared to be very much in love.

It was easier for all of us on land, where we all had a chance to take a break from each other. But once we were back on board, the same problems would crop up. Will seemed to be wrestling with inner demons, and I felt that he was not enjoying the trip and perhaps blamed us for putting him in this position. It could have all been imaginary on my part, but I worried about his sullen moods. Perhaps in this respect he was like John, who had been far from cheerful in the Caribbean, but with John I understood the reasons for this. Besides, John's mood was lifting all the time, whereas Will's unhappiness was here and now. I didn't want ill feeling to spoil what was going to be an extraordinary experience that John, with his drive, had made possible for us all. But this was all very petty, and I knew that if we were faced with a crisis, everyone would do their utmost to help. We couldn't really have been with better people.

I could, I think, see my own faults all too clearly: I was inclined to bury myself in a book and be rather subdued. And I could have been more straightforward about the food: I was always hoping people would be careful and not use too many of the goodies when it was their turn to cook. Bec and I were hoarders, agreeing that we were almost happier having the treats in the cupboard than actually eating them. This had often resulted in the treats going bad, which was intensely annoying for the others. As always, John and I had our rows, but these were now out of necessity conducted in public; the others must have found that offensive.

REBECCA

Dad asked Will and me to make a trial run through the canal, acting as line-handlers aboard a small wooden ketch owned by an Aussie, Captain Don ('Crocodile Dondee'). He had been a real croc-hunter during a racy life which included searching for gold in Papua New Guinea. Disease had forced him out of the jungle, but maybe he'd found a bit of gold; he'd certainly lost the tops of a lot of fingers to the crocs. He had been sailing the world for a few years with Natalie, a determined and much younger Frenchwoman, and their dog, Strainer. Because their yacht was so small and slow, they had to anchor for the night among the alligators up in the Gatún Lake. During supper, while Natalie gave me some new 'New -Age' recipes, Don took the opportunity to study Will's charming manners. The cunning Aussie thought he'd detected an opportunity to supplement his boat's coffers with a few spins at backgammon. But in his time, our boy had done a bit of number-shuffling himself, and he picked up on the Aussie's speed before any damage was done. They both looked at each other rather differently after that.

The trip through the canal was not without incident. A canal worker's heaving line broke at a fairly critical moment, then a furling headsail jammed so the sail couldn't be wrapped away. And finally, the engine broke down on the middle yacht in our raft of three – just as we were entering the first of the descending locks, which made for a few tense moments.

Will and I caught a bus from the Pacific to the Atlantic and Dad listened closely to our report. At last we found *English Rose* 'on the list', and made our way out to anchor for the night on the flats on the edge of the main fairway. It was like sitting in the dentist's waiting room, and nerves were rather frayed. Will and I had something of a set-to on the foredeck while we set the anchors in the dark, and things were not running very smoothly as we approached the canal.

JOHN

The sheer majesty of *English Rose* crossing the American continent next day was not lost on us. Tossing and turning at anchor on the flats that night, I thought about the builders of this modern wonder of the world. Ferdinand de Lesseps had come out here in 1881, fresh from his triumph with the Suez Canal, and the following year he started work on a sea-level canal along the Chagres River and the Rio Grande. Six years later, the company crashed, with barely 20 miles dug and 22,000 dead from disease. In those days, Panama was a department of Colombia, but it declared independence in 1903, paving the way for America to build the canal. America paid Panama US$10 million for the Canal Zone, a 5-mile-wide strip on either side of the route, and the first step was colossal: to clear the whole strip of malignant tropical diseases. By the time the first ship steamed through, on 15 August 1914, the canal had cost US$387 million.

During the 1970s, Panama steadily gained control of the canal, and a final transfer of ownership is promised for 2000. Until then, America retains majority representation on the Canal Commission.

Nowadays, around forty ships a day pass through the canal. From shore to shore it is a little over 40 miles long, but 23 of these are in the Gatún Lake, which is 84ft above sea-level. To reach the lake from the Atlantic, we would be lifted by three locks, together with a ship, and after crossing the lake we would be lowered by two more locks to the Pacific.

Dawn came at last, dull and misty. Fernando and Gerardo, our two swarthy young Panamanian canal pilots, got my nerves twanging by not turning up until seven, an hour late. And once aboard, they lost no time in telling me that they were only trainees, gathering experience before being allowed on big ships. They would be in control of manoeuvres in the canal, but ultimately I was responsible for my own boat. I'd just read an insurance advert boasting of how they'd settled a £1 million claim in seven days, for a yacht crushed between an out-of-control canal tug and a lock wall. As I was uninsured, I was less than keen on this scenario.

According to the schedule, *English Rose* was to be the centre boat in a raft of three. I waved cheerfully at the German skipper whose smart steel yacht was lashed along my port side. He nodded grimly and continued chomping and puffing on his pipe. My ex-Para friend, David, was strapped along my starboard side, and while he'd got over the mugging incident, it came as no surprise to see him chain-smoking. We moved very cautiously towards the yawning gates of the first lock. It was quite an event, what with busy tugs, the flooding of the lock and the turbulent wash from an enormous yellow Japanese car-carrier. There was plenty of dashing about, securing ropes to bollards to hold us in the violent backwash. In the steaming heat, this was a time when we six needed to be communicating at our very best, and it didn't happen. There were storms of family tears. We were beginning to feel the effects of the long time we'd been together at such close quarters.

David's engine broke down when we reached the Gatún Lake and our pilots asked if we'd go back and give him a tow, to avoid a surcharge if he failed to make it through the canal in a single day. Already heavy-laden, *English Rose* had never been in freshwater before, and now we sank even lower without the buoyancy of seawater. The race against time with the tow was hard work on the faithful Mercedes engine, and we had to ease back on the throttle when the water-cooling needle nudged up into the danger sector of its dial.

We remembered the tens of thousands who had died building the canal, without which we would have gained the Pacific only by sailing through the North-West Passage or rounding Cape Horn. As well as the sheer size of the locks and the ships we met in them, it was very strange to be sailing through the jungle. When the dam was built to raise the level of Gatún Lake, the animals fled to an island in the middle, which remains a biological reserve for research.

But for me the finest memory was passing under the Bridge of the Americas at the western end of the canal. Now we were in the Pacific Ocean, and I just knew life would begin anew.

Tying up to trots in a strong ebbing tide, we hitched a lift on a launch and headed for the bar in the colonial-style Balboa Yacht Club. Perched there on tall stools, we supped litre glasses of iced beer and peered into the setting sun at the vast and mysterious Pacific. What a day.

I had planned this voyage for our family, perhaps a last chance for us to share a grand experience; to slip away for a while from the bureaucratic enmeshments of modern life. Far away now were accounts and VAT, licences and laws, rules and regulations. As far as possible, I wanted to avoid the tedious logical planning which beset our life at home. We were living in freedom, but by its very nature, this freedom resulted in frequent changes of plan, reacting on impulse to people, places and weather conditions as we encountered them. But I appreciated that this chopping and changing presented difficulties for Andy, and particularly for Will, to whom this way of life was something new. The glory of the voyage was that it presented us all with a major struggle, something worthwhile and difficult to try to achieve. But in the midst of it, it was easy, sometimes, to lose sight of the grand design and see only the petty irritations.

6

A New World

On 6 January we took off into the Pacific, threading our way through the buoyed navigation channel on a low, slumbering swell. While the skyscrapers of Panama City slid slowly below the horizon, we ate fried steaks from a small tunny we caught on our 35-mile trip across the gulf to Isla Bayoneta, the most northerly island on my new chart of the Pearl Islands, which I'd bought that morning, along with a spear-gun.

It was already late on a grey afternoon when we arrived at the low, overgrown islands. Gulls were squawking with delight, fighting over shoals of fry in the heaving grey waters of the channel. Squadrons of ungainly pelicans dived noisily into the tide rips. Turtles, manta rays and sharks abounded, and in spite of the sticky heat, there were no volunteers to swim ashore. Bayoneta Island was a sinister, deserted place. Sinuous branches and roots from its jungle trees came creeping right down the rocks like thick serpents, sliding into the little bays of silt-covered rock. Marie Christine, Isso and I raced about, scattering waves of hideous shore crabs in our vain attempts to catch a glimpse of the mysterious birds calling from within the tangled rainforest. Above us, spiny iguanas 2ft long gazed contemptuously down from their crevices in the cliffs. This was no one's idea of a tropical paradise.

After dark, we spotted half a dozen dim lights shining from a little settlement 3 or 4 miles away, over on an adjoining island, and during supper we all agreed that we must sail there next day to see what kind of people would live in such a place. Meanwhile, we had an uneasy night, fearful that we might drag our anchor and be swept ashore, ending up as food for the battalions of scuttling shore crabs.

We caught a shimmering dorado on our crossing, and anchored in the bay before the village of Pedro Gonzalez, the only settlement on the island. A couple of small Indian boys paddled out in a short dugout canoe and we followed them ashore. The islanders seemed cheery enough, though we heard later that they more or less lived on the marijuana they grew there. We bought oranges, bananas, papaya, maize and drinking coconuts, and watched them stewing iguana, which they hunted with dogs.

As the day wore on, a few battered wooden fishing boats came to anchor near us in the bay. Each had a crew of around a dozen villainous-looking fellows who sat about smoking, mending nets and eating vast platefuls of boiled rice. They told us they were resting until dusk, when they would go off to fish right through the night. We hoped they were telling the truth. In fact, we waited up to see if they really were going to leave, and Isso began ripping the feathers on our orange hand line, up and down in a pool of light I made with the searchlight. She was becoming a real little chatterbox now and this did much to keep up our morale in the heat. Hideous grey catfish came swirling up the beam out of the depths, chasing after the feathered hooks, and Isso screamed with delight, until it came to unhooking these horrible monsters; then it was a heartfelt 'Thanks, pal!' when Andy came to the rescue.

Still uncertain about the fishermen, Marie Christine and I lay in the doghouse reading until we heard the very last of the engines chugging away into the night.

Next morning there was quite a tide running through the bay, but we decided to scrub and polish the hull all the same. Never feeling entirely safe from sharks, I swam up and down the waterline, scrubbing the weed from above the red line of boot-topping with a long-handled washing-up brush. In the unventilated boat, my prickly heat was causing more and more irritation and I found prolonged immersion in the sea the only way of cooling myself and thus dulling the itching. Shortly before leaving Scotland, we'd given the boat a coat of white anti-fouling paint, but this seemed to have washed off during the past four months, and the growth of weed in tropical waters was phenomenal. Our main problem was that as we were carrying all the paraphernalia for eighteen months at sea, we were lying too deep in the water, and weed soon grew on the bare fibreglass above the boot-topping. Undaunted by the heat from a cloudless sky, the ladies toiled away in the dinghy, first with hull-cleaner and then polish. Poor Marie Christine suffered sickness from the fumes every time she cleaned the hull.

Meanwhile Will and Andy went about other tasks. Sweltering in the galley, Will baked a chocolate cake for tea. He was in better spirits now, and we all tried to keep him cheerful. Marie Christine and I were struggling with the obvious close-quarter irritations of Will and Bec's romance. Luckily we had each other to confide in, and this helped ease our tension.

Andy serviced the engine for a while before trying out the new spear-gun. He'd spent a lot of his childhood in the swimming pool, and now he found the warm, tropical water especially appealing, soon showing that he could dive deeper and hold his breath longer than any of us. After a few trial dives, he came shooting out of the water with a large green parrot fish impaled on the spear.

Our greatest difficulty with Andy was dealing with his certainty. He had a strong personal view about everything, and there was seldom any expression of self-doubt. But when I say 'our' greatest difficulty, that is my own view, and perhaps that of Marie Christine, with whom I discussed things on watch. Looking to myself, I considered what effect I was having on the other five – and I was not very impressed. I had had a fair bit more experience of this kind of pressure, and I knew about 'reeling out and reeling in' my emotions, to prevent ever coming up against the stops, so to speak. But while this 'softly, softly, catchee monkey' approach might have helped me to cope with the pressures of confinement, it was hardly the stuff of leadership, and I was only too aware that facets of my own personality might not be too attractive, either. And I realised that my being so gloomy couldn't be helping very much. But when you're gloomy, you're gloomy – there is nothing for it but to struggle to overcome the difficulty. For myself, and for Will too, physical exercise was the best antidote to gloom. But physical exercise is not easy on a boat in the tropics when you are tortured by prickly heat. I have never liked the heat, but if I hadn't included the Caribbean and Polynesia in our itinerary, Marie Christine and my two daughters would never have come on the voyage. Prickly heat was something I was having to come to terms with. Most of the time I wore only a *pareu*, loosely knotted around my waist to minimise chafing of my already raw skin.

After washing the decks and getting shipshape, we prepared to head south in the gathering heat the next morning. But the tripping line came undone on the anchor and we were lucky to be able to raise it. This was a knot Will had tied. Nothing serious, perhaps, but it came on top of one or two other mistakes – admittedly not many – which probably sprang from his inexperience at sea. Nevertheless, a fair few of my overly optimistic friends had been dead for some years now, and I was certain it was only my own attention to detail that had saved me thus far. I suppose, if you row across the North Atlantic and sail it alone, it might make you a little finicky in the eyes of the average voter, but I had a creeping feeling some of our nine lives were already slipping away and we still had a long, long way to go.

As ever, it was Marie Christine who was the heart of the whole team. She had the same ability to see wonder in simple things that had so entranced me thirty years before, and it still lifted even the drabbest day into delight and perked up everyone.

The southern tip of San José Island resembled paradise. Like the close-cropped frame of somebody else's too-perfect photograph, the rock formations were too extraordinary, the blue of the sea and the green of the jungle too vivid. Closing the end of the island, we found a big swell trundling along the inside of the headland and crashing in brilliant white on the reddish lava rock.

'Looks like the *Orion*, that German boat we came through the canal with,' murmured Andy, nodding towards a small white ketch lying close under the shore. We noticed that the dinghy was still aboard, but couldn't raise any response on the radio. 'Too hot, Mama. Maybe they sleeping,' offered Isso, palms up, as she called the depths on the echo-sounder.

Will was setting up the anchor. 'That's a funny-looking flag,' he called back from the bows gesturing towards the island. 'It's a black bear or something; I think it's a pre-war German flag.' There was a flag there all right, run up a pole among the trees above the shore, and right beneath it was a flimsy shelter, made mostly of plastic sheeting.

We were over rocky ground and had to make a couple of attempts with the anchor before we got a good grip. After lunch it was decided that Andy and Will should stay aboard in case the anchor dragged in the swell while the family foursome paddled ashore. We landed at the mouth of a stream on a sheltered sandy beach. On either side the ground rose sharply, covered with dense undergrowth. Somewhere up above us, and not far away, was where the flag must be. By a path which led into the trees, rough lettering on a driftwood sign proclaimed 'El Paradiso'. This was a good start, at least. Nearby lay a rusty pair of scales with rocks painted in kilos. Perhaps this was some kind of shop. We rang a tarnished bell which hung from a bough and followed the path into the shade, followed by a few scrawny and inquisitive chickens, seemingly indifferent to the iguanas and the revolting, scuttling shore crabs. Translucent sandflies were dotted about the place and it was stinking hot.

A single log bridged the stream by the water-hole, where a sand drum filtered muddy water which dribbled from a perished red rubber hose. Reaching the far side, and grasping convenient roots, we hauled ourselves up a steep bank and on to a narrow path which led up through the trees. A tall grey-haired woman, slim and sallow, intercepted us as we neared the hut with the clear plastic walls. In her early fifties, Gerda was preoccupied – 'Harassed of Hamburg' was our nickname for her. She'd sailed away from Germany with Dieter eleven years before. They'd been on their way round the world but they'd found their *el paradiso* right here. Now they were truly Mr and Mrs Robinson Crusoe, and this was as far as they were going.

'I have no time!' she barked, explaining that Dieter, now sixty-five, had gone to Panama City in their boat, leaving her to care for everything. 'Please. You will come back in the morning.' I sensed there was little compromising on the road to Gerda's horizon. A bit ill-tempered, we retraced our steps, filled our folding water bags and Isso, Marie Christine and I swam back to *English Rose* while Bec paddled the dinghy.

Just before dark another smaller sloop came in and anchored on the far side of the bay. The German flag flying from her stern warned us to keep clear. What with the *Orion* and Gerda's homestead, it was beginning to look as if we were Englander intruders in some sort of German hide-out.

Leaving Bec and Will to watch the anchor, we took Andy with us next morning and austere Gerda seemed in rather better humour. She informed us that the new yacht belonged to a famous German sailing couple who were rather elderly; the man was ill and they planned to rest up for a while. She led us through the trees on to a large flattish orchard full of fruit trees. No wonder Gerda was harassed. Cashews, oranges, grapefruits, avocados and bananas . . . I wondered why it is that we all doggedly take on so much more than we can manage. These things come to own us, and we become their prisoners.

Returning to the boat, Will and Bec went ashore. Then Hartmut and Mona Braun hailed us from the *Orion* and Marie Christine and I paddled over. Our first and abiding impression was one of German efficiency. Far from Hamburg and well on their way, they'd sold their all and headed vaguely towards New Zealand, and now the *Orion* and her open-ended voyage was all they had in the world. Inside, the *Orion* was spacious and immaculate, with much heavy teak. At fifty-two, Hartmut had retired from careers in the merchant navy and marketing. He was quiet and content to puff on his pipe while Mona, who was forty-three, chattered and giggled with delight at having someone new to talk to. A handsome blonde optician with a ready smile, she was not quite as keen on the sailing life as her husband. Lighting one cigarette after another, she explained her anxiety lest Hartmut should fall ill or be injured.

'I am a weak swimmer, also frightened of the sea.' Her heavily accented voice quavered a bit. 'I'm unhappy at an unending life on this boat.' They shared the ocean crossings in two twelve-hour watches, Hartmut working the nights and Mona managing things by day. I wondered whether these very long watches were increasing her boredom.

A man of firm opinion, Hartmut declared the poorest and now least self-sufficient islands in the Caribbean to be the ex-British colonies. Bonaire, he judged, had come off best from colonial rule, a result of Dutch interest and funding. I imagined a different story in Whitehall, but each country has its own view of history. Troubled by German materialism, he was deeply interested in finding a simpler way of life and took the time to befriend Indians so he could learn their ways of catching fish from dugout canoes. Poor Mona just worried that he might be eaten by a shark.

Next morning, we found the gaunt figure of Dieter, pacing up and down the shore like a man possessed. Standing by his 'El Paradiso' sign, in faded denims with a képi shading his piercing blue eyes, he looked the complete fanatic. But it was just his normal self; he wasn't even cross. However, I never dared ask what the flag represented. Newly returned from Panama City, Dieter was celebrating the German government's decision to post him his old-age pension each month: his working days were officially over. Proudly, he showed us his grotesque collection of bottled snakes, bats and reptiles. Sitting there in his shelter, toasting his new-found prosperity in home-made rum, we looked out through the startling green curtain of jungle foliage, across the pale blue waters of the bay, and on to a lonely rock eroded into the shape of a Pacific *tiki*, a lesser God. I didn't envy him his castaway life. Weighing it up, I preferred our Scottish stone croft, with its rain, sea loch and midges to his plastic-lined shack, sun, surf and sandflies. I didn't think he'd make old bones – this was no place for the white man. But one of his photographs I will never forget: an enormous storm swell surging into the bay. *English Rose* would not survive those conditions in her present position.

Thanking Dieter and Gerda for their hospitality, Marie Christine, Isso and I accompanied Hartmut and Mona on a walk into the interior of the island. As soon as we were out of earshot of our hosts, Hartmut burst out: 'He'd have been no more than a janitor in Germany, now he's living a lot worse than the Cuna Indians. He could have learned a great deal from them, but he ignores them.'

On a ridge overlooking the open Pacific, on the far side of the headland, we found a grassy lane cutting straight through the jungle. It was rather like an almost abandoned bridleway on an English country estate. Hartmut told us that the island was criss-crossed with these tracks, which the Americans had built, together with an airfield, in the Second World War. The idea had been to deny the Japanese the Pearl Islands, just in case they tried to use them as a base for the invasion of America. He hinted darkly that nowadays, the whole set-up was being used for Colombian drug business. But everyone says that in South America.

It was a long hot day. We arrived back at the beach from our ramble exhausted, our clothes full of thorns and sticky plants. Isso had had more than enough of listening to grown-ups talking their nonsense. For hours we'd been looking forward to the long, cool swim back to the boat, but now a much higher swell was rolling up the steep, sandy beach, its foaming fringe almost reaching the rubber dinghy. We'd tied it up by both painters among the trailing branches of a huge jungle tree. Perhaps it was time to stretch Isso's swimming a bit.

Waiting for a run of smaller waves, we all rushed down the beach and pulled the dinghy as far out as we could. Marie Christine, Hartmut and I stayed in the water while Mona and Isso pulled themselves aboard and began paddling backwards towards the approaching wave. Then it all went wrong. The wave reared up, flipped the dinghy upside down and dumped itself on top of the fearless five. I felt something bump beneath me, then my head burst free of the sea and, seeing Hartmut with Marie Christine and Isso, I grabbed the dinghy and Mona and struggled up the steep sandy beach. Everyone was giggling – except Mona. She was the bump I'd felt, and now she had a mouthful of sand and looked rather bedraggled. This was not doing her confidence much good. I waved to Andy and Will on *English Rose* and they paddled to the edge of the surf in the second dinghy. Isso swam out through the surf with her mother and me and I was delighted at her bravery. When she was safely in the dinghy with Will and Andy, Marie Christine and I swam back to get the first dinghy and Mona and Hartmut. We weren't hot and sticky any more.

When the sea eased a bit, Hartmut took us snorkelling in a narrow channel between the headland and a small island, and it was there that I had my first encounter with a shark. The tide was flooding quite strongly through the channel and I was lifting and falling on a long, lazy swell. Diving down a couple of times, I bounced the spear off the armour-plated scales of a couple of parrot fish and became completely absorbed in trying to outwit the wily creatures. I felt very much at home in this beautiful place with its multi-coloured coral and curtains of fish.

The shark and I met each other at the end of a small canyon among smooth grey boulders. He was cornered. We looked at each other. I think we were equally surprised. He was a handsome fellow, about 6ft long, grey with a white tip to his dorsal fin. Then he charged straight towards me, sinking as he came. His speed surprised me, and he was long gone before I could bring the spear-gun to my shoulder to defend myself. Feeling both foolish and rather shaky, I swam about a bit, wondering if I should tell Bec, who was snorkelling quite happily only 50 yards along the shore. In the event, assuring myself that the shark was harmless, and not wishing to cause alarm, I told no one until we were safely back on *English Rose*. And I decided I'd better not tell Mona at all.

It was time to leave the Pearl Islands, pressing on south-east towards our point of departure from the Americas. On a gentle beam reach, we covered the 80 miles in a day, stemming the current which spills up into the Gulf of Panama.

My heart lifted as we closed the Darien coast, coming under virgin rainforest, trackless green, blueing away up into cloud-covered mountains, with no sign of roads, nor any sort of habitation. It was late afternoon by the time we found the tight little Bahia las Piñas, cut into the otherwise straight line of primeval coastline. We anchored there for the night, hemmed in by steep jungle-covered mountains on all sides.

Darkness fell quickly. The generator lighting the exclusive fishing lodge in the bay rumbled on for a while, then fell silent, and everything was swallowed by the menace of the jungle night.

We'd come for the fishing, and next morning, Mike Kettridge, the cheery American manager at the lodge, gave us some tips for fishing the offshore reef. As we gathered excitedly round the workbench in the big-game fishing workshop, the comforting thud of ball on leather glove drifted across manicured lawns. A couple of pro baseball players from the Cleveland Browns were lazily swinging their throwing arms in deadly practice.

Mike told us the bonito gorged on dense shoals of something like sand eels. And lantern fish, coming up from the depths by night, were stunned by the dolphin's sonar and then eaten at leisure, while dorado, tuna and the like joined in the feast. In turn, feeding on them, the marlin and sailfish went black as they attacked, only assuming their natural brilliant colours afterwards. Amid the carnage, shoals of butterfly fish arranged themselves like car-wash curtains through which the dorado, tuna, amberjack and other similar fish passed to be cleaned.

An hour later, we were pulling clear of Los Centinales, the two jungle-covered islets guarding the entrance to Bahia las Piñas, the point where the Spaniard, Balboa, first stumbled down through the steep mountains to discover the Pacific. A black water spout was writhing down from dense black clouds close inshore and all around the surface of the sea was a whirlwind of spray being drawn upwards. We watched it warily, painfully aware of our slow maximum speed. On the Canal a retired US Navy man had told me how a water spout had once passed over a cruiser he'd been on, sucking off aerials and signalling lamps – anything at all loose. And now, nobody was able to come up with an entirely convincing explanation of what would happen to us if it should pass over *English Rose*.

Seven miles offshore, beneath clouds of fluttering grey terns, we came over the reef in 90m of water, right on the edge of the continental shelf, where food-rich cold water sweeps up from the 3,000m depths. From up in the crosstrees, Will spotted dolphins jumping out to starboard and as we raced towards them Andy's rod bent to a 10lb yellowfin tuna. Then Bec caught a 10lb dorado and Isso took a 4lb bonito.

It was exciting stuff, and, anchored by the lodge once more that night, Bec cooked delicious fresh tuna and rice with a fine sauce. With the fish still in rigor mortis, the filleting had taken a long time out at sea.

Later, we motored 3 miles round the corner to Las Piñas, a Cuna Indian village, which we found well laid out. The locals looked healthy and cheerful. Cheeky hyperactive children used our upturned dinghy as a trampoline while we bought eggs and vegetables at the store. On our returning to our anchorage in sultry steaming heat, the visit sparked off a stormy argument about the rights and wrongs of megabuck Americans in a wild jungle place like Las Piñas. While Will contrasted what he saw as the extreme poverty of the village with the incongruous luxury of the lodge, Marie Christine felt the Indians were in heaven on earth and it was simply up to them to make what they chose to make of it. Andy avoided argument as ever, as if he'd read somewhere, and wisely remembered, that silence is the recipe for successful voyaging. I wondered if the answer to poverty is not quite as simple as having a lot – these Americans had a lot, but many had found ways to be impoverished in other respects. And I began to wonder what Will would make of the millions of poor people in Lima.

We went ashore to say our goodbyes the next day. Mike gave me an old chart, persuading me to make our departure from South America from Chiquito Guayabo, a seldom-visited little bay further down the coast. Moving close inshore as we travelled south, we had the strange feeling of going ever deeper into the unknown. Folds of jungle-covered hills in all shades of green ranged away up to the misty mountains inland, only the occasional coconut grove and a sparse scattering of thatched huts on stilts betraying any human presence. It is extraordinary to think that there is still no road link between North and South America at this point.

We caught several bonito on a yellow feather Mike had given us, and this thrilled and exhausted Isso. The fish, with its deep red meat, looked just like steak; Marie Christine and Bec cut it into thin strips, coating them with soya and garlic or salt and spicy sauce before stringing them on a line to dry in the sun, ready for our journey into the Pacific.

Rounding into the small bay I'd noted on Mike's tattered old chart, we caught our first sight of paradise, or the nearest I'd seen to it on this earth: a small rocky island on the north shores of Chiquito Guayabo Bay, linked to the mainland by a crescent of sand and rock to form a perfect shelter from the ocean outside. A football match was underway, made possible by the low spring tide, on the gently sloping beach, across which meandered the dry-season outflow from the all-important river. A short, powerful man paddled over in a dugout canoe to show us the best anchorage. In the bow knelt a small one-armed boy. The CQR bit cleanly into firm sand and Andy paid out 40m of chain on the windlass as I motored gently astern. Ciro and his son Luís clambered aboard and welcomed us with gentle smiles; soon two women came out with four more children. All these people were Choco Indians.

In the absence of roads, movement between houses around the bay, as well as up and down the coast, was all by dugout canoe. And with plenty of fruit and fish available, they had all the ingredients of an easy life. But all too soon our visitors were telling us they were *pobres*. Now and then rich Americanos came down in their big-game fishing boats, and that's how they'd found out they were *pobres*. I thought of the conditions I'd seen in the copper mines of the high Peruvian Andes and the sprawling slums of Lima. We had stumbled on a magical place.

'HAPPY 50TH BIRTHDAY' the ribbon proclaimed gaily, spreading across the saloon bulkhead. Wobbling balloons hung from the handrails. Marie Christine was queen. And, gathered round the rickety table in the centre cockpit that evening, it was plain to see how her subjects appreciated just what she was contributing to the voyage: she was the heart of it all. Andy produced a box of chocolates, Will an embroidered Cuna Indian *mula*; Isso shyly brought out a bottle of rum wrapped in special paper, which she and Bec had bought at the little store in Las Piñas. And Bec's finely woven panama hat fitted her mother perfectly. Heralded by great gusts of heat wafting up from the open galley windows, Bec and Will's birthday meal emerged, piled high on the plates. Steaks of dorado in a creamy sauce surrounded with yams and plantains from the *pueblito*. There was a splendid birthday cake, baked by Val Greenhalgh at home in Manchester and iced by Bec. Rum punch was followed by champagne, and then Will, with a daring flourish, produced his banana and zabaglione pudding.

Everyone enjoyed the opportunity of a lie-in next morning. Although it was the coolest part of the day, when deck jobs and clothes-washing were least irksome, we were all thinking of the broken sleep to come when we pushed off into the vast Pacific and began the night watches again. We were carrying our home with us, and the Choco Indians seemed to set great store by this. Sitting in the saloon, they would gaze in wonder, murmuring 'Bonito casa!'

Marie Christine, Bec and Isso went ashore to look at the woven baskets the women made in the village, but I was too sore to move off the boat. There were only half a dozen thatched huts on stilts strung along the strand. The women looked anaemic, perhaps as a result of having six to nine children each.

Marie Christine loved the baskets and wanted so much to help the mothers that she bought the few they had. Then she explained that many more were needed to contain all the flowerpots cluttered along the window sills at home. The women offered to work nights to make more and everyone was very happy. I tried to imagine what the village would be like when all these children had six or nine of their own.

The coarse grass was dotted with orange tagattees, like those we'd seen in Nepal. But the orange, lemon and banana trees looked sickly, their curling leaves patched with black. The women shook their heads and muttered, 'Pestes'.

In readiness for our voyage into the Pacific, all clothing was washed and rinsed in the river and strung out along the guardrails to dry. The women now paddled out with jaguar skins and monkey teeth, but we politely declined – 'Importado a Britannico es prohibido' – and the women smiled sadly, and, maybe, knowingly. As long as they could sell skins, I doubt if anything but extinction would stop the Chocos from shooting everything they found.

That afternoon, Andy and I set off for the Big Stone, as the Indians called the steep island lying just offshore. This was where they caught their fish, using hand lines from the dugouts. We wore masks, boots and fins. T-shirts protected us against the sun and gloves minimised cuts from the razor-edged coral, which festered fast and healed slowly. Andy carried the spear-gun, rigged with both rubber bands for maximum power. There was some swell out on the ocean shoreline and the place carried its own special menace. I was glad there were two of us. The bottom was in sight all the way across to the island. We encountered a dense shoal of small jet-black fish being herded by a few slightly larger black fish with pale grey heads. There were plenty of wary parrot fish: although they were the best-sized quarry, they were also very good at keeping their distance. I felt a bit frightened and wondered if it might be my age; I've always been familiar with fear, but I seemed to feel it more often these days.

As we swam through the narrow channel between the island and the mainland, the underwater rocks became the size of houses. Some of them may have tumbled from the island in the 1976 earthquake. The Chocos spoke vividly of that day: the tremors began just after noon and lasted for thirty terrifying minutes. Enormous rocks hurtled down the mountainsides and mud from giant landslides had coloured the sea red for years. Although the sea was disturbed, they were eternally grateful that there had been no tidal wave. It is more likely that the earthquake sent one rolling away across the Pacific.

Finning slowly south, Andy and I passed along the outer side of the island. We were swimming along the side of a cliff. On our right-hand side the water dropped steeply into an inky blackness from which funny-looking fish swam up to look at us. I stuck close to Andy with the spear-gun, and I noticed that he seemed to be looking below and behind him more often now. What else might swim up?

With the freedom of the days now, my sense of wonder was growing. I tried to puzzle out how the parrot fish had got from the Caribbean into the Pacific. Surely they couldn't have swum round Good Hope? Had their eggs been carried across the isthmus by seabirds? Would we find them in Polynesia, and if so, did this mean that these reef fish swam across deep water, or did the eggs get carried away on currents?

We found a dozen villagers aboard the yacht when we got back. They'd brought Marie Christine the biggest chunk of yam I'd ever seen – it looked more like a log – and there were piles of carrots and coconuts, plantain, onions and potatoes, too.

Will fell ill shortly after a morning run along the beach with Andy. He went to bed for the day and we thought it was probably sunstroke. Even Martinez, the youthful *gobernador*, or village chief, was worried by the awful heat. He told us his brother had been sick for a couple of days now and all the Choco Indians were complaining that they were getting blacker.

Lying at anchor, we'd noticed that *English Rose* was heeling some 3 to 5 degrees to starboard, and we all felt it was important to bring her on to an even keel before we set off into the Pacific on the port tack. So Marie Christine, Bec, Isso and I spent the morning heaving stores around to correct the balance.

There was a social cost for all this sweat. By lunchtime our party was in disarray: Marie Christine was throwing shoes at Isso, who was having trouble maintaining interest in moving stores, and Bec was in a state because Will was ill and because her stowage book was being changed around so much. Our courses at home in Scotland concentrated on team-building, communications and leadership. I looked at the situation and decided that the problem was my leadership. We needed better organisation. The day was saved by the timely arrival of Martinez in his dugout *kayuka*, together with his little daughters, Elizabeth and Lucy. We had nearly finished our stowage-day lunch: a rescued rusting tin of cannelloni and some kidney-bean salad. Martinez liked it, but the children were not so sure. They giggled and pulled faces over the strange food. Martinez told us he paddled out to the Big Stone at six each morning and was always home by nine with enough fish to feed the village, his day's work complete. This morning he'd wrestled with a shark, jamming his hand into its gills and hauling it into the narrow dugout. 'Sopa – bueno por Japoneses!' he chuckled, jabbing his finger at the picture of the shark on our coloured chart of tropical game fishes.

We began talking of the next leg of our voyage, and he looked very solemn. 'Don't go any further south,' he said, shaking his head, 'En Colombia hay mucho piraticos!' It didn't take long to translate this. I drew my finger slowly across my throat and Martinez nodded grimly.

I decided to lay a course pretty much due west, at right angles to the shoreline, when we left Chiquito Guayabo. I wouldn't turn south until we were several hundred miles out. I was concerned about the nonchalance of the rest of the crew. We were about to set out across the ocean which covers one third of the earth's surface, and the others were treating it as if it were just another hop down the coast. Why did I always feel anxious about these things?

A few days earlier, Will had promised Martinez he'd play football on the sloping beach at low tide. The game began a couple of hours after lunch when the sun was still high. Our sick hero towered head and shoulders above the rest, and for a while he dashed around with the best of them. But this was an open-ended game, and eventually Will sank back on his heels and walked. How often I'd done just this in the past – found the game or the training impossible to resist when I should have been resting for the main event.

After the game, Martinez brought Will back to the boat in his dugout. Sitting in the centre cockpit under the awning with us, at the rough table we'd had made in the Piñas, our new friend politely chewed his plateful of spaghetti. He seemed genuinely sorry to see us go. Swinging in his hammock at night, safe under a velvet tropical sky, he tuned in to the seductive adverts on his prestigious Japanese transistor radio. They whispered of all the material things he hadn't got, and convinced him he was a poor man. I compared him with Roberto, our friend in the Peruvian Andes. Why did I always feel such a bond with these people? Was I hoping they were real friends, direct and without ulterior motive? Yet surely much of their friendship stemmed from the material things I could give them. But then, what they were giving me was not material. Perhaps that was the key to it.

We made the most of our last lie-in, finally weighing anchor at 9.30 after a good breakfast. Pulling away from the village in the fresh morning light, it looked even more attractive than when I'd first seen it. Martinez, his year-old son in his arms, waved sadly from the water's edge. I would remember this place for much longer than the Caribbean.

7

The Galapagos

JOHN

As South America slipped beneath our eastern horizon, Isso and I were very chirpy at the wheel. *English Rose* nodded out into the Pacific, heeled nicely to port under a fresh north-west breeze. The GPS blinked 880 miles to the Galapagos and a further 3,000 to the Marquesas Islands at the northern end of French Polynesia. I did a few quick calculations, estimating that it would take us about a week to the Galapagos and maybe another three to the Marquesas. We'd be looking forward to a few days' break in the Galapagos, all right.

Will was red all over and his pulse rushed up to 90. Feeling far from cracky, he was persuaded to get off his feet and into his bunk.

Seasickness set in. 'Reel out, reel in.' When Andy relieved us at two in the morning, his ashen face matched the eerie nightscape as we galloped headlong under a clear sky and a full moon. We covered 185 miles in the first twenty-four hours and already our old chum Martinez seemed a world away.

Then, in the late afternoon of our second day at sea, the wind died and we were back to a centralised mainsail, to prevent rolling, and the hot rumble of the faithful Mercedes engine. Headed south-south-west now, we searched in vain for the south-east tradewinds.

Five days of almost uninterrupted motoring followed. It was the longest period the engine had ever run. We reckoned we were clear of the pirates now, but we kept a good look-out all the same: this place had a bad history of whales ramming yachts and books by the Bailey and Robertson families, survivors of whale sinkings, were suddenly compulsive reading for all hands. At least Will was on the mend, and we all conspired to restrain him from overdoing things for a few days.

On a glassy calm, we passed through a swathe of rubbish so dense we could count fifty pieces of plastic at a time. Soon the windward shores of the world will look like the rim of a junkyard. And the big patches of oil were none too encouraging, either. Marie Christine even spotted something like a mine in our path. 'Head to starboard!' she cried back to Andy at the wheel. But it turned out to be a huge dark brown turtle, which simply rolled its shell a foot or two to port and lay floundering in our wake. As Will's recovery continued he returned to take up his share of the cooking. The long stalks of green bananas were slow to ripen, so crusty home-made bread and fish were the mainstays, with beetroot and a sort of mashed potato made from the huge yam log Martinez had given us.

There was a fair bit of wildlife now. 'Oh, my goodness me!' Andy would cry at each new sighting, racing through the bird books his mum had sent out to various ports. Petrels increased in numbers, and frigate birds, too. A booby even rested on the bow for a night. When it flew away at dawn, something like a young white cattle egret perched on the port lower spreader. Maybe it was an immature tropic bird, because a mature white long-tailed tropic bird flew around a few times. Only when Isso moved up to the foredeck did the egret take to the air, and even then it soon landed again at the foot of the main mast for a while before flying off to the north.

We passed the occasional billfish and many sharks – we even lost one on our line. Once, a great cloud of vapour from a blowing whale about a mile out on our starboard quarter had us all on edge. Small whales were frequently reported in the log, and from our reading we were well aware that any one of these could easily sink *English Rose*. Will claimed a UFO but this was put down to the sunstroke. To celebrate our crossing of the equator a flock of masked boobies performed aerobatics as if trying to catch flying fish in the air.

Heavy doldrum rain squalls were now the order of the day and Marie Christine set about collecting rainwater in every container we had. In the first light of dawn on 29 January, we were close enough inshore to make out a line of heavy surf breaking on the low, black volcanic cliffs of Santa Cruz, one of thirteen major islands in the Galapagos group, which includes half a dozen minor islands and over forty named islets. As the equatorial daylight improved rapidly, we cruised a mirror-like sea along the southern shores of Santa Cruz.

'There's much more vegetation than I thought,' exclaimed Marie Christine as we all peered ashore from the shade of the doghouse.

'Yes, it's so green,' Bec agreed. 'I thought they would be desert islands. It looks like mostly dense scrub and cactus.'

'Maybe it rained recently,' I suggested, reading out loud from the pilot: 'The islands are greener where the rain falls, but some are in the rainshadow of others.' The almost round island sloped gently up into the grey cloud which covered its centre. In these central highlands, patches of green fields among moorland gave an impression of the fringes of Exmoor. But there really were sea lions wobbling about on the beach here.

An hour later, safely anchored, bow and stern, off the little village of Puerto Ayora amid a cluster of flashy charter launches, I was astonished at the size of everything. The pelicans were huge, and the frigate birds too; even the fish jumping all round the boat. A turtle drifted by on the tide and then ungainly aquatic iguanas swam past in twos and threes. These short-sighted black creatures hardly seemed to notice us. Catching one would be only too easy.

I was a little anxious about arriving at Santa Cruz. New Ecuadorian rules required visiting yachts to pay US$200 per head per day, and there was no way we could afford $1,200 every day. Paddling ashore in the dinghy with the ship's papers, crew list and all the passports, I ended up crawling through pale, smelly mud in my smart khaki shorts and new blue shirt. Crabs and iguanas crept up the black volcanic rocks, keeping just ahead of my careful but awkward progress. 'This isn't much of a bloody entrance!' I cursed my prickly heat, hobbling along under the palm trees towards the low white port captain's office.

As is customary in South America, I was kept waiting for a while. Then, with a broad smile of welcome, Alfonso Zambrano Almagro, adorned with the crisp tropical whites of the Ecuadorian navy, positively swept up the steps, waving expansively for me to follow him into his small office. For a young officer, so keenly aware of his appearance, the white plaster on the bridge of his nose looked curiously out of place. Surely no one would dare smack him one.

'I am a sailor, I wish to help you,' be began, 'but first I must warn you of the situation here. My government has enacted a new law: unless you have permits from the Department of the Navy and the Department of Agriculture, I cannot grant you entry into Galapagos waters.'

I stayed silent, looking suitably glum. Captain Alfonso went on: 'Unless . . . unless your boat has a mechanical fault or you have problems of health . . .'

'I have the two permits, and I have a mechanical fault with the pump used for changing the engine oil, which I must put right before attempting the three-thousand-mile passage from here to Marquesas, and . . . I have a health problem,' I finished rather lamely, thinking of my interminably sore crotch from the prickly heat.

'Well, if you have the permits, no problem. You must pay two hundred American dollars per day for each member of your crew.' Capitano Alfonso shook his head sadly. He appeared to be under the impression that I had rejected his offer of help.

'Captain, I am an ordinary man. We are six, I cannot pay twelve hundred dollars per day, but I must repair my ship and my health before I sail on.'

The smile returned to his swarthy features. 'In that case, perhaps I can help you,' he replied nasally. The plaster on his nose made him look like Peter Sellers. 'I am permitted, under exceptional conditions, to grant you three days in this port to correct your faults.'

'But it is Saturday. I cannot get anything fixed if the shops are closed for the weekend.'

'Not closed. Open! The finest supermarket in all the world,' proclaimed the lord and master of all of Santa Cruz, 'OK, I give you until Tuesday afternoon. Please, where you are coming from?'

'Great Britain,' I replied hopefully.

'Ah!' he beamed. 'I was in the Devonport Dockyard for one year. Very good place.' And searching through his drawer he came up with a photo of a Leander-class frigate, now renamed Fragata Presidente Alfaro.

I left the office feeling lucky. It had cost £100 to anchor for four days out in the bay. Now I could hope to get diesel, water, supplies, the small pump to change the engine oil and cream for my prickly heat. On my way back to the boat I paused to buy myself a folding panama hat in a balsa wood box to celebrate my new life of freedom.

'I sure done it! We've got four days!' I crowed up at the anxious faces as I clambered up the wooden ladder on the back of the boat.

'Oh, well done Johnny!' Marie Christine smiled with relief. They'd been waiting before putting the sail covers on, just in case we had had to sail straight out again.

Inevitably, a shopping expedition was soon mounted. The fearsome trio, Marie Christine, Bec and Isso, were about to storm the Galapagos. I needed to find the honorary British consul, so they dropped me off on the 'other side' of the creek and paddled away through the throng of charter boats, landing on the small stone mole guarding the tiny tidal harbour. Before the tourist invasion of the past five years, the island had needed no better facilities.

I picked my way up the slippery concrete steps leading past a well-used electric derrick. A workman told me that Señor Balfour was out on one of the boats in the bay. The busy Ecuadorian secretaries in the office smiled in a friendly way and promised to tell him that John Ridgway, correspondent for the *Daily Telegraph*, would be in touch as soon as the weekend was over. 'Oh, wow!' I thought. 'The big time at last.'

Turning to leave the office, I waved my arm vaguely in the general direction of the cactus and scrub at the back of what seemed to me to be a sort of builder's yard. 'Er, where's the road back into the village, please?'

'No road,' the girls giggled. 'You have to go by boat.' Now I realised why the strip of private houses and wharves was called the 'other side'. Although it extended for only half a mile or so, the honeycombed volcanic rock was covered with impenetrable thornbush and dotted with tall cactus: this place was, to all intents and purposes, an island.

I hobbled back to the slimy steps and waited for a lift, perching on a dry bit of concrete and trying to persuade the breeze to blow up the legs of my shorts to cool me down. Suddenly, in the dirty green water below me, I saw a creature even more ill at ease than myself. A hideous black iguana, some 3ft long, was just managing to keep afloat as it struggled towards the steps. It wasn't really swimming – its feet were motionless – all of its horribly slow progress across the bay had been achieved by a clumsy swaying movement of its body. The poor thing looked as if it hated the water. It had no chance of catching anything itself, but it would be a tasty morsel for a shark. Gaining the steps, it began to haul itself up towards me. I sat still, hoping not to frighten it. It fixed me with a pitiless, beady red eye and kept coming. I realised I was directly in the path of an oncoming pocket dinosaur. Sheer concrete slab was no obstacle to it: those same feet which had proved useless for swimming now revealed long, black claws which gripped every slimy niche in the fast-diminishing gap between us.

I found myself wondering if its bite might be poisonous. What a twit I'd look if I were bitten by an iguana, the slowest thing on earth next to the tortoise (would even that catch me?). I sat perfectly still, my back to the volcanic rock wall. I decided to fend it off with my dad's old black leather briefcase like a sort of weary, sore matador in khaki impress-the-port-captain shorts. Its eye was so small I couldn't tell if it could see me. It crawled past me and disappeared into a crack in the rocks. Then I looked around to see if anyone had been watching.

Later, Bec told me how Darwin's men had thought the aquatic iguana very stupid indeed. When driven to the water's edge it would not go in, and when picked up by the tail and thrown in, it simply turned round and swam back to the same place on the rock. Pity I hadn't known that.

Eventually a passing boat took me to the mole and I walked gingerly into the scruffy-looking chemist's. There was nobody in the shop, so I coughed and a surly-looking youth came in, just the sort with whom I didn't want to discuss my sore crotch. I fished out the empty packet which had held the tube of Fucidin cream. The youth glanced at it. 'No hay!' he said insolently, turning to leave.

'Usted un doctoro?' I asked sharply in pidgin Spanish.

'No'.

'Yo necessito vista un doctoro.'

'Cinco minutos.' And he was gone.

The pharmacist didn't look too pleased at being summoned. Quickly, he sold me a tube of quite different cream and held out his hand for US$7.50. I forked up and stalked out – straight into an empty ice-cream shop, where I bought myself a soft vanilla cone. Then I saw the fearsome trio advancing down the street from the market, so I gobbled up the ice-cream as quickly as I could. Being soft it was easy but it was also very cold. It gave me a terrible pain in the bridge of my mouth and I realised I had just wasted another dollar on more pain. Worse: I knew I'd have to buy them ice-creams too.

On leaving the shop we met the pharmacist and his son. I noticed he avoided my eye. I felt I'd paid too much for the cream for my crotch, but I knew I'd better cheer up fast or the fearsome trio would be on to me for being miserable and getting them all down when they wanted to enjoy their shopping. This would be a really expensive place for them to fly home from.

We entered a gruesomely expensive shop called the Black Lady, which seemed to contain everything the trio wanted. I stood out in the road, trying not to look self-conscious. There was a lot of oohing and aahing and talk of how this skirt or that blouse could be regarded as a present for a birthday six months ahead. I just thought ahead to all the expensive black pearls waiting in Tuamotu, only three months hence. Maybe we could spend more time at sea.

'That's fine, we'll come back tomorrow, after we've decided,' said Marie Christine. I sighed with relief.

But the Black Lady was quick. 'No tomorrow! I fly to Guayaquil in Ecuador tomorrow. For restock the shop. You must decide today.' She returned her languid attention to the girl chiropodist who was rubbing away at her heels.

Price tags once more confirmed Isso's unfailing taste in expensive clothes. I was leaking dollars again.

MARIE CHRISTINE

So good was our custom that the Black Lady's chiropodist even took a look at the verruca on Isso's heel. And when she shook her head, the Black Lady said grandly, 'My husband will help – he knows about these things.' I had been unsuccessfully dabbing it with acid ever since we'd left Scotland. Whatever it took, the offending wart had to be gone before we reached Peru, where Isso would have to walk great distances to see her family. She could not be held back by a sore foot.

We followed the self-taught medico husband in his green Dr Kildare tunic. His house lay directly behind a newly constructed shop which sold the latest shiny electrical goods. I guessed it had been built in the front garden for one of their sons. The husband led us through a cramped courtyard shadowed by a huge palm tree, where shells of long-dead giant tortoises added to the charnel-house air of the place, and on up an old staircase to the front door. On each turn of the steps were more bones, shells and skulls. Isso held my hand tightly.

Unlike his somewhat overpoweringly persuasive wife, Dr Kildare was softly spoken, and we conversed in a mixture of Spanish and the English he had learned while driving tourists up to the Darwin centre. I didn't understand everything he said, and when he began muttering Spanish incantations in the darkened living room, I rather panicked. But he refreshed us with chilled papaya juice and sharp cherries from the largest fridge we had ever seen, and assured me that the 'eye of a chicken' was only the Spanish term for verruca.

He laid Isso out on a squashy sofa and I winced as he started cutting away with the scalpel. 'Let us know, Isso, if it hurts,' I muttered. I had to speak loudly – Isso was already lost in a Peruvian TV game show, which seemed several steps on in bad taste from the American variety. Knowing Isso's stoical qualities, she would probably just endure it. But how kind and gentle the Black Lady's husband was as he applied the smoking acid. Then out we went into the dazzlingly bright late afternoon and on to the white street, lined with the scarlet flame trees, and beyond, the turquoise bay and *English Rose*.

We returned twice more to Dr Kildare's house, and looking back, it seems as if we spent most of our four days in the Galapagos in his cool dark room. I studied old photos propped up on a heavy mahogany sideboard, trying to imagine the past. History here was so recent, progress had come in a rush. The 'doctor' was Ecuadorian, but he'd spent most of his life here in Puerto Ayora, and of course he knew all the European settlers about whom I had read so much. While he worked on Isso's foot he gave me a history lesson.

In 1535 the King of Spain sent the Bishop of Panama to report on Pizarro's progress, but his galleon was becalmed off the coast of South America. For weeks it drifted helplessly westward on the current until, by chance, he came across the Galapagos, where they found much-needed water. It is thought that some of their cattle and goats escaped and multiplied, intruding into this previously undisturbed ecosystem. Later, English buccaneers used the islands as a place to hide or lie in wait. William Dampier described in his journal his capture of three Spanish ships laden with treasure from Peru. When chased by Spanish warships, he'd fled to the west and hidden among these little-known islands where there was all the fruit, fish, meat and water his men needed. But even so the Galapagos Islands had still been virtually untouched by man when Darwin arrived in 1835 aboard the *Beagle*, and it was what he saw here that confirmed his ideas about the evolution of species.

Many people followed: seafarers, American whalers and sealers. But as dangerous to the islands' rare species were the animals – pigs, dogs, cats and rats – they brought. Even plants they introduced had ravaged the natural vegetation. The giant tortoises suffered most, killed in their thousands for their excellent meat and oil. Ships would plunder the islands, storing the tortoises in their damp holds, where they could survive for up to a year without food or water.

Ecuador claimed the Galapagos as part of her territories in 1832 and set about colonising them with penal settlements. One of the islands, Floreana, had a dark history. A Peruvian megalomaniac brought there with him eighty settlers and a pack of ferocious dogs. Those who tried to escape from the job of building him a city from the clinker rock were hunted down by the dogs. As the numbers got low, so sailors were lured off their whaling ships into the regime. A bloody revolt ended this reign of terror, and the self-appointed king was chased into the interior and eaten by his own dogs.

Isso, who has an unquenchable appetite for human drama, listened avidly: this was indeed a different way to learn history.

The arrival of the Baroness Wagner-Bousquet with her retinue of three admirers in the 1930s was another dark period for Floreana. A spoiled, demanding lady in her forties, with prominent teeth, she saw herself as empress of the island. This greatly annoyed the other two families living on Floreana. The German Dr Ritter and his companion, Dora, had been practising their 'nature philosophy' there for two years. Nudist and vegetarian, they had had all their teeth removed before leaving Berlin, hoping to prove that they could live to 140 years of age. Also struggling to survive were Herr Wittmer and his pregnant wife, Margret, who had given birth to a son shortly after she had arrived. They had followed Ritter out from Germany but were barely tolerated by him and his disciple, Dora.

Early on, one of the Baroness's three lovers escaped with his life. Then she and her current favourite disappeared, and no trace of them was ever found. The last of the three swains was shipwrecked while trying to escape, and his remains were found on another island. He had starved to death. Next to go was Dr Ritter, who died suddenly in terrible agony. It was thought he'd been poisoned, but nobody was ever charged. This left only three people on the island. 'Who could have done the murder, if that was what it was?' The doctor's sinister voice intoned. Isso's eyes were like saucers. 'Dora or the Wittmers? Frau Wittmer still lives on Floreana. She is very elderly now. Maybe she knows the secret.'

Our friend cured Isso's foot, asking nothing in return. A bottle of

Scotch whisky and an *English Rose* T-shirt seemed a poor gesture of thanks for his kindness, but maybe one day he will come to Scotland with his 'Black Lady' and then Isso can tell him some of the stories of murder and mystery which abound in the Highlands.

Just as much as the fine views and strange customs, it is the friendships made along the way that make a journey memorable. Isso was learning this, and we were reminding ourselves that it is what you are that matters, not what you have.

JOHN

We had a delicious and inexpensive steak at a café-cum-bar on the bend where the road from the village of Bella Vista curves left on meeting the sea. No more than a village itself, Puerto Ayora sprawls along the bay front, centred on this bend. Seedy little Bella Vista, probably so-named to encourage settlement, lies a few kilometres inland and really doesn't have much of a view at all.

With 40,000 visitors in 1993 – almost ten times the number who'd come in 1970 - the islands were struggling to manage the latest in a series of human intrusions. After the capital village over on Isla Cristobal, Puerto Ayora is the second most important settlement of the Galapagos Islands. All around there were signs of change. Nobody could be precise about the population of this island: it was somewhere between 6,000 and 8,000. Big wooden cruise boats which would take a year and a half to build were under construction on the shore. There were small hotels at all stages of completion, and supermarkets too, along with souvenir shops, mostly selling hand-painted T-shirts of Galapagos wildlife, and lots of little cafés. Most shopkeepers moved about as if in a trance, bewitched by the island's newly installed television service. They gazed through their transitory clients to the coloured screens, blinking violence and romance around the clock from all over South America. It looked as if they practised the violence, too: there were a lot of people with plasters on their noses. Out in the bay stood some forty or so boats of all shapes and sizes. There were rumours of a Mafia cartel controlling all transport: the airline, the cruise ships and even the ritzy steel gin palaces specially built for the 'blue-rinse' clients rushing to see the doomed wildlife. But who could tell?

'We call them cattle,' a local laughed. 'You see, to begin with they came here in cattle trucks from the airport over on Baltra Island.'

Next morning, Captain Alfonso issued us all with torches and drove us along bumpy red dirt roads to visit Furio Valbonesi, an eccentric Italian who, twenty years before, had bought a farm up on the gentle mountain slopes of the interior, wanting to get away from it all. But when we arrived at the solitary wooden farmhouse, there was no sign of its mysterious owner. The place was wide open, even to the most casual glance. It had a modernistic Mediterranean atmosphere, with spacious if raw and simple rooms.

'The trappings,' grinned Will, yuppie stockbroker of the eighties, nodding knowingly at the Louis Vuitton attaché case lying casually among books by Salman Rushdie and P.D. James. Pinned on bleached plank walls, the Rolex posters of polo matches and one advertising an Ernest Hemingway memorial regatta vied for eye-catching space among photographs of the owner's racing catamaran. Pale armour-plated shells of long-dead giant tortoises served as seats in the living room, and a pair of small-sized shiny black leather riding boots stood tall beneath a rail of smart saddles. The massive kidney-shaped wood surface of the table was supported centrally by a single whale's vertebra, no more than 2ft clear of the timber floor. Marie Christine summed it up: 'He's not married.'

'No, solo,' the good captain agreed laconically.

We set off on foot, up a rocky track towards the mountains in the centre of the island. 'This section, it is just for the tortoises,' smiled Alfonso, as we struggled through a dense undergrowth of cactus and wiry bushes clinging to broken lumps of lava. In considerable discomfort from my soreness, I was more than relieved to halt at last by a clump of bushes. 'Now the adventure begins!' Alfonso explained excitedly, beckoning us to follow him down a crude log staircase into a black void. At the bottom, our torch beams blinked down a long sloping tunnel about half the diameter of a London tube station. 'Furio discovered this, about one year ago. It is a lava tube – an underground river of lava.'

There was a note of drama in Alfonso's voice. 'Come, we go!'

We crept along the tube, which soon divided into different levels, leading up and down and around, until we didn't know where we were.

'What do you think, Isso?' I whispered, after a particularly slimy descent down a long sodden log ladder.

'I don't know what to say, Danny,' came the anxious reply. Her hands were trembling with fear. It was all very spooky, just the place for one of Isso's ghosts.

I tried to find my bearings amid Alfonso's commentary on the depth:

'Er, at this moment, we are fifteen metres below the surface.' How would he know?

'What's the barbed wire for?' asked Bec.

'Oh, Furio, he's trying to make electric light come along the wire, but he no have much money.' We plodded on, and after a while, I couldn't see any more barbed wire. At least we wouldn't be electrocuted if the owner turned up. The great lumps of jagged rock lying jumbled on the bottom of the tube looked as if they'd fallen from the roof of the tunnel, and quite recently, too.

'That looks like a mosquito,' called Bec, flickering her torch beam at the wall, where an unfortunate insect wriggled on a trickling patch of yellow slime.

'It is the first time! I have seen nothing here before!' protested Alfonso.

'It'll be Injun' Joe and bats next,' I muttered, watching the mosquitos spiralling up in the beams of light, homing in on our slime-covered hands.

At long last we spotted a glimmer of daylight, far above, and crawled to freedom. Hobbling back to the house, I was relieved to see Furio entertaining a handsome island lady on the balcony. I felt sure he'd come up with a drink of water at the very least.

A slim fair-haired fellow in blue jeans and a cream shirt buttoned at the wrists, Furio spoke perfect English. Abandoning the lady, he quickly produced a giant bottle of Pepsi and half a dozen glasses, waving us over to a bare wooden table. We flopped on the benches, mopping the sweat. Even Alfonso went strangely silent now, as if demurring to a greater intellect.

'Welcome to the Mutiny Restaurant!' laughed Furio, lighting another cigarette. 'I'm fed up with cooking cannelloni for tourists. I spent four months down that lava tunnel last year, but I'm giving it all up now, I'm finished. I'm alone, and it's not worth it. I've started studying legumes.'

It was rather difficult to follow that, but Marie Christine was pleased to have the chance to speak English. 'Why are so many of the people on this island wearing sticking plasters on their noses?' she inquired.

Furio laughed. 'We've just held a world conference for plastic surgeons. One of them, with exceptionally strong fingers, offered to demonstrate the breaking and remodelling of noses, using the islanders as volunteers. It's astonishing how many came forward.' Alfonso joined in the laughter.

Furio told us he'd had the farm, which was on the 20 per cent of the island reserved for agriculture, for twenty years. He'd been away for quite long periods but always returned. 'I like the country, the people, the space. Europeans, they all fight over everything, don't they? What for?' As we turned to leave, I wondered whether Bec and Will might settle in such a place.

'The bow anchor's been dragging all day!' Andy called down to us in the dinghy when we returned to the yacht. He was miffed at having drawn the short straw for anchor watch, but I could understand what a worrying day it had been for him.

We should have made a better job of anchoring in the first place – it was another instance of us shooting ourselves in the foot. Now I immersed myself in soothing the team through the tricky manoeuvre of relaying the anchors. Everyone was tired and tetchy, and I realised this was just one of those moments when everything could go wrong.

'John Ridgway?' The shout startled me. Shooting out from behind one of the anchored cabin cruisers, steering a small wooden tender with a little Jap outboard, came a tall, elderly and distinctly English figure with a white beard and glasses. 'I'm David Balfour. Can I help you with your stern anchor?'

'That's very sporting of you.' It was rather a good way to meet the honorary British consul, avoiding all that stiff formality which wastes so much time. David made short work of relaying the stern anchor with Will and Bec, and I invited him aboard for a drink.

'Here comes the port captain's boat,' called Andy.

'El doctoro!' announced the petty officer, attired in smart whites, from the stern of the power boat. And there was the pharmacist and his surly son. He almost smiled. It was a tricky moment. I had no idea Alfonso had arranged this medical visit. The British consul was sidetracked on deck by my wife while I went below with the pharmacist and his son. There was no time to waste. I dropped my pale blue *pareu* and pointed to the raw patches on the insides of the top of both thighs. The son bent forward with interest and the father began a lengthy medical tutorial in Spanish. I was ignored, impatient and humiliated.

I thanked him, readjusted my *pareu* and we repaired to the deck. 'La plancha, la plancha!' said the pharmacist. The British consul translated: I must iron my underwear. The crew was rocking with laughter, I was the laughing stock of the Ecuadorian navy and all face was lost. I ushered pharmacist and son into the dinghy with promises to return to his shop for further purchases in the morning. Then I signalled David below and got out the malt whisky.

David's story could so easily have been my own. The same age as me, he had abandoned a law degree in 1963, and set sail with a friend for Australia in an old Brixham trawler. But the Galapagos was as far as they got. They tried to charter the boat for scientific work, but there wasn't enough business. So David went back to Britain, returning in 1969 aboard a Baltic trader with plans to start in the tourist business. Here he was, twenty-five years later, resembling every child's idea of a favourite uncle, hectically busy in the boom which had begun in 1983 with an encouraging push from the Ecuadorian government, frantic for US dollars after the sucre fell victim to inflation. He was presently involved in setting up a proper school to prevent island children from drifting back to Ecuador. Santa Cruz had become his life, and he looked fulfilled.

David kindly arranged for me to meet the directors of the competing Parque Nacional and Darwin Foundation. So next morning I set out to estimate the survival chances of the fabled Galapagos wildlife. After all, it was only the wildlife which brought all these people to the islands. I was not very encouraged. An early casualty of the accelerating tourist boom had been the Parque Nacional itself, which nominally controlled 97 per cent of the land mass as well as the territorial waters surrounding it. But the park lacked the manpower to exercise that control. Talking with Arturo Izurieta, its dynamic new director, at his office on the outskirts of Ayora, he was quick to assure me that the 'global plan' for the future of the Galapagos was safe in his hands. All construction was to be frozen, concessions halted and fishing regulated out to 200 miles offshore. But he admitted he still hadn't the manpower to enforce the regulations.

I allowed a brief pause in the monologue to grow into a silence. 'I want you to understand,' Arturo burst out suddenly, 'Parque Nacional will control. Darwin Foundation must learn to do science and forget about meddling in the administration of the islands.' I sensed a personality clash. The prestigious Darwin Foundation's research institute was situated but a few hundred yards away, and its American influence did not please the Ecuadorians.

It was a long, sore walk back to the village, where I lunched alone in an empty tourist café. Arturo had got one thing absolutely clear in my head: I now felt I did appreciate the unique value of the Galapagos.

Over thousands of years, man has bashed and burned just about every part of the planet. In fact, he's made such a mess of it that it is very difficult to puzzle out how things might have evolved without his influence. But by sheer fluke, although he colonised all the other thousands of islands in the Pacific, until comparatively very recently, he never colonised the Galapagos Islands. And of course, they had little to recommend them – just baking-hot heaps of black lava, covered with leafless shrubs and ugly cacti, inhabited by birds, reptiles and a few Ecuadorian political prisoners. But in 1835 Charles Darwin realised that he really was in a place where species had evolved untouched by the influence of man. He had a sudden flash of original thought: 'Here, both in space and time, we seem to be brought somewhat nearer to that great fact – that mystery of mysteries – the first appearance of new beings on this earth.'

The English pirates, American whalers, Californian sealers and animals introduced by the convicts followed, and as with everywhere else, man is steadily watering down the magic. But tourists will prove the most serious threat the islands have faced. Then there are the colonists to service the tourists, with all their own economic pressures.

Limping back along the track, I felt rather sad at the idea of the islands being exploited as a short-term resource. The timber buildings of the Darwin Research Institute were drab and the place looked in a bad way. World recession had curtailed funds, morale was low and qualified staff were drifting towards the higher salaries now being offered by the Parque Nacional. Chantal Blanton PhD, *la directora*, as she was called, welcomed me into her spacious office and sat me down on a sofa. Tall and slender, perhaps in her late thirties, her long, fair hair was swept up on top of her head, balancing the effect of her big, round 'scientist' glasses. Emphasising her energetic approach, she was wearing a white Darwin T-shirt, shorts, long white socks and trainers. In sharp contrast with the hangdog look of other members of staff who had passed me in the gloomy corridors, Chantal radiated confidence and enthusiasm, and I thought of all the times I'd had to put on just such a performance. Coming round to the front of her desk, she leaned casually back on it, looking down at me and putting me in the sort of inferior position you're supposed to try to escape when you're stopped for speeding.

I began by mentioning the new charge of $200 per person per day for the cruising permit for visiting yachts, but she countered immediately, in a crisp American accent, 'The movement of yachts really does need to be controlled, you know. A French yacht was recently discovered by an official tour boat in one of the anchorages on a remote island. The crew were playing football on the beach – using a penguin for a ball. Unfortunately, there are only a couple of hundred of those birds in existence.' I was stuck for a reply.

And she smiled when I suggested that the Ecuadorians might like to see the back of the Americans. 'Our problem is that we must produce scientific answers to problems: sometimes government doesn't like what it hears. The Parque Nacional people have little experience. Everything may be fine as long as the government supports Galapagos, but there are elections every four years. What if another government diverts its funds elsewhere? There is only one Galapagos in this world.'

I asked if she'd seen much change in the islands. 'Well, I've been here eighteen months now. I've seen the growth of supermarkets and the arrival of television and video. People coming here often remark on how unremote it is. The message which needs getting across to people is: make the most of where you are. It's getting to be the same everywhere. Even the pressures are only slightly different.'

MARIE CHRISTINE

Four months out from home, and here we were in this extraordinary setting. Around the boat would swim the awkward stick-like black marine iguanas or a brown turtle, as old as time, returning from the huge ocean to mate. And in the air, dark angular frigate birds wheeled high above, waiting to hijack another bird's catch, and boobies and scarlet-beaked tropic birds dived into the fish-rich water. Flocks of huge grey pelicans flew in low, like bombers on a raid. Sometimes they would perch on our pulpit, quite unconcerned by the ever-present array of flapping washing along the guardrails; one even had the affront to sit on the top of our 70ft mast, crushing the wind vane.

Inland, the hills were green – I could almost imagine Dorset – rolling clouds fed them moisture, and around this time of year the *garua*, a soft rain, was expected, nurturing vegetables and fruit in abundance on the fertile volcanic ground. But down on the shore the scenery was lunar. Either side of the rapidly growing village spread a tangle of thorny scrub and Opuntia cactus with its brown trunk, like any tree, but sprouting from its branches spiny cactus plates. Black and red fly-catchers and

Darwin's finches hopped about quite unconcerned by us gawping humans.

Among Andy's mum's carefully thought-out supply of birthday and Christmas presents, along with the book on Galapagos birds, was another intriguing island story of five brothers who escaped Nazi Germany in a small boat their parents bought to start anew out here. With Teutonic grit, they carved out lives among the volcanic clinker and thorn. From where we were anchored, we could see Carl Angermeyer's home clinging to the steep shore. The house, which matched the picture in the book, was constructed of clinker blocks, which made it look as though it had just grown out of the twisted lava. How much more in keeping with its surroundings it was than the mushrooming developments across the bay. I wondered how Angermeyer, an old man now, viewed the enormous changes which had taken place during the fifty years he had spent on his island refuge.

JOHN

Unlike at Chiquito Guayabo, there was nobody waving sad goodbyes from the beach as we sailed out of Puerto Ayora, late on the morning of 3 February. All the characters we'd met were busy; after all, Ayora village was no longer a sleepy paradise. Tourists came and went, two a penny, and pennies were what mattered most on Santa Cruz.

Just half an hour out, we came upon a pair of turtles locked in a compromising position. I hoped it might be a good omen for our 3,000-mile, three-week voyage, but it didn't work out that way.

Amid the high, misty islands, tide, wind and current all seemed set against us. While the sea was glassy calm, it was being ripped up in places by conflicting currents in the narrow channels between islands. Barely 30 miles out of Santa Cruz, up ahead of us we could see Crescent Island, the 600ft-high rim of an uninhabited extinct volcano, lying just off the south-east corner of Isla Isabela. Setting the GPS so that we'd leave Crescent a mile to our right, I squeezed my sweating body down through the hatch in the doghouse and went below for a nap, hoping to bank a bit of sleep before the night watches.

'Something's wrong with the GPS!' Andy's blunt Yorkshire tones brought me swimming sleepily back to life. I crawled back up on deck. Sure enough, Crescent Island now lay well to our left. We were heading for the rock-strewn channel between it and the towering bulk of Isabela.

We couldn't understand it; a strong current appeared to be running in the opposite direction from that shown on the chart, and we were convinced that, if anything, the tide was running the wrong way as well.

'Alter course thirty degrees to port,' I grumbled, tugging at the blue cotton *pareu* wrapped round my waist, and clumped off to stretch out on my bunk once more. Daytime sleeping always seemed to bring on ill humour. We passed Crescent as required, but not as planned.

A moonless midnight found us creeping across a flat sea, wreathed in wisps of eerie mist. We were now close under Isla Isabela, and right on the western edge of the Galapagos Islands. A ghostly feeling pervaded the boat. The scores of reckless plunging blue-footed boobies had long since flown back to land, leaving only mysterious dark silence, interrupted now and then by the heavy splash of breaching sea lions and dolphins and the longer sigh of whales.

The whole place exuded pre-history, it was as if we were in Conan Doyle's *Lost World*. Bobbing along in very poor visibility, I visualised *English Rose* skirting round the upper slopes of Isabela's Cero Azul, a 16,000ft volcano. We were only about 5,000ft below the summit: the rest lay below the waves.

'Keep the engine running, Johnny,' urged Marie Christine, her voice edged with anxiety. 'I don't care about the fuel. I just don't want us to be swept on the rocks by some freak current we don't understand.' Now even the radar seemed to be playing up: an ectoplasmic sort of patch was growing on the left side of the screen. I glanced at Isso, our ghost enthusiast. Huddled beside the radar, she was keeping very quiet, peering out through the side windows of the doghouse in the way she always did when she didn't want to make eye contact with anyone. The three of us managed a bit of singing to try to cheer ourselves up, but it didn't do much good. The Galapagos Islands just wouldn't go away. We were only too pleased to scuttle below when Andy finally came quietly up the ladder to relieve us at two o'clock.

When we came on again at six in the morning, it was already broad daylight. But the great bulk of Cero Azul was still only just astern, and that was where it was to stay, looming over us, for the next couple of days. Although we were out of the immediate danger of running ashore, we daren't use any more of our precious diesel so early on in this long passage, so we just tacked to and fro in an almost flat calm. We found fifteen baby squid and five flying fish on the deck. The squid might have been a clue to the presence of numerous whales: they reminded me of a radio programme I'd done years before, with Maurice and Maralyn Bailey, whose yacht had been rammed and sunk in these waters by a sperm whale. Their 118 days was then the longest recorded time spent in a liferaft, and now everyone was reading their book whenever they were off watch. How would we perform in our two eight-man liferafts? Yet again, we checked Bec's list of abandon-ship duties, posted on the chart-table bulkhead. She was for ever updating the parcels of food and water we kept attached to the rafts for emergency. We ought to have kept a copy of the Baileys' book there, too.

That evening a spooky white patch swam round and round *English Rose* on Bec and Will's eight-to-ten watch; some sort of large fish making a phosphorescent trail, and eyeing us as a potential snack. Shining Andy's torch at it seemed to frighten it away, but only for a while.

Sharks and whales were everywhere. One large shark cruised around us, its triangular dorsal fin cutting the surface, followed, some way back, by the tip of its tail. To begin with there were plenty of turtles too; on 5 February we saw eight, but that evening we finally got the sails up and we saw no more after that. 'We're on the way! Shooting stars amazingly bright!' Bec recorded gleefully in the log. Later she added: 'One small and one large monster.' Whatever the luminous white patch was, it was coming with us.

8

The Great Ocean

JOHN

We covered only 89 miles on each of the first couple of days under sail, but steadily our daily runs climbed to around 150 a day. As if wishing to join in the lifting of our spirits, a large school of dolphins crossed our bows, a hundred or more, jumping with joy as they headed south. On this leg, there were no time pressures, no having to get Brian, or Bruce and Rita, or Richard and Jink, to their plane. And from the outset I cultivated an attitude which was absolutely the reverse of the regulated computerised rush which is becoming the main feature of modern civilisation. It seemed to me that all you really have in life is a short period of time, nothing more, and I was determined to make the most of mine. In any case, there was no point in hurrying: we did not want to arrive in the Marquesas before the end of the cyclone season.

And so a week flashed by. On 10 February, with 2,200 miles still to go, the sun disappeared behind thick cloud. The sea got bumpy, we got queasy and Marie Christine got glum. As we sped along at night under well-reefed sails, with distant lightning flickering on the horizon and dolphins rushing along our sides like luminous sea serpents stitching the waves, she told me straight: she hated sailing, and in particular, she hated being stuck with other people.

Two days later we saw the first glimmer of returning sunlight in the morning. Isso went below to fetch bread and marmalade for our breakfast, wondering what all the seasickness fuss was about. Marie Christine and I fed the red and white muppet over the side on its wire trace and paid out 100yds of plaited green line, winding in a bit to set the tension on the reel.

The strike came within seconds, wrenching the perspex handle from my hands and racing it into a whap-whap-whap! against the shock-cord preventer. Far astern, an arc of silver burst from the sea, shaking its head violently. All of a fluster, I eased the sheets while Marie Christine brought *English Rose* into the wind. I worked away on the reel until Andy, responding to our frantic cries of 'Fish! Fish!' came hurrying up and took over. Then I slipped the hook of the gaff under the line to make sure it was feeding flat on the drum.

After a lot of paying out and reeling in, we saw an iridescent flash, deep down and some 20ft astern. This was something different. A few moments later, using my legs as levers and with my hands safely inside the leather gloves, I heaved aboard 4ft of shimmering wahoo. It fitted exactly along the whole length of the seat on the port side of the aft cockpit. Marie Christine abandoned the wheel. Thrashing about in the boat, it looked a good match for us. A cross between a giant mackerel and a marlin, with a back of electric blue and bright blue tiger stripes flowing down into the silver, it stared at us with a baleful eye, its vicious teeth and the twenty or more spines along its dorsal fin giving it the look of a crazed killer. But it was soon in the pot. It had never reckoned on a meeting with our band of Inverness Technical College-trained salmon-filleters.

I stabbed it through the head with our sharpest kitchen knife, severing the backbone and pinning it to the breadboard. Andy pounced next, slitting it from vent to gill and removing the intestines. His two years running the salmon farm at home made for swift work. Marie Christine chopped it into steaks and fillets. On deck, Will, who had lifted a few tons of salmon on the farm himself, worked with Isso, swilling buckets of seawater over everything, and a blur of scrubbing brushes washed the blood straight out of the self-draining cockpit before it had a chance to coagulate.

Down in the galley, Bec fried the steaks with pasta, grated cheese and parsley sauce for an early lunch. The fresh flesh was finely grained and sweet, but there was a snag: having no fridge, we had to eat an awful lot. And we'd have to eat the fillets for supper. We hated killing fish unless we could eat them.

*

The Pacific is a big ocean. It was only mid-February, and we worked out we'd come 6,000 miles from Ardmore; yet by our intended route through Polynesia, we were still 6,000 miles from our mid-July rendezvous in Valdivia, Chile.

Our six-to-ten morning routine was simple: crawl sleepily up into the doghouse, listening to Bec's hand-over briefing. Check and tune the rig as necessary. Slip out on to the stern, hang on to a mizen-mast backstay and really clean the teeth. Morning PT on deck for A Watch. Pay out the fishing line for the day, then rig the aft cockpit awning over the mizen boom and rig up a groundsheet between the mizen backstays – all this before the sun could cook the doghouse. Then I would wash out the aft cockpit and sweep the doghouse, while Isso or Marie Christine made breakfast. Then we would take turns to go below for an all-over wash, with a pint of water each.

The whole crew was much more at ease on this leg. Will was freer now. The black moods, so upsetting for everyone else, were fading, as was his unusual and irritating habit of somehow, even in so small a boat, managing to absent himself from all formal crew briefings. He spoke of his early life on the family's Gloucestershire farm; he told how he'd always been under-sized at school – so much so that his biology teacher had told him to drink seawater because it contained iodine, good for his thyroid, which would surely help him grow. I'd never heard of such a tonic, but it had certainly worked in Will's case. He was intensely physical: each morning would find him up on the foredeck, braced against the main mast, grinding through a punishing circuit-training routine.

Enjoying a respite from seasickness for a while, Andy mellowed, became less blunt. He and I struggled away with noon sights and moonsets, and he was always good at combing through handbooks and finding solutions to technical problems. He loved the feeling of being at sea alone at night, far out on the Pacific. He was quite at home on his own: since graduating from university, he'd lived alone in the Watcher's House at Ardmore, hardening his pipe-cleaner-thin frame with two physical years of single-handedly moving hundreds of tons of feed and fish in all weathers, and depending on his wits and boatmanship skills for his safety in the winter storms. He was now close to what could be termed 'self-reliant'. Clad in the scantiest of black swimming trunks, he maintained his fitness by working out with my Heavy Hands dumbbells by day and doing what he called his 'nightly walk from Ardmore to Kinlochbervie'. This was measured in steps up on to the plank of heavy Panama hardwood used by Isso and Marie Christine to gain extra height to look over the doghouse roof while steering.

Isso was still transfixed by 'Anderew', as she called him, always hoping he might tread on her as he got into his bunk above hers, or ask her to rub suntan oil on his back. She engaged Marie Christine in daily conferences about how she might win his favour, and perhaps even leave our watch to join his. Nail-polish appeared, and, becoming increasingly figure-conscious, Isso consumed much less food. There was no more talk of buying jars of strawberry jam or Coca-Cola. And although our younger daughter was still likely to fall asleep on the midnight watch, she always insisted, no matter what, on staying up until Andy came to relieve us.

Battles between mother and daughter were fought out in frequent tantrums. 'Yep, yep, yep, yep!' signalled impatience; 'Mama's a witch!' or 'I cut you neck!' meant war. 'Okey-dokey,' sounded the all-clear and a joyous cry of 'Ooh! I want to cuddle Mama!' declared peace in our time and an eager return to her mother's greatest enthusiasm: teaching Elizabeth to enjoy reading. Enid Blyton, Anne of Green Gables and the Borrowers provided an everlasting source of discussion.

I continued with my own daily struggle, only inching towards my goal of teaching Isso to learn and recite her multiplication tables. And yet she had an uncanny ability for automatically knowing the date, in all weathers, no matter how tired she might be. 'Wednesday sixteen February 1994!' she would trip off her tongue at any time of the day or night.

Rebecca was in charge of maths. She concentrated on Isso's dream trips to the glittering shops of Inverness and how she was going to manage the change from her pocket money at the counter in Seconds and Firsts, her favourite dress shop.

Although Isso was always thinking up new names for herself, like Suki or Blossom, Bec had taken to calling her Dolly, because nowadays, our Inca princess was always laughing. Gone was the paralysing anxiety which had been so much a feature of her life at boarding schools in Scotland, the turning to face a corner of the room when people called unexpectedly.

The barrel-chested Quechua people have developed superhuman stoicism over the centuries. Their ritual chewing of coca leaves is aimed at overcoming the main features of life in the bleakness of the high Andes: cold, hunger, exhaustion. Stoicism was Isso's standby for every occasion.

Rebecca was very cheery and open too, crying 'Oooooooh!' at each wondrous oceanic revelation. She was always cool and sensible, and the realities of being watch-leader, particularly on bad nights, underlined her ability to reason coherently. While she had a strong bond with her mother and her little sister, Bec found it hard working with me. She hated it when I shouted at Marie Christine, or, worse still, at her. Then the little lip would go down and there would be a battle to stop the tears and maybe screams of rage. I remembered those awful days when, holidays over, it was time to go back to boarding school. My only blood relative, putting her on the empty mail bus in the morning and walking back to the boat waiting at the end of the loch. The Highlands have a terrible silence for the lonely. It was no easy thing to find a balance of loyalty between boyfriend and father within the confines of *English Rose*. And all things considered, she was looking as happy and settled as I'd ever seen her.

These were the days of ease, linked by gentle starry nights and a flat-bottomed crescent moon ascending from the horizon in the early hours, while the sea chuckled along the hull in velvet darkness. Marie Christine and I were enjoying our first bit of real relaxation for a long time. Life was close to perfection. If only the awful prickly heat would go away. As we three came on watch each morning, the sun would rise up out of the sea like a burnished copper disc. With mainsail and Yankee boomed out on either side, we were running some 160 miles downwind each day, under blue skies, heading in the very wake of Cook, Melville and Stevenson, directly along the latitude for Hiva Oa at the northern end of the Marquesas Islands.

It's true, there were spiders nesting in the bunches of yellow bananas hanging from the mizen rigging and little black fruitflies hovering among the pineapples tied to the handrails in the saloon, but we looked on them as fellow voyagers into the unknown.

On the night watches we rattled through our songsheets and held poetry recitals from my battered prep-school copy of Maxwell's *Verse Worth Remembering*. Isso would recite her two-times table, then I'd spout Masefield's 'Sea Fever' (sometimes several times, to get the delivery just right from the steering wheel). Isso's three-times table would be followed by Marie Christine's breathless rendition of Wordsworth's

'Daffodils', Isso's four-times, my version of Tennyson's 'Eagle', Isso's five-times, Marie Christine's 'Sea Fever', Isso's six-times, my Newbolt's 'Vitae Lampada', and so on. There was oceans of time, and we took to spending a lot of it out on deck, in the shade of the sails, eating lovely long lunches and talking about family matters. 'If you don't enjoy this, Ridgway,' I kept telling myself, 'you won't enjoy anything. This is *it* – there's nothing on earth better than this.'

And yet, I wondered, did my feeling of wellbeing owe more to my blessed release from the unscrupulous society from which I'd temporarily escaped, than to any real hope of an earthly paradise just over the far horizon? Being paranoid didn't mean the buggers weren't after me. Out here, I was right off the roundabout of other people's expectations. I could put up more sail, alter course, and simply disappear . . .

I was counting heavily on the presence of my family; I really loved, best of all, being with Marie Christine, Bec and Isso. I welcomed the inactivity, encouraging my mind to wander without constraint. But how could any but the most blindly complacent be happy while the world sank into a deeper mess? The only firm decision I'd ever taken to help was to marry and have only one child, and that was pretty simplistic.

The Pacific is vast, but not always empty. A couple of thousand miles west of the Galapagos, we encountered fleets of Japanese and Korean fishing boats – fishing ships would be a better description. At night it was like arriving at a small town. First we'd see the loom of their lights, way out in the middle of nowhere, then the garish white islands of floodlight. At 8.25 am on 18 February we sighted two fishing buoys, one on top of the other, and at 9.25 two more just the same, about seven miles apart. We wondered whether they might be connected by some kind of drift net which would kill every living thing – fish, bird or mammal – caught in its mesh. At other times we saw what appeared to be radio beacons, marking what might be the end of a long line of drift net. We could catch nothing ourselves now. There were no dolphins about any more; the sea had become a desert. Even the flying fish seemed to shrink. The only ones we saw were a mere couple of inches long.

Rebecca

Sitting at one end of the long black table in the office at home in the croft, I drew a wobbly line from dot to dot across a map. Britain was now only a small squiggle in the top right-hand corner. Most of the map was taken up by the emptiness of the vast Pacific Ocean, which gave it a lopsided look and dwarfed our own great Atlantic. It took me a while, paging through the index of our aging *Times Atlas of the World*, to find the groups of islands I had never heard of: Marquesas, Tuamotu, Society, Australs.

My fingers sailed through the Panama Canal and further eastwards across seas of green and blue – the Pacific. The Gulf of Panama, Cocos Ridge and East Pacific Rise were all in shades of greeny-yellow, indicating depths less than 4,000m, while the second half of our passage would be deeper – at least there were no 'fracture zones' or 'trenches' to cross. Anyway, what is the difference between 2,000m and 4,000m, except that corned-beef tins take longer to sink to the bottom? I tried to think positively as I scattered a few ink dots, marking the Society Islands, far too far to the east. Here lies Tahiti. Yes, Tahiti, surely everyone's dream of paradise. My mind drifted off into visions of beauty: giant hibiscus flowers tucked into thick black hair, grass-clad hips swaying in the warm night air on deserted coral strands. How romantic it would be in the south seas.

It had been a long, hot Leg. I never knew it was possible to sweat as much as I did standing in the galley in my bikini, just dripping. We kept the hatch in the foredeck open as long as possible, closing it only when the sea picked up and broke into our precious, small, dry space. The canvas windscoop did its best to push air through. If the wind died completely, we would sleep on deck to escape the extra heat created by our trusty engine; otherwise, I lay in my narrow pipe cot bunk with a sheet below me and my head as close as I could get it to any passage of air, resting on the scaffolding pipe that held the outer edge of my bunk in place. I knew this trusty pole would also serve as the weight to carry me down if burial at sea became necessary.

We called our home the library ship: books were stored in every available locker and under the saloon seats, and once one had been thoroughly read it was put away. Reading was our main pastime when we were not on watch, cooking or in the heads. The rather cynical *Happy Isles of Oceania* by Paul Theroux was handed round – this was where we were headed. Will read and reread an ancient guide to sheep husbandry, his heart well and truly on the land. He searched for help in *The Psychology of Sailing*, but I think it only confirmed his worst fears with its case studies of people who had been driven to murder as well as suicide. Andy discovered a love of reading, gobbling up sailing tale after sailing tale. Isso followed suit with ghost stories. I was engrossed in Isabel Allende's haunting *The House of the Spirits*, then John Steinbeck's *East of Eden*. I found their descriptiveness and minute detail such a refreshing contrast to the vast, empty sea and open sky around me.

Mum read everything at high speed, particularly enjoying William Trevor's short stories. Dad was stuck into *The Prize*, a huge tome covering the history of oil. Anyone who would listen was told in detail how it was oil that had decided the outcome of both world wars. He found even a huge biography of Aldous Huxley rivetingly interesting, and this led on to another, of Ottoline Morrell. In our situation reading could be managed without that awful feeling of guilt you usually get at home, where there are so many other things you ought to be doing. For Mum and Dad, the days and nights were filled with their very individual interpretations of the books they were reading, usually punctuated by furious rows. 'That's it, I'm finished,' Mum would scream, dissatisfied with Dad's not quite so romantic views, and waving her arms across her waist to signal the final cut-off.

I longed to reach land, and felt my life was in limbo on these long passages. Yes, there were some truly great moments: the change of night to day, and day to night, which luckily fell on our watch in the tropics, was always spectacular and uplifting. Sailing westwards meant we kept in line with the sun. It rose off our stern and set ahead of our bows, leapfrogging us every day. After supper, which was usually cooked by Will, Mum or me, and the steamy washing up, Will and I were off watch until 10 pm. It was dark, and we didn't have enough battery power for lights, so we either lay as still as possible and stewed in our bunks, or slept. I preferred the latter. Before getting into my bunk I would climb out through the forehatch with our small plastic washing bowl containing a cup of precious fresh water. This was my favourite time of day. The cooler night air returned and I could wash away the salt while standing naked on our nodding bow as the blazing sky slipped below the horizon.

During balmy evenings on deck in the Caribbean, Will had taught me to play backgammon, and after weeks of being beaten, I was beginning to get the hang of it. Now we were more or less level-pegging. The board needed to be propped up to keep it flat and held on to in case of a sudden roll. No one else would play. Andy was not a games player, and Mum and Dad knew only too well from previous experience how even an argument resulting from a harmless game can be blown out of all proportions in this hothouse environment. Although we were fiercely competitive, I hoped Will and I knew each other well enough not to let such pettiness interfere. Backgammon became one of the highlights of the day. 'Just one more game, one more game,' the loser would plead. Sometimes the loser would have to promise to act as 'slave' to the triumphant one for a whole day, though I wasn't much good at this.

It was not long before our watch time came round again and Andy would leave his post in the doghouse to come and wake us. Towards the end of the leg we became worse and worse at getting up. Often Will would appear in the doghouse at strange times, imagining that he had been woken, and sometimes he would call down from the top bunk to see what time it was. My rather irritable response was usually, 'Not yet, sshh, go back to sleep!' We seemed to become confused between imagined calls and real calls, until Andy's unmistakable, harsh 'Are you two getting up or what?' brought us back to reality.

The night skies were amazingly clear. Every few minutes long-tailed shooting stars and satellites criss-crossed our inky ceiling. I wore a T-shirt or cotton jumper over my swimming costume, but needed little else. We kept a good look out for ships, but saw very few, and then mostly their lights or just looms. We believed them to be Korean tuna boats sweeping the ocean of every living creature with their massive net walls of death.

As we inched closer and closer to the mysterious Polynesian islands, Will and I would talk of the past and plan for the future. Sometimes I read for a bit while he kept watch, then I kept watch while he did his exercises: sit-ups on the doghouse roof, step-ups and weights in the cockpit and press-ups on the lazarette on the stern of the boat. He was always much more cheerful after his exercises: he was like a caged animal without them.

Will and I kept our toothbrushes in a horrible green plastic mug on the fruit-and-vegetable bunk below the doghouse. Once, when my Macleans squeezed dry, he insisted on using a cheap brand of toothpaste which tasted grim, but always caused a joke. We turned toothbrushing into a ritual, brushing for ages in the cockpit before lunging over the side to spit out the paste. This ceremony helped us to wake up properly for the night watch. I was very jealous of the ability of our male crew members to pee over the side, cutting out all the valve-opening and pumping involved with using the heads. So I worked out a way in which I could do it, too. This was made easier, if a little more exciting, if the boat was well heeled over, but it was only possible in warmer climes where I wore little clothing.

For an hour or so each afternoon I tried to teach Isso some basic maths. I am no great mathematician, so I tried to put it over in shopping terms. She loves shopping. I hoped that by using the age-old trick of getting her interested in what she was 'buying', she would forget that we were actually practising mental arithmetic. Sometimes it worked, and she managed no bother, but on other occasions it just didn't. This Peruvian child had no interest. Her people had no concept of numbers greater than ten – they preferred to barter. Anything over ten was 'many'. How could I change this underlying natural force? I wished I had more patience.

We started the multiplication tables. Learning by rote, Isso was better: we went forwards, backwards and every other way to try to get the hang of the first, easier, ones. It reminded me of my own early days at Kinlochbervie Primary School – all chanting, and then people being picked to answer on the spot. I used to shake with fear: how terrible to be disgraced in front of the class. I sympathised with Isso.

Apart from the change-over of watches, when we brought the next team up to date with anything new, there was little chat between us all. We scarcely picked up the World Service on the radio and our tapes, although old favourites, were getting a little stale after five months of continual use. One of Isso's roles was 'music officer', but she interpreted this by hiding her mass of tapes in her bed, so that only she could listen to them on her Walkman. Still, dance album after dance album might have been a bit much for the rest of us. Instead, Fleetwood Mac ran again and again, the list of tracks long since rubbed off the cassette by hot, grasping fingers.

Lunch was our conversation time. The sight of food always brightened us. We had a phase of hot soup. Will often tried to sneak in a few bits of the fish we had dried in Panama, which we all loathed. I liked a good, thick vegetable broth with lots of bite to it, but with few fresh vegetables, crunchiness was a texture hard to find. We did have a little cabbage and yam, and there were some potatoes, onions and garlic left on the almost-bare fruit-and-vegetable bunk.

Bread was baked every day, either by Mum or Will. I think Will enjoyed kneading: it gave him a chance to use up some of his pent-up energy. When the dough squeaked and looked like freshly dead skin-covered flesh (these were my mother's words), the bowl was wedged into the warmest place aboard to allow the dough to rise – sometimes on top of the gimballed cooker in the galley, or in the corner of the cockpit with most sun, but usually under the saloon table, on the floorboards above the engine. Once the dough had doubled in size there was a second kneading, followed by the shaping of loaves or buns, which would be left to rise once more before they were cooked.

One afternoon I was just disappearing down the hole leading from the doghouse into the aft cabin and galley to get the barometer reading for the ship's hourly log, when Will, with a note of authority in his voice, asked me to check the dough while I was down there, and to do the second knead if it was time. This was quite a responsibility. There was pride at stake in any of our cooking, but particularly in the age-old skill of baking. After tapping the barometer and taking the reading, I checked the operating-theatre bowl, half expecting to see human organs under the teatowel instead of dough. It looked all right. Carefully carrying the bowl to the galley, I set it down and called up the instrument readings to Will. I told him the dough looked good and I would give it a second knead. 'At least ten minutes,' he called back. I took a few deep breaths, washed my hands and began kneading. Feeling faint and ready to collapse after ten minutes, I divided the dough into two and shaped each half into a round, placing them side by side on a floured baking tray. I put a teatowel over them and put them back under the saloon table. I lit the oven to warm up, and shot back to the doghouse, feeling rather pleased with myself. Thanks came from Will and I glowed inside with pleasure. I checked the bread fifteen minutes later, it had not risen enormously, but I thought it would be fine to cook. Into the oven it went – but by the time it came out, it was just the same size. It was like a rock to cut and needed superhuman jaws to chew. The ragging began . . .

I felt such a flop. I decided to make iced buns the next day to prove that I could make dough that would rise. I was gratified that my buns rose into light, fluffy clouds, topped off with thick, white icing – just like the ones Gran used to give me for tea on weekends home from school.

Nevertheless the giggles continued until a few days later, when, after the subject of 'Bec's bread' was brought up yet again, Will's sniggers suddenly died on his lips. He turned to me and said: 'Do you know, I don't think I put any yeast in that mixture!'

We had all read Marcia Pirie's *Travellers on a Trade Wind*, written in the late 1980s, which gave a descriptive view of the beautiful Marquesan Islands we were heading for. We hoped they had not changed too much in the intervening years. Mum even dreamed of the tropical fruits Marcia described: mango, papaya, banana, orange, lime and the extraordinary pamplemousse – a very large, greenish grapefruit which can be peeled and eaten like an orange, its huge segments bursting with flowery grape-fruit-tasting juice.

While we stewed and drank warm water, we longed to see land grow-ing out of the horizon.

JOHN

The time rushed by. Entering our fourth week at sea after leaving the Galapagos, and still 500 miles short of the Marquesas, the wind began to die, making it even hotter. Our nerves began to twang a bit, and we seemed slicked with sweat most of the time. The Galapagos ointment was containing the prickly heat fairly well, but the sciatic nerve in my left leg was making my foot jump whenever I lay down, an irritating legacy from having had a disc removed from my back a dozen years before.

My nightly faxes to my father in Wimbledon were part of the routine now that we were in our fifth month on *English Rose*. We were now nine hours behind British time, which meant I had to send my message at nine in the evening – if I got the transmission times to Ardmore wrong, Rita would send testy replies warning me not to wake Bruce by setting off the fax machine in the middle of the night. By then it was already six in the morning in Wimbledon. Home seemed far away.

We were tootling along parallel with the equator, just 600 miles on our right-hand side. But Marie Christine and I often gazed the other way, towards the vast emptiness to our south. There was no land between us and the edge of the Antarctic ice, over 3,500 miles away. Before too long, we'd be heading down there ourselves, and my wife was none too happy about the prospect. 'You've no right risking your fam-ily by taking them to Antarctica!' she'd spit. I hadn't much of an answer to that, and it was a real weight on my mind. The best I could do was take on a couple of extra crew. I had plenty of time to think about pos-sible candidates among the 10,000 people who had been to the adventure school over the previous twenty-five years. Now I needed just two good men . . .

I faxed Rita at Base Camp in Ardmore and asked her to trace two ex-instructors: Jon Williams (known as J.W.) and Bruce Gardiner. Rita is some ferret. Within a few days, J.W. and Bruce had agreed to meet us in Valdivia at the end of September.

The wind died altogether with 300 miles still to go. Dripping sweat, I put in my earplugs and switched on the faithful Mercedes for the last couple of days, turning the boat into a furnace. The noise in the saloon drowned the crash-bang-wallop of Will's preparations for a complex lunch of canned peas, chick peas, etc., but it was like living in a bottle. Tapping away on the computer was one long drip of sweat. Bec had to shout when she was reading us Hal Roth's account of his yacht being wrecked near Cape Horn.

On deck we began to see solitary white-tailed tropic birds flying high above us. Then we passed through a big patch of feeding boobies, black terns and frigate birds, and the muppet was hit by a good fish on a short line. It escaped, so I lengthened the line, and within seconds we had an 8lb tuna on deck – just as Andy was about to open the curry packet for supper. Within half an hour we were tucking into tuna steaks and rice with parsley sauce.

Things were looking up. Everyone but Isso slept out on deck when not on watch. Isso was impervious to heat, noise and just about anything.

In the early hours of 25 February 1994, a wind came up from east-north-east and Bec and Will put up the mainsail and a full Yankee. Soon we were flying along at close to 8 knots. We had come a long way. At 8.15 am, after twenty-two days and 3,000 miles of open sea, we could make out the jagged skylines of Hiva Oa and Motane. These islands, growing out of the vast blue ocean, were reputed to be the most beautiful on the face of the earth. We were all on deck, so excited – there can be no better way to arrive in truly foreign lands. We sheltered behind the mainsail, but the sun still burned us through its reflection off the choppy sea.

During the hours between our first sighting of steep black-sided Hiva Oa and our entering its little port in Traitor's Bay, we came to see three of the six inhabited Marquesas Islands. Yet in those seven hours we saw no fishing boat, no house, nor any trace of mankind – just flocks of feeding birds and seabirds wheeling over a white-capped deep blue sea.

'Today I am wiped out, defeated by misery and mostly sickness . . . I think that there, this really savage element, this complete solitude, will give me, before dying, a last spark of enthusiasm which will rejuvenate my imagination and make the conclusion of my talent.' Paul Gauguin wrote this of Hiva Oa in 1901. He was to spend the last two years of his life on this island. I thought I understood what he was saying.

9

Earthly Paradise

JOHN

From its volcanic fang, the crater rim of Temetui swung down and around in a sweeping semi-circle, cradling the village of Atuona, beside the sea. Traitor's Bay lay a little to the east of the village, on the other side of a spur marking where the crater rim had subsided into the ocean.

The bay was really the mouth of an overgrown river valley, and, to our eyes, tired by weeks of fierce sunlight reflected off the sea, this choking vegetation was a rolling riot of wonderfully restful green punctuated by a black sand beach and black volcanic rock along the shoreline. The jungle valley sides rose steeply, gradually thinning to grass, rising and merging with the mountainous hinterland.

In the bay, we found eight visiting yachts tucked away inside the breakwater, but none bearing the ugly 3ft-wide band of yellowy-brown slime and barnacles that we were now carrying above our waterline after the passage from Galapagos. We were the first boat across the Pacific that season, but this novelty brought no one on deck to greet us as we came in, and we laid our anchors bow and stern on our own. Everyone seemed pretty torpid under the pitiless tropical sun.

Anxious to get clearance before the weekend, Marie Christine and I grabbed the six passports and hurried ashore late on a Friday afternoon. We hitched a lift from a huge tattooed Marquesan, who said nothing as he raced his macho-red Toyota stationwagon over the shoulder of the crater and plunged down into the luxuriant foliage almost burying the village of Atuona. Nobody spoke English here, only French or Polynesian. Curtly, he nodded at a smart red, white and blue sign which read 'Gendarmerie' in black letters. Thanking him in French, we jumped out and walked into the compound, with its twin flagpoles and neat bungalow quarters.

The two young gendarmes were smartly turned out in well-pressed pale blue shirts and dark blue shorts. In checking our every detail, and preparing the green passports for our three-month stay in French Polynesia, they were most helpful, yet firm in a typically brusque Gallic manner. Our questions were invariably answered with 'Of course!', palms upward, and a shrug, as if they couldn't comprehend how foreigners didn't know how to behave. And when a young Polynesian wheeled his bike through the gate and asked quietly if his passport had arrived, he was greeted with a sharp 'Non!', which carried with it no trace of public service. But then, the French occupation of the islands had not been of much public service to the indigenous Marquesans. In 1800 the population was some 80,000, but by 1900 there were only 2,000 still alive. European diseases had been the biggest killers.

'Go to the Banque Socredo and pay your bond. Return here with the receipt, and we will issue you with the visa for three months – of course!' The bank was already closed, but a quick chat soon had a little over £8,000 from our bank in the High Street, Inverness spirited to Hiva Oa. There was to be no interest paid on this three-month loan we were making to the Banque Socredo. That gave us something to chatter about.

Leaving the bank in fairly high dudgeon, we strolled along the narrow strip of concrete road which ran a little inland from the bay, almost overarched by the lush vegetation. After five months of voyaging, we had at last reached the 1.5 million square miles of Polynesia, which has been under French rule for a little over 150 years, lying 3,500 miles north-east of Australia. If a map of French Polynesia were laid over one of Europe, Hiva Oa would be close to Stockholm, Mangareva by Bucharest; Rapa would be west of Naples, Mopelia at Brest and Rimatara on the Franco-Spanish border. Here in the Marquesas, at the northern limit of the territory, there were no skyscraper hotels, no cruise liners, no charter yachts or package deals. And the cyclone season, only a few hundred miles to the south, would prevent us from leaving these islands for several weeks. There was nothing for it but to relax and enjoy this earthly paradise. And yet I was by no means sure we could manage relaxation on such a grand scale: it was quite new to our experience in life so far.

Paddling out to the boat, with long rolls of delicious French bread tucked under our arms, we were thrilled to see great preparations under-way for life in port. The sail covers were on, the big awning was rigged over the main boom and the small one over the mizen boom. And the old carpenter's table from Puerto Pinas was standing groggily ready for sup-per in the centre cockpit, its after end resting on the two stacked liferafts.

We did indeed have a relaxing weekend. On Sunday afternoon the two neighbouring villages of Atuona and Taaoa held a regatta in the harbour. From noon to nightfall, the sleek six-seater outrigger canoes – or pirogues, as they are called – raced out to sea, round a rocky island and back. Times varied between sixteen and twenty minutes of total commitment. The champion crew raced three times, their superiority evi-dent from the first thirty seconds of each race. These six men were from the road-building department, and they dug their shovel-shaped paddles into the water with the same shiny-shouldered rhythm they used to fill the cement-mixer, forever entwining Atuona in a ribbon of concrete road. With their blue peaked caps firmly jammed on their heads, they kept their smart red catamaran tantalisingly ahead of all comers.

It is said that Polynesian culture has been destroyed on the Marquesas, that the islanders could not survive without the patronage of French family subsidies, not to mention the free health service and edu-cation. But it seemed to me that any people which can paddle pirogues with the kind of ferocity I saw in the harbour that evening would not lie cowed for long. Both male and female crews whizzed around us, bend-ing forward as they drove through their training circuits. As they surged past, straining faces broke into the broadest smiles I've seen, roaring out challenging cries of greeting. I was glad my rugby days were over: I wouldn't like to take the field against that lot!

Half a dozen pétanque matches raged along the dockside, truly gigan-tic men and women tossing silvery steel balls as if they were no more than ball-bearings. And the families, each averaging half a dozen chil-dren, splashed around in the muddy water or washed down egg-and-tomato baguettes with the fresh milk from chilled coconuts. Half the population of the Marquesas was under twenty years of age. It was all something like village Highland Games at home in Scotland; but better – this was no tourist trap. Here the villagers were the competitors and there was no beer tent. I never heard a harsh word all afternoon. And quite unlike South America, there were no runny-nosed children nor any signs of poverty.

The Gauguin Museum was smart and new. Of course, there were no original works in it. Raddled with syphilis, the wreck of a man who died here in Atuona had painted stuff far too valuable to be left in the middle of the Pacific. The young Frenchwoman sitting by the till had sailed out eight years before. Her husband taught at the village school which served the three southern islands of the Marquesas group.

She'd returned to Paris only once. 'I hated it. The people are so . . . nervous!' she said, puffing at her cigarette beside a brimming ashtray. Above her the sign read, 'Comité de Tourisme'.

Still smarting from the business with the bond, we sailed away for a few days of local cruising. The Canal de Bordelais was only 3 miles across, and we came to anchor in a sandy palm-fringed bay on the north-east corner of Tahuatu Island. Protecting us from the lively southeast tradewinds, the high hills were covered with rolling grassland offering a pleasant home to herds of wild horses and goats, the descendants of animals put ashore by pirates long ago.

We found it strangely difficult to shake off the harbour community mentality we had so welcomed on our arrival in Atuona. We felt vulnerable here, so far from home, and the Pacific seemed so vast. Jan van Drunen from Holland and his French wife, Nanou, came aboard from their 33ft sloop to discuss their plans for cruising the Magellanic channels. For three years, Nanou had been teaching in the long-established Catholic School in Atuona, run by the nuns of St Joseph of Clunie. 'Marquesans carry the same red EEC passport as you and me,' she cried passionately. 'The updated Treaty of Rome of February 1986 says it is forbidden to discriminate between nationals of member countries. All you need is a passport, and for the skipper of the yacht to hold "tickets" for your next destination.'

After they returned to their boat, something of the tension of Nanou's exasperation remained, eventually spilling over at lunch. The common cause of crossing the Pacific to the islands together was over. Now we were in a sort of limbo, obliged to enjoy paradise together. Andy made the odd caustic remark but he was wise enough to practise a policy of avoiding confrontation on the boat, preferring instead to listen in silence. Bec knew that, for her, heated arguments often led to tears, so generally she kept silent, and Isso soon grew bored unless things turned theatrical. This left Marie Christine, Will and me.

So far, Will had masked his thoughts with the excellent manners which came naturally to him, but now we began to argue. Politics was usually the bone of contention. Will was aware of my doubts about the Common Market and my suspicions of Germany's intentions within the organisation. We were from two different generations. I'd worn either naval or army uniform from the age of twelve to twenty-eight, and I'd heard a good deal about the two world wars. Will was all for a clean slate and optimism. I'm afraid our disagreements fuelled a building mutual resentment.

Over the next couple of days we sailed south down the sheltered west coast of Tahuata Island, passing the village of Vaitahu, where Captain Cook anchored. Andy and Will put the rest of us ashore in Hapatoni Bay, where screaming children with flowers in their hair greeted us wildly as we came wobbling over the swell.

The four of us walked delightedly in the cool shade of overhanging trees along a narrow grassy road lined with an old stone wall. There were no hills along the shoreline and there was no hurry. A big woman, pregnant with her seventh child, appeared out of the undergrowth, bearing a basket of pamplemousse, mangos and lemons for us. Shyly, she gave each of us a flower and Marie Christine gave her a miniature bottle of Ralph Lauren perfume and asked if we could pick up the fruit on our way back. A little further along, we came across a carpenter sawing a hardwood log and a couple of women fishing in the clear waters with their small children. They asked if I was Captain Cook's grandson. I told them I was not and asked them where we might anchor safely. The sawing stopped and the man pointed to a small bay, more of a bend in the coast, really, just a couple of miles up the coast. 'Bon sable à Hana Tefau!' he croaked. I grinned with pleasure: my O-level French recognised the word for sand, the very best substance for our Simpson-Lawrence 75lb CQR anchor.

Further along, we came to a cemetery on a slope and an old church with a tin roof, where a small paraffin light burned, as if in memory. The simple building was quite empty, but well cared-for, with neat pews and clean purple altar cloths. A green bronze bell was inscribed: Paris 1873.

We retraced our steps, and found the carpenter waiting for us with a big hessian sack full of pamplemousse. The pregnant woman asked us up to her new bungalow, explaining that they were still rebuilding their homes in the wake of the 1987 cyclone. Her six children were covered with flies. She gave us a box of bananas, mangos, oranges and avocados, asking if we'd like to trade earrings or a plate for the new house in return.

Perhaps we needed to have sailed for five months to really appreciate that family walk along the shore.

Taking the carpenter's advice, we sailed up to Hana Tefau and came in close under the precipitous slopes of the island. The virgin forest was unbroken, except for one small very rusty tin hut where a few men were busy clearing a ledge in the undergrowth to build a small timber house. It was just high enough above the shore to stay clear of a tidal wave. Rising as they do, straight up from the seabed 4,000m below, the volcanic Marquesas have no protective coral reefs and are therefore completely open to ocean swell. I anchored cautiously. There was a fair bit of open sea for the waves to build up – I made it about 4,500 miles to Australia and 3,600 to South America. I felt particularly vulnerable here.

It was baking hot and so we all took to the water, pulling ourselves along the rope which moored our stern to the coconut tree, and passing on our way through a shoal of small green and black striped fish as densely packed as a shoal of sardines. We larked around for a while, but through our masks we could see we were swimming in a biological soup which was stinging us continuously with little pinpricks. All the same, I was enjoying the exercise, and when the others climbed back aboard *English Rose*, I stayed in the water. I set about scrubbing the hull once more with a plastic saucepan brush, which had a sort of scraper which helped remove barnacles from the hull and around the rudder stock casing. I was exhausted by the time I clambered up the stern ladder, but pleasantly relaxed, as if I'd been for a run.

We all needed some space. The next day Will set off alone, climbing up through the forest to the ridge, returning covered with scratches and nono bites, and not in the best of humours. Calling in at the copra-drying box among the trees, Marie Christine invited the five house-builders to supper and straight away they set about catching food for us to cook. Fishing just off the surf line with hand spears, they tossed red and black fish into a red plastic washing-up bowl which they pushed along in front of them, and as it grew dark the younger fellows brought out the fish, together with four stalks of green bananas and a sack of coconuts. In return they asked for bullets for hunting the wild goats. There was William, who'd looked as if he'd soon be a real walloper, his younger brother, Elli, and a half-Spanish nephew, St Croix. Gideon, his piratical long black hair secured with a red ribbon, was from Fakareva in the Tuamotus. The previous night, on a spring tide, they had caught twenty langouste by lamplight as the creatures crawled about in the moonlight on the rocks at low tide, but earlier in the day they had taken them all to a community storage tank to await the inter-island supply boat.

Etienne, the leader, needed some coaxing to join us. He'd stayed ashore because he felt he'd never fit in the dinghy – he weighed 135 kilos (21 stone). Andy and Marie Christine paddled ashore to persuade him. A huge bear of a man, with a vast mop of curly greying black hair, he wore a great bath towel wrapped round him like a multi-coloured cloak. His enormous fingers and feet had difficulty with the wooden ladder on the stern and his calves were bigger than Will's well-developed thighs. Carefully, we slid him under the awning and shoe-horned him into the aft end of the centre cockpit. His broad face, lit by the hissing Tilley lamp, broke into a great smile. He was on stage. He began by wrapping and rewrapping the towel around him, measuring it in precise arm lengths. Then the deep baritone voice boomed out as he pointed at his audience with a middle finger like a marlin spike, and we all fell under his spell.

After a while a rising wind blew the rain under the flapping awning, so we went below, Etienne barely squeezing into the companionway. 'Hana Tefau was once a village. My ancestors lived here. I am returning to start again,' he laughed. 'My third wife is arriving from the Tuamotus next week, we must have the house built by then!' It seemed the reason Hana Tefau no longer existed was because, a while back, it had chosen the wrong side in a local war, joining with Hapatoni against the village of Vaitahu. 'The losers were eaten, or they could build a platform and head out to sea. That's how the Polynesians discovered Hawaii and Easter Island,' our guest explained. After this we never doubted Marquesan cannibalism. More unhappily, he recalled a particular nuclear test on nearby Muraroa, which had been delayed to suit De Gaulle's busy schedule. By the time he arrived the weather had changed, and after the explosion, the mushroom cloud tilted towards New Zealand.

REBECCA

I enjoyed the feeling of cold tear-like raindrops on my cheeks as we left Tahuata Island and headed for Hanamonu Bay, back on Hiva Oa. Dolphins played around us and, lifting my eyes heavenwards, I watched one of the most beautiful birds alive – the delicate, snowy-white long-tailed tropic bird – dancing above us.

Mum, Dad and Isso were back in the aft cockpit by the big stainless wheel. Isso looked really happy, laughing and joking, and moving about the boat quite confidently now. Mum loved the green land all around, and the sacks of fruit we had been given made her feel much more secure. Our vitamin C cravings were being satisfied at last. Dad seemed in good spirits, too; he enjoyed the real cruising sailors we were meeting now, each with their strong views on how the world could be made a better place, and their great fondness for the homelands they were escaping. He also enjoyed the larger-than-life – in both size and personality – locals.

Andy, Will and I hung over the bows, marvelling at the stunning creatures of the sea that came so close, but never quite touched our boat. This sort of existence suited Andy well. He enjoyed relaxing in the heat of the sun and watching the goings-on around us. He was now living the life he had dreamed of and read about in his big collection of sailing books. He seemed truly content.

Will, on the other hand, hated the intense, airless heat and found life on board stifling. Apart from the brief cool spell at the start and end of each day, the searing heat made his customary physical activity impossible. He could do nothing but boat-maintenance jobs under the shelter of the great white awnings, where we were continually stepping over each other. Whenever possible he would swim long distances to the shore to go for a run, desperate to release his pent-up energy and enjoy a bit of his own space. Living so close to five other people was difficult for everyone, but it was torture for him. When Will was down, he would retreat into himself and become quite silent. Withdrawing seemed to be the only way he could cope. He was normally so cheery and outgoing. I knew how difficult these long silent periods were for the rest of the crew. We had been through it all in the Caribbean with Dad, who had been gloomy and depressing, but in spite of his terrible prickly heat he was cheering up now. I could cope with Will's huge mood swings because I cared so much for him. I even felt responsible – after all I had lured him into this situation.

Will was a different human being ashore. He didn't really like hopping from one place to another. He was not a keen sightseer and would have preferred to spend longer in one place, getting to know the people better. He always seemed to strike a good rapport with those we met; he spoke good French and soon won friends with his natural, extrovert joky personality. It made me happy when I saw how the local people warmed to him and enjoyed his company. However, I understood Dad's schedule. He wanted to get as much out of this voyage for us all as he possibly could, and there was so much to see. Will accepted that it was Dad's boat and therefore his plan, and he never complained, but it didn't make things any easier for him.

Above all else, and what mattered to me was that Will and I got on well. Of course we had the occasional tiff. I knew at the outset that this journey would put our relationship to the test, but I wanted us to share this extraordinary voyage and visit these places together. And perhaps the fact that I knew Will found it so hard made me care for him all the more. We loved our time together.

But on a sailing boat with four other people – three of them members of your family – there wasn't ever a time when we were completely alone. Our best time was at anchor, when we slept on the cabin roof with the small white canvas sun awning tied tightly under the boom and stretched out to the guardrails on either side, forming a low tent over us. We were constantly refining it. It was lovely to lie together breathing in the cool, night air after weeks at sea below decks in the gaggingly stuffy cabin. We were often woken by tropical rain deluges at night and, with the boat anchored bow and stern, as it usually was, one or other of us got soaked as the wind and rain blasted in under our 'tent'. If it got really unbearable we would abandon camp and scramble below with our bundles of bedding to collapse in a damp heap on the cabin floor.

On our three-week passage across the Pacific each of us had slipped into a routine around the watches. During those long hours of sea dreaming, we imagined what it would be like when we reached land. Perhaps our expectations were impossibly high; in any event, for each of us they were different. It would take time for us all to adjust to the new order of things.

I loved the land and our home being anchored in calm water so it did not roll continuously. Slipping into a swimming costume for breakfast in the cockpit was great. And for a treat I ferreted out some of the precious Brooke Bond jam portions Mum and I had been saving to enjoy with one of the best things the French had brought to Polynesia: the baguette.

JOHN

Dolphins led us into steep-sided narrow Hanamenu Bay shortly before noon and we anchored bow and stern in black sand. We gulped down a bowl of soup, anxious to meet the fellow who was pacing expectantly up and down the beach like a shipwrecked mariner. As we paddled ashore, the swell was dumping unpleasantly, but we managed to time our run up the black beach well enough to avoid a soaking.

Coming up to the abandoned coconut plantation at the top of the beach we were met by Nicholas Chimin, a wild-looking thirty-five-year-old Marquesan. He could hardly contain his energy, chain-smoking and jumping around with a manic enthusiasm which reminded me of myself. Enthusiasm always excited me.

Nicholas had been starved of human company for a couple of months and now he drenched us in hospitality, proudly showing us around the ancient ruined settlement. Central to everything was the ample supply of sweet water from a spring. Gushing noisily from the valley wall, it came bouncing down over black rocks, gurgling through tangled trees of vivid green and chuckling into a flower-shrouded bathing pool, conveniently studded with smooth volcanic boulders.

'This source, twenty feet high.' His hands drew the geyser. 'Big man. Big stone. He drop it on source – water come out other valley.'

Not so long ago, 2,000 people had lived here, but now there is only Nicholas and his four dogs. We followed a narrow grassy lane, short and straight, bordered with lumps of coral and black volcanic rocks. Soon dwindling to a narrow path, it wound up the valley through the heat haze and on over the mountains to Atuona, the island's capital – a full day's walk for an athlete.

Occasional visitors came round the coast by boat from Atuona, big Marquesans yearning to escape the frozen chicken legs from the USA, the Toyota credit traps from Japan and the whole honky-tonk video jangle of materialism which has them stitched into dependence on French subsidies for everything from health to copra. Submerging into the hunter-gatherer life of their recent forebears, they had shot out the cattle, but wild pigs, goats and horses were still plentiful.

Where the forest wall converged on the end of the lane, the giant tangle of a banyan tree stood beside a derelict cemetery, its spreading branches shooting tendrils, taut as bowstrings, into the rich soil below. The chief who capped the geyser was immortalised by the wall round his tomb and the raised stone plinth which once formed the floor of his house.

Here, under the great mango trees, seven pigs had so far tripped the fatal branch and brought Nicholas's heavy timber cage trap crashing down on themselves. Pausing to examine muddy marks on the tree trunks, indicating the shoulder height of pigs which had rubbed themselves there on recent nights, he grinned his huge savage enthusiasm. 'Soon, big moon. We hunting many pigs!' While his dogs could find their way only on moonlit nights, the pigs could snuffle about among the coconut and mangos undisturbed in total darkness.

In Nicholas I saw that unleashed spirit which I'd barely glimpsed in myself since leaving the Parachute Regiment nearly thirty years before. He was the most generous man we'd met: he chopped down trees to get pale purple orchids for Marie Christine to put in her jug vases on *English Rose*. He picked huge green pamplemousse, shook lemons from their bushes and disappeared into tall dark-leaved trees with slippery branches to select ripe mangos for us. Using his sharp eyes, he pounced on little maricuja fruits from the forest floor for Isso to stuff down her T-shirt and charged barefoot into the undergrowth at a glimpse of special red and black berries for Rebecca to make into a necklace.

Just upstream of the sandbar, at the mouth of the 100m stream which flowed from the cold, clear spring, he nodded toward a string of twenty grey mullet drying on a nylon fishing line stretched between palms at the top of the beach. 'Very good! Tomorrow night we catch. They come up from sea, to eat weed. I tap with knife.' The latent violence in his grin held out little hope for the soft-mouthed fish. Then he showed us the fat, black freshwater shrimps which he speared in the river at night and told us we would go snorkelling for lobsters by moonlight.

Exhausted, we took Nicholas back to the boat for tea, where he sang his songs to the accompaniment of Isso's small guitar, shaming us into singing John Denver songs to Andy's guitar. The tropical night came quickly, and Nicholas took Bec, Will and Andy off to spear shrimps, returning a couple of hours later with a panful. Marie Christine steamed them simply in their own juice. When they turned red we gulped them down with garlic and butter sauce. This was the life I'd read of as a boy, it was Coral Island and Swiss Family Robinson all rolled into one.

Nicholas, dark and brooding, told us he had lived alone out here for a year, since his wife was killed in a car crash in Papeete. He held firm opinions. It was the Marquesans who had discovered the Marquesas Islands, he told us, going on to explain how the planets controlled the world; how volcanos caused the clouds and made trees and plants vibrate. Then he demonstrated an extreme version of meditation: after first expelling all air from his lungs, he held his breath for two minutes until, he claimed, his blood thickened and his veins began to break up, overheating his brain. None of us was keen to have a go at this.

REBECCA

Andy, Will and I went ashore before it got light the next morning. Nicholas was waiting with his dogs, sucking on a cigarette breakfast and raring to go.

'We hunting, we eat many peeg!' he barked, explaining in broken English that conditions were perfect. The torrential rain of the previous afternoon had softened the ground, ensuring that trotter prints would be visible; there was no wind, so the five dogs would be able to fill their scarred liquorice-coloured nostrils with the scent. If we were lucky, we might surprise a pig still dozing under the heavy-laden Makomako trees above the valley.

Nicholas set off at a cracking pace through the 'lost' township; smothered in a tangle of undergrowth, it was the perfect setting for Indiana Jones. My running shoes were too tight and I knew I would be the slowest. Thank goodness we still had a few hours of cool. Turning off the main path through a copra plantation, and crossing a clear stream on flat stepping-stones, we climbed up the side of the valley on a well-defined track where the occasional cotton bush burst with miraculous seed for no one to pick. All was quiet; the island looked green and beautiful.

We climbed steadily, stopping too rarely for the odd breather, as the lithe dogs moved silently this way and that, noses down. 'Peeg! Peeg!' cried Nicholas, pointing out a couple of trotter prints. His face had the harsh, determined look of one who kills without remorse.

We reached a plateau covered in chest-deep undergrowth and the odd tree. Nicholas stopped and sniffed, looking around, fingering the butt of the sheath-knife at his hip. I watched him for clues. All five dogs were gone.

We had just begun walking again when some piercingly loud squeals stopped me dead. 'Cochon! cochon!' Nicholas screamed, crashing through the undergrowth. We followed, quick as we could, the thorns and bushes tugging at our cotton clothes.

My heart was pounding. There was a bristly black female pig, as long as my arm, pinned to the ground by its throat. Dogs growled as it screamed with all its might. Nicholas quickly plunged his knife into its heart. Thick red blood oozed out as the squeals subsided, and after a few grunts a peaceful, glazed expression settled across the beast's face. The dogs snuffled around, lapping up the blood.

We were amazed to have caught a pig so quickly, and Nicholas was thrilled. If it had been dry, he would have lit a fire to burn off the bristles, but today, he skinned the carcass instead. He tied the pig to a branch by piercing its lower jaw and threading a shoelace through the hole. Will remembered his blissful childhood days on the farm, while Andy hopped uncomfortably from one foot to the other, thinking of the domestic pigs they had kept at college in York. I just imagined the feast that would ensue.

The dogs disappeared, and suddenly there was more squealing, further away this time. 'Peeg, one more Peeg!' Nicholas cried with delight, dropping everything and rushing off again. We disturbed some wild bees which stung us in their fury, and by the time I reached the second pig, its right ear had been chewed away by the frenzied dogs. Once again the knife silenced the terrible squeals. This victim was male. Nicholas sliced off the testicles to prevent tainting and threw them to the dogs; then he swung the pig round his neck and retraced his steps to deal with the first one.

Nicholas loved posing for photographs, holding a pig in each hand like giant dumbbells. He began skinning the female, stripping off lengths of bristly black skin which the dogs leaped at. Leaving the head complete, he then gutted the pig. I insisted on keeping the liver and kidneys, handing over a plastic bag from my rucksack. 'Good food costs less at Sainsbury's . . . please recycle', it read. I doubted that this was the kind of recycling they'd had in mind. The dogs relished the pig's intestines, but the stench was appalling. I got the feeling that no pig meant no food for them. Nicholas opened the pig's stomach to find that it had been living mostly on guava and makomako berries, which the Marquesans often used to make glue.

In a quarter of an hour, any loose bristles had been scraped away and the pig was clean. The blood-stained dogs licked their wounds, and one limped. A large boar fighting for its life is very fierce, and some dogs lose their nerve. Nicholas put the pig into a makeshift rucksack made from a hessian sack with shoulder straps of cotton *pareu*. He insisted on carrying the male pig as well.

He stopped at a lone orange tree groaning with fruit. 'We pick oranges. Green ones. One week, they be sweet to eat.' The good-hearted

Nicholas was thinking way ahead, to after we had sailed over the horizon and left his world. Reaching up for bunches of five and six oranges, we greedily picked as many as Will could carry. When his legs could not support any more weight we stopped piling them into his pack and headed triumphantly down to the bay. It was still only 8.30 am.

Nothing to this pig-hunting, I thought as we found our way back. But during the next two full and exhausting days, we never got another.

Arriving back at the shore, we found that a handful of Nicholas's young relatives had arrived by boat to enjoy the wild bounties of their land. Nicholas immediately put them to work preparing a feast, while we were sent off to bathe in the cool, crystal pool. What paradise. All the same, I was a bit alarmed to think of all those shrimps lurking there once the silty bottom was stirred up.

While one of the pigs was put in a pit of hot rocks covered with banana leaves to bake, *umu*-style, for three hours, I went out to the yacht to collect tomato paste and a loaf of freshly baked bread as our contribution to the feast, which was set to last some days. Mum and Isso were drawing each other. They could hardly believe my tales of the pig-hunt. When they'd seen us back on the beach so early, they thought something must have gone wrong.

Then Nicholas took us off to help pull rhubarb-red stalks of taro from the wet soil close to the river. But it was very hot by now, and we were relieved to go back and sit in the shade around the *umu* pit, staving off hunger with Nicholas's French army-issue coffee, biscuits and cheese while he boiled up the taro roots to make a starchy potato substitute. A delicious coconut, onion, garlic and lemon sauce was prepared by Domingo, a rolly-polly, friendly telecom worker who was only too pleased at the chance to practise his English and impress his beautiful girlfriend, Tahia. After a while, Andy walked off along the sand to soak in the perfection of his surroundings, and Will went off with Domingo to see the plants the Marquesans used for healing. I was content to sit, and in between swatting nonos, I tried to draw.

At last Nicholas announced that the 'peeg' was ready, and we all gathered round as he scraped away the sand, peeled back the steaming banana leaves and revealed succulent joints of pork that had been running around that morning.

He insisted we helped ourselves first, laughing at the small portion of meat I took. 'More, more – you must eat more peeg,' Domingo cried, rubbing his own large belly. They loaded their own plates piled high with meat and came back for more. Cannibal ancestors or not, they certainly had a taste for flesh. Nicholas himself ate little, preferring to chain-smoke, but we had not eaten pork for months and returned for more ourselves. Any meat was a real treat: it was way above our budget and without refrigeration on board the boat it was impossible to keep in any case. When at last everyone had eaten his fill, Nicholas and his relatives lumbered off for a long siesta while we returned to the boat, promising to pick them all up in the evening for a party.

Life continued in this blissful way for a couple of days – more pig-hunting, feasting, bathing and taking it in turns to go ashore and enjoy quiet times on the boat. At last, we seemed to have found harmony in this remote bay. But it was not to continue.

One afternoon Will and I were on boat duty, watching four pilot whales bobbing up and down together like bottles right by the boat. The others were ashore having a crab feast with Nicholas and some other yachties who had arrived. It was late afternoon by the time they returned, bringing with them some of the relatives – to our surprise, the Marquesans had come to say goodbye. Apparently, we were leaving.

There was little explanation for this sudden departure, except that the wind was favourable for the passage to Fatu Hiva. Isso gave one of her precious Abba tapes to Nicholas's relatives, and after a bit of chat, Andy took them ashore. Will and I – particularly Will – were not pleased with this snap decision to leave. We were all loving Hanamenu – there was plenty for us all to do – and we had agreed that changes of plan needed to be discussed beforehand, rationally, if at all possible. A tense atmosphere developed between the six of us on board. Will and I started getting the boat ready for sea, while Mum prepared a light supper to keep us going through the night. Then we all sat silently around the saloon to eat. Mum, in her usual role as mediator, began to test the water. She asked each of us how we felt about the sudden move. Andy, in his non-committal way, said he did not really mind, except that he hoped he would not be sick all night. Tough little Isso shrugged her shoulders and nodded. I added that I did not mind either, but I knew it was hopeless. From the tone of my mother's voice and Will's mood, it was obvious that someone was going to snap.

When it came to Will's turn to speak, he said that he was not very happy: this sort of sudden change of plan was exactly what we had talked about trying to minimise only a few days earlier. Mum turned to Dad and asked him why he had not told us all the reasons for this sudden departure. She was pretty cross with all of us by this time, and her fiery Irish temper was only just warming up.

I was sure the inevitable row could only end in disaster for me: the big split between boyfriend and family. I had been through this before, with a previous boyfriend who had lived and worked at Ardmore. I often felt I was the cause: that the root of the problem was the age-old tendency of parents, particularly fathers, to feel that the man their daughter has chosen is not good enough, and never will be. Losing your 'child' to someone else, and coming to terms with the fact that he or she is grown up, is something I would have to experience myself to fully understand. But perhaps it was all a case of males fighting for supremacy.

Everyone shouted – except for Isso, who sat there silently, and Dad, who muttered the odd quiet word about 'seeing it through'. I ran up on deck, not able to bear it any more. Will said he was going to leave the boat as soon as possible and fly home.

After a tear-filled night on deck, watching Orion slide across the sky, we sailed in the early morning. We were to call at Atuona before setting sail for Fatu Hiva. Will packed his kit and we both sobbed. Having spent every waking minute of the last six months with him, I could not imagine life without him. He would return to England, find a job and begin to build something for our future together. I was torn between wanting to be with him and my determination to see the trip through. But if I stayed it would be a whole year before I saw Will again.

Back in Atuona, we spent the day trailing to the gendarmes' office to sort out the return of Will's part of the bond and booking a flight out for him. We were miserable. Not wanting to return to the boat, Will and I spent the night ashore with his rucksack and bag, sleeping out on an old concrete landing stage. *English Rose* was to sail next day. We talked and talked, unable to sleep, huddled beneath my small duvet. The stars went out and heavy raindrops began to fall. We pulled the rubber dinghy over us to make a shelter, but muddy water welled up from underneath. We moved up into the trees, sodden, shivering and wretched, and slept fitfully.

At some time during this terrible night, we decided to try again. We would talk to Mum and Dad in the morning and, Will would eat humble pie. Maybe that's what a good soaking does for you.

JOHN

I had known it was time to go when two young Swedes sailed in. Thomas and Lars wanted to discuss a television documentary they'd seen in Sweden. It was that film again. It unsettled me. I had sailed for six months to get away from it and I wasn't going to hang around talking about it.

When we got back to Atuona I calmed myself by getting into the sea early next morning and scrubbing away at the waterline with my washing-up brush. Bec and Will paddled the dinghy out from the shore. 'John, can I have a word?' called Will as they passed.

'OK. Just let me finish the scrubbing, then we'll have a chat.' I wanted a breathing space to consider possible courses of action. We had 4,000 miles of South Pacific winter to cross before we reached Chile. If Will did leave us now, I'd need to call out a replacement from the UK. In the event, Will announced that he'd reconsidered his decision. Now he apologised and asked to rejoin the team. We shook hands. Marie Christine and I were heartily relieved. For me, it had been nothing more than one more storm in a teacup and I realised Will would have had to be a saint to put up with me.

While we were in Atuona Nicholas appeared. As a small way of thanking him for all his hospitality at Hanamenu Bay, we offered to take him with us to Fatu Hiva, a day's sail to the south-east. It was a bumpy trip, and Nicholas was seasick – he'd had a few celebratory drinks since returning to civilisation and needed a bit of a rest.

The first of the Marquesas to be visited by Europeans (in 1595, by Mendana), Fatu Hiva is the Marquesan island I most wanted to see. I took anchor watch while everyone went ashore. I sat up in the bows, looking inshore through the palms, and between the brooding grey needles of basalt rock. Way up on the misty ridge, the south-east trades tumbled their fluffy white clouds over the watershed. It had taken me thirty-four years to get here; the thirty-four years since I wrote to my hero, Eric Hiscock, from the musty teak saloon of *English Rose II*, lying on the trots off the leafy Elephant Boatyard, far away in the Hamble River. I think it was only the fact that he answered my letter that kept me from giving up on this dream. It had been worth the long wait – and all the bumps in between.

Next morning we went to church. 'Jesus was a demon!' laughed Nicholas, wading through the surf with us, flexing the pagan tattoos on his biceps. He was dressed in ex-French army fatigues, his arms full of the breadfruit he'd be roasting on the beach while we were on our knees.

Afterwards Marie Christine bought a *tapa*. Painted in black on the bark of a breadfruit tree, the Marquesan fighting man looked rather less fearsome than Nicholas himself, who explained this ancient fighter lived by killing and then eating people. And yet Nicholas was truly a gentle man. We left him at the church elder's house while A Watch walked inland to find the waterfall. Up in the virgin rainforest, I crushed one of the venomous centipedes with my heel while Isso munched her way through six windfall mangos and Marie Christine found an 18in eel in a stream. On the way back we bought a wooden bowl, a large *tiki* and five hairpins from an ex-boxing champion called David. Then Marie Christine and I went off to celebrate our pearl wedding anniversary aboard a large green schooner also anchored in the bay.

In the middle of the first course the foghorn sounded and Bec called us on Channel 12. 'We're dragging!' I rushed up on deck, trying to move calmly. In the moonlight, I could just make out *English Rose*, close under the cliffs on the north side of the bay. Our host loved a drama: in a flash, we were in his rigid raider, across the bay and back aboard our boat. I slipped the engine into slow astern while our host pushed us off the cliffs with his dinghy. Bec and Marie Christine worked the winch to haul us off with the stern anchor and Andy helped Will take in the bow anchor. I was pleased with the team-work. But as much as I liked Fatu Hiva, the anchorage was unsafe: it was time to leave.

After returning to Atuona for a couple of days, to drop off Nicholas, we sailed for the rockbound island of Oa Pou. No bigger than a sixpence on the chart, it lay some 70 miles to the north-west.

We left Atuona just after dark. Andy and Isso helmed for the first couple of hours, taking us through the Canal Bordelais on a windless night with a full moon. The south-east trades gradually reasserted themselves in the early hours and a grey and windy dawn found us 16 miles south of Oa Pou. We gybed and raced north under reduced sail on a beam reach, heading straight for a great white fang of rock. Passing through dense flocks of seabirds, our fishing line caught a blue beaked booby, towing it under in sheets of spray. Ornithologist Andy admonished the poor bird with severe cries of 'No! No!', as he struggled to unhook our red and white muppet from the wildly flapping creature's wing. Once released, it managed to fly around for a bit before settling on the rising swell to groom its ruffled plumage.

I went in too close to the vertical face of the rock spire and we were knocked over by fierce downdraughts. Marie Christine had a dreadful cold and this latest bit of foolishness was just too much for the Irish temper. She struck out at me. I parried the blows with my left forearm and steered the boat with my right. Everyone else was stunned by her outburst: looking down at the deck, they scuttled forward and left the two of us to sort it out. I went rather quiet; no doubt I was largely to blame. This was not the fence-mending we needed to weld the crew together after the battle with Will. But it was just the way to lose concentration and sink the boat.

In silence, we motored gently up the west coast of the island, passing several attractive inlets before anchoring in Hakahetau Bay. Behind the village half a dozen volcanic plugs reared thousands of feet up from the crater in the island's centre. Some were covered with dark green bushes; others were the simple sheer-sided needles of rock which inspired Jacques Brel to write one of his last songs, 'La Cathédrale'.

'These spires *are* the Marquesas to most people,' murmured Andy excitedly.

I'll remember the 'spires' of French bread more, I thought dejectedly, still glum from the row. Except for Isso, who caught half a dozen fish, we were all exhausted by this short voyage from Hiva Oa, so we spent the rest of the day sleeping and did not go ashore.

Hakahetau could be no more than a temporary anchorage, for we needed better shelter from the Pacific swell. The next day we came into the island's capital, Hakehau, just a few miles along the coast. There we found a handful of small French long-term steel cruising boats, gently bobbing their weedy waterlines in the diminished swell in the shelter of a fine rock breakwater built by 500 Foreign Legionnaires in 1988. We anchored bow and stern and gazed open-mouthed at the beauty around us. The surf thundered in at the end of the beach unprotected by the breakwater, and the mountains looked even finer, if that were possible, their spires arrayed in gradually ascending levels, looking ever more like the fabled cathedral.

Going ashore, we found quite a substantial village shrouded from the seafront by swaying palms and a luxurious growth of trees. But the few shops were uninspiring, and the people simply seemed to lie in the sun or drive their Toyota pick-ups round and round, going nowhere.

It was only 25 miles across from Hakahau to Nuku Hiva, the most northerly of the six inhabited islands in the Marquesas group, but it was another squally trip and we were relieved to see the great sheltered bay on which stands Taiohae, capital of the Marquesas.

Going ashore with the ship's papers, Marie Christine and I had an excellent *poisson cru* in the butcher's shop where we bought a leg of goat for Easter. Further along the waterfront we encountered young Adolphe, a Chinese boy looking after his Dad's video-hire shop-cum-food store. Already a whizz with the calculator, he was only too pleased to practise the English he was being taught privately. It was as if he were being groomed for success, to be a jump ahead of the Marquesans, when the waves of American tourists eventually hit these shores.

By keeping the date – 1 April – from the rest of the crew, we escaped Will's tricks until after noon, when a truce is traditionally called on April Fool jokes. Henry, a burly twenty-seven-year-old Marquesan who taught at the Catholic primary school, offered to drive us up on to the rim of the crater. From the top we could see the whole grand sweep of the bay. The smell of the heat, and the red track winding up through brilliant green vegetation, reminded me of Peru. I'd been reading Simon Strong's *Shining Path*, an informative but chilling account of the terrorist movement there. What chances I'd taken, searching for Isso's family. Soon it would all begin again. How many lives has a cat?

'What did Marquesans eat before Captain Porter brought the goats?' Marie Christine asked.

Henry's face broke into that great beaming happy smile so typical of Marquesans. He pinched his bicep between finger and thumb, and roared, 'We ate Captain David Porter as well!' Careering down the mountain, his young son opened the car door with his teeth. 'A true Marquesan,' laughed the delighted dad.

For Easter, we sailed round to Taipivai Valley, some five miles to the east. It rained, cold and heavy, during this short trip, but we caught a 25lb yellowfin tuna on the way, and gave this, as a contribution to the Easter feast, to Daniel from Martinique. We found him, with wife and friends, in his spacious unfinished plywood house on stilts, roughly a half a mile up a muddy track, beside which gruesome land crabs crawled over a seething rubbish tip on the banks of the sluggish brown river.

A retired gendarme on a pension from Tahiti, Daniel was, he told us, unwelcome in the valley as a representative of the French. 'They call me Seke. It means black,' he smiled ruefully over a can of beer. 'They say I am not Polynesian and they don't want me here. But I came eight years ago with two bags and now I have this!' He nodded towards his new wife from the valley and the neat, small market garden he had carved from the forest by the brown river's edge. And I wondered if unpopularity wasn't based as much on his background with the hated gendarmerie as anything else.

A couple of trading schooners and an old blue-painted Breton fishing boat, which was collecting empty beer cans for scrap from the islands, joined us on a stately procession to the adjoining bay, where the village people had been going for the Easter feast for many years. While the children had fun with treasure hunts and the like, Isso stuck to Marie Christine and wouldn't take part. Still very shy, she dreaded the panic which overwhelmed her when events began moving too fast for her. How I sympathised with her.

At the end of the day, fearing we were moored too close to the beach, we left the other three boats and motored back into the shelter of Taipivai Bay for the night. A pair of large manta rays cruised open-mouthed through the muddy waters, sifting the plankton. The locals told us they were easy to harpoon and good to eat.

In the morning Will went off on a goat shoot with Thomas, a lively half-Chinese Marquesan in his early thirties. They visited some stone *tikis* up on the hillside above Tikapo Point, passing a curved rock where people were beheaded in the old days. Later, Thomas joined us for roast leg of goat, playing his ukulele while a pair of hammerhead sharks cast luminous trails around the boat in the darkness. He told us they'd been attracted by the gutting of the goats earlier in the day. He asked Marie Christine and me to visit his home among the bananas by the shore. His pretty wife, Marie, who'd been married before, grieved for her daughter, who had remained with her father. Living in paradise is no more a guarantee of happiness than wealth. She cooked us supper, and when it began to rain very heavily they asked us to stay the night in their little home by the sea. With its concrete floor, and a black-painted timber frame clad with corrugated iron, it was no more than a simple conversion of a copra-drying shed, but we were happy on the mat they slung on the floor for us. It was a lot bigger than the doghouse.

In the morning, after walking round the copra sheds, we returned to the yacht and weighed anchor. Thomas and Marie waved from the trees above the rocky shore for a long time. Isso steered as we motored back up the coast to Taiohae.

A nono bite on Will's arm had become infected, so he went to the hospital, but there was no doctor there. By now pretty groggy, he returned to the boat and started a course of antibiotics. Things were grinding to a halt. Finally Bec got him to a doctor, who probed the infection. Will fainted, and was told to come back to the hospital after the festival weekend. Feeling rotten, he slept for most of the time and I became concerned that the infection might neither be cured by the antibiotics, nor come to a head for lancing. The resulting stalemate, hanging about in harbour, was like being becalmed: none too good for morale.

I tried putting people ashore in relays, to relieve the growing sense of being stranded, but drinking beer and chewing cheeseburgers was less than inspiring. Poor Will was, not surprisingly, far from in his best spirits, and the weekend festival got off to a slow start. By a white mobile food stall, next door to a Chinese store, Marie Christine and I munched a chip supper with a stick of five bits from a New Zealand sheep's heart. The French world news on the television at the back of the counter and the friendly Chinese Marquesan made it a pleasant evening, but walking back along the beach was not quite the Pacific Island experience of popular imagination. The stars were clear on a moonless black velvet night, but the sea was muddy after the rain and the grey sand shoreline crawled with creatures of the night.

Jerry Landon, recently arrived from Easter Island, and Jean, his sixty-eight-year-old companion, came aboard from their yacht, the *Wandrin' Star*, for supper with Marie Christine and me. We asked Edward C. Judd as well: he'd just come in, too, alone on a 32ft green steel cutter he'd built ten years earlier, 3,000ft up in the mountains behind San Diego in California. Edward was slightly built and quietly self-sufficient, with the big white beard befitting an elderly single-hander. Jerry was a retired nuclear-waste-disposal man who would have liked to have seen that problematical material lodged deep in the downward-trending plates of the earth. Jean was rather lame, but had a great heart, which must have stood her in good stead for the forty years she'd run a dockside restaurant in Seattle (where, as it turned out, Edward used to eat in 1947, when he was in the US navy).

These boat people inspired us in their quiet gritty way. Anyone who'd come this far was well aware of the danger slumbering just beyond the breakwater. And this well-respected common adversary forged a bond among fellow voyagers in remote places like this. Yet they kept their distance. Self-reliant and independent, they asked for nothing; their boats and finances were models of resourcefulness.

'Crocodile Dondee' arrived, his little wooden ketch nodding to the Pacific swell, at the end of a thirty-day passage from Galapagos. Thrice married and fond of the 'tinnies', he soon disappeared ashore with his twenty-nine-year-old French girlfriend. Bec and Will, who had worked as line-handlers aboard their boat on the way through the Panama Canal, remembered Don's speed at backgammon. We caught up with him shaking the dice in a bar that evening. He'd spent four years hunting crocs in the darkest interior: shooting them was too noisy, and he'd had a few narrow escapes surprising them with an axe by torchlight. A man of philosophy, Don had a profound belief that Japan had been planning the outcome of the Second World War since the end of the nineteenth century. I found it difficult to understand how any nation, let alone Japan, would deliberately seek such humiliation, but Don insisted that his best friend, whose father had been a speechwriter for the Emperor Hirohito, maintained that, by retaining their culture and keeping the support of America through the critical years of economic growth, Japan would come to rule the world, according to their 'destiny'.

At last, Will was able to get into hospital. He was given a general anaesthetic for the poison to be drained from his right forearm. Bec looked rather drawn when she returned from his bedside. We resigned ourselves to several days more at anchor. But they passed pleasantly enough.

When Will was finally given clearance to sail, we left immediately for Raroia in the Tuamotu group, 446 miles to the south. By late afternoon we came once more into the wind shadow behind Oa Pou. I switched on the motor and immediately we caught a 5ft-long 40lb wahoo on the red and white Panama muppet. It was filleted and fried in minutes, while Isso prepared her special squeezed-lemon drink for us all. We were on our way.

10

The Low or Dangerous Isles

JOHN

We came on watch at 6 am, just as it was getting light, on Monday 18 April. I clambered on to the doghouse roof for my first glimpse of a real South Pacific atoll. It was more than forty years since I'd read *Coral Island*, and seen Jean Simmons in *The Blue Lagoon* at the Granada in Slough. And now, at last, the spiky outline of palm trees, almost a mirage, was bobbing on the silky horizon. Very slowly, it firmed up into a hazy smudge and then a sage green line. A couple of hours later it had consolidated into a fresh, bright green and we were close enough to hear the rollers crashing on the reef. Only 300yds from the shore, the echo-sounder still showed more than 600ft of water beneath our keel.

This was isolated Tepoto, one of the Disappointment Islands. It lacked a safe anchorage, and, duly disappointed, we turned south, heading for Raroia Atoll on the eastern fringe of the Low or Dangerous Islands, otherwise known as Tuamotu. Very different from the precipitous Marquesas, these atolls were low-lying, circular coral reefs built up on the slopes of long-submerged volcanos. Many of my boyhood heroes had been shipwrecked in these parts, each spending months, or even years, repairing their stout wooden boats with the help of friendly Polynesian islanders. The very lowness of the atolls, which deceives radar, combined with sudden calms and treacherous currents to make our night watches a serious business.

Strandings were common even now: indeed, travelling between the Marquesas and Tahiti, most cruisers skirt the western fringe of this huge, scattered group. We, on the other hand, had chosen to explore east and centre. As we rumbled south under the faithful Mercedes, it was hot as ever down below. In the bright sunshine, pale grey smoke twisted thinly up from the charred plywood covering the exhaust at the back of the main companionway.

Abandoning the saloon, Marie Christine and I slept out in the open, wedged along the seats on either side of the main cockpit. 'For me, this is the most wonderful part of the trip so far,' enthused my wife, after we'd watched the biggest shooting star either of us had ever seen whizzing right across the sky from east to west.

Fearful of running aground on Takume Atoll in the hours of darkness, and in order to time our arrival to coincide with the flooding tide at the narrow entrance into the Raroia Lagoon next morning, we switched off the engine and drifted. Rebecca and Will were on watch as we slowly cooked on the shimmering mirror of the afternoon calm. For some time Marie Christine and I had hardly been able to communicate with them. Bec was very tense, and Will, nursing his bandaged arm and knocked out by the great doses of antibiotics he'd taken, remained woodenly silent, as if he were enduring torture. Now, the frustration of going nowhere, brought things to a head again. I suggested an alteration to the sails, which were slatting noisily against the rigging. 'Everything I do is wrong, isn't it?' Bec screamed, bursting into tears of rage. Mum and Dad shrugged unhappily as she stamped below, abandoning her command of the ship. Blimey.

This tantrum cancelled the discussion Bec was about to lead on liferaft drills and duties. Here we were, in the most treacherous place I had ever visited, and wobbling dangerously. I thought of my hero 'Bully' Forbes. During the last century, when the mighty sailing clippers, laden with Australian wool, raced home across the Southern Ocean and round Cape Horn, 'Bully' Forbes was the hardest-driving captain of them all, encouraging his crew forward with a brace of pistols at the wheel. But in 1994 it was a bit different: the crew wanted to stop and admire the view, soppy things like that. There were six of us, and 400 days still ahead. I had to consider the hopes, fears and aspirations of all. Nobody had a monopoly on sensitivity. And in my heart, I knew I'd never have a better team. From bitter experience, I knew how much I'd miss them if they weren't aboard.

With the coming of darkness we got underway. I altered the watch times to ensure that I would be running operations, with Marie Christine and Isso, from the moment we neared Raroia Atoll until we passed through the treacherous Garue *passe* and into the blue lagoon of my dreams. But as a result of the row there was a misunderstanding, and by the time Marie Christine and I took over the watch from Bec and Will at 3 am, our speed had dropped off and we were running late. The half-moon was long gone from the night sky and now a freshening north-east wind was hurrying us along. Lightning flickered, but it failed to illuminate the twin atolls of Takume and Raroia. Fewer than a dozen miles ahead now, they were too low-lying to appear on the radar screen. This was no time to get the maths wrong. All sophisticated electronic gear is subject to error – human error. It is so easy, through fatigue or simple distraction, to enter the wrong figures into a computer, and all it takes is one incorrect digit . . . My hands clenched on the wheel.

Lively as ever, in the cool darkness Marie Christine passed steaming mugs of coffee and guava sandwiches up from the galley and into Isso's outstretched hands in the doghouse. I had schooled myself to treat every entry into port as carefully as if it were my first. The tropical dawn seemed terribly slow in coming. Imperceptibly, the black pearls on our eastern horizon linked to become a necklace of palm-covered islets, each fringed with white sand and curling, thundering breakers. And on a rising tide, all six pairs of eyes straining, we shot through the narrow Garue *passe*. Inside, the lagoon was the palest blue, running to green and indigo in the deeper channels between the coral heads. We followed the inner edge of the atoll for a mile or two and anchored before a low village of barely sixty souls.

Ten miles away, across the lagoon, on the windward side of the atoll, just beyond the scattered clumps of coconut trees, lay the terraced red reef on to which Thor Heyerdahl had steered his raft of balsa logs. Named after the Quechua sun god Kon Tiki, it had come crashing and grinding through huge surf in August 1947. Not much has happened on Raroia in the fifty years since: perhaps half a dozen boats call in each year. I felt I understood about *Kon Tiki*, and I felt again that surge of exultation which had lifted Chay Blyth and me, nearly thirty years before, when we landed on the Aran Isles off the west coast of Ireland after rowing our open dory for ninety-three days across the North

Atlantic from Cape Cod. I was so glad we'd come to Raroia.

We were tired and it was windy. So we didn't go ashore, anxious the weather might be changing. And at two o'clock the next morning, Marie Christine nudged me awake in the doghouse. 'There's a lot of lightning, Johnny!' I thought of the 70ft mast sticking out above all the palm trees. We woke everyone and dismantled the computers and GPS. Then we put the spare GPS in the pressure cooker, hoping that the cooker would act as a sort of Faraday Box in the event of a strike. We practised with the fire blanket and extinguishers and ran through the liferaft duties once more. Then we went back to bed, everyone moving away from the main mast, out of the forward sleeping compartment and into the saloon to sleep on the seats or floor.

The thunderstorm cleared the air and we felt a good deal fresher over our porridge in the morning. Marie Christine, Isso and I put on our best kit and set off with the ship's papers. Grateful to be on our own, we made our way to the low, red-roofed village hall, complete with flagpole and terrifying government posters detailing cyclone procedures: the atoll was only 6ft above sea-level at its highest point. Our documents were cleared in near silence by Marcel, the gendarme's son, who explained shyly that his father was away in Tahiti. After a few minutes heavy footsteps clumped along the balcony and in came Martha, the mayoress, a very large Polynesian lady moving with stately grace. There was no doubt who was running this atoll: she carried a mighty right hand, like a leg of ham. As a little girl, Martha had found on the beach the box of stores which had been blown across the lagoon from the stranded *Kon Tiki* raft in 1947. Her husband, Rogo, a grave, square-built fellow in his late fifties, hovered silently at her shoulder. He was the radio operator, the community's only link with the outside world.

I remembered three names from Heyerdahl's Kon Tiki book, two of them, the chiefs, must surely be dead. 'What about the little boy, Huamata, who was dying with the abscess on his head. Did he survive?' I asked.

'I am he!' Rogo grinned triumphantly, bowing his grizzled head and fingering the scar. 'The Norwegians saved my life with their penicillin, but they got my name wrong. Huamata is a girl's name.'

Martha took us on a conducted tour of the village. Among the swaying palms scattered along the lagoon side of the 400yd-wide strip of sand lay a handful of neat single-storey buildings, mostly painted in pastel blues, yellows and greens, each built to withstand a cyclone. There was a dispensary, a school and a church, all just inches above sea level.

Fairly stomping across the sand, Martha left A Watch scampering along in her wake, wondering if the locals were really all that interested in us, or simply frightened of their mayoress. Raising her right arm like a battering ram, she pointed at a little bungalow with stormboards resembling a cricket scoreboard and rapped out orders in Polynesian. Instantly, dutiful maidens appeared and lovely necklaces of mottled cowrie shells were hung around our necks. 'Welcome to Rarioa!' Martha boomed. Our hosts smiled weakly.

Through a half-open door I caught a glimpse of a dissolute youthful figure lying face down on an unmade bed, a thin line of cigarette smoke curling up from a dangling wrist. Evidently time passed slowly on a desert island.

Martha snorted angrily at rubbish piled in the coarse grass. We shook off our shoes at the shop and crossed the clean cement floor. Neatly stacked in a long glass cabinet on the wall were the alternatives to the monotony of fish and coconut for breakfast, lunch and supper every day: canned sardines, pilchards, pork and beans, sweetcorn, peas and sweetened condensed milk. There wouldn't be much shoplifting here.

Arriving back at her neat and tidy blue bungalow at the root of the low concrete pier, Martha threw open the double front doors and flicked up the louvred glass window slats. Before disappearing into the kitchen, she presented us each with palm-leaf straw hats plucked from her sitting-room wall, and gestured for us to sit on a low settee. She returned with drinking coconuts in glass bowls and Rogo in tow. Marie Christine took the anchor brooch from her own dress and pinned it on Martha's. The gift was accepted without thanks, as if an exchange of gifts and unthinking generosity were normal procedure on a real Coral Island.

Perhaps Isso was not the first Quechua Indian to visit the island. I suggested; maybe her ancestors, theirs too, had come on a balsa raft like Heyerdahl's? The huge mayoress peered intently at Isso. 'Possiblement!' she smiled.

Then Rogo unscrewed the lid of a little jar, spilling black pearls across the white tablecloth. After studying the pool of gleaming gems for a moment, he picked one up between finger and thumb, bit it to test the quality, and gravely presented it to an embarrassed Isso. 'For the first Inca to visit Raroia!' he said solemnly. Then he bit another pair. 'For your ears,' he smiled broadly at Marie Christine, 'and here is one for Rebecca.'

The centrepiece of the sitting-room wall was a framed montage of family photographs. Martha pointed at a smiling sophisticated young girl, sitting by a dressing table somewhere in France. 'Our daughter,' she said, proudly. 'We wanted her to have opportunity.' They'd given her up for adoption, to a childless French couple in Papeete, at two days old. We explained how Isso's maternal grandparents in Peru had asked us to give her *opportunidad* after her father had been murdered by terrorists from the Shining Path. Then she burst into a very untypical fit of giggles, rubbing the corners of her eyes and pointing at the matching slant of Isso's eyes. A full-blooded Polynesian, she was quite certain that if the soft *Poppae* (sunburned ones) had managed to raft here from South America, then hardy Incas with the same looks as Isso and herself could surely have done the same. Isso was most impressed.

Rogo's father had visited Raroia with the French navy and had fallen for his mother, a Raroian girl, and so he was a *demi*. He kept an open mind on where the Polynesians had come from. Various religious groups had their own ideas, too: some even said they had come out of caves. Others claimed they originated in Asia some 30,000 years ago, migrating north and crossing the narrow Bering Straits. From there, perhaps, they'd spread south, through Alaska and all the way through the Americas down to Cape Horn. *Kon Tiki* had shown it was possible to cross the Pacific from Peru on a *paepae*, a platform or raft. Spanish historians in Peru told of many such voyages made in pre-Inca times, and several 'ologists' had come to Raroia since Heyerdahl's expedition, each with their own pet theories to prove but with little or no experience of the sea. These people made a big thing of rubbishing Heyerdahl's ideas, maintaining that the Polynesians had come island-hopping against the winds and currents from Asia. Some of them took Polynesian treasures back to America and Japan with them.

'We know the South American balsa logs of the *Kon Tiki* survived, but there is no balsa in Asia. They make their *paepaes* of bamboo, and that doesn't last, because the sea worms eat it.' Rogo smiled. 'I don't know, maybe we came from all directions!'

A couple of days of heavy rain and thunderstorms confined us to *English Rose*, the squally winds changing direction from north west to south-east. We set anchors fore and aft, keeping the bow heading out into the lagoon with the palm trees of the atoll covering our backs to the west. We spent an entire morning unwinding the bow anchor chain from the coral heads. This was no place for anchor warps – the rope would chafe through in no time.

We never quite worked out when the work was done on the atoll. The bell called people to church at dawn; at noon everything appeared to stop for the day while adults slept through the afternoon before returning to church in the evening. And it was hard to imagine how the islanders managed the isolation and monotony: it was a cheerful scene in bright sunlight, but grey skies soon transformed it to sadness. The population had dwindled by 70 per cent from 200 to sixty in the fifty years since *Kon Tiki* landed here, and perhaps 70 per cent of the motivation had gone with it. Emasculated by French copra subsidies, family and unemployment benefits, many people were drawn to the slums of Tahiti, leaving a lot of the houses unoccupied, in ruins or locked up.

Nevertheless, some building was taking place. Since 1985, the cultivation of pearls in giant black-lipped oysters had provided a living for maybe a dozen men. Rogo and his friend Rémy took us out on to the blue lagoon to see their *petites maisons*. These little thatched huts on stilts were set on broad coral heads which reached up from the crater floor like pale yellow mushrooms through a 100ft or more of turquoise water. From the huts, buoyed lines stretched out like a spider's web with vertical strings suspended from them, each holding half a dozen or more huge black oysters. Each little hut was a family farm; each family first collected the spat and then 'grew on' the tiny bivalves in wire cages. Later, these were hung in plastic netting, and finally tied individually to the lines. Between them, middle-aged couples, often grandparents, managed the whole operation, sometimes living for days far out on the lagoon. There was much monotonous labour, first seeding, then scrubbing the shells clean and finally harvesting the pearls from each of thousands of oysters. The whole operation, even down to the black plastic netting, was strikingly similar to our own scallop- and mussel-farm at Ardmore. It would be rewarding enough when the operators were on top of the job, but it could so easily become a nightmare of befouled shells and sinking, stinking, weed-clogged headlines.

In mid-afternoon our two friends came out in Rémy's green speed-boat to take Andy and me fishing. We raced along the shore and close under the coconut palms growing almost into the water. In ten minutes we reached the Garue *passe*, the only channel from the lagoon to the ocean. It was a maelstrom. Outside the atoll, the level of the ocean was falling with the ebb tide. The calm lagoon contained an area of water 15

The Crew

Isso setting out

Marie Christine - New Yachtie

John - Leader of the Pack

Bec

Will

Andy

Isso and slave hut in the Caribbean

Will and giant tortoises in the Galapagos

Summertime, and the fishin' is easy....

Bec sail-mending

A day's work done,
Martinez in Chiquito Guayabo

Polynesian fighting spirit ~ Hiva Oa,
Marquesas Is.

Yacht in Polynesia ~ Tahu Ata, Marquesas Is.

Nicholas skinning a pig at Hanamenu Bay

The pool at Hanamenu Bay

Bora Bora

Isso on the path to her past

John and Josefina

All that was left in Lucmahuayco,
Isso's birthplace

Isso with Mum and Granny

JW

Igor

Ship's cat

The Southern Ocean in midwinter

Breathe in, breathe out - keep fit in Tierra del Fuego

English Rose beneath a glacier in the Beagle Channel

Camping in the Patagonian Channels

High above Estero de las Montañas, Chile

Gentoo penguins, Waterboat Point, Antarctica

Waterboat Point

Old bones, Port Lockroy

Blue-eyed shags, BAS Faraday

The southernmost yacht in the world, BAS Faraday

Elephant seals, South Georgia

King penguins, South Georgia

Bec and Isso, Grytvicken, South Georgia

Bruce greasing the winches

John sights home, April 1995

Back at Ardmore

miles long by 10 wide which was squeezing out through the *passe*, an opening barely a couple of hundred yards wide. Raging overfalls formed a huge rooster tail which rolled and roared for a mile or more out to sea. Formed by great up-wellings from the seabed, whirlpools swirled along the margins among the undulating glassy flats.

Eyes afire, Rémy crouched in the square stern, perched on half an ancient cork lifebuoy. Steering the outboard as if it were a racehorse, he took us streaming down the very edge of the current and out into the ocean. 'This is my refrigerator,' he shouted above the roar. 'Now I'm going to open the door!'

While Andy and I paid out trolling lines down each side of the bucking boat, Rogo sat cross-legged on the sharply pointed plywood foredeck, threadbare denim jacket flung across his shoulders. He bellowed instructions at Rémy. How these two boys came to life out on the tide race: copra- and pearl-farming were nothing compared to the serious business of a hunter-gatherer.

'Maany, maany mahos in the passe, Johnny! You get feesh, you pull in line *fast*. Like boxing, Johnny: one-two, one-two!' Rogo tucked his chin into his shoulder, demonstrating the combination punches. 'You too slow, maho take fish!'

The sun dipped slowly towards the western horizon and the giant sky changed from blue to yellow to red. Here and there shoals of small bonito and tuna came leaping from the boiling waters, pursued by the predators of the deep. The waiting clouds of noddies and boobies raced towards them, shrieking as they dived. Rémy coughed incessantly in the stern, his bloodshot eyes bulging from his massive square head, which jerked up and down on his broad shoulders. Rogo, chain-smoking his pungent roll-ups, dished out the orders from the bow, tapping the wood: 'Tuuuna, tuna, tuna, tuuuuna . . .' he crooned enticingly. What power in these two men; what dignity and presence. Yet there was a sense of emptiness: one motor and no paddles, and no other trace of mankind in a vast seascape. The gin-clear water hurtled by as we raced along the margin of the reef, skimming over great mottled slabs of coral.

'I've got one!' I shouted, hauling in the line, hand over hand. 'Bonito! One-two, one-two, one-two!' bellowed Rémy.

There was a big bump and the line went slack. 'Maho!' Rogo grabbed the line, but the shark had grabbed the fish. I was too slow.

Soon it was Sunday again. Always susceptible to excess and extreme, I've

tried to avoid things which might consume me, addictions like cigarettes, alcohol or even religion. Nevertheless, when Isso woke us at 5.30
am we four hurried ashore in our best kit.

'I think we're late!' Bec called over the usual family shouting match,
as we dodged the overhanging bushes trying to nudge us into the sea.
But there was no one waiting outside the church – just one thin brown
dog lying on the rain-swept gravel. And the church itself was empty too.
So we sat on a long wooden bench, swatting mosquitos as they settled
on our bare legs. Soon the little children for whom Bec and Will had
organised a sports day on the school playground began arriving, dressed
in their fine bright clean Sunday-best. They giggled about our blue eyes,
and imitated the way I stood with my hands on my hips.

Martha came rolling along the sandy path in crisp white blouse and
brown skirt. Smiling broadly, she kissed each of our three ladies on both
cheeks. Rémy, in tan slacks and floral shirt, appeared and sat down beside
us. As everyone arrived, they shook our hands; the bell was rung seven
times and we all filed in through the double doors. The aisle was covered
with a long strip of bright tile-pattern linoleum; the lower walls washed
blue, like the sea, while the upper walls were white like the daylight. And
the whole length of the black ceiling was scattered with gold stars. Many
triangular flags were strung across the body of the church in brightly
coloured bunting, and two silver-painted candelabra hung over either
end of the aisle. The centre one was missing: in its place was a red plastic
fishing buoy. It reminded me of the vastness of the ocean surrounding this
circular coral strand. A mother-of-pearl heart fashioned from an oyster
shell adorned the cross on the simple altar, lit by one guttering candle.

The pastor walked round from behind the altar. Astonishingly, it
was my fishing friend Rémy, transformed by a long white cassock. A
glorious, soaring female voice – Martha's – filled the church, joined by
deep male voices, rumbling the great surging swell of the surf out at the
tide race. I was overcome. Was I dreaming? We all sat down, and Rémy
intoned the beginning of the mass. Three rows in front of us, Martha
was trembling with exertion, as if she had malaria.

Whatever else might happen before we reached home, I hoped I
would always remember the generosity of spirit in this place. And I
promised myself that when we got home to Scotland, whenever I felt
down, I'd throw open the windows up in the tower and play Polynesian
music to remind me that I was truly alive. It was the most wonderful
sound I had ever heard.

At the end of the service we walked to the little pier and paddled back to the boat. Rogo and Rémy came out and prepared a delicious *poisson cru* in the main cockpit. The secret was to force the soft pulp of a drinking coconut through a sieve to form a sort of cream. This cream, together with fish they'd just caught by casting a net in a small bay a few hundred yards from where we were anchored, and the juice from the fresh limes we'd brought down from the Marquesas produced a treat we were never able to quite equal ourselves.

Promptly at eight next morning, Rogo arrived in his green plywood speedboat. Andy drew the short straw and stayed behind to work on the boat while the rest of us set off on the 10-mile trip across the lagoon to Kon Tiki Island. The journey took just under an hour, as Rogo's outboard was playing up a bit. I brought the dinghy oars, just in case. The coral heads were few and far between and, as it turned out, we could easily have brought *English Rose* and anchored off the tiny palm-covered mound of shattered coral where the six-man crew of the *Kon Tiki* lived for four days early in August 1947 – before young Martha found the box of food on the beach and alerted the old chief, who rounded up the villagers to paddle their pirogues across the lagoon in search of the *poppae*.

The dazzling water and blinding white coral sand seemed to redouble the power of the sun. Clouds of snow-white fairy terns took off in alarm, circling and screaming above the coconut trees as Rogo gently beached his boat on the soft sand. Isso jumped out, splashing her feet in the cool water. 'Non, Isabel! Viens ici!' Rogo shouted, as I pulled my daughter back from the water. Sure enough, a small brown shark came racing into the shallows, looking for a mid-morning snack.

The tall palms and the darker green bushes beneath gave off a fresh and welcoming smell. Very few people had ever visited this place and Marie Christine and Rogo agreed it would be nice to mark the occasion with our own palm tree. So we searched for a place to plant the coconut we'd brought from Panama, which had been the major plant in Marie Christine's expanding conservatory, its green leaves adorning the saloon right across the Pacific. Rogo helped Isso and Marie Christine with the planting, promising to return in a few weeks with some lime and a stake to help it grow.

Reddish boulders of broken coral lay strewn across the 400-yard-wide reef, hurled up by the pounding tradewind surf on this windward side of the atoll. As we paddled out along the channels towards the ocean, the advancing tide came splashing up to our knees. The crew of the *Kon Tiki* had been saved by hanging on to the raft as it smashed on this reef; its nine huge balsa logs stayed connected only because the natural fibre lashings were set in deep notches in the trunks, beyond the reach of the grinding coral.

'Johnny, you stay – I go on. I spear fish for lunch!' Rogo grinned. The black tips of small shark fins broke the surface as they circled round us. We watched Rogo stalking forward; like an old grey heron at the edge of the loch at home, he moved silently out towards the coral step where the surf bumped in from the ocean. After a while he tensed, crouching forward with his throwing arm trailing well back, like a cocked weapon. Suddenly the arm lashed forward. Even a hundred yards away, we heard the seven steel prongs of his spear crash into the coral and glimpsed a flash of vivid blue as a parrot fish raced across the shallows over the red of the reef. Rogo splashed after it, loudly scraping the prongs along the reef, herding the fish before him. Foolishly, the parrot fish sheltered under a lump of coral. Rogo cocked his arm again and let fly. This time he had got the main ingredient for our lunch of strips of raw fish soused in lime and bathed in coconut milk.

Paddling back across the reef towards the boat, we searched for shells for Bec's collection, turning over the smaller lumps of coral lying in the channels, undeterred by Rogo's warnings of vicious eels. But then one streaked out and thrashed through the shallows. I leaped into the air, accidentally kicking off a shoe and landing barefoot on the coral. We went off shell-collecting after this.

We found a crack like a fault line leading across from the ocean to the lagoon. 'I live here a few more years, then maybe I have to leave,' Rogo told us, shaking his grey head. 'The volcano is moving.'

Rogo had several theories for the failure of pearl farms. The thinning of the ozone layer could be heating up the sea, and this would kill the oysters. The melting of the ice caps would raise the sea-level and drown the atoll. We'd read that the first experimental pearl farm had been established in 1963, in the lagoon of nearby Hikueru Atoll. Now, in 1994, the oysters there had all died. Rogo believed this was because the volcano was smoking underwater. Rising wisps of steam caused a yellow substance to build up on the lagoon bed; this fed the algae, which in turn depleted the oxygen and killed the oysters. In other places the oysters were simply becoming sterile.

While the sun beat down on white sand and turquoise water, Rogo nursed his outboard along the inner shores of the atoll. He pulled into the stubby remains of an old coral pier. A coconut palm, blown over in the last storm, lay collapsed on the water, sheltering shoals of fish from the sun in the shade of its trunk, which was held on the surface by its branches, sticking down into the sand. A large black shark came cruising along the shore. Rogo turned the boat to chase it away. Then he speared another fish under the palm tree and splashed it around, but no other sharks came for it.

'This is where my grandmother's house stood, before the village was moved to the lee side of the atoll at the beginning of this century.' He pointed to a patch of coral mortar. 'This is my land, and over here' – he paced a few yards through the palms – 'is Rémy's land.'

Wandering across the island, swatting mosquitos, we paused for a drink of coconut milk from nuts Rogo nudged from a low tree with a convenient pole. Bright red hermit crabs were everywhere among the tapioca plants. He said there were a few coconut crabs lurking in the undergrowth which could crush a coconut shell with their claws. Apparently they made excellent eating, but he didn't tell us how he caught such monsters in the dead of night.

Emerging from the tangled trees at last, we found twisted rusting iron plates and ribs scattered all over the reef. This was all that remained of a sailing paddle-steamer wrecked here towards the end of the last century. The thick black steel, massively riveted, sheltered all manner of small fish. After the ship broke its back, it seemed the crew had managed to get ashore in a small boat. Then two-thirds of the hull had fallen backwards and slipped off the reef, dropping into the deep and taking the safe with it. Rogo's granny had seen it all.

It was already afternoon by the time we returned to *English Rose* and made *poisson cru* from the two fish Rogo had speared.

I was determined that Isso should see a shark while snorkelling: overcoming your fears is an important part of education. We swam out to the edge of the coral, where the water blued away down towards the floor of the crater. I sensed we were not alone: he was out there somewhere to my right, gliding between two coral heads. I grabbed my daughter's elbow and pointed ahead. If he turned left now, he'd be coming straight towards us. He did. I felt Isso tense. She stopped swimming. The grey shape of the shark kept coming – straight at us. Then he stopped and turned broadside, waiting. Isso shook off my hand and swam straight at the shark. It turned and fled. She had come a long way from the little girl who wouldn't get out of the dinghy in Bequia. I was proud of her. But I didn't want to do it again.

We wanted to do something to repay the islanders' kindness. We'd heard that Rémy was building a little house for one of his several daughters. Leaving Andy on the boat, the rest of us set off through the village to see if we could help. We found the little party in a clearing by the beach, a couple of hundred yards beyond the nearest house. Rémy was being assisted by his son-in-law, a mighty young man of Danish descent referred to as the Viking, and Marcel, the gendarme's smiling son. Rémy had already had a long day. He'd been out fishing for lunch at three in the morning; at five-thirty he'd conducted a church service, and by the time we arrived he had the site all laid out, 16ft long by 12 wide. We five set to work filling in the coral hardcore with long-handled shovels. The Viking brought coral and sand to the site in a noisy dumper, and Rémy worked the cement-mixer. By lunchtime the concrete foundation had been laid. We'd done this many times at home, but how seldom in such perfect weather. People came through the coconut trees with bowls of food, covered with cloths to keep off the flies, and laid them along a wooden trestle table, and the feasting began.

11

The Society Islands

JOHN

It's all of 500 miles from Raroia to Tahiti, part of 1.5 million square miles of French territory, the largest area of sea owned by any one nation. And it was calm as we motored on the long, low swell of a slumbering ocean, sleeping out under the stars in the main cockpit as we passed through the channel between Fakareva and Faaita and turned east to head directly for Tahiti.

At first light on the first day of May 1994, three days out from Raroia, A Watch spied Tahiti lying steep and deliciously green on our western horizon. Oh, the romance of it all! Captain Cook named this group the Society Islands, after the Royal Society, to which he had been elected in London. Why did he return so often? Did he have a *vahine* sweetheart to lure him back from faraway Europe and his desperate voyages searching ever further south for the fabled southern continent, which turned out to be no more than the icy wastes of Antarctica?

I fancied I could see slabs of rain-wet rock at the northern end of the earthly paradise. The illusion began to fade as soon as I peered through the binoculars: the shiny rocks materialised as white-walled California-style luxury bungalows. A Jumbo jet came rumbling out of the clouds from the north. I remembered my disappointment in the Caribbean and wondered if paradise was lost after all.

As we approached land, the sea which had been an empty place for us for so long began to fill with boats. Windsurfers raced out to greet us; sailboats and even a hydrofoil ferry came sweeping past. Rounding Point Venus, we followed the reef to the oil-tank farm and nosed through a tranquil *passe* into Papeete Harbour. The leading marks lined up on a large modern church in green, white and café-au-lait, which could have been a greeter for some Polynesian Disneyland. But at least there were no glaring signs for the Hilton, Sheraton or Hyatt.

As we motored along the line of long-distance yachts moored stern-to against the edge of the harbour road, a sleepy French voice called over the radio. 'This is like Europe. Everything is closed over the weekend. Just anchor wherever you like, then come into the office in the morning and ask for Gerard.'

We anchored between a neat Swedish double-ender and an abandoned-looking French boat, hitching our heavy mooring lines to neat black bollards beside the tree-lined road. Cool fresh water gushed from taps on the shore, free showers for yachties and the teams of islanders training in racing pirogues.

Our new neighbour, Jürgen, came for lunch under the awning. Once a company analyst for a Gothenburg bank, he'd reinvented himself as a lean and capable solo sailor. 'I was divorced a dozen years ago, and I needed to feel confidence in my boat,' he smiled shyly over the macaroni cheese. 'I'll just sail on until the money runs out.' I guessed he might come sailing into Ardmore one day with a Tahitian *vahine* in tow.

Isabel, a middle-aged mum, came swimming out to her faded white boat in the mid-afternoon, her long mousy French hair piled high to keep it from the murky harbour water. Scrambling aboard, she untangled the mooring lines and pulled her aged pram tender towards the shore for the ungallant Hugo, a long-haired brat we'd met in Hiva Oa. Pulling himself out along the line, he jumped on to our boat, sliding his muddy trainers down the white front of the doghouse. I was not a happy bunny. 'Fantastique! Ze women here are like diamonds!' he leered through teeth green from sixteen years of neglect. 'I have three thousand dollars. Zis place is wonderful after midnight.' His mother's boyfriend had died somewhere along the way, and now their battered steel boat had a heavy list to starboard.

Bec asked him where he was going next. 'Oh, simple. I leave my mother here to get a job, then I sail back to New Caledonia. There I will sell the boat, or if this is impossible, I will run it on a reef and claim the insurance. It is easy for me: I am only sixteen, an accident is always understandable, non?' Isso looked on, captivated by the French teenager's awful charm.

The French certainly knew how to run a waterfront café, and Papeete provided a matchless setting. But the true charm of Tahiti lay in the generous-spirited, ever-smiling Polynesians, and if the ambience were not enough, then the girls were surely the most beautiful in the world.

I took a bus along the coast, looking for an old man recommended by Rogo and Rémy. A few miles out of town I found a secluded bungalow standing alone by the sandy shore. It was cool inside, more like a library than a home. Now in his seventies, the anthropologist Bengt Danielson had settled here after wading ashore on Rarioa from the *Kon Tiki* in 1947. Thin, with a wispy beard and the rather pedantic manner of a man who has written a six-volume history of Polynesia, Bengt was fiercely anti-French. 'As you most certainly know, they have destroyed the Polynesian culture,' he snorted. 'There has never been a French anthropologist here – there is no money in Polynesia for them, it is worthless except for nuclear testing. Independence is the only way forward.'

By contrast, Bob Withers held a realistic commercial view. Bob, a steady Kiwi, had retired from New Zealand Airways and become the honorary British consul, running his car-hire firm in the back streets of Papeete. He was the antithesis of Bengt: quietly spoken and down to earth. He described a serious situation in which 40 per cent of the economy had disappeared with the end of nuclear testing. But the Polynesians had French passports and the French had invested heavily in the Pact Progree with the aim of creating an infrastructure to help Polynesia stand on its own feet. As a result, government workers had disproportionately larger salaries than the rest of the islanders now flocking to Tahiti for work. Fishing, copra and vanilla were insufficient resources. Bob shook his grey head. 'Danielson was persona non grata with the French all right, but it needs more than just idealism.'

Tourism is a possibility, with Japan, Australasia and USA the market, but these countries have sophisticated needs and numbers would need to double from 150,000 to 300,000 a year to sustain the fancy infrastructure Polynesia would need to compete in the marketplace of global tourism. Yet compared with the teeming poor of South America, the Polynesians seemed very fortunate. In a way the French nuclear programme, the motor which has driven the economy, has saved their innocence. The withdrawal of the French might yet see the Tahitians slide down the beach into the murky, resentful waters of tourism, as has happened in the Caribbean.

Marie Christine and I went ashore for an evening out to enjoy the cosmopolitan atmosphere along the waterfront. A perky, elderly Glaswegian couple, small and round, eyed us suspiciously. 'You're from Scotland, aren't you? We saw a TV film about you at home. Then it was the in-flight movie on NZ Airways across the Pacific, too. You must be some kind of nutter.'

'What are you doing here?' I asked lamely, with sinking stomach.

'Well, I read about a company selling the Duchess of York's book.' They grinned at one another. 'I thought, royalty, scandal, helicopters, kids . . . it can't fail! I bought shares at five pence and sold at one-seventeen. And here we are, catching the two am flight to New Zealand.'

After a pizza we turned for home. It was nearly midnight and things were quietening down, and it was dark under the trees along the harbour road where the raffish cruising yachts lay scattered. Andy had paddled the dinghy back to *English Rose* after putting us ashore earlier in the evening – we didn't want to risk having it stolen – so I swam out to the boat to fetch it for Marie Christine. As I hauled myself up the wooden steps, Isso let out a cry from below and I knew something was wrong. Will came up from the saloon, looking serious. 'I'm afraid we've had visitors, John. It happened while Bec and I were ashore. They swam out with a bag, but Isso and Andy heard them and came up on deck, and they jumped in their dinghy, paddled ashore and left it untied under the trees.'

The previous night, a Danish boat had been robbed of tear gas and knives. We reckoned the thieves must be watching the yachts, maybe from the buildings on the other side of the road, and waiting until the crew went ashore before making their raid.

Sunday again. Marie Christine, Bec, Isso and I sat on an airy balcony in the large church beside the harbour. Below us were islands of white straw hats and the booming singing floated upwards. After church the French military marched through the streets, all bands and antique uniforms. To an ex-soldier like me such a scene had a magnetic appeal. I thought about how badly recent wars had gone for France. Defeat in the Franco–Prussian war of 1870 was followed by Verdun and the trenches of 1914–18. But all the outrage the Americans felt after the Japanese bombing of Pearl Harbor couldn't really compare with the bitter humiliation of the German occupation of France in the Second World War. Given that background, I felt it was little wonder that France insisted on nuclear tests for their independent Force de Frappe. Some memories fade only slowly.

MARIE CHRISTINE

In a remote harbour like Papeete, we always found the atmosphere around long-distance yachts a bit heady. It's a little like being on leave during a war: the battles are going on over the horizon, but for the time being we and our boats were all safely at anchor. Barriers fell easily, regardless of boat size, age or nationality. But even so, when the smart cruising boats of the Europa Round-World Rally arrived, to an official welcome of Polynesian dancing, garlands of flowers and a gunfire salute, I felt we couldn't just rush up and introduce ourselves.

I suppose most husbands and wives have a different approach when meeting people. Perhaps to compensate for John's bullish tendency, I prefer to hold back a bit and let events take their course while he fights our battles, pushing forward, not wishing to miss an opportunity.

Miss Muppet was a sister ship of *English Rose*, known as the 'green moneypot' – they had everything on board: a washer-drier, a 100-litre-an-hour water-maker, video-player, electric keyboard, ice-maker, hot showers, state-of-the-art galley.

'Wouldn't you just love to wake up to newly baked bread and fresh brewed coffee? We just set the machines the night before,' Jody miaowed at me. I had also heard that Carl had to get up in the night to alter the air-conditioning: Jody liked a blanket on her bed. I thought of us sweating pints on a damp sheet.

'I wasn't prepared to go on this trip unless we had all the comforts possible,' she said. Why hadn't I taken that approach? How sensible and easy she made it all sound. I had obviously gone wrong somewhere at the planning stage. But, living in the north of Scotland, and not seeing other boats or reading yachting magazines, until this trip I had never heard of water-makers, nor even considered washing machines and showers. I thought our windscoop was pretty state of the art. I chuckled over our image – the poor country cousins – but I sensed that Carl understood and admired our intention to sail down into the Antarctic, where comforts would be of little value compared with our strong rigging, sails and back-up procedures.

Tiki, a Polynesian lesser God, had recently joined us. Walking back from the centre of town, I had noticed some young boys throwing something into the air. It looked suspiciously like a small animal. 'Arrêtez!' I screamed, instantly falling into the stereotype of an Englishwoman abroad, protecting all animals. 'Ca c'est méchant!' I fully expected their parents to jump off their boats and harangue me. The missile was indeed an animal: a very small ginger kitten. Once free from its tormentors, it ran off and hid under a kiosk. What a fighter, what a survivor, I thought. I had managed to hold it for a moment: it was tiny, its serious blue eyes seemed to measure me up in an instant. Surely it was too young to be parted from its mother. It must be living off scraps.

'Whose is the kitten?' I asked. The oldest child told me it was a stray. They thought it had been thrown from a car window into the bay. I felt compelled to take care of it. I wondered if John would ever consider us taking on a cat. He does like them very much, and he wept a tear when he heard of the death of Pussy Ridgway, one of the five we had left behind. But a kitten on a yacht? Why not? It was too small to survive for long on its own, but small enough to adapt to life on a boat. I would have to persuade the others that we needed a ship's cat. This plucky ball of fluff was surely destined to be a Ridgway.

Bec jumped at the idea, and the next day she and I picked up the kitten from an elderly French couple in a nearby boat, who had given her a temporary haven while I put the idea to John and the rest of the team. They were entranced with her and would have liked to have kept her themselves, but they would soon be flying back to France. Introducing a cat into the equation of seasickness, squalor and lack of space would affect everyone on the boat, so the decision to take her had to be unanimous. We paddled her over in the rubber dinghy to meet the team. Bec and I held our breath as we watched the sharp, pricked-up ears and alert blue eyes. She was small enough to sit in the palm of a hand and to melt the stoniest of hearts.

'Well, all right, then,' John agreed, as did Andy and Will and Isso. Bec and I were overjoyed. We took down the picture of a cat, cut out from a magazine, that had dominated the port side of the saloon. Now we had a real one on board. Now, even if we had water shortages and no air-conditioning, each of us could snuggle up to this ginger scrap, which purred continuously, when we needed a touch of comfort. In one swoop Tiki turned our boat into a home.

JOHN

The charms of Papeete's French food prompted me to start running again. I 'ran' lengths of the local swimming pool, kitted out in a special flotation jacket. This logical development of swim training for race-horses allowed extra exercise without wear and tear on the joints. As usual, as my fitness improved, so did my morale.

After two weeks in the fleshpots, we cruised across the Sea of the Moon for half a day to Mooréa, Tahiti's heart-shaped sister, the most beautiful island in the world. We came to anchor in Cook's Bay, a shel-tered deep inlet edged with blinding white coral sand. Steep green cliffs rose up to six shark-toothed sentinels, remnants of an ancient 3,000m volcano. In the valleys grew pineapple, vanilla, coffee and coconuts, stitching intricate patches of vivid colour on to the landscape. Legend has it that Mooréa was formed from the second dorsal fin of the fish that became Tahiti, and that a hole through the summit of Mount Mouaputa was made by a spear tossed from Tahiti by the demigod Pai, to prevent it from being carried off to Raiatéa, the most ancient and sacred island in Polynesia, by Hiro, god of thieves.

The days were long and hot. It was too soon yet to be heading for Chile, and there was nothing for it but to laze. The daughter of a 1930s Hollywood star and her ex-racing-driver/Texas oil man husband invited us aboard their luxury 50-footer to celebrate his fiftieth birthday. The drink flowed, and there was a fair bit of chat about the increasing prob-lem of robberies from boats all round the world. As the guests were leaving, the oil man nodded his head towards the aft cabin. 'Come and see our security arrangements,' he whispered. Secreted in various places were weapons, clean, dry and lightly oiled, including a pale grey .222 Austrian assault rifle, a crossbow and an Israeli Uzi machine-gun. I would have added an anti-tank bazooka rocket-launcher myself, together with a discreet firing position, open at the back for the blast.

It seemed to me that some breakdown of law and order was an inevitable by-product of increasing freedom, democracy and liberalism. We carried no weapons, however. Our only defence was to try to fore-see possible difficulties and circumvent them in some way.

Bill, my American chum from the Marquesas, was here. He and I went diving together out around the reef, while Rebecca manned the dinghy above us. We saw octopus, nurse sharks and moray eels and gathered huge shells. Bill was a pro, and diving with him was the stuff of dreams. He could charm the birds off the trees, yet now his third or fourth marriage was in difficulties. Sue was quieter than she'd been in the Marquesas and seemed near the end of her tether. 'If only Bill could just say a little thank you when I cook his meals,' she'd remark.

At forty-three, Bill was running to fat, his looks were bloating and his hand was never without a bottle of the local beer. One day I asked him about the gold coin on the necklace he perpetually fingered with his spare hand. The beer ran away with him. 'Jaahn,' he drawled, taking a long suck from the bottle, 'this is a piece of eight.' When he was twenty-four, no more than an assistant diver, really, a boat he'd been diving from drifted off the edge of the dive limit. His young buddy began waving, pointing down at a Spanish cannon sticking up from the bow of a wreck stuck in the bottom of a gully in the seabed. They'd discovered a treasure ship. There was $\frac{3}{8}$in gold chain, a huge mound of gold pancakes and all sorts of stuff.

In the boat above, the US marshal was blind drunk, quite unable to help them as they loaded gold treasure aboard. When they couldn't get any more on the boat, they returned to base. Bill's friend phoned his lawyer father. 'Git the marshal drunker,' came the order. 'Git him unconscious. I'm on my way.'

That evening they left a much smaller pile of gold, loading the rest on to three container trailers and driving away into the night.

'That pile was much bigger!' roared the sore-headed marshal next morning. Bill and his friends were charged with stealing treasure, and for a while, things looked bad. But their lawyer, produced film evidence in court of the drunken marshal peeing on the small pile of gold. Clearly, he was an unreliable witness, and the defendants were cleared.

'My son Jim – and his son, too – they'll never have to hunt no pigs on the Marquesas, man,' grinned Bill, slugging from the bottle.

The day before we sailed west, Sue flew back to America with baby Jim for a 'break', and Bill was left alone on the boat with his beer.

MARIE CHRISTINE

What had we done to deserve these months in paradise? Now I could understand the allure of cutting our ties with home and leading this gypsy life. Our boat was our caravan, and the wind our horse. There had to be some funds, of course, to pay for food, harbour dues and other contingencies, but with careful housekeeping the cost of living could be kept to a minimum. Some of the people we'd met had sold their homes and were living off the interest from their capital. Very few escapees were of Bec's, Will's and Andy's age – most were middle-aged and older, free to do whatever they wished within the vast limits of their own capabilities. Their courage was an inspiration to us and the fun of it was that, by chance, we kept meeting up with friends we had met at other anchorages.

'That's *Wand'rin' Star*, that is!' Andy pronounced. He was seldom wrong. We were sitting in our usual motionless noon state, under the awning, waiting for a cooling breeze and just watching what everybody was up to. The familiar outline and rather worn sails became clearer as the yacht pressed into the bay and dropped anchor nearby. Five months had passed since we had first met Jerry and his companion, Jean, in the Galapagos at the end of January. In mid-April our routes had crossed again when they dropped anchor in Nuku Hiva.

While we had sailed direct across the Pacific to the Marquesas, they had decided to drop south and visit Easter Island on the way. After a good sail they had managed to get ashore to see some of the 600 huge stone figures up to 9m in height. They had been delighted by the friendly welcome they received, and by way of thanks they had taken aboard, for the voyage on to Polynesia, a vivacious local woman who wanted to trace her Polynesian ancestry. They had enjoyed her company and her tales about her rather confused personal life.

Jean, over sixty-eight, had told us over huge plates of her delicious vegetable lasagne and apple sauce how they managed in bad weather. 'When it's real stormy, we just batten down, sit ourselves on the bean-bags and turn on *Fantasia*. It's real soothing,' she said in her drawly, comforting west-coast voice. We were amazed. On *English Rose*, storm procedure was altogether different, more like London in the Blitz. Those on watch were fighting to keep the boat going forward; the rest waited uneasily for their turn on deck, oilskins close by, mentally prepared for capsize, abandon ship or at least the end of the world.

By Mooréa Jerry and Jean had lost a bit of their serenity. Their first port of call after Easter Island, with their guest in tow, had been Mangaréva in the Gambier Islands. Within a couple of days their new crew member, who already had a husband and children at home, had seduced a local man. She decided to stay on Mangaréva with this new man, who gave the two sailors a beautiful black pearl as a thank you present for bringing this magnificent creature into his life.

But Jean and Jerry's good deed caught up with them in Tahiti. The ships' papers showed that three persons had left Easter Island, therefore three had to pay the bond and three should ultimately leave Polynesia. The lady had tricked them. She was eventually found. Clearly well aware of the situation, she had gone into hiding. She was brought to Tahiti and then flown back to Easter Island, all at Jerry's expense. He was a sadder, poorer man for the experience. I hoped that in the end he would be rewarded for his kindness, that the black pearl would turn out to be a priceless gem, but somehow I doubted it.

We heard later that Jean and Jerry had married in a simple ceremony on a remote Pacific island. We will remember them when the wind blows and think of *Fantasia*.

In Raiatéa, Captain Cook's favourite Society Island, John became obsessed with his mistress's bottom. The boat demanded so much more of his time than I did. We had made complicated plans to have the boat lifted out and 'anti-fooled', as the French call bottom-painting. It had last been done nearly a year before, between the tides at cold and rainy Ardmore. Whenever there was a moment and the water wasn't completely toxic, John would be over the side, scrubbing away at the barnacles and fouling. Along with the cavalier French, he ignored all warnings of sharks and the danger of skin and ear infections which the Americans were always keen to talk about. Often he would feel quite sick afterwards, mildly poisoned by the cloudy anti-fouling water which he had created. It would be good to get the job done properly so that he did not have to torture himself so, or make us all feel guilty that we weren't down there suffering with him.

'You're overweight – by two tons,' Dominique, owner of the careenage, shouted over the creaking lift that was unceremoniously dumping *English Rose* back in the water.

'Well, never mind. Maybe you'd like to join us at the barbecue tonight,' called a shy voice from the quay. Seeing our disappointment, Austin Whitten, a Canadian amateur weather forecaster, brought us right into the boatyard community. Those on a tight budget lived on their hauled-out boats, negotiating precarious ladders. And tonight was their weekly party. The place had the air of a bombsite in spite of our hosts' efforts. A string of olde-worlde coloured lanterns hung in a line illuminating a meagre driftwood fire, surrounded on three sides by propped-up planks for seating. Crouched near the action were the fellow guests, nut-brown, lean and leathery: the long term sailors. Every few minutes a great deafening gush of water descended from a nearby boat, like a great grey elephant emptying its bladder. The skipper was flushing a patent treatment from his blistered GRP hull, working night and day in case it seeped through. Over the chat I could hear that John was in difficulty. 'You're a moose?' 'No!' Austin's wife Patricia squealed.

'Ah, a muse?' John suggested, to more Canadian screams. 'A nurse!'

Isso giggled her head off and I leaned closer and closer to Austin, who spoke hardly above a whisper. 'Can I hear drums?' I caught myself whispering back.

'Why, yes. It's the local dance group practising.'

Later, filled with burned sausages and steaming breadfruit, we scurried like rats, past the empty paint tins, over a single plank bridging a ditch and into the dense undergrowth, trotting towards the compelling drumbeat. A single neon strip tied to a coconut palm barely illuminated the grass clearing behind a bungalow where about forty young men and women were performing a complex and erotic dance.

Last year's lead dancer was breastfeeding her baby amid a band of fierce drummers. A group of generously sized older women sitting in a knot with their wildly excited children, their smiles like melons, called us over. In charge was a proud *mahu*, who moved swiftly among his troupe communicating his wishes with a mere twitch of his *pareu*, which he wore more elegantly than the most beautiful of the *vahines*. His command was total though he spoke rarely. His spare male body demonstrated the precise provocative movements he required from his dedicated dancers. Lissom girls swirled their hips to the staccato beat, their graceful arm movements spelling an ancient legend, while gymnastic rubber-legged men mirrored their steps. The heavy stench of pigs in a nearby pen wafted over us, mingling with the sweet fragrance of waxy white tiare flowers.

Bec, Isso, John and I watched, spellbound. It was all so spontaneous; I wondered what we had lost back in Europe along the way to our neurotic, sophisticated computer age.

'You will be visiting Pora Pora, won't you?' – the letter B does not exist in Tahitian – the friendly boatyard manager asked John and me as we motored out to a mooring. I held my breath and gazed entranced at

Bora Bora, its magical misty outline floating above the horizon. I desperately wanted to visit this beautiful island.

'Yes, I think we'll have to go there,' replied John, 'I've been told we can fill up with tax-free diesel and cash in our bond.' It was either that or return to Tahiti, and none of us liked going back.

Yet I knew that Bora Bora was a tourist trap with luxury hotels and a past that drew Americans in their droves. In 1942 the USA had set up a refuelling and regrouping base to serve allied shipping on the route between the Panama Canal and Australia. Thousands of American troops had been stationed on this 10km-long island and on board the 100 US navy transports at anchor in the secure lagoon with only one *passe*. When the base was closed two years later 130 mixed-race babies were left behind, many of whom died when they were switched from American formula milk to island food. It was on this island that a young naval officer, James A. Michener, set his haunting love story *South Pacific*, which was made into the film which had moulded my notion of Polynesia and the South Seas. It was enough to lure us there.

This mystical Bali Hai beckoned us from across the 25-mile-wide channel, the most entrancing sight of all the many islands we had visited, scattered across an area the size of Europe. Dramatric seven-million-year-old basalt peaks, dominated by Mount Otemanu – the 'sea of birds' – a mighty volcanic plug over 700m high, soared above the varied aquamarine hues of the lagoon. 'Pora Pora' first born.

We slipped easily through the Teavanui *passe* in the reef; through the *tapetape*, the line where the deep-sea indigo pales to breaking white and then on into the welcoming turquoise of the shallow, calm lagoon. Our anchor rattled out 50m of chain off an impossibly green uninhabited island, with the guardian basalt plugs rearing up behind. Hot from our anchoring, all but Will, whose arm was slow to heal, jumped off into the warm lagoon water. Knowing this would be our last chance to swim and snorkel, we decided to spend a couple of days doing just that. But we had been warned of a type of streptococcus in this water that could cause infection to open wounds. My heart went out to Will, forced to sit quietly reading on deck.

We snorkelled out towards Motu Tapu, a tiny 'forbidden' islet – just coral, sand and palms – reputedly inhabited by devils, which was popularised in Murnau's 1928 film *Taboo*. But it was what we found below the water that held our attention. Andy had discovered telltale 10m trails leading across the seabed to cone shells. Digging quickly, he uncovered beautifully marked brown and white 6in-long pointed shells. John soon got the knack and found nine, while Bec was hell-bent on getting a giant clam to take home for a soapdish. They nestled safely between coral and rock, to which they were strongly attached. The curvy lips were lined with an iridescent purple-blue-green, held half-open while they sifted in the food that floated by on the tide. Once under attack from the fierce blonde Bec, they shut tight and hung on grimly. Isso and I dipped down and up following shoals of coloured fish in and out of their coral, picking up treasures that never looked quite as lovely once they were out of the water.

Swimming back to the boat, Isso struggled against the tide, which was sweeping her directly away from the stern of *English Rose*. Bec swam with her to give her encouragement. From going backwards, to remaining stationary, to inching forwards, she finally made it after an hour-long battle. She had learned a tough lesson the tough way.

We had read of cone shells with a deadly stinging dart, and later that afternoon, the five of us, swimming in ragged formation, came upon a patch of rocks harbouring a large steel-grey moray eel. John, in front, turned and signalled to us. Not knowing what he meant, we swam towards him, pushing him nearer the vicious creature. It bared its sharp teeth and stared with beady eyes before stealthily recoiling into its lair. The sun, blue sky and warm, clear water had made us confident, but dangers lurked all around.

Lenny and Colombian Jane, more fellow travellers whose path had crossed with ours several times, joined us for supper one evening. By the light of Andy's blue Chinese hurricane lamp we ate the flat fish he had speared in the lagoon, while ginger Tiki tossed and patted her own brilliant yellow and black fish supper along the scuppers.

Lenny's talk centred on his return to the States after he had sold his boat in Australia. I looked across at Jane. She volunteered an answer to my unspoken question in a quiet, sad voice. 'I go back to Colombia and start living my life there again.' I remembered her bright eyes at the water trough in Atuona three months earlier, when we had first met, and how she had described Lenny, twenty years her senior, as *muy bonito*. Bored with life as a cashier in a Cartagena supermarket, she'd answered an ad in her local newspaper for a cook and shipmate and was chosen from twenty applicants. I am sure she had hoped then that this would be her passport to another life. Lenny had enjoyed a compliant, sweet-tempered young female crew for his voyage through the

Pacific, and that was the deal. Now it looked as though she was headed back home.

The following day we sailed away on a fine north-east breeze. Our bodies were browner than they'd ever be again, and our boat was filled with shells gathered from the turquoise-green lagoon. Stored within ourselves were pictures of paradise into which, in our minds, we could escape on the cold grey days ahead.

12

Roaring Forties in Winter

REBECCA

After leaving Bora Bora, we returned to Raiatéa for a couple of days to prepare for our trip to Chile. We hoped to visit the Austral and Gambier Island groups in the first week or two, but the idea of a month in the Roaring Forties in winter caused a few flutters. Andy paled at the very thought of the inevitable seasickness; poor Dad couldn't wait to reach the cold weather to relieve his prickly heat, but Mum wasn't looking forward to leaving the sun. 'Better get on with it, Bec!' grinned Isso, stoical as ever. As for Will and me, we'd settled into the routine once more. At last the open wound from his operation in the Marquesas was beginning to heal with the cooler weather, but he was still worrying about where this was all leading him. The months were passing, and he wanted to get on with the agriculture training he'd promised himself on leaving the City. We discussed it endlessly. I was torn both ways. I wanted to be with Will, and yet I was keen to see the Chilean channels and experience Antarctica. I would stay with the boat and other three Rs. There was a chance that Will could still get a place on a year-long course at Cirencester if he returned from Chile before September.

After heading south-east for six bumpy days, we arrived off Raivavaé. While Andy chanted over and over from the pilot, Isso called the depths from the echo-sounder and Will, high in the cross trees, kept a look-out for coral heads, we rode a huge swell through the seething breakers at the gap in the reef. Anchoring by two small French yachts, both storm-damaged from their long trip up from New Zealand, we discovered that we were the first yachts to visit the island in over a year.

We were all excited by lovely Raivavaé and invigorated by the wonderfully cool weather. Sitting below, around the saloon table, for the first time in months, we discussed Brian Cunningham's new Tao theory of abandoning hope in survival situations. Brian, our rock on Leg 1, from Ardmore to the Canaries, faxed us weekly from Paris. He claimed that his good spirits on that difficult journey had been due to his resigning himself to enjoying the continuance of the storm rather than just waiting for it to end (and, it must be said, to his lack of seasickness). I knew the chance to give this approach a try would not be long in coming, and I decided to give it a go.

A gendarme drove us the half-mile to the gendarmerie in his official black Peugeot estate car. Eric, a round-faced man in his early thirties with thinning hair and glasses, was the embodiment of a friendly and reassuring policeman. He was so pleased to see someone new that he drove us round the island the next day in his car, complete with blue light and unusually high suspension.

Still accustomed to the months of hot weather, I shook off my shoes to cool my feet and lay back in my seat to enjoy the drive. Hugging the coast, the road was flat at first, but, crossing the root of a small headland, we climbed gently through dense woodland on to a low saddle. I was just thinking how perfect the climate was when the car stopped in the middle of nowhere. 'Madame Tiki,' murmured Eric, jumping out and disappearing through a small gap in the wall of trees lining the narrow road. In single file, we followed him into the darkness, heading for the lesser god.

There was something about the angle of her mouth, a single cruel slash across the oval disc of her face. Madame Tiki looked tricky. Astride a rough stone platform, she was almost buried in a tangle of undergrowth, where a falling tree had just missed her, a squat figure of reddish rock some 5ft tall, arms folded and minus her left ear. Isso moved eagerly forward for a closer look but Eric grabbed her arm.

'Don't touch her! If you do, they say you will die soon after!' We all stopped. The place grew darker now, assuming a rather sinister atmosphere, as if this foreign policeman had brought us into the wood to identify a mutilated corpse. Plump mosquitos gorged themselves on our bare legs while Eric described Madame Tiki's vindictive personality. 'There were three tikis, but two men came and took a couple for the Gauguin Museum outside Papeete,' he explained with a policeman's clinical gravity. 'I'm afraid both were dead within a couple of months.'

'Mmm!' someone remarked. No one went forward to touch Madame Tiki. The wild lemons we had picked up slipped from our hands.

'You can't get the islanders to say a thing about the tikis, but they always keep a light on at nights, to keep the phantoms away,' Eric smiled grimly as we made our way back through the trees, half-expecting the car to be gone.

We drove on in silence for a bit, skirting the sandy shoreline. But our spirits just had to rise. It was as if we were driving through one of those advertising scenes which cover long sections of wall, always out of reach, on the far side of the track in London Underground stations.

The road led on round the enchanted coastline through tiny hamlets of shining Protestant churches and simple cyclone-resistant bungalows. Each home displaying its smart front room for all the world to see: gaudy curtains, bright *tifaifai* cushions and a centrepiece of family photographs. Groups of women sat chatting by the roadside while their menfolk huddled in other groups nearby.

Eric came to dinner on Isso's birthday, bringing Lanvin chocolates and a doll from his home town, Valenciennes. Proudly looking at our map of France while we played our wobbly Edith Piaf tape, he emphasised that the gendarmerie was a military force. The boat was alive in the cool beauty of the place and Isso was beside herself with excitement, the centre of attention, all dressed up, the lovely shell necklace from Raroia completing her outfit. The cake, balloons, whistles, sparklers, pressie-opening and all the 'Happy birthdays' made it a night to remember.

At sea once more, we headed for the Gambier Islands, settling down to the old routine for another week at sea. To begin with, speeding along under blue skies in a steady north-north-east breeze, we enjoyed some of the best sailing we'd had since leaving home eight long months before.

But our new crew member was beginning to make herself some elbow room. 'The kitten needs to sleep for twenty-two hours a day,' Jean-Pierre – a Swiss vet, circumnavigator, marathon star and cat maniac – had told us when he'd looked her over in Papeete. Well, Tiki seemed to get by on less. She hurtled about all day, growling ferociously if she caught so much as a glimpse of a flying fish on deck. During pilotage a member of the crew had to look after her in the doghouse, and we muttered about making a harness. And at night she never failed to appear in the dark, like a wraith, jumping on my bunk. One minute there was nothing, the next she'd be there, soundless as a cloud and stock-still, but only for a while. Growing impatient, she'd crawl up to my head chew my hair or climb into one of my bunkside lockers. Of course, Mum was always keen to have Tiki in her bunk but the kitten was fast becoming a small cat and she was restless, needing action night and day. In the space of a few days she developed jaws and claws strong enough to draw blood through the sheets covering my legs. Will played with her each evening after supper, but he had taken to wearing a leather glove to do so.

The weather changed shortly after lunch on the fourth day. Under blue skies, Andy called us on deck to take a look at a strange line of dense cloud rapidly catching us up from the south-west. 'It might turn out to be heavy rain,' he said, looking towards the giant tumbling over-falls of black and grey reaching up into the heavens. 'But it looks as if the wind at the leading edge is whirling upwards.'

'Let's wait and see,' said Dad, going down below, happy with the mainsail shortened by two reefs.

'We've gone aback!' Andy called a few moments later, his voice rising with anxiety. We slipped the headsails round to the starboard tack and pulled back the running backstay in an ominous calm. This was our chance to take down the mizen and roll away the headsails, but we dithered.

Seconds later, the wind slammed through 90 degrees and we were racing along in a 40-knot south-easter. Everything went dark as we dis-appeared into the heart of the black cloud. Pelting rain sheared the tops off the old waves still running weakly in the wrong direction. We'd left it too late.

'Don't shout!' I screamed with rage at Dad as the Yankee sheet slipped through my hands and the big sail thundered out of control. Andy struggled with its furling line on the aft deck. We dropped the mizen sail and then the main, stowing away the boom and setting the storm trisail on its own track up the main mast. Eventually we achieved a snug rig, but it had taken too long. We were wet through and getting cold – just what we should have been trying to avoid.

We had four more rough days. It was a good lesson for us all, learned in warmish weather: reduce sail area ahead of time; don't get wet; and don't wait until you are wet and cold before getting your waterproofs on. Life descended into a grey lumpiness. The wind generator whined alarmingly in the gale, so we lashed the blades of the windmill, but we couldn't silence the ghostly wail of the wind in the rigging. Visibility was poor for much of the time and we were in the moonless sector of the month, so there was little chance of seeing the low-lying atolls as we flew by. Dad pored over the chart time and again.

Andy began to get over his seasickness, but he still had to make a dash for his bunk as soon as he went below, rushing for the heads if he could not make it. Even so, his interest in the sea, the boat, and the places he was visiting helped him through it. On watch, Will and I were pretty glum; again, just waiting for land. Will found it very difficult to lift himself. 'I think this is making up for everything I've done wrong in all my thirty years,' he'd mutter to himself. The rougher weather made it harder for him to do his exercises, which did not help. The luxury of forgoing waterproofs had passed, but at least this change in climate had brought Dad into better humour. Our forward sleeping compartment was draped with plastic bivvy bags in a vain attempt to protect our precious bunks from saltwater drips and gushes where the sealant around the perspex skylight hatches had been cooked over and over by the tropical sun. I had loved the colours, shells and beauty of Polynesia and dreaded the stormy weeks ahead, but now, the thought of Will leaving when we reached South America uppermost in our minds, we tried to make the most of just being together.

MARIE CHRISTINE

Now we were getting into cooler weather the holiday atmosphere was evaporating. We'd been eating lotus blossoms for long enough: now we were ready for the fresh challenges which would undoubtedly come our way on our long and lonely route across the Pacific to South America. Amateur meteorologist Austin from Raiatéa, who kept vigil with other yachts sailing up from New Zealand, warned us that no one ever took our proposed route in the winter.

The boat had been our home for nearly a year now and we were familiar with its every nuance. It had become almost a physical extension of each of us. Confidence had sneaked in and replaced my doubts and fears, I felt I could sail the boat single-handed if I had to.

Few parents can have had the good fortune to spend as long as we did in the company of their grown-up children – at least, that is what Isso thought she was, and she certainly seemed to have grown up a great deal since the start of the voyage. She was so cheerful, willing and keen to please. Swimming, steering the boat on watch and paddling the rubber dinghy to collect people from the shore were her greatest accomplishments; self-confidence her greatest need. Sometimes she still panicked when suddenly asked to do something. A mental block seemed to prevent her from understanding instructions. Perhaps it stemmed from the fear and confusion of her early childhood. Although she'd later learned to read and write in good Scottish schools, they had been unable to help in this respect. Her beaming smile and deep laughter lit the long hours for John and me. We tried to make the most of it. The endless singing, poetry and multiplication tables continued. This was no ordinary child – who knew how she might develop? What she lacked in learning she'd have to make up in originality. I wanted to help her learn to read fluently and with interest, to write clearly and accurately, to be able to perform simple mental arithmetic. Beyond this we groped for a way to develop her imagination and dormant sense of curiosity.

Early on, we reached the conclusion that most of the schooling Isso had received in the eight years she had been with us had been wasted. We remembered the primary schools adviser for Sutherland confidently assuring us, before Isso had even left Peru, that within six months she would be speaking perfect English. Eight years later we realised just how wrong this assumption had been. She could read, but it took such effort that she had no idea whatsoever of the story. She was unable to form a complete sentence, and her vocabulary was very limited, but she never asked when she failed to understand the meaning of a word. With hindsight, we should have concentrated on the English language first. All the other learning had gone right over Isso's head. She hadn't really understood half of what her teachers had been saying over eight long years.

John wasn't the same person as the one who had set off nine months previously, either. The hurt and pain almost forgotten, he seemed to be thoroughly enjoying the voyage and being with us all. Never could he be described as a patient man, so I was surprised at the endless care he took when teaching Isso. 'I'll teach that girl her multiplication tables or die,' he promised. On, and painstakingly on, they went. Then, one day, we realised that Isso had finally got it. Up and down she went, sometimes faster than John could keep up with. He declared that it was one of the most rewarding things he'd ever done. For light relief, Isso and I delved into the Indiana Jones atlas of South America. Our quest to find her real mother in Peru was probably going to be as exciting as any of John's adventures.

Six days out of Raivavaé, a gale was blowing as we approached the huge atoll containing the ten islands which make up the Gambier group at the very south-eastern tip of French Polynesia. This was our most difficult entry so far. The afternoon was wearing on, and we wanted to be sure of anchoring among the coral heads before dark. Steady drizzle turned to curtains of rain, obscuring the channel. From the plumes of surf exploding along the rocky shore we realised that the missing section of reef on the far side of the atoll was allowing a heavy sea to run across the lagoon. Only the islands themselves diminished the swell. Slaloming through the final set of coral reefs, we found ourselves in clear water at last, in a sheltered bay on the east coast of Mangaréva – 'floating mountain' – where swaying, writhing trees clothed the hills, rising steeply from the sea and disappearing into the racing grey cloud.

Creeping through the coral reefs in growing darkness and incessant rain, we came upon a big white square rigger. Lying there, shrouded in mist, she could have been the London Missionary Society ship *Duff*, whose captain had named this group of islands after the English Admiral Gambier in 1797. Wind-blown figures in heavy oilskins waved as we ran in close, comforted to see fellow humans in grim weather. 'Colchester!' I gasped in astonishment, reading the port of registry on her stern.

'Feelthy British!' John laughed into the wind, unable to catch the reply as we swung by.

We dropped anchor 100yds away and went below to get dry and try to warm ourselves with a cup of tea. 'It was in the *Onedin Line* television series, was that,' said Andy authoritatively, his seasickness forgotten. 'The *Soren Larsen*. From her stern right out to the end of her bowsprit, she'll be all of a hundred and fifty foot.'

The stove was just lit when, to my dismay, a large inflatable bearing half a dozen burly figures roared over. But they surprised us with a kind invitation. 'Would you all like to come to dinner, tonight, seven-thirty?' We had no hesitation in accepting. Bec, Isso and I dressed up in our most exotic *pareus*, which we fastened with beautifully carved Polynesian black oyster shells. John chickened out of wearing the jazzy floral shirt I had bought him in Papeete, which he thought hideous, and he certainly did not intend to wear his *pareu*. He settled instead for a white shirt and duck shorts, muttering, 'It is a British ship, after all.' And as we were moored close by, just this once we left no one on board and all six clambered into the inflatable that came to pick us up. Tiki was in charge.

Eager hands helped us up the wooden walls and friendly English voices greeted us as we emerged, blinking into the bright light on deck. What a lovely shock it was to suddenly find ourselves among our own countrymen again. A huge 'Happy Birthday' tinsel streamer proclaimed the occasion being celebrated – in fact it was three birthdays on this ship with thirty passengers and crew. John needn't have worried about what to wear because everyone was in fancy dress. Our three fellows looked rather strange in their 'correct' attire.

What a change of mood this was! We had felt grimly anxious during the previous few days on our voyage here, and until that moment I don't think we realised how much we had missed the English sense of humour, irreverent jokes, sharp innuendo and the grumblings we understood so well. People of vastly different age and background, used to the comforts of their own homes, gave vent to all the prickles developed over weeks, and in some cases months, of being penned up in the confines of a sailing ship. The drips from the decks, the surfeit of bananas, the cramped damp of the cabins, the peculiarities of other people, the heat, the boredom of the long passages and all the 101 other irritations we had endured ourselves. But soaring above the trivial was the impression that this was the place to be: where the action was. This was no grey day at the office, but glorious Life.

There were two other guests, both shaven-headed private soldiers in the Foreign Legion. They were working on the island, building roads and other permanent facilities. Thin as a whippet, the narrow-faced Portuguese soldier spoke little English, but the bull-like Scot, clad in a black shirt fastened at the throat with a Harley–Davidson brooch, barked harsh responses to the inquisitive. He was prepared to reveal that he was from Fife, but little more, except that he wouldn't recommend anyone to join the legion.

'Is it true you can join the legion to avoid a jail sentence elsewhere?' gushed a pretty girl.

'Aye!' glowered the legionnaire.

'Would you say the romantic image of the Foreign Legion is justified?' asked Will conversationally.

'Aye, if getting yer balls broken every day is romantic.'

Next morning rain and wind still swept the anchorage. Our new friends on the *Soren Larsen* sailed at noon, and the anchorage seemed empty afterwards. It was too windy to paddle ashore, so we got on with preparing the boat for the rigours ahead: leading sheets and furling lines to the winches around the aft cockpit, servicing winches and running rigging, sealing any leaks which had come to light. We stowed away our summer gear and the snorkelling kit, aired the heavy red Henri Lloyd sailing suits and rooted around to find the fibre-pile clothing to wear beneath them.

The Mangarévan people believed that magicians would come to their island, bringing with them an all-powerful god. So when French Jesuit priest Honoré Laval, of the Congregation of the Sacred Hearts, arrived from Chile with another priest in 1834, the islanders submitted completely to his ruthless and inflexible moral code. As virtual slaves they built the vast 1,200-seat white coral rock cathedral whose twin square towers I could make out from the doghouse, dominating the heavily wooded shoreline among a scattering of flimsy huts. During Laval's joyless thirty-seven-year reign, the population dropped from 9,000 to 500. Laval was eventually taken away by a French warship, tried in Tahiti for murder and declared insane. When he died his body was brought back to Mangaréva for burial in his beloved cathedral.

Yet history records that he banned the rampant cannibalism for which these islands had been renowned, increased cultivation and improved living standards. The dramatic decrease in the population could have been caused by the European diseases brought in by foreigners, rather than by Laval's regime itself. To dispel the all-pervading superstitions, with his own hands he overturned the feared stone *tikis*.

When the weather eased we went ashore and walked around the empty cathedral. Light filtered through tall windows and we had to keep reminding ourselves that we were in the Pacific, not in Europe. In the silence we found the plaque dedicated to the memory of Laval. As we wandered around the precincts of the cathedral, where there were more remains of fine buildings and arches, we wondered what must it have been like trying to survive on a remote island with people literally wasting away all around you. What had driven Laval to achieve so much. Can it have been faith alone?

In our search for the meteorologists' advice, John and I walked up the steep muddy track to the weather station, which sits astride a headland to the west some 500ft above the village. Passing through dense woodland, we came upon a small cemetery containing the noble mausoleum for the thirty-fifth king of Mangaréva, whom Honoré Laval converted to

Christianity, and the ruins of the convent where young Mangarévan virgins would have spent their lives in devotion. The convent grounds were now being used as a market garden. An old gardener showed us the large stone-lined pit which is all that remains of the breadfruit store traditionally maintained in case of famine.

Cyclones are very expensive, and the regional government takes very seriously the weather reports which come from the south-eastern tip of its 1.5 million-square-mile territory. At the station we found Dominic Devaux, a slim gentle Frenchman, one of three meteorologists manning this fortress-like building on the very rim of the world. Dominic had softened the station's concrete drabness by adding gentle coloured photographs of Pacific wildlife to the alarmingly graphic posters detailing procedures for surviving cyclones. Handing us the latest forecast, he smiled, 'If Honoré Laval had never come to Gambier, it would not be the place it is today. Bon voyage, mes amis.'

There was no time to waste. We had only a few hours before the next front was expected. We cleared the reef just before dark, heading for the lonely British outpost of Pitcairn, a couple of days further south.

'Dad, I think you should come up and take a look. We can see the coconut trees and hear the surf,' Bec called anxiously to John, an hour before our watch was due to begin at midnight. She spoke softly, as always, and I knew he had trouble hearing her. He was muttering as I followed him through the galley and up the vertical ladder into the doghouse.

'There it is – listen,' said Bec urgently. The surf boomed in the dark, glowing luminous white all along our port bow. Beyond lay a dark line of palms. Bec flicked the radar range to 3 miles and we saw the whole atoll grow greenish-white on the black screen. John called a course alteration to Will out in the blackness and pointed out the projection of our new course on the screen. Now we should clear the Portland Bank, which lay unseen to starboard.

Pitcairn came up for us, early one morning, a grey wind-torn smudge on the horizon, 300 miles south-east of the Tuamotus, just as it had for twenty-four-year-old Fletcher Christian aboard the *Bounty*. His chronometer had told him that this little dot was incorrectly plotted on the chart. 'This is where we'll stay, hidden for ever!' I could almost hear the triumph and desperation in his voice as he rallied his nine mutineers and the Tahitian beauties who'd come with them.

Everyone knows the story of Pitcairn and the mutiny on the *Bounty*, and Clark Gable, Marlon Brando and Mel Gibson have all played Fletcher Christian. Now we were going to meet his family. Approaching the islands I tried to put together the pieces of the story and understand how it had all happened.

It seems that Lieutenant William Bligh was a determined man. He'd learned his business under no less a figure than Captain James Cook. Sent from England by King George III in 1787 to barter for breadfruit in Tahiti and take them for replanting in the West Indies, Bligh commanded a 100ft merchantman with some forty crew. An authoritarian figure Bligh may have been, but Cook was more severe in the matter of discipline: he never hesitated to have his men flogged if they broke the rules, and native islanders who threatened his position were quickly put to death. With Captain James Cook everyone knew just where they stood. Bligh, however, was not quite as straightforward. His quick temper and sarcastic tongue deprived his men of their dignity and created resentment.

John favoured the theory that the mutiny occurred because Bligh was too soft. Cook believed in the strict rotation of shore parties to avoid permanent attachments forming between his men and the captivating Polynesian women. Bligh allowed his men to stay too long ashore. They did more than gather breadfruit cuttings; they fell under the spell of beautiful women they couldn't bear to leave.

Off the island of Tofua, on 27 April 1789, three weeks into their voyage to the West Indies with the breadfruit plants, Bligh hounded and humiliated Christian in front of the crew, who whispered that they would support him if he led a mutiny. He agreed. No blood was spilled, and Bligh, along with eighteen loyal crewmen, half the ship's company, were put off in an open boat with rations and a sextant. After putting some of his men ashore, Bligh made one of the greatest of all open-boat voyages, covering 3,600 miles and landing in Timor, now part of Indonesia. He returned to England, where he was court-martialled for losing his ship and exonerated. The Royal Navy commenced its relentless search for Christian and his mutineers, dispatching *HMS Pandora* to Tahiti. Bligh, meanwhile, was given another ship and it was he who eventually brought breadfruit to the West Indies after all.

The mutineers had returned to Tahiti aboard the *Bounty*, haunted by the knowledge that the Royal Navy would hunt them down. Reunited with his Polynesian sweetheart, Fletcher Christian told his followers they must find somewhere to hide. Some chose to remain in Tahiti; the others set off with the very latest chronometer to help them find their way. First they tried Tubai, not far from Raivavắe, but they abandoned the island after killing sixty natives. Then they discovered Pitcairn, barely 1.5 miles long. It was impossible to anchor safely, much less maintain the three-masted *Bounty*, so they set her on fire. She duly sank in Bounty Bay and they were stranded.

The island appeared quickly. By mid-afternoon we were sliding along under reduced sail, close under the east coast. A dirt track wound up the 'hill of difficulty', which rose steeply to over 1,000ft. More than a dozen little houses, all different, poked out from various levels on the mountainside, each sheltered among the trees and bushes.

Foolishly, Fletcher Christian shared out all the land among the Englishmen, ignoring the Polynesian men who accompanied them. So the two groups lived separately. The mutineers began to fall out with each other and fight, and one killed himself with drink. On learning that the Polynesians were planning to kill the Englishmen, Christian staged a pre-emptive strike which wiped out the natives and killed him, too. Within three years of the arrival of the mutineers in Pitcairn, there was only one man left alive: John Adams, a patriarchal figure in a community of women and children.

HMS *Pandora* rounded up the mutineers who had remained on Tahiti but failed to find Pitcairn. She sailed for home with the prisoners chained in the forecastle. Several of them were drowned when the ship was wrecked on the Great Barrier Reef, but three men were eventually hung at the yardarm in the Royal Navy Dockyard in Portsmouth Harbour.

Eighteen years passed before another ship called at Pitcairn. The crew of the American whaler were astonished when a young man paddled out in a canoe and hailed them in English.

'Echo-sounder, Isso. On "times one", please.' The little figure scuttled into the doghouse to switch on and begin her chanting. Peering over the rail, I could just make out patches of rock among the sand 50ft below. The water was a deep violent violet and I shuddered at the thought of the remains of the *Bounty* lying snug somewhere down there within a few yards of us.

A big easterly swell was bursting all along the cliffs. Over the radio we told the islanders we'd brought them sugar from Mangaréva. They had run out and were desperate for it.

'Just you go round the corner into Long Rope Bay. There's another yacht there, and a fishing boat. You drop your anchor there. We'll be round in twenty minutes.' The voice was strong, the accent an old-fashioned west-country burr.

Long Rope Bay was bounded by fearsome rocky teeth. Like the jaws of some giant dog, they slavered white with the long swell running in from under the black clouds now gathering in the western sky. The cavernous throat was backed by sheer black cliffs. There was no shelter. A lovely blue ketch, smart as paint, lay snubbing dangerously at her anchor. A small fishing boat, all tarnished aluminium and tall chimney stack, was circling uncertainly, bristling cranes and line-hauling gear. I read *Maclachlan* on her stern and assumed she was from New Zealand. I could see only two crew. The bare-chested young fellow on deck kept waving to us as if he'd seen no one but his middle-aged skipper for a very long time. John dropped the revs and we circled, too.

Then the islanders appeared, coming round the rocks from Bounty Bay, the same way we had. I think they called their boat the 'Tub' – it certainly looked like one; a dull, aluminium ship's-open-lifeboat sort of thing, built like a warhorse and trailing a plume of black smoke from dirty injectors.

'I hope they have an auxiliary motor,' John muttered, but everyone was gazing at the islanders. There were at least ten of them, bright as buttons, and every last one looked capable of mutiny. There were a couple of huge Polynesian men; several could have been English fishermen. The women were capably built. The helmsman moved his giant wooden tiller as if it were a toy. They were all whooping with joy.

Then the front crashed through. A dense black line of cloud crossed the island and the wind direction changed 180 degrees from north-east to south-west. Everything was suddenly back to front. The wind shrieked and it was raining cats and dogs.

The tub drew near. 'Bounty Bay'll be in the lee now, better go back there, then,' called another Olde English voice. But the wind would be following us, picking up from the south-east. Darkness was coming, and this had all the makings of a dirty night.

'We'll be heading on, it's too risky here. They gave us sugar for you in Mangaréva,' John shouted into the shrieking wind. 'Can we give it to you?' In a trice the man had hopped into a skimming dish of a tender and come alongside us, his curly head appearing and disappearing over the toerail on the swell.

'Ah well, maybe next time,' he laughed, lobbing a couple of shopping bags full of fruit on to our deck. 'You can never tell what this swell will do.'

We heaved the sack of sugar on to the skimmer. 'Have a good trip!' he called, and was gone. Dodging the bucking blue American, we headed into the darkness, bound for Easter Island, more than 1,000 miles on our way to South America.

'*English Rose* this is *Mai Tai*,' the radio called. It was the blue American. 'I just wanted to warn you. We left Easter Island ten days ago. All four yachts there lost anchors to the swell. The six-monthly supply ship lost both her anchors. I'm kinda surprised you're headin' that way at this time a year!'

The point was not lost on us.

JOHN

The six of us were performing better now. It may well have been the cooler weather, and there is no doubt that stroking Tiki soothed our nerves, but there was a new atmosphere of expectancy. The violent passage of the frontal systems, reminders of impending Southern Ocean winter storms, really forged the bonds.

For ten more days we persisted on our course for Easter Island, moving cautiously east and south, keeping the mainsail smaller than really necessary and generally taking care to avoid damage. But *Mai Tai*'s radio warning of storms haunted me and finally persuaded me against visiting Easter Island.

By suppertime on 27 June, we were 2,047 miles west of Valdivia, our winter refuge on the west coast of Chile. We had seen no shipping in over a month. We all agreed it was time to take the plunge and tack south into the night, heading for the Roaring Forties. Once in the Southern Ocean, we could turn towards the great barrier of the Andes, riding the westerly winds which run along the northern sides of the depressions in those desolate wastes.

The immediate change of climate saw the departure of one visitor and the arrival of another. The red-tailed tropic bird, beautiful and lonely, with his silky white plumage and long red tail streamers, had occasionally appeared at dawn or dusk, like the dove of peace, far, far out from land. But he liked the warmth and now he was gone. In his place came the cheery Cape pigeon with his unmistakable chequered mantle, wheeling to and fro across our wake, searching for anything the racing keel might churn up.

The moon was on the wane, already down to half-size. I shuddered at the thought of a full two weeks of black nights and pencilled a general warning in the log:

> We are approaching a danger area. Exceptional storm tracks are marked on our path on the US pilot chart for the month of July. We need to get it RIGHT FIRST TIME. Recent errors include: main vang led wrongly, winch handles not secured in pockets, topping lift left caught round main backstay. Below decks, ensure all locker lids beneath seats are fastened and taped closed. Nothing should FLY if we get knocked down. THINK.

Bec made a bright new flag for the Dan buoy pole. And at her position in the doghouse, Isso was tested on hitting the blue 'man overboard' button on the GPS. Such a grim eventuality would spell the end of the family of cockroaches which, seeking warmth like the rest of us, had recently had taken up residence in the casing of this instrument. By night they could be seen shinning up and down its shiny black case in the creditable cause of physical fitness. Yet again Bec had us talking through the abandon-ship procedures and I wondered how we'd cope with the mizen staysail and all the jerrycans of drinking water she was insisting we took with us.

The weather deteriorated sharply as a grey north-east gale pushed us south, and it wasn't long before I was protesting about the wet state of the logbook. As if to remind us that we were in the Roaring Forties, a rogue wave burst over us in the middle of the night, sending a jet of cold water backwards down a ventilator and drenching poor Marie Christine as she lay asleep in her bunk.

We changed the rig to my old Southern Ocean favourite: small Yankee, small staysail and trisail. All sheets were now operated from the aft cockpit, using the shelter of the new doghouse as well as the new four winches on the stern. With the main boom lashed to the deck and both running backstays led aft, we dealt more easily with the violent wind shifts which came with the passage of each front.

There was no other way but east, and, close-hauled on a north-east wind, we were moving like a surfaced submarine. As I snatched at sleep, the bows thumping into the grey seas sweeping the boat, sneaking doubts began to fester. But up in the cosy new doghouse, well wrapped up and snug by the glowing GPS, the name of Arun Bose, master crafts-man, was sung to the highest.

'BEC SIGHTS THE FIRST ALBERT!' I read the log entry with chagrin. Ever since she was little, I'd always won the Penguin chocolate biscuit prize for a first sighting of land and such like. Now I'd missed both the Cape pigeon and the albatross. Swinging his 10ft wing span across our wake, the wandering albatross symbolised independence and a free spirit, the whole purpose of this long voyage. In 1887 an albatross was found dying on the beach at Fremantle, Western Australia. Tied to its neck was a tin on which French sailors had scratched a message, appealing for res-cue after being shipwrecked on the Crozet Islands, 3,500 miles to the west. I love the whole idea that maybe, riding the westerlies, albatrosses circle the globe every two years or so, living for eighty years or more, quite independent of man.

In the early hours of Sunday 10 July, our barometer slid below 1,000 millibars for the first time in nine months, and our first Southern Ocean blow commenced in pitch dark. We dropped both trisail and staysail. Now only a scrap of Yankee, high on the forestay, pulled us along by the nose. With over twelve hours of darkness in every twenty-four, there was time for fear. The waves grew and the sea became stippled with white which glowed and crept in the blackness. The roar of unseen overtaking rollers could silence any conversation. Welded by danger, everyone pulled together.

We stretched two forestay rigging screws on this voyage and the threads were stripped when they were undone. I often wondered at the weight of the fully furled Yankee wrapped round the forestay. It shook the entire boat much too heavily for my liking. For stability, I began to unfurl a little staysail and a bit of Yankee. Maybe a new heavier forestay and a bigger rigging screw should be fitted along with furling gear.

Running along the northern edge of the Roaring Forties, we were kept close beneath the South Pacific high-pressure zone. And, helped per-haps by our strategy of patience, we were let off lightly, escaping with no more damage than a chafed furling line. And for the next week we crept steadily east, overtaken by a succession of shallow lows and drawing ever closer to the Andes, which stretched directly across our path. Unlike the Polynesian islands, behind which we had always found shelter, there was no way round the great barrier lying before us. In the absence of weather forecasts in this deserted part of the world, the barometer became the crystal ball in which we tried to read our future. We must not arrive in a storm.

Dawn came slowly on 17 July, a misty, moist morning of universal grey. A Watch were hand-steering – minus Isso, who had transferred to Andy's watch to help out with providing food, reading the barometer and filling in the log. Marie Christine and I missed the volatile South American presence. At the wheel we fortified ourselves with mugs of hot cocoa, home-made bread and pamplemousse marmalade. Shortly after eight, I glimpsed the outline of a rocky headland, dipping into the sea far out on our starboard side. This was Punta de la Galera. After thirty-one days at sea, we were less than a dozen miles off the mouth of the river, leading up to Valdivia.

The sea changed from ocean blue to muddy green and we were surrounded by more birds than I had ever seen at one time. In the near, middle and far distance, varieties of albatross, clusters of Cape pigeons, pairs of storm petrels, shearwaters, black back gulls and terns all wheeled about their business. And flocks of heavy black birds with wedge-shaped tails settled on the water between patrols.

I have found no means of arrival to compare with the thrill of the first landfall after long weeks at sea.

'I seen it! At last!' crowed Isso, when we hauled her on deck. And she went scuttling forward to sit alone, peering through the murk at the first shades of 'My Country' and looking for signs of 'My People'. Our daughter, now fifteen. From my position at the wheel, I looked along the length of the boat wondering what might be going through the mind of the little figure huddled in her red oilskins up in the bows. She had left Ardmore a schoolgirl; now she had blossomed into a young woman, intensely aware of her appearance, turning out each day in a different outfit. Her glossy dark hair framed her oriental features and her shadowed, slanting eyes hid from us the secrets of unspeakable cruelties visited on her 'People', in the name of religion, politics and civilisation, by her own kind and by European colonists. I'd been reading Isabel Allende's *The House of the Spirits*, and after many visits to this turbulent continent, I'd come to appreciate just how hideously truthful an account it was.

13

Ranches and Ruins

JOHN

The coast loomed out of the mist. Below a thick mantle of dark primeval forest, covering even the hilltops, a ragged quilt of fields linked isolated farms. Providence had smiled on us. We had indeed arrived in calm weather. Passing the ruined forts of Morro Gonzalo, we entered a wide estuary. Squadrons of black cormorants came flying low over the steep brown seas to meet us.

'Good waves for kayaking, John,' chortled Andy, his thick black moustache riding up and down with pleasure at the thought of three months' relief from seasickness. I shuddered and Bec giggled at the memory of the Cape Horn canoeing. A steady cold drizzle set in as we opened up the little port of Corral. All but destroyed in 1960 by the most severe earthquake ever recorded, it appeared to be no more than a scattering of bleak huts lying among giant heaps of yellow wood chips bound for Japan.

Turning to port, we entered the river, safe at last from wind and sea. A great load lifted from my shoulders. Will passed up mugs of steaming coffee from the galley and I increased the revs, letting the eighty Mercedes horses push upstream against the flood of black winter water between steep forested riverbanks. Poor Isso looked glum. She'd hoped for a little more warmth from 'my South America'. Any notion of leaving *English Rose* in a cradle on the shore while we visited Peru vanished when we passed a wreck left stranded by a tidal wave a couple of miles upriver from its home port.

Some ten miles inland we came into marshes where the river grew wider, meandering through islands of tall winter-bleached rushes: a haven for jostling moorhens, black-necked swans and flights of huge grey and white pelicans, which came skimming downstream on their way to some Sunday lunch rendezvous. This marshland had been prime pasture until the riverbed was raised by the earthquake in 1960.

Slowly, distant spires grew into churches as we came into Valdivia, which looked for all the world like a small European town. Near the centre, on a tangle of ancient wooden pilings, stood a sentry box, standing guard over a handful of small yachts. And written in tall black letters on the end of a long, white corrugated-iron shed, we saw the Holy Grail: 'Club de Yates Valdivia 1912'. We were home.

The storm swept in from the coast just three hours later.

MARIE CHRISTINE

That evening we walked into town. It was dark and raining. 'Looks like Poland,' said Will despondently. The streetlights reflected in the puddles illuminated a dismal scene: concrete road slabs lifted and broken, shanty houses leaning haphazardly in any direction. It was as if the earthquake had happened only recently, not thirty years before. We had built up such high hopes of Valdivia, and this was not how we had imagined it would be. I wondered how Andy was feeling. He would be staying here for three months.

Soaked through, we arrived back on the boat after a greasy first meal ashore. But these disappointments couldn't quench my excitement. I was just so happy to have arrived. John and I soon reassembled our doghouse bed. The three dusty planks were passed up from the floor in our tiny cabin and the red vinyl cushions placed on top, then our two musty duvets and extra sleeping bags for insulation. It was a miserably damp, cold night, so we fitted the blue canvas storm curtain outside the hatch dropboards, lacing it well to keep out rain and wind. Tiki was delighted with the new arrangements, and soon commandeered our bunk in the doghouse. It was perfect, for she saw herself as guard cat: watching out of the windows, her lower jaw would tremble as she uttered a strangled squeak when anyone came along the pier, or a bird had the temerity to come near.

Horizontal rain battered us all night and the black riverwater gushed and gurgled past our safely secured home, nestled against slimy wooden pilings on the outer side of the old wooden dock. I realised how lucky we were to have arrived when we did.

Over the INMARSAT, Rita confirmed that J.W. and Bruce were flying out to join us at the end of September. Knowing them both very well, we were confident that we would be a strong crew by the time we reached Antarctica in January. John and I had discussed endlessly what was best for Will. I am sure he would never have let us down, but it was obvious that he hated being on the boat. With the extra two fellows coming, he wasn't needed as crew. His idea of trying for a place on a course at Cirencester released him from *English Rose* with his honour intact. I couldn't decide how Bec was feeling – she was a closed shop on this affair of the heart. But I knew that with Will absent when we resumed our journey in October, she would miss him terribly.

Next day, we sat in the saloon surrounded by piles of mail that had been awaiting our arrival. The yacht club must have wondered who this English Rose was as parcels and letters from our loving families at home filled and overflowed a big box they had marked 'Yate English Rose' in the club secretary's tiny office. We were munching happily on fresh food – bread, cheese, tomatoes and milk that Isso and I had rushed out to buy – when there was a loud knock on the roof and gruff voices called for Ridgway and Burchnall. We peered up through the main hatch to see who it could be. Surely we had seen all the officials? But these visitors burst into hoots of laughter. It was Will's cousin Ed and his fellow student Cedric, who had driven overnight from Argentina, just getting through the snow-covered passes in the storm.

Bec and Will had decided to see some of South America before he returned to England and ever since we arrived they had been in and out of town trying to make plans. The invitation to Cedric's family *estancia* in Argentina would be a perfect start to their tour. In a whirl they packed, and set off the next day with their two pals.

Will was wearing his broad-brimmed South African hat and Bec brightened the greyness of the wet day in a turquoise and lilac jacket, the multi-coloured scarf that she, Isso and I took it in turns to wear wound around her head and neck. We waved them off, wondering whether we'd ever see Will again. 'The most dangerous thing they'll encounter on this whole trip is driving on these roads with those two!' John muttered through clenched teeth.

'They'll be all right, don't worry.' But it was pointless saying anything. Bec and Will had a bit over a month to travel around Argentina,

Paraguay and Bolivia, and neither we nor they knew where they were heading. It would be the first time we had ever been out of touch for so long.

'Make sure you're at the Hostal Familiar in Cuzco by the beginning of September!' John shouted out final instructions for the hundredth time to Rebecca. We so wanted to go together as a family to Peru, to be there with Isso when she met her Peruvian family. But I rejoiced for Will and Bec. At last the two of them were away from the claustrophobic atmosphere of the boat and us. We all needed a break from each other.

REBECCA

Cedric had invited us to stay at his stepfather's *estancia* just over the border for as long as we liked. He loved the *estancia* lifestyle, and the more the merrier: four would not rattle around as much in the big house as two. We could travel back with him and Ed in the hire car, sharing petrol and the rental fees. Will and I had planned to go off skiing at Antillanca, perched up at the end of a dirt track on a volcano on the Chilean side of the Andes, but we could do this on our return.

Our only form of contact with the boat was by fax via Ardmore. I faxed Rita, who faxed Andy on the boat. He could fax anywhere to Mum and Dad, but some South American machines are not all that reliable. At least Rita and Andy would know if any of us were overdue or in trouble.

We all needed a break from each other and the boat, and I was dying to get out and see the green fields and primeval forested mountains of the Andes.

The dull, grey morning brightened as we loaded the car. Already a great weight seemed to have lifted off Will: once again he was the amusing person I had fallen in love with a little over a year before. Our relationship had certainly been through some tests since then.

To see something of the country, we decided to take minor roads. The hire car had limited kilometrage, but we had sufficient time for a few detours. We soon learned that minor roads in South America are dirt farm tracks at best, and within ten minutes of leaving Valdivia, we were all out pushing. There were lots of jokes, and I could see that Ed and Will were very fond of each other after many summer holidays spent in the Scottish Highlands as children. Will and I were just thrilled to be out in the lush countryside, which was a sort of unkempt version of the

Scottish borders. Huge poplars and oaks stood silent and silvery-grey waiting for spring; sheep and cows grazed on the rich grass. But the people looked downtrodden and poor, grubby urchins hitting skinny dogs with sticks by ramshackle wooden houses. There were no solid stone farmhouses with smart country cars parked outside. But after the grey rolling seas of the winter Southern Ocean, everything appeared fresh and alive and growing.

We had no luck in finding snow chains, so we stopped for the night in an old wooden *hostal*, where we showered to the roar of the gas water heater, an unparalleled luxury. Without chains but with great hope, we set off for the pass over the Andes into Argentina. Higher and higher into the dripping forest we drove. Sawmills sat outside the small homesteads, rickety steam engines on the sodden grass providing the power. Some people sat high and straight on fine horses wearing ponchos and wide-brimmed sombreros; others walked. The local class system was obvious to all.

At a roadblock a smart uniformed man stepped out of his wooden sentry box and told us that the pass had been closed the day before due to heavy snow. It would not be opened again until the spring. He suggested we tried the next border crossing to the south, which was not quite as high. There we could catch the daily ferry across Lago Pirehuelco and cross the Huakum Pass into Argentina.

There had been very few cars, but now there were none, only the odd heavily laden lorry carrying timber down from the mountains. Back in the dripping forest, we passed a lone man hitching. He wore a yellow plastic jacket, wellies and a hard hat. I insisted we gave him a lift. He answered my pidgin Spanish questions shyly. He said he was lucky to have a job three days a week at the large sawmill, where the ancient forests were being chipped and sold to Japan for paper. He had no transport, so he had to walk the 11 miles to and from work.

It was late, dark and snowing when we arrived at Puerto Fui on Lago Pirehuelco, a single street of wooden shacks with nowhere to stay. Cedric and I walked to the kitchen door of one of them. Through the cracks between rough planks, I could see two buxom teenage girls, their thick, black hair tied back, in skirts and bare legs. The man of the house sat slouched over the table, weary from work or drink. Cedric and I looked at each other and he knocked loudly.

Cedric asked the wife if we could stay there, while I added the odd 'Por favor, señora,' and shivered. Eventually she agreed and brought glowing embers from the stove in the kitchen and placed them carefully in the pot-bellied stove in another room. The daughters rushed into two back rooms and straightened beds; there were no sheets, so they did not need changing. Bedpans were emptied and all was set. The fire slowly began to put out some heat as we huddled round it. Will and Ed reminisced about the family holidays during which, it seemed, Ed was always in trouble.

Supper was tagliatelle and a couple of fried eggs. I felt content. I would far rather stay in a shack with real local people than in a smart hotel. Just as well, really, as I never have the choice.

At 3.45 am a typical South American commotion began outside. Lights were flashing, horns beeping, engines revving. Someone began banging on our window shouting, 'Gringos, vamos!' The ferry had decided to leave at 4 am instead of 7 am. We were up and out in double-quick time. We crossed our fingers, the grey Renault 12 started and we rolled on to the open ferry. It was still pitch dark when we drove off, two hours' sleep later, in the bitter cold. Up, up into the snow-covered Andes. The border was not yet open. I fingered my British passport, wondering how fondly these men remembered the Falklands conflict. The multitude of checks made me feel nervous, but with a nod and rubber stamp, we were through.

Up higher still, every branch and twig was coated with frozen snow. The sun rose on the Argentinian side of the Andes, piercing the forest with its brilliant golden rays. The trees began to thin as we hairpinned our way up through fresh snow, having to get out and push occasionally. Snowball fights were inevitable.

Once we were over the Andes, the weather and vegetation changed dramatically, the rain shadow creating an arid landscape of tall separate pines. The mass of moss and lichen ended with the dripping Chilean dampness. Suddenly we were in an alpine land and the air was dry.

Way down below the pass we came to San Martin de los Andes, a modern European-style ski resort, years away from Chile's steam-operated sawmills. Four cups of coffee and four slices of unexciting cake cost US$14 – more than double what we had paid for supper and a bed the night before in Chile.

By late afternoon, and after several wild-goose chases down roads that turned out to be blocked by snow and hours of dry open plains, we turned off the main road to San Carlos de Bariloche at a large gate with 'Estancia Rincón' carved into it, just like something in the movies. Up a

bumpy drive and through some trees, we arrived at Cedric's 'bungalow' – single-storey, yes, but some 25m square with a courtyard in the
centre. On the walls of the courtyard hung dozens of mounted stags'
antlers. In the dusk they sent a shiver down my spine.

Ruben, the Chilean retainer, lived in two rooms filled with boxes
adjoining the main house. Short, unshaven and unkempt with a wild
light in his eyes, he looked after the dogs, fed his ducks and watched the
trapped trout grow in their pond. He shared his *maté* gourd, a grubby
bulb of herbal tea while chatting about his passion for old Indian arrow-
heads which he found close by. People rarely listened to poor old Ruben.

Soon Mr Touyare, the manager of the *estancia*, arrived from
Bariloche with the keys to the house and apologetically let us in. Will
and I gulped at the luxury. A corridor led round the inside of the square,
its inner-facing wall almost completely consisting of windows and the
outer one leading into various luxury en-suite bedrooms. There was a
large drawing room with great ships of sofas and a 3m open fireplace.
Old leather trunks ornamented the room; large modern oil paintings
hung from the walls. One wall held bookshelves with a few books,
lumps of crystal, stuffed birds and an array of *maté* gourds. Through a
swinging door was the dining room, furnished with a heavy, thick dark
wooden table and a dresser. Through another swinging door was a
large pristine white kitchen with white tiles on the floor. The rest of the
house had parquet flooring and underfloor heating. I gasped, trying not
to look too out of my depth. If we had not been living in an 18m tube
for the past year, I am sure this would not have looked so amazing, but
the space! Our whole boat would have fitted into the kitchen alone.
Maybe I could get used to being Lady Muck.

We spent the next ten days running or walking before breakfast;
shooting, or trying to shoot, hare in the small fir-tree plantations; looking for partridges in the rough bush. I was always the beater, hoping the
innocent would get away. We rode with Juan, a one-eyed peon, a real
gaucho in short leather boots, baggy trousers gathered at the waist,
leather jacket, scarf round his neck and fedora hat. The effect was completed by a pair of Ray-Ban sunglasses. Here, I was a little nervous.
Pony-trekking during school half-terms and mules in Peru were the
extent of my riding skills, while the boys had ridden since early childhood. I was reassured and given a nice white horse.

Assuming this was the calmest out of the bunch, I climbed aboard and
off we went. Cantering was something I never really got the hang of, and

I had the bruises on my bottom to prove it. When the other horses took off, I found it impossible to restrain mine, so I had no choice but to follow. Of course, there were no hard hats or anything like that, so I just hung on. Hares often hid in or behind clumps of icchu grass, and would suddenly dash out causing the horse to start. It was not until several days later, when we had ridden over the hills through horse armpit-deep snow to a hut they called the refuge, used for stalking expeditions, that I discovered the horse I had been given to ride was specially selected not for its calm nature, but its colour - a woman must ride a white horse.

We stalked on horseback too, but here we saw the deer before one-eyed Juan. The highlight to his day was catching an armadillo-type creature. He raved about what good stew it made, and how we must all share it. It was hardly a substitute for venison.

We took a dinghy downriver, climbed high hills for barbecue picnics, slept whole nights in still beds, relaxed in long baths, used stationary loos without valves and pumps – and when the generator spluttered into life each evening, we used the washing machine and could always have clean clothes.

Sometimes we went into Bariloche to buy more food and have a drink in the buzzing ski town, but I preferred a quiet evening playing backgammon in front of the great log fire and laughing over dinner, just the four of us round the heavy jungle-wood table. We took it in turns to cook. We ate Cedric's Belgian-style whole chicken in a pot – his mother was Belgian – Ed's mince, into which he poured half a jar of strawberry jam, Will's steaks and my efforts at hare and chicken stewed in red wine.

After ten days, Will and I left for Buenos Aires with an invitation to return for Cedric's birthday in a couple of weeks' time. Our luxury stay in the hills had been equivalent to a city-dweller's break at a health farm.

Bus is really the only way to travel in South America, unless you can afford to fly. Our twenty-two-hour, 1,600km journey to Buenos Aires took us northward, across vast yellowy-brown cattle plains. We stopped for a while before darkness fell at a remote town built of uniform concrete houses, mushrooming around what seemed to be an ugly gasworks or chemical factory. Dawn found us still batting along the dead straight road. Every now and then a band of poplars would appear in the distance like giant spear heads in a great long row, as if lining the drive to the 'big house'.

Then we were engulfed by the sprawling mass of Buenos Aires, a city of 11 million inhabitants – almost a third of the country's population. There was not much 'good air'. Thousands of people thronged the bus station. I had heard that this was a dangerous city, so we hung on to our bags tightly, especially as my rucksack had a Union Jack sewn on the front. Will's friend Harry, an electrical engineer who imported robots and French shoes, had given us his address. Back and forth along the smart residential street we went: the address Harry had given us was a building site.

'Maybe Harry is working on the site,' Will suggested. We peered in through the open section of boarding that separated the site from the street. Twenty or so men, stripped down to their trousers, exhibited fat brown bellies as they drilled and mixed cement. At one side was the *parilla*, or barbecue, where great sides of beef sizzled for lunch.

A quick telephone call eventually traced Harry. Tall and slim with fair hair, he smiled readily and made us feel very welcome. Playing the old-style English gentleman abroad, he spoke excellent Spanish and seemed to fit easily into the cosmopolitan lifestyle of Buenos Aires. He never stopped to draw breath, telling one funny story against himself after the next. I'm still not sure if the wrong address was a joke or genuine mistake, but knowing Harry . . .

We enjoyed the masterful architecture of Buenos Aires and ate vast quantities of beef at Harry's favourite restaurants. It was surely the best beef in the world, eaten with the most creamy pureed potato or chips, seldom any vegetables, apart from a few leaves of salad. I'm sure this was because they could not fit them on the plate. Harry took us to the Sunday market in the San Telmo district, where the tango and beef-eating seemed to dominate life. We visited Evita Peron's tomb, perpetually decorated with sumptuous flowers, at the cemetery of the Recoleta, and saw the Casa Rosada, President Menem's offices, which are linked to the port by a tunnel. Then there was the grand Teatro Colón, built in 1908, with its marble staircases, red plush and gilt, and a warren of corridors leading to subterranean workshops.

People stopped us in the street and asked us if we needed any help, keen to show how Anglophile they were. Anyone mentioning the Falklands War did so apologetically. Will and I made a two-day excursion to Uruguay, chugging across the muddy delta of the Rio Plata aboard an unwieldy ferry. We stayed for a couple of nights off a cobbled courtyard filled with geraniums in the old fortified Portuguese town of

Colonia del Sacramento. Out of season it was deserted, apart from a few locals with their ancient cars. Blue and white Portuguese tiles proclaimed the names of the sycamore-lined streets where the inhabitants liked to stroll along discussing the past, a thermos flask of hot water under one arm and *maté* gourd in the other hand.

A generous-spirited shopkeeper gave us a bottle of wine to welcome us to his home town, and took us to see the old disused bull ring, the thriving racecourse and his two horses. When we came to leave, the old ferry had broken down, so our tickets were upgraded to enable us to take the modern British-built Sea Cat.

Armed with two Uruguayan cheeses, we crossed the Plata delta to Buenos Aires and headed south to watch right whales mating off Peninsula Valdis in Patagonia. These enormous majestic creatures seemed to be performing for us, so close that we could see the whiskers on their chins. We barbecued steaks and drank cheap wine before boarding the bus back to Estancia Rincón.

We got off to a bad start with Cedric's mother, who had just arrived from Europe. She was upset that we had left our kit on an unmade bed and a rucksack leaning against the bedroom wall. She screamed at the Peruvian maid and cook until they cried, and then it was our turn. We both apologised profusely, and Will, always courteous and often overly polite, was horrified by the outburst.

Dinner was served after drinks in the drawing room – sweetbreads and a vast bowl of apple sauce. I knew Will would have difficulty eating this but he gulped it down with the odd pained glance at me. The conversation was a little stilted. Even Cedric and Ed were pretty quiet now. I felt uneasy with the servants, seeing Isso in their frightened eyes.

Next day I stayed in bed, trying to sleep off a bad cold, while the boys went off skiing for the day. They returned full of exciting tales and Will brought a large box of hand-made chocolates for Madame, a small one for me and a smart cap for Cedric's birthday the following day.

We had asked Cedric if we could put our dirty clothes in the washing machine. The generator stayed on all day now, and he told us vaguely that if we just left the dirty clothes in a heap in our room, the maids would take them to be washed when they came to clean. Instead Will took our bundle along to the utility room on the other side of the courtyard, where both maids were hand-washing at the big stone sink. In his best Spanish, he asked if it would be possible to put the bundle of clothes into the machine. The maids looked blank. Eventually one of them nodded, indicating that he should leave the clothes on the floor.

We met in the drawing room before dinner. Our glamorous hostess, just back from Bariloche, came whirling in, still wearing her fur hat and long coat, and offered us all small savoury doughnuts from a crunchy paper bag. She left the room, but a moment or two later the door flew open and she was back, still in hat and coat, and began shouting like she had the day before, only worse. In a mixture of Flemish and English she let rip. At first none of us knew what it was all about, but then it became clear that our washing was the problem.

'How dare you ask my maids to wash that enormous pile of clothes! Don't you think they have enough work to do as it is? Most of those clothes should be dry-cleaned anyway. How dare you treat my house like a hotel!' Madame's eyes flashed between Will and me.

'I am most terribly sorry, Madame. I thought they could all go in the washing machine. It's my fault, I didn't mean . . .' apologised Will, but Madame turned and was gone.

Cedric's stepfather broke the awkward silence, smiling as he lay back on the sofa. 'Don't worry. As they used to say in Arabia, "When the camels pass you must wait till the dust settles." Everything will be all right in a minute.' I had a feeling that this was not an unusual scenario.

But a minute later, we heard Madame shouting louder and louder, and in she burst again. We all stood up this time. In her arms, she held our dripping clothes. Will again bent over backwards to apologise, but to no avail. After much ranting Madame turned to leave the room and Will followed, insisting that she give him back the washing so he could do it himself. This made her even more furious. Educated people, she declared, had no business doing their own washing.

Cedric and his stepfather tutted and shook their heads.

'Bec, I think we ought to go.'

Back in our room, Will and I packed, shocked by the row. Then Ed and Cedric appeared, ashen-faced by the turn of events. Cedric implored Will not to leave, but he was adamant. Raised voices could be heard from the drawing room. Supper would be a nightmare.

Then Madame arrived. 'Don't leave. Let me give you a kiss, and we'll forget about it all. Cedric so wants you to stay for his birthday. Won't you?' She pleaded in broken English.

'I think it's best if we leave now, Madame. Thank you for your hospitality. I was going to give you these when we left, so you might as well have them now.' Will handed her the box of chocolates.

Cedric gave us a lift into town. And as we drove along in the dark, I wished I had said to Madame: 'I thought my family was difficult, but now I've met you, I'm not so sure!'

Next morning, we caught an early bus for Chile. We were both quiet, stung by the events of the night before and wondering what we had done wrong. In the end we felt we'd had a lucky escape. On the way back to Valdivia, we stopped for a couple of days' skiing on perfect slopes on the uncrowded Chilean side of the Andes. Antillanca proved a great antidote to Cedric's mother's wrath. We skied all day and each evening swam in an outdoor pool, surrounded by snow-laden pines, to ease our tightening muscles. Back on *English Rose*, Will assembled his kit for England, while I whittled mine down for the weeks ahead with the three Rs. Then we boarded a bus for the long haul north to Peru.

Passing through the Atacama Desert, we visited Chunquicamata, the world's largest open-cast copper mine, 4km long, 2km wide and 600m deep; the El Tatio geysers, at 4,500m in a bitter dawn, and in the sunset, the stunning, eroded salt mountains which form Valle de la Luna. Crossing the border at last, we were thrust from the order of Chile into the chaos and colour of Peru.

Our time together was running short. We dreaded our eight-month separation. In the couple of days we had, I wanted to show Will something of true Peru before we took the tourist train from Puno to Cuzco. Again, we travelled through the cold night, in an old Peruvian bus whose passengers buried themselves in sacks and blankets for the journey. The bus broke down periodically until we arrived at the small market town of Llave, close to the shores of Lake Titicaca. Quite by chance, we had arrived on market day. We booked into the only *hostal* in town, a flat-roofed, unfinished-looking concrete building on the main square. Our room had two beds with plastic-covered mattresses and sheets that were not quite long enough to tuck in. The bathroom had a cold hose shower and a bucket for flushing the loo.

We stood on the roof watching the town coming to life. Women bearing great bundles tied up in striped cloths shuffled along with a rolling gait on the way to their pitches on the street. Children towed pathetically small sheep on the ends of ropes. The men had cheekfuls of coca leaves and *mantas* tied around their waists. Three small alpacas with coloured wool in their ears grazed on the smartly segmented square. Within an hour, the place was choc-a-bloc. One whole street was filled with women selling 'haberdashery' – fabric, powdered dyes from battered old tins, fancy threads and tapes and other brightly coloured wools. The next street sold herbs and spices of varying earthy colours – some from vast sacks with the tops rolled down, others in great lengths of small plastic sachets attached to one another – and plastic bags stuffed full of garlic.

In this area of town, all the traders seemed to be wearing traditional dress. Beneath their jaunty white stove-pipe hats or round felt bowlers, the women were round-faced with dark slits of eyes and rosy-chapped cheeks, their thick black hair hanging in two long plaits down their backs, tied together at the bottom with ornate woollen tassels. They wore layers of thin jumpers and cardigans, often brightly coloured, with the odd safety pin or needle tucked into them in case it were needed. They wore thick woollen skirts gathered at the waist and reaching below the knee. It appeared that each new skirt was put on over the old one for extra warmth, making it impossible to tell whether babies were imminent or not. Feet were often bare, or clad in practical sandals made from old car tyres. Great wads of banknotes were tucked into their waistbands, while anything else – wares, food, plastic sheeting and children – was carried on the back, wrapped in a *manta*. This hand-woven third-world rucksack, which often had to take much weight, was folded in half diagonally, then swung up on to the back. The men were less exciting in their dress, preferring Western clothes, but usually topped them off with a felt trilby hat and a beautiful hand-woven poncho with black, brown or grey background, whose lines of coloured design revealed the area its owner came from.

On the other side of the square was the less traditional market, stall upon stall of synthetic Western-style clothes sold by smart young traders with digital watches, flashy grins and gold teeth.

On our way to Cuzco, we visited the pitiful Uro–Aymara Indians living out on the floating islands of reeds on Lake Titicaca. There are no pure Uro Indians left as they have all intermarried with the land-dwelling Aymaras. Most of them have been beguiled by Puno's bright lights, but those who remain on the lake are almost totally reliant on tourists, reduced to selling model reed boats and sending out their snotty-nosed children to beg. We bought some deep-fried fish from an old crone and headed out into the lake for another four hours by open boat. At 3,855m, the altitude and brilliant glare from the lake gave me a splitting headache and I was much relieved to see the extraordinary island of

Amantini growing out of the haze ahead of us. Every patch of ground was turned over to the staple diet of potatoes.

With Abimael Guzman, the leader of the Shining Path movement, now safely behind bars, tourists had returned in great numbers to view what remains of the mighty Inca kingdom. The train to Cuzco was packed and vibrant, and even the market, where Dad had had his trouser pocket slashed by a pickpocket five years previously, seemed quite safe.

By now I was counting the hours to the dreaded moment when Will and I would have to part. I could hardly imagine what this gypsy life would be like without him to share the highs and lows, without the quick glances we exchanged whose meanings could not be explained in a thousand words. I would miss Will's jokes and tricks so much. We had been together almost every moment for over a year, just about as intense a relationship as any human could experience – and it had worked, it had grown. We were very much in love.

The bleak, bleached Altiplano with its patchwork of beige and brown, held together by low walls and thatched mud houses, stretched as far as the eye could see. Everywhere we looked we saw Isso.

On my way to meet up with the three Rs, I wanted to take Will to see Machu Picchu, which gives such an insight into the tortured history of this extraordinary Latin country. We woke early on 11 September, Will's thirty-first birthday and our last day together. It was as if our internal clocks knew we should not miss even a precious second of each other. I could hardly open my eyes, so red and swollen were they from the tears that had eventually turned into exhausted sleep the night before. I began to sing 'Happy Birthday' to Will, who lay next to me, holding me tight, but halfway through my quavering voice faltered and the sobs took over.

Machu Picchu, 2,280m above sea-level, was rediscovered in 1912, by an American, Hiram Bingham. The Quechua people told him of the ruins, but their grandeur and significance was not understood until an archaeological expedition from Yale explored them fully. Believed to be the last Inca stronghold, Machu Picchu was never found by the Spaniards. It seemed larger and more fantastic now than it had the previous time I had visited it, nine years earlier, just after we found Isso. The stunning setting – a jungle spur whose sides drop away almost vertically for thousands of feet to the Urubamba Valley below – added to my wonder at the amazing engineering feat created here by the Incas and their slaves – my sister's forebears. Temples, palaces, staircases, fountains, the famous sun dial and the knowledge that human sacrifices had taken place here all increased its power.

We wandered along grassy terraces held in place by smooth, sculptured walls of grey rock, with ten or twenty more above and below us, as the heat of the day began to build. The strains of 'El Condor Pasa', played on panpipes, drifted on the air. Choked by the splendour of Machu Picchu and the emotion of our last moments together, we hardly knew what to say.

14

A Prison and a Mine

JOHN

After Bec and Will left for Argentina, we spent another week in cold, wet, midwinter Valdivia. It rained incessantly. The yacht club was deserted on weekdays, the boats lying silent in the deluge. After our long stay in the tropics it felt like being in an unheated houseboat alongside the Thames towpath in January.

The names on the list of the yacht club committee members were all German; men descended from stalwart farming stock, who had come out from the Fatherland 100 years before. Their signature was every-where – on the land, in the factories and in the city. Their imprint was order, agricultural methods and architecture. The German College was just for Germans, and the faithful alumni funded it for as long as they lived. In many ways, Valdivia was like a small agricultural town some-where in the Germany of seventy years before.

MARIE CHRISTINE

It was with great joy that I stepped ashore in Chile. We had three hard months ahead of us, searching for Isso's family, but at least I was back in my own element. I could walk, run, jump; I could smell the earth, trees and grass, see the colours of the land. The desert ocean was behind us for a while. The hardships of living rough and bus travel would be nothing after what we had been through.

The yacht club had been established in 1912, when Valdivia, boosted by German immigrants, was at its most powerful and even today the members really only spoke in German. I dredged up my rusty finishing-school version of the language if I couldn't think of the right word in Spanish which, I think, confused matters even more. But when the moment was right I would launch into 'The Erlkonig' by Goethe. At the age of seventeen I had learned this off by heart to ensure that I would be allowed to go to the Schischule evening hop. I was quite infatuated with one of the older ski instructors and had to be there or die. The poem has stuck fast in my sieve-like brain and I am always confident that I can chant the verses mantra-style, even if I don't quite understand what I am saying. It never fails to impress: it's a bit like a foreigner reciting to an English-speaker Shakespeare's *Henry V* battle speech in its entirety.

The rain continued to pour down. As ever, the jobs needing to be done to prepare the boat for its greatest test, Antarctic ice, were legion. John, his half-specs resting on his nose, talked endlessly with Andy about possible problems and ordered new stronger paddles for the dinghy, a cabin heater and spares for everything. Valdivia, with its engineering bias, was going to be the place to get equipment made and jobs done, but very few people spoke English and Andy was quite worried about having to communicate such precise and vital requirements in Spanish. None of us could work out the Valdivian accent, which seemed to involve swallowing the ends of words. John's method was more pantomime than exact translation, but his antics and enthusiasm had the engineers and shop assistants enthralled and usually he got just what he wanted. In a cooler climate now, with the prickly heat finally gone, there was no stopping him. He had me and Isso out running each morning before breakfast. I quite enjoyed these trips, since they gave me a chance to see the gardens along our route, which were just showing signs of spring, although the bluebells, daffodils, pansies and primulas reminded me of my abandoned garden at home.

From the yacht club it was about a ten-minute walk into town. On our first night we had inadvertently walked through the back-street slums, but the direct route lay along gracious Avenida General Lagos, following the riverbank. Set in gardens with the finest camellias I had ever seen were once-fine townhouses, extravagantly styled in corrugated iron, using every variety of shape and decoration that could be imagined. But the 1960 earthquake had left some of them tilting rakishly, looking quite unsafe.

Isso and I spent most days in town, running errands and getting wet. First it was the washing. We carried the big bags between us, feeling quite ashamed when it was emptied out on the counter in the pristine Walther Heck Chic Laundry. Walther's daughter, dressed from head to toe in creaseless beige, fixed her disdainful ice-blue eyes on me as she listened to my lame story about having been at sea. I think she just dismissed us as dirty vagrants, which is what we were.

Packing our rucksacks on board the boat was a monumental task. We were going to need clothing for both heat and bitter cold. John had long detailed lists, but Isso had her own ideas about what she would wear, based more on style than on survival. She kept her kit in a thousand plastic bags beside, behind and in her bunk and fiercely resisted any interference. She coped valiantly, but without sweet Bec, the boat seemed gloomy and dank.

Early one morning, I caught Isso standing forlornly on the wet floor in the saloon, gazing at the tarnished brasswork on the bulkhead, which was beaded with condensation. Very slowly, fat tears squeezed from the corners of her slanting eyes and rolled silently down her cheeks. 'This is not my country,' she muttered. The Europeanness of everything was a huge disappointment to the little Quechua. My heart went out to her as she sobbed, 'I'm going to miss Tiki.' We all would. But I knew she meant she'd also miss Andy, whom she adored, and was already missing Bec and Will.

Were John and I doing the right thing, taking her back to meet her family? She was just fifteen, but in many ways more twelve going on seventeen. John was confident she would cope, but Isso herself was becoming anxious. Before leaving home I had felt she was too young to understand and handle the huge emotional hurdle of meeting her natural mother. We had agonised over the wisdom of bringing her back to Peru while she was still so young, but time was short. In November 1992, five days' walk from the nearest dirt road, John and I had found her mother and maternal grandparents living high in the mountains. Josefina, the granny who had cared for Elizabeth from the moment she was born, had begged me to bring her back to Peru so that she could see her one more time. 'I have not long to live,' she said.

We left the yacht that had been our home for ten months on Thursday 28 July. In the rain and dark we wobbled up the slippery plank to the shore and Andy passed over our heavy rucksacks. Calling goodbye, we staggered off to catch one of the rickety buses into town.

Would I get stronger? I wondered as I felt my legs buckle when I tried to step up into the bus. The bus station was a mass of people: families, students, businessmen and begging pregnant women.

Our shiny green bus had two drivers and two smiling conductors, all dressed smartly in green uniforms. From our seats I watched dark, stocky women unloading bunches of long-stemmed white, purple and blue scented stocks destined for the market. I longed to be where these had grown. But our 1,500-mile drive north would take us through these temperate lands and beyond, through the nitrate-rich deserts which comprise one third of Chile; then we would make a detour through Bolivia to show Isso a bit more of 'her South America', before heading north again into Peru, where our daughter had spent the first six years of her life, quite unknown to us.

Resistance soon sets in with a teenager if the message is stressed too heavily. Isso was below par anyway with a cold, so we soft-pedalled our fascination with the country unfolding before us as the bus sliced through vivid green fields on that straightest of roads, the Pan-American Highway, which, except for the Darien Gap in faraway Panama, stretched all the way to Alaska. Too soon we passed the yellow mimosa trees, blue wood smoke, oxen pulling carts, gnarled winter orchards and snow-lipped volcanos sleeping on the eastern horizon. After weeks of grey monotonous ocean, this bountiful land, with all its variety, was what I thirsted for.

Isso, however, was captivated by the television screen above her head, which beamed videos of oriental sex and violence day and night. Fortunately, I discovered that it was almost impossible to see the screen from the front seats, which were never in demand as they were in the most dangerous position. Struggling to explain the Falklands War to poor snuffling Isso on a bus map of South America, I realised just how big the gulf between our perspectives was.

JOHN

After a dozen hours we reached the sprawling, smoggy suburbs of Santiago. In the darkness of early evening, steady rain dimmed the lights of commuter traffic. It was a long time since we'd been in a capital city. This one lay in a bowl with a pall of pollution hanging over it. Several floors up in an old colonial building, we found a grim room for the night. The high walls were bare, save for a crude tortured painting of a giant eye crying unnoticed into a drain. By now, we'd all read Isabel Allende's account of the horrors of modern Santiago in *The House of the Spirits*. We felt glum and far away from Tiki.

In the morning we huddled under a dribble from a water pipe, our first shower since leaving Raiatéa in the Society Islands. Then we clambered up countless steps on Marie Christine's cultural tour. Gaining the ramparts of an ancient fortification and peering through the upper layers of smog, we could just make out the radiant white majesty of the Andes towering above the city.

Lunch was soggy brown paper bags of Chilean grapes, plums and bananas, eaten on a park bench, then it was time to dash for the bus station.

For twenty-four hours we bumped north before I was flattened by Isso's cold. We stopped for a couple of days at a flophouse in Arica, close to the Chilean–Peruvian–Bolivian border. At last, bum-sore and weary, we arrived in La Paz, capital of Bolivia, at 12,000ft. For the first time, in spite of a thumping headache from the altitude, Isso began to look excited. While Chile, with its German settlers, had seemed more like Europe than Latin America, here were the Altiplano people she recognised from her early life: women with their long black plaits, multitudes of skirts and babies slung over their backs in brightly coloured *mantas*.

We'd come here to get used to the altitude before heading north for Cuzco in Peru, visiting Lake Titicaca along the way. My wife lay in her bitterly cold bed, a flannel over her aching head. For a change she was suffering more than me from the altitude. This was my chance for a preemptive strike: to win the Bolivian programme: 'Now we are in Bolivia, we must visit a prison, a mine and a football match,' I suggested. Not for me soppy trips to colonial cities, still more ancient churches and sipping Pisco sours in shady orange-tree-lined squares.

'OK,' she muttered weakly.

'Good. First we'll try the prison.'

It was just another dusty beaten-up *plaza*, a square with a few dried-up trees and a bandstand. At least the sun was shining. Across the pestilential brown bowl containing the sprawl of La Paz, the snows of distant Mount Illimani glistened white and inviting. I thought for a moment I could see a route up the 20,000ft peak.

'Desculpe. Por favor, donde está el cárcel?' I asked a wizened old man of about fifty. He eyed me suspiciously, then his gaze softened, as he spotted the glimmer of an opportunity to sell some fruit from his stall. Smiling hopefully, he pointed at a grim grey wall lining the whole far side of the square. By way of thanks, I looked interested in his wrinkled tangerines.

'This is the right square, flower,' I called, sucking at the thin air. Marie Christine came plodding gamely round the corner, grey-faced from the altitude. It had been a long pull up from the main street. At her side, Isso looked bright enough, but I could tell she was still worried we were all going to spend the night in jail. Before crossing the road into the *plaza*, we bought some oranges and tangerines, thinking vitamin C might help some political prisoner.

This was a visiting day, and the square was thronged with waiting families gazing unhappily at the prison. Thick plaster peeled in huge flakes from the long castellated walls flanking the tin-roofed central block. From rifle slits and barred windows, frantic prisoners were signalling to loved ones and accomplices in a sort of racecourse tick-tack.

The stone archway was simply engraved with the year 1895. We jostled among the babbling crowd of Aymara and Quechua Indian visitors. Flourishing my large blue British passport, I looked as old and senior as I could, shouting above the din, 'Gran Bretaña! Gran Bretaña! Necesito visitar un hombre Norte Americano!' It was no good asking to see an Englishman: the embassy had told us the most recent British inmate had died in the jail.

It worked. Recognising someone at least as arrogant as himself, a young officer called to one of the guards at the table, who resentfully snatched our passports. Our right forearms were marked with a purple stamp. As we were led through, prisoners waved desperately at the steel bars, calling 'Americano! Americano!' I ignored them.

The guard left us, pointing at a suave-looking fellow facing the wall and speaking heatedly into a public telephone. Wearing a smart grey leather jacket and neatly pressed slacks, he looked oddly out of place. Noticing us, he put the phone down – a little too quickly, I thought. He smiled. 'Hello, I'm Nick Bozaninos. Which state are you from?' The voice was smooth and charming.

'I'm afraid we're feelthy British,' I replied, shaking hands and introducing Marie Christine and Isso. Nick suggested we take a look round the prison. We plunged into a maze of evil-smelling tunnels and winding passageways, passing several cells which doubled as stores, selling all manner of things. Here the prisoner-cum-shopkeeper slept in the gap between the ceiling and his stock. One tiny corner cell was even converted into a parlour for chess matches.

It may have been apprehension, but I had the feeling that the cells on the second floor were leaning over us. It was like some decaying village in the Middle Ages. Squat Indian women came barging through like pocket battleships, their long black plaits flying from under their brown bowler hats as they bent forward under huge loads wrapped in their *mantas*. It was all bustle. Children wailed and loved ones sobbed; shoddy lawyers hopped about like crows, with brown cardboard files under their arms. The male visitors looked just like the prisoners. We weren't pestered quite so much now we were with Nick.

'This place was built in 1895 for three hundred, but they've added bits on here and there,' he said, nodding at the rickety brickwork above us, 'and now there are sixteen hundred prisoners in here.' He looked nervous; his pale blue eyes were red-rimmed and watery, as if he were on the brink of tears. The combination of smart haircut, businesslike glasses and neat grey beard with consumptive cough and slight shivering made him look both urbane and vulnerable. I guessed I was more at home in this rough place than he was.

Stopping for a moment in a small open space of easily hosed concrete, I was glad to be out in bright sunlight. The surrounding cells, two storeys high, seemed less oppressive.

'How long have you been in here, Nick?' asked Marie Christine.

'It's six months now. It's all been a terrible mistake.' The words came jerkily, accompanied by an overpowering smell of garlic. Nick was a sick man. He'd been the Greek consul in Bolivia and ran a small import–export company which had gone bankrupt. Apparently, the Bolivian army owed him a lot of money for explosives. 'I am the first person to be extradited from America to Bolivia,' he shrugged hopelessly.

Eager to change the subject, he set off once more through the warren, explaining how the prison was run like a large piece of real estate. 'When you come in here you have to buy a bed or a cell from someone leaving the prison. The best cells cost two thousand US dollars. I share with one of the biggest mine owners in Bolivia.' I could see that the Mediterranean charm was beginning to win over my wife, but Isso remained inscrutable.

Passing through a heavy steel gate beneath an arch in the white wall, we came into a more refined enclave. 'This is Alamos, here live an ex-general of the republic, an ex-cabinet minister, an ex-bank owner, and several others . . .' Nick's staccato squeak trailed away. 'It is rent free and tax free. A girl visitor knifed one of the residents to death recently, but they were drunk. Generally, we live quietly.'

Taking a Yale key from his pocket, he opened the door to Cell 19. In the dark hallway a couple of bricks, each containing an electric element, served as a crude kitchen and provided employment for a poorer prisoner-cum-cook. A few cans of food lay on bare wooden shelves and steep wooden steps led up to an unfurnished bedroom above.

'Miguel, we have visitors,' Nick called through an open doorway. His tone betrayed his inferior role in the prison hierarchy. I guessed he would be sleeping in the bare room upstairs.

'Oh, hello. I'm Miguel Orlandini.' The deep confident voice was more English than ours. Our host turned away from the television at the far end of the room and came to greet us, a short, hugely overweight figure, almost round, in a vast red Gucci polo-necked sweater. We all shook hands and sat down on a sofa in what was little more than the dead end of a well-furnished but windowless low tunnel. Miguel had done his best. Four expensively framed prints of old-English pastoral pursuits lined the fresh cream walls, a couple of black cocker spaniels dozed on the ample bed beneath the television, and a pair of slatted wooden lampshades provided tastefully subdued lighting. Ignored, poor Nick was left hovering awkwardly by the doorway.

Perching on a wooden stool in the centre of the room, Miguel prepared to deliver – as he must have done on many previous occasions – the case for his defence. Thinning grey hair atop a massive pointed head led down to a full white beard; above it expensive rimless glasses pinched a big nose. His face broadened into a thick neck. This was a man used to power.

Miguel Orlandini Agreda was an oligarch, old Spanish. His family had come to colonise the new Spanish territories in 1600. Principally landowners around Cochabamba, they had been in mining for over 100 years. Miguel had had every advantage. He told us he was born in America in 1945 and sent to an exclusive Thames Valley prep school in England. From there he'd moved on to Downside, one of the best Roman Catholic public schools in the land, where he'd won an exhibition to read modern languages at Cambridge University, which led on to further studies in Geneva.

He had luxury homes in Florida and Madrid and he'd owned six

Rolls–Royces. He showed us a personal letter from George Bush, thanking him for contributing to the 'Fund for America's Future'. Miguel had always followed the good life, believing in the old adage, 'South America is nice from afar, and far from nice!' But while he travelled the world, visiting tin-smelters and developing the family business, the main battle was being fought in distant Bolivia.

As early as 1952, when Miguel was only seven years old, a Trotskyite government, fearful of the power wielded by the mining companies, had begun nationalising the mines, and as successive governments showed more interest in the money than in good management of the mines, the process continued to replenish dwindling funds. On 24 June 1985, the Orlandini Tortoral Group of fifty-four mines was nationalised, without compensation to the owners, together with a US$6million shipment of tin. Miguel fought back, obtaining a ruling from the Bolivian Supreme Court on 3 December of that year denationalising all the mines and returning them to Orlandini Tortoral. His tin was aboard a French ship heading for Holland. His Dutch lawyers assured him that it belonged to Tortoral, so Miguel had the cargo seized as it entered Rotterdam.

The Bolivian government was not amused. 'Miguel, do you want the government to look like highway robbers?' asked the minister of mines on the phone.

'No, I just want my mines and tin back!' retorted Miguel.

'OK. To save face, we'll give you the mines immediately. But let us have the tin in Rotterdam. We will give you more tin in Bolivia to make up the amount of the shipment.'

But they didn't. Instead, when he returned to Bolivia, the government sued Miguel for US$3.4 million in costs for the trouble in Rotterdam, and a lot more besides.

Six months in prison was breaking Nick, but Miguel had been in this windowless tunnel for twenty-nine months without trial. He was fighting back, playing a patient game. Within a week he hoped to have the mines restored to him. 'I'm an empire-builder!' he laughed. On his release, he would open new offices in La Paz, build a house by the mines, open new tin mines and bid for the great Huanuni mine which had once belonged to his great-uncle.

'The world is rushing into the twenty-first century. Bolivia is the geopolitical centre of South America, with unfathomable reserves of natural gas. Within ten years, just across in Argentina, São Paulo will be the second largest city in the world. Chile is doing beautifully, thanks to Pinochet.' Miguel warmed to his subject. 'Paraguay, Peru, Ecuador – we must all join together to build a pipeline to America. It will be a great chance for the richest nation to finance the poorest.'

'What about the Indians, Miguel?' Marie Christine interrupted.

'Look, North America progressed as it did because they killed all the Indians.' There was no stopping him now. We sat quietly. I hoped Isso understood what was being said. 'We must educate them, so they can catch up. It's the same in Peru, Ecuador – everywhere. I'd give them all twenty-four hours to get into European clothes and make Spanish the only language taught in schools. Bolivia needs half a million white European families out here to dominate. It's not a big problem – the total population of this country is only seven million. You know, five and a half million commute into Lower Manhattan daily.'

It was time to go. Visiting hours were over. Leaving our oranges in the darkened hall, we made our way back to the prison gate. Unsurprisingly my best folding sunglasses were stolen from my jacket pocket in the melée.

The all-night bus ride from La Paz to Potosi was inexpensive but cold. Choking dust blew in through a window which wouldn't close. In spite of many layers of clothing, with scarves, hats and hoods pulled right over our faces, we were still chilled to the bone. In the middle of nowhere, at 1.30 am, and well over 14,000ft up, we got a puncture. Ignoring the anguished cries of his passengers, the driver bumped on into the nearest *pueblo*.

We rumbled into Potosi, the highest city of its size anywhere in the world, just as dawn was breaking. Sprawled at the foot of a brutally scarred reddish-coloured hill in the middle of the most barren terrain imaginable, it looked dreadful.

Only a dozen years after they first landed in Peru, the Spaniards stumbled on the Indian mine workings here in Potosi. The hill was a volcanic plug of silver. '*Cerro rico*', they called it. Even today in Spain the word 'potosi' is still used to describe anything superlatively rich.

Raoul, an ex-miner, agreed to take us down the mine where, he told us, all his brothers had died. A Quechua himself, he soon befriended Isso, entrusting her with a couple of sticks of dynamite in brown grease-proof paper, half a dozen detonators, a small plastic bag of yellow ammonia nitrate, a box of matches, some lumps of carbide rock for lamps and a few packs of cigarettes. On our way to the mine, he suggested we bought bags of dry green coca leaves for the Quechua miners who lived in bleak rows of huts on the edge of town. They helped deaden pain, hunger and fatigue.

While we struggled into helmets, oilskins and wellington boots, Raoul poured fresh water on to the carbide rock in our hand-held lamps, creating thin flames with a match. There was a low rumble and a shift of exhausted miners appeared, blinking in the daylight, pulling and pushing their small railway truckloads of silver ore. This was a co-operative mine. The Indians were working old Inca tunnels, much smaller and more dangerous than the government workings which had been closed down.

The stone archway was stained dark with blood of llamas. 'Three men were crushed to death here last month.' Raoul spoke rapidly in broken English, directing Isso to stick right behind him as he led us down. The strange guttural sounds which accompanied his speech gave us a clue to why our adopted daughter had found English so hard to learn; it was completely different.

Often bent double, we stumbled and crawled through narrow tunnels and scrambled down rickety wooden ladders which took us down to different levels. Our throats grew sore from the crystals of arsenic and ammonia that lay in the shaft. The Incas had done without ladders, simply reaching down with bags on 100m ropes to all six levels.

We came to a place where the side of the shaft had collapsed, leaving a gaping black hole. Somewhere down there lay the bodies of several miners who'd fallen over the side, probably when drunk.

'Theo is hungry,' said Raoul. 'Not enough llamas have been sacrificed.' Our lamps played flickering light over a life-sized image of the Devil, crudely fashioned in mud. A half-smoked cigarette dangled from his cruel lips and serpents twisted around the horns which sprouted from his head. Gruesome offerings of llama foetuses lay scattered around. 'We eat the mines, and the mines eat us!'

Hungrier even than Theo, the Spaniards had, in a little over 200 years, extracted 46,000 tons of silver from this desolate hill. The cost was unbelievable: 8 million lives. After they'd used up all the Quechua and Aymara Indians, the Spaniards imported luckless negroes, who, because of the cold, didn't last as long.

'Pacha Mama, Mother God of Earth, she too is jealous,' Raoul went on. 'No woman may work here – only men and boys.'

'How old?' asked Isso, her eyes widening beneath her yellow miner's hat.

'If they have no family, they work at twelve,' said Raoul. 'They help carry for us. Towards the end of our shift, we drink the boys' piss – it gives us strength.'

Stumbling back up the shaft, claustrophobia only just in check, I thought of our visit to the jail in La Paz. 'You know,' Miguel had said, 'when there's a fatal accident in a mine, we usually strike a rich seam soon afterwards.'

15

Isso's Return

JOHN

Elizabeth Ridgway. Place of birth: Lucmahuayco. So reads the entry in the red British passport. The words, and the document itself, encapsulate our adopted daughter's life. To return to her native land to look for her natural mother and see again the place where she had come from was what she wanted. And for me, the journey would close a circle of twenty-five years.

Those particular troubles in Peru began in 1970, the year I first visited the country, leading an expedition from the furthest source of the Amazon to its mouth; the year of the agrarian reforms which broke up the huge family *haciendas*, freeing the *campesinos* from serfdom, and shared out the land among them. It was hoped they would form their own co-operatives to grow and sell their produce. From this might come a developing national pride and an increase in Peruvian exports. All this could help poor Peru's deplorable balance-of-payments situation. But for the most part, the reforms brought corruption and a chaotic drift into semi-self-sufficiency, with large families growing up on small patches of land.

It was also the year I first met Elizabeth's father, Elvin Berg, three parts Quechua Indian and one part Norwegian.

Elvin was then twenty-two and lived in the 'eyebrow of the jungle', the remotest spot we visited on my expedition down the full length of the Amazon. He took us hundreds of miles through the rapids, and in doing so, he more than once saved my life. When we parted, I gave him my watch and promised I'd return some day.

MARIE CHRISTINE

Fifteen years later we decided to visit Peru. Rebecca had just left school and it seemed a good time to make a family trip to meet Elvin. I had joined John on his 1970 expedition further down the Amazon, after their raft was wrecked, but I missed the earlier part of the journey in the Andes, and consequently had never met Elvin. Over the years John had enthralled Bec and me with tales of the Berg's Swiss-Family-Robinson lifestyle at Osambre, where a half-Norwegian called Abel Berg had carved out a farm from virgin forest. Elvin, the eldest of his five children, hunted with the Campa Indians for jaguars, which preyed on their cattle. We were fascinated by the details of their self-sufficiency, which included washing with nuts which fell to the ground from a soap-nut tree planted beside a stream running through their compound.

So in 1985, at the end of a busy Ardmore season, we flew out to Peru, only to find ourselves in the middle of a terrorist war which had barely been mentioned in the British press. The agrarian reforms had weakened the grip of the right-wing oligarchy and a Maoist movement called the Shining Path had stepped boldly into the power vacuum, determined to begin history again. They planned to destroy all foreign influence in Peru and restore full power to the proletariat. It was hardly the place for a family holiday, or a good time to be searching for a long-lost friend.

To reach Elvin's Osambre, we would have to travel into the Red Zone of the emergency in the Apurimac Valley. Our five-strong party was not the most experienced ever: eighteen-year-old Rebecca, two instructors from Ardmore and the two of us, and John decided we would need at least three weeks toughening up in the thin air of the Altiplano. Fitter and more efficient at moving quickly with all our kit, we returned to Cuzco amid rumours of terrorist successes everywhere. But John was determined to find his old friend whatever the risks. We left secretly at night, avoiding the Guardia Civil outposts by using an abandoned back-door route into the Red Zone which John remembered from his 1970 expedition.

Within a week we had been taken captive and marched overnight to military headquarters set up in a village three days' walk from Osambre. We narrowly avoided being lynched by a large gathering of the Ronda, the local civil defence, who believed we were delivering arms to the terrorists. We were saved by John's suggestion that our rucksacks and emergency belt-order should be publicly unpacked and the contents held up for scrutiny. Later in the day things took another turn for the worse when the black hooded military scouts returned from a foray in the surrounding jungle. John drew himself up to his full height and, in limited Spanish, explained to the officer that he had served as an officer in the Parachute Regiment. With this tenuous brotherhood established, the reason for our journey – our search for Elvin – was believed. The lieutenant instructed us to leave the area and not return. He told us what we had been fearing: terrorists had crossed the river to Osambre, had surprised Elvin, who knew them personally, tied him to a chair, set fire to him and then burned the farm to the ground. 'Your friend is dead,' he said bluntly. We were too late.

It was fate that stopped us a day later at the scattering of huts called Accobamba, a refugee village on our sombre route back towards the snow-covered passes between us and the nearest road end. And fate that led us to a crippled girl who told us that Elvin had a daughter, being cared for by her elderly grandparents in this village. 'They have suffered much,' she warned us. 'Her mother is unable to look after her. Be gentle with them.'

Isso sat hunched on a dirty sheepskin rug, hungrily drinking thin soup from a chipped enamel mug. Dark eyes stared out from a thin face, suspiciously peeping up at the three gringos who had walked out of the jungle into the simple adobe hut and were now talking with her granny, Josefina.

This six-year-old girl had good reason to be wary of strangers. Here, in the ancient Inca Kingdom of the Clouds, 8,000ft up in the Peruvian Andes, her short life had been filled with horror. Her father had been murdered, and her mother's family had fled from the Shining Path terrorists who had taken over Lucmahuayco, the village where her grandfather was head man of eighty families, only a three-day walk from Accobamba. He had escaped into the jungle, and in reprisal the terrorists had slaughtered his only son, Isso's uncle. Many innocent people were publicly slain. The women had their hands tied behind their backs and their throats cut, so the soul could not escape the mouth to betray their killers. More appalling mutilations were carried out on the men to ensure a slower death. And the terrorists were moving fast. They had promised they would capture Accobamba within the week, and Isso's grandparents were on their hit list.

Hyperventilating with fear, Granny Josefina begged us to take the child. Her suggestion was a bolt from the blue, but in an instant I knew it would happen. It was meant to be. This was John's chance to repay Elvin for saving his life. And sweet, compassionate Rebecca never faltered in her wish to help this small girl from the jungle to take the *opportunidad* her grandparents craved for her. Besides, Bec had always wanted a brother or sister. John had strong views about the exploding world population and believed we should do our bit by limiting our own family to one child. His principles could not be challenged, but in my heart I had always wanted more children. And here was Isso, already born into this world, alone but for her ailing grandparents, in need of a secure home and family and, above all, love.

We didn't take Isso back to Ardmore straight away. Granny Josefina and her husband decided next day that the danger of heavy snow on the mountain passes along our route to the road was even greater than the risk of staying in the village. And we felt they should take time to consider their decision. But our hearts were heavy as wearily we began the four-day walk over the mountains, accompanied by Isso's grandfather. It was hard for us to leave these vulnerable people to their fate. We learned later that the terrorists had come the following night. Terrified, Josefina and Isso hid in the forest, only re-emerging when they learned that the terrorists had been routed by the villagers.

For my own peace of mind, I had to find Elizabeth's natural mother. We eventually discovered her living in the village at the end of the road being cared for by relations. Although in her late twenties, Leocadia was more like a child than a grown woman, her dark, wavy hair tied back in a bunch. She smiled wide-eyed at us from a smooth, open face. The only sign of anxiety was the wringing of her hands. Her father explained that she couldn't look after herself, let alone her child. Had the terrorist war maimed her, the horrors affected her mind? She smiled and nodded sweetly when her mother's suggestion was put to her in Quechua. The language barrier prevented me from talking to her directly, and I could only put my arm around her and tell her in English that if her daughter came to us I would love her as my own. I worried that she didn't understand what her parents were suggesting. Further on, in the jungle town of Quillabamba, we sought out the travelling priest who had baptised Isso. He strongly urged us to go ahead. But Leocadia was always in my thoughts.

And so it was, nine months after we briefly met Isso in a jungle hut in

Peru, that she came to our home in Scotland. A short stay in Lima had cured her chronic malnutrition. She had weighed under three stone, her hair was infested with lice and her stomach with worms. Her baby teeth were so blackened by decay that they had to be extracted under general anaesthetic.

One late October afternoon the small figure ran across the green of a neighbouring croft to meet us and take the short boat trip to our remote Highland home. She was dressed as Snow White, an outfit she had chosen from a book of fairytales: white frilly blouse, tightly laced black waistcoat, a white pinny over a full red skirt. She had a lot to adjust to. Until recently she had never seen everyday things like wheels, glass or electric light. She understood no English and we could utter only a few words in Quechua. Now I quaked at the sudden realisation of the enormity of my job. But it was only for a moment. As we crossed the loch she sat squarely on my knee, held my hand tightly and called me Mama. This was nothing special, for all women in Peru are called Mama, but it was reassuring all the same. And so began the long journey of getting to know and love each other.

The feelings created by adopting someone else's child are complex, both for the new mother and for the child. I felt that what Elizabeth needed above all else was an abundance of love. There had been little scope for this in her previous life, with her father murdered, abandoned by her natural mother and her terrified granny grieving for her own butchered son. Loving isn't something you can pretend. The three of us knew we had to love Isso all the time, even when she was naughty, sulky, or unresponsive. The first few days were filled with excitement. Thrilled by everything, Elizabeth would rush up and down stairs, switching the lights on and off. She changed her clothes several times a day, delighted with so many new things. There was a whole retinue of dollies. Her favourite would be wrapped up in a *manta* and slung over her back, Indian-style. It was enchanting, and our compassion soon turned naturally to love. For Isso, I think it was a dream come true. She was suddenly very much the centre of attention, and the hunger and fear slowly faded into the past.

The honeymoon period couldn't last for ever, of course, and as Isso started to feel more secure she would quite understandably test me by not doing what she was told. She was very clever at playing us off against each other. 'Where is Ribeeka?' she would ask crossly if I met her for the half-hour walk round the loch from the school bus; or 'I want

Mama,' if it was the other way round. Sometimes my patience was sorely tried and we would get cross with each other, and then she would turn away and sob heartbreakingly: 'I want Mummy Lima,' her name for her own mother. 'I'm going back to them on a horse.'

I often thought of 'Mummy Lima' and Granny Josefina, and of what they had given up so selflessly in the hope that Isso would receive the *opportunidad* of an education and a good start in life. But could Isso really understand this? When school was difficult, or people stared at her in the street, she hated it, even though I told her they did so because she was pretty. I know she sometimes felt she didn't belong in our world, and we sometimes wondered whether we had done the right thing. She worried that she wasn't like her friends. Above all, John and I wanted her to have the confidence to be herself. Gradually, she built an idea in her mind that Peru was perfect, and her family paragons who never raised their voices. But that emerged only on a very few grey days; most of the time she filled our home and strengthened our family with the sunshine of her personality.

Over the next nine years John made four more trips to the Red Zone of the emergency in the Apurimac Valley to trace family survivors. He even hoped to bring to justice Lucio Orrosco, the terrorist supposed to have been responsible for burning Elvin to death. It was a worrying time – Elizabeth could so easily have lost a second father. In the autumn of 1992, John and I made the journey to Accobamba together. I wanted to reassure Granny Josefina and Leocadia that Isso was healthy and growing up in a loving family. Josefina looked older and frail. This was when, through our guide–interpreter, she beseeched me to bring her granddaughter to see her before she died. She felt she had not long to live.

Now the fourteen-year-war was over and it was safe to take Isso back. After eleven eventful months at sea, we hoped we would be in time. She was so excited at the prospect of the big walk into her world, but I was apprehensive. What would she think of her family? She had become so used to comfort at home, and I wondered what she would think when she saw that her family didn't wear shoes and had no running water in their simple two-room adobe hut, even though I had explained all this to her. I so hoped she wouldn't think less of them. How would she react to her mother, whose condition had seemed no better two years before? Was she too young to manage this huge emotional hurdle? I felt that, with our love and support, things would somehow work out. But my own feelings were in a turmoil. Isso had been my daughter now for nine years, and I didn't want to lose her.

A Watch arrived in Cuzco on a warm August Sunday in 1994. From the steps of the cathedral, the mayor was reviewing the army, goose-stepping higher than shoulder-level. Inside the dark heart of the ancient cathedral, a relic of the appalling Spanish Inquisition, motes of dust glittered in narrow beams of sunlight, shafting down from lofty windows. The congregation, mostly devout Quechua Indians in traditional dress, waited in stoical silence while a plump, pale European priest in horn-rimmed specs fussed at his high golden altar. Could all that suffering have been for nothing? The great organ pipes began to snort: 'The answer my friend, is blowing in the wind . . .'

There was no sign of Bec, so we left a note at the Hostal Familia and pushed on, trying not to worry. We took the rickety train from Cuzco to the end of the line, squalid, steaming Quillabamba, 10,000ft below Cuzco on the jungle fringe. A brief baptismal entry in the Dominican Mission's registry there is the only evidence of Isso's birth. Everything else was burned by terrorists in Lucmahuayco. Her grin broadened as the dust greyed her face during eight more hours in the back of the truck which bumped us back up into the Andes. There had been no rain for four months and the leaves on the coffee bushes hung limp and vertical. Whole mountainsides were on fire, burning to create fresh pasture for cattle. A pall of smoke reddened the sun, choking the *campesinos*.

We found Roberto and Celestino waiting for us in Lucma, having received our postcard from Panama. At thirty-three and twenty respectively, they were short, wiry and innovative, and had travelled with us before. A small brown horse called Napoleon stood by to carry the 50 kilos of gear needed on our three-week trek. But there was no sign of Bec. We had had no contact with her since she'd set off with Will to Argentina. We had hoped we would all meet here to be with Isso when she met her family. We left another note and hoped she might catch us up. There were any number of likely explanations for her absence, but it was terribly worrying all the same.

The walking was not easy. We reached Roberto's Uncle Marcelo's home at 14,000ft after eight hard hours, a lone smoke-blackened hut beneath a glacier: no books, no music; just ten cows, some milk and thin, cold air. Our heads throbbing with the altitude, we slept poorly on dirty sheepskins.

Next morning, Isso was sick three times on the long drag up to the Chuquito Pass. 'Better just get on with it,' she muttered bravely. At least the pass was clear of snow.

Descending several thousand feet, we plodded along a parched valley before beginning the long haul back up to Yanahuanca, a bleak village where glaciers feed a green lake dammed by moraine. The afternoon sun disappeared and the cold fell on the miserable collection of huts. We had potato soup again, and crawled into our bivvie bags, wearing all the clothing we had with us. When the crippled old woman blew out the candle, a horde of guinea pigs came rushing along the mud floor and crawled all over us. Exhausted, we slept better.

Poor Isso was sick again on the way up to the Huamus Pass, but soon recovered on the descent to Choquetira, where we ate boiled potatoes while waiting for a hailstorm to pass. And she led the way as we began the 5,000ft descent to Accobamba, running through the cloud to keep warm. Rounding a bend on the 1ft-wide path, we surprised a bent old woman minding sheep. Clad in ragged brown skirts, with a thick plaid *manta* across her thin shoulders, she was barefoot in the cold rain. There was a dirty bandage twisted round her right calf. Suddenly she screeched with delight at the sight of the plump English schoolgirl in her navy sailing jacket. With a stream of Quechua, she hugged the startled Isso, straightening her smart red bowler hat so the big white marguerite daisies faced the front. It was Isso's great-aunt.

Descending quicker than I wanted, we were soon among clouds of brilliantly coloured butterflies in steaming rainforest. Isso was enchanted by the spectacular scenery, and thrilled to see that now John and I were the ones people stared at.

On down the ancient Inca path, scattered with deep purple petals, we raced in single file to keep up with Isso.

'There it is – Accobamba!' cried John as we rounded the end of a steep wooded spur and the scatter of thatched huts came into sight beneath us. So nearly there. I felt my courage failing me.

'I may live here!' Isso said, as much to herself as to any of us.

The air was filled with the scent of swaying blue eucalyptus trees. How had I forgotten such a detail? I had so often thought of this place when telling Isso the story of how she came to be with us.

'Of course,' I answered breezily.

I knew that I must stand back, I must not influence her. This was the moment for her to meet her own family, and I was not going to turn it into some kind of tug-of-love situation. The sacrifice that Leocadia and Josefina had made nine years before might prove to be one that John and I would have to endure.

The snug village was tucked on to a green shelf above a rushing river with steep forested mountains soaring on either side of the valley, reaching high into the snowy peaks of Choquesafra – the beard of gold. This had been one of the last Inca communities to hold out against the Spanish conquerors. We stopped to catch our breath. Once again Elizabeth straightened her red hat, now matching her glowing cheeks. She wanted to look her best. Her voice was firm. 'Come on, Mama.' And we proceeded, with her in the lead, towards the huts and the family she had left so long before.

Then we were there. Just below the path, where a thread of water had been diverted from the stream by a carefully cut agave stem, stood the house: a simple thatched hut made of sun-dried mud blocks. Nearby old Josefina sat cross-legged beneath a small peach tree, absorbed in sorting some coffee beans which lay pale on a dark cloth *manta*. On hearing our voices she looked up, startled, and touched her throat in the nervous way I remembered. Then her care-worn face broke into a wide smile; calling out with joy, she hobbled to her feet and rushed to embrace Isso. We had come in time.

Hearing the commotion, Don Juan, Elizabeth's grandfather, emerged from the shadows, hardly believing what he saw. This old man who had lost so much that was dear to him hugged his granddaughter, wiping away tears of joy.

With the greatest courtesy they invited us into their home and laid out sheepskins for us. In the smoky hut, Don Juan stood up and welcomed us formally. 'Thank you for coming. How long can you stay?'

'Four days,' John replied in halting Spanish. Their faces lit up and Don Juan clapped with joy. 'It's been a long time,' he said, looking at Isso, the lines of suffering etched on his face. Josefina hobbled away, returning with mugs of sweet, black coffee grown in the surrounding forest, and, to Isso's delight, an enamel bowl full of *oncucho,* a delicious starchy vegetable which she straight away declared she remembered. She had handled meeting her grandparents well; what would her feelings be when her mum arrived?

Today, as every day, Leocadia was working in the fields. We waited. My emotions were still a tangle. How could I face this woman whose child had given us such joy? Her deprivation had been our blessing; it seemed so unfair. She must surely resent me, and I desperately wanted her approval.

Just as the light was fading we heard her step outside. Suddenly, there were mother and daughter facing each other, both too stunned to make a move. It was between them, this meeting; I was an outsider now. Eventually, Leocadia let the farm tools fall with a clatter and stepped towards her fine, healthy-looking teenage daughter. There were no tears, just smiles.

I caught Isso peeping at me. 'Go on, darling, hug your mum.' The two strangers embraced awkwardly. I felt a pang of violent guilt. I couldn't guess what either of them was thinking. Wiping my eyes and steadying my camera, I took lots of photos, as much to cover their embarrassment as to record the auspicious moment. Isso towered above her tiny mum and granny; Leocadia giggled and gazed at Isso's glossy hair and strong, white teeth.

We stayed with Isso's family for four days. I wanted her to spend time with them, for them to enjoy seeing her as she was now, so fit, healthy and happy, to build memories that they could all draw upon later. It was difficult, for they had no common language – Isso had quite forgotten her mother tongue. But she helped her granny and mother with the daily tasks at which they were so adept, peeling the potatoes which were the staple of every meal and scattering what little was left over for the ever-hungry hens who came into the house unbidden when our backs were turned. She helped to sweep and wash the few tin plates from which we ate. We washed clothes in a wooden trough fed by the stream beside the path, and in the evening, as it got dark we sat close together and tried to talk, watching the fireflies pierce the black velvet of the night.

On our last day we bought a pig from neighbours and baked it with sweet potatoes in a clay oven we built in a field above the river. And there, on a lovely afternoon on the mountainside, we had a feast and listened to Don Juan's tales of his jungle village of Lucmahuayco: of fat snakes in coils 18ins high among the sugar cane, monkey raids on the maize, and of black bears and jaguars eating the cattle. By a purple-flowering bush, a bottle-green hummingbird hovered, drawing pollen, and in the background, away across the Apurimac Gorge, layer after jagged layer of mountain ridges stretched up in shades of grey, blurring into the bubbling white clouds.

Peace had returned to this place, and it was an idyllic time for us all. As Don Juan said, nine years is a long time, and just as Isso had forgotten all of her Quechua, mercifully, the bad memories of the past seemed to have been buried as well. Preparing for bed on our last night, I whispered to Isso, 'Say goodnight to your mama, darling.' As ever, the whole family were watching, fascinated by our complicated process of getting undressed and laying out our bivvy bags on the piles of sheepskins covering the dirt floor. She answered me slowly and thoughtfully. 'You are my real mama now.' We hugged, and I hoped my tears of joy did not show in the candlelight. I never wanted Isso to have to make a choice between me and her natural mother, but at that moment I couldn't help but feel a great wave of relief and gratitude sweep over me.

Elizabeth had decided that Scotland was home now, but we will go back again and visit this beautiful land and these kind, gentle people who have suffered so much, and who are her family. Perhaps being more certain of her past will help her to face the future.

JOHN

I awoke at 2.30 next morning, when the black cockerel began his strange dialogue with an unseen acquaintance further up the valley. Don Juan had agreed to accompany us on the four-day walk back to Lucmahuayco. It was now ten years since he'd fled the village, and none of his family had been there since. Not only had his son been butchered by the Shining Path, but even his son-in-law had been sent on a mission to search him out and kill him, merely to prove his new-found commitment to Maoism. The six of us, Roberto and Celestino, our two guides; Don Juan, Marie Christine, Isso and myself, set off in the cool of early morning but as the sun rose and the day began to roast, I began to feel far from my best. Perhaps it was too much roast pig, I thought. I drank some fresh orange juice from a kettle passed to us by a large lady along the path, and moments later I had to jump down into the bushes as three weeks of accumulated diarrhoea culminated in an explosion.

I needed a couple of hours' sleep in a nearby hut before I was able to continue. At supper I was unable to face the smelly dried fish from the river. Our hut was infested with fleas, and by morning the liners in our bivvy bags were speckled with blood.

Luckily, Isso's twenty-three-year-old cousin, Norberto, also born in

Lucmahuayco, agreed to help cut a way through to the village. Now we were seven.

We managed one more day with Napoleon the horse, whose flanks were now running with blood from nightly vampire-bat attacks. The resident family in the single house at Sondor treated us to papaya, bananas and chicken stew and agreed to keep an eye on him. They produced the hide of a huge puma or mountain brown lion they'd shot recently after it had killed several cattle and goats.

From now on the route was overgrown, and the continuous chopping made for slow progress. 'I can't wait to get home, Danny,' cried Isso. 'How far does this forest go on?'

'For about three thousand miles, as far as I can remember,' I replied. Far beneath us, white bands of rapids barred the pale green waters of the broad Apurimac River. For the most part, the tangled path followed a gentle decline along the steep walls of the valley, but now and then we were forced down to cross a stream bed and struggle up the far side. We killed a small brown snake and came across recent bear droppings containing deer fur.

From a vantage point high on the valley wall, we could see across the mighty Apurimac and into the little village of Chapi, hiding in a hanging valley. This was the *pueblito* from where 1,000 terrorists had crossed the river on balsa rafts by night on their way to capture Lucmahuayco.

Norberto fell ill with the fever which was soon to spread to most of the rest of us. His limbs ached, he felt cold and sweat poured off him. Aspirin and a short sleep helped, but, still far from well, he struggled on. We plodded through cactus, bamboo and clumps of kapok, avoiding a hornet's nest only after Roberto was stung on the ear. We lost the path while descending steeply to cross a river, and had to camp for a night tormented by insects.

Next morning we found a large tarantula spider in the bedding, and shortly after setting out, we came across the first of the defensive pits on the path. These deep holes had been dug by the terrorists, designed to kill or capture unwanted visitors to the training camp they'd set up at Lucmahuayco. Vertical sharpened stakes would impale the unwary as they fell through the concealing mat of grass and sticks. We didn't know where there might be more. Norberto, in the lead, moved cautiously.

Much of the day was spent battling head-high pollen-laden grass. 'Can't do anything about it, Mama,' called Isso. 'Better just go for it!' Rations were low, and lunch disposed of the last of the festive pig: bits of jaw complete with teeth. I couldn't eat it. By mid-afternoon, after long delays for chopping, we were looking down into a deep side valley. Lucmahuayco lay somewhere at our feet. Three hours later, at the end of the eleventh day and desperate for water, we staggered to a halt in the darkness, our way forward blocked by agave and cactus.

Norberto and Don Juan reconnoitred forward and found a stream cascading through a hole in a low ruined wall beside the overgrown path. This was all that remained of Lucmahuayco. Exhausted, we spent a good night under a canopy of trees, with two smoky fires to deter the mosquitos.

Next morning various parties explored the ruined village. Everyone was shocked at the extent of the secondary jungle. It had choked everything, blotting out the sunlight, preventing anything from bearing fruit. Amazingly, there was nothing at all to eat, as everything the village had ever planted out had been overwhelmed by jungle.

Apart from a few rusted cooking pots and digging tools among the ruined walls, nothing remained of the eighty families who'd lived here, save for a few skulls, separated from their skeletons to prevent the spirits of the dead from following their assassins. When, at last, the army had attacked the terrorist training camp by night, they had killed every man, woman and child. 'That's Doña Angela,' whispered Don Juan, recognising the location where one skull had been found. 'She was seventy. They tied her hands and cut her throat.' He sat apart from us, and we could only imagine what thoughts and memories must have been going through his mind, the last headman of the village.

'Children throw hand-grenades,' growled Norberto, who'd served here during his national service, eager to avenge his dead relatives. They both talked of returning, but Don Juan knew he was too old to start clearing his land again. He reminisced and told us of the school, of the village street lined with houses, of the good coffee they had grown here, the livestock and fruit which flourished. Now he had only an acre or two, back in Accobamba, no status and no family, apart from his aged wife and his dependent daughter.

Elizabeth took it all philosophically, even managing to tell ghost stories at night. She was now quite clear that she wanted to live in Scotland.

Out of food, we only stayed a night. I didn't want to linger in this place which had seen such terror. Death seemed to hang in the air. Norberto explained how the terrorists had purposely allowed all the paths to become overgrown to dissuade attack. So now there was no way forward, either, to the ruins of Osambre. Reluctantly we had to return the way we had come, abandoning my plan of a circular route around the mountains, back to Lucma via Isso's uncle's jungle hideout at Capiro, further down the Apurimac.

Early next morning, before the fierce sun was up, we were back on the tortuous route back up to Accobamba. The journey took us three days and we were lucky to pick up food at Sondor on the second day. Marie Christine and I were both sick, but Isso, born to this life, walked strongly onward without complaint.

We said goodbye to Josefina, Leocadia and Don Juan, hugging them silently. Even if we had known the words to say in Quechua, they would have been inadequate. We left the family with small gifts which we hoped would help them – some chickens, two pigs and a cow in calf. From Lucma, Roberto was going to send them some apple trees on one of the mule trains passing through, and from Cuzco we promised to try to send seeds and medicines via a trader friend. They hugged Isso one last time, and we left as quickly as we could. We had set their minds at rest that their granddaughter was loved and cared for.

We'd discussed the possible outcomes of our trip to Accobamba often enough, but somehow, I don't think I had ever expected Isso to become hysterical and refuse to leave her natural mother. Perhaps, if I had thought such a reaction likely, I wouldn't have taken her to Peru until she was a little older. I hoped that everything we had experienced on this journey together would help her to understand better who she was and help her to cope with the jungle of Europe.

REBECCA

'Ribeeka?' The young Peruvian boy's clear, questioning voice in the darkness was the reassurance I needed as I jumped stiffly down from the rickety truck which had brought me up to Lucma, a dusty eight-hour journey from Quillabamba, where I had left the train. Jordan, the fourteen-year-old son of my friends Eliseo and Hilda led me to their house. They were expecting me. I had stayed here twice before, and their welcome was warm.

They handed me the note I anticipated. 'Dear Bec, We waited a week and have gone on. We leave tomorrow, 5 September. Hope to see you at Accobamba. Love Mum, Dad and Isso.' It was now 12 September. Faxes

from all over South America had not found their target and I was two
weeks late.

That night, lying in bed covered with heavy, dust-filled ponchos, I
decided I would set off into the mountains and down into the jungle to
try to meet them on the way back. I would give myself one day to find
a local man who would come with me as guide-cum-interpreter -
Quechua Indian is the only language really spoken in the *campo*. It was
a big decision to go on my own, but I had travelled through this country twice before and felt I could handle the physical side. Besides, I
needed something challenging to help ease the great sadness I felt at having parted from Will. I felt relatively safe from the Maoist extremists
who had cleared the area where I wanted to go of nearly all its sparse
population. After his capture, Abimael Guzman, whose superstitious
followers had endowed him with supernatural powers, looked depress-
ingly human, and the Shining Path movement had collapsed.

Eliseo searched for a guide, but by 8 pm the next day, no one had
come forward. Nobody knew the route I wanted to take, the one I had
travelled five years earlier with Dad. At 8.30 pm there was a knock on
the door and, blinking in the bright light after the darkness outside, a shy
young man entered. Basilides Quispe Botanes, a street clothes-seller and
tricycle-taxi operator in Quillabamba, was stocky and strong with a
brush-like fringe that stuck straight out from the roots. Eliseo patted him
on the back, and told me he was the best. Before the terrorists had driven them out, his family had lived in the area I needed to get to, and he
assured me he remembered the route. Basilides would come with me.

Before I went to bed, I wrote a quick letter to Will. I told him of my
planned journey – at least he would know where to come and look if I
didn't return. I calculated that it would have taken Mum, Dad and Isso
three days to reach Accobamba; if they had spent four days there as
planned, they would now be walking to Lucmahuayco. Now that the
war was over, I knew Dad wanted to show Isso Osambre; then, descending the Apurimac River, they would return to Lucma in a great circle
round the mountains, via Capiro, where Isso's Uncle Olaf lived like a
bandit chief. Dad never liked retracing his tracks, so I gambled that this
would be his plan. I would go round the circle in the opposite direction
to meet them.

We set off at 7.30 am. Basilides was on time, and I sensed that he
would be a good man. Armed with a small saucepan, a kilo of sugar,
pasta and some biscuits, we began our week-long trip – journeys here are

judged in walking time, not distances. I am sure he thought *la gringa* was
bound to be slow going up to the steep mountain passes, and the first
day did indeed nearly finish us both: we walked hard for ten hours with
barely a break. As darkness was falling we arrived at a single house
where Basilides' aunt lived. Antonia, with her squat, cracked bare feet,
was thrilled to see us; she and I had met five years before, when her husband Antonio had been our guide. Sadly, he was far away, down alone
on his tiny jungle coffee plantation, which he loved the most. We spent
the evening in her smoke-filled, tar-covered cooking hut, our eyes
streaming. Antonia added some pieces of ancient tripe to the potato soup
and placed an extra piece over the fire to cook for the two travellers.

The following day we left the Altiplano and descended down, down
into the forest. Faded yellows and browns turned to great green trees
with flowering bromelias draped in long pale moss and the ground was
choked with sprawling bamboo. The narrow path became a deep green
gully, leaving ground-level way above our heads, eroded by tropical
rains and years of mule trains carrying the coffee harvest on the long
three-day journey to the Lucma market. Butterflies of all colours fluttered away from our big feet.

About 1,000m below, we reached the Toroyunca River, washed our
sweaty clothes and stopped for the night. My first impression of
Basilides had been correct: we were getting to know each other by now,
and, typical of the country people, he was polite and generous. He set off
with hand line and spinner to catch our supper. 'Bastante truchas' –
plenty of trout – he had been murmuring all morning, in between playing his Chinese-made Lark harmonica up and downhill. I got a fire
going, heating water for his return by a ruined stone wall where great
lizards caught flies doped by the afternoon sun. Soon it would be dark,
and those lizards would be walking around my bivvy bag.

Basilides returned, proudly swinging a great bundle of trout, and
taught me how to descale them using hot ash. We ate a delicious meal
together in the dark, before the cold night set in. With no blanket or
sleeping bag, I slept with my thermal longjohns and top on under my
clothes and a down waistcoat over them, then climbed into my bivvy
bag and sleeping-bag liner, put my feet in rucksack to keep them
warm and hoped for the best. Nevertheless, I woke up freezing, several
times.

Next morning we left early to make the most of the cool. Basilides
didn't know the route from here on: we would have to ask anyone we

met. The landscape had changed considerably in the five years since I had last been here. With the war over, already people were returning to the jungle to build homes on their small *chakras*, and those we met on the path, although shocked to see a lone gringa, were friendly when they got over their initial suspicion. Great blue butterflies, 10cm from wing tip to wing tip, flopped slowly away; I rhapsodised about them to Basilides, who did not quite share my enthusiasm. The path followed the tumbling Toroyunca River downstream through thick jungle. Once, I stopped dead in my tracks, sure I could hear the cry of a sheep; Basilides chuckled and pointed out a brilliant red bird high above us. I wondered where Mum and Dad and Isso could be. I hoped I'd meet them soon.

We came upon Antonio, on his long haul back up to his home on the Altiplano. He hugged me warmly and gave us each a large welcome slice of juicy papaya. Next to him on the path was a huge heavy bundle, a sack containing among other things his miaowing cat and a machete. Over his shoulder he carried his faithful .22 rifle. Not long ago he'd shot a bear with paws the size of his hands. Antonio was a frontiersman, daring and hardy. I photographed him and his nephew, standing no more than 5ft tall, but straight and proud, with his rifle slung over his shoulder. We chatted excitedly, about the fierce jaguar that had attacked us from under a bridge in 1989 and which we had eaten for three days, and about the terrible new route that Antonio had cut out of the jungle to avoid the terrorists. Then, not one to waste time, he reloaded his bundle and we said goodbye, promising to stay overnight with him on our way back – along with the three Rs, I hoped.

The day became hotter and hotter as we dropped lower and lower. Great areas of trees were being chopped down and burned to make way for coffee plants, which can produce beans for 100 years or more. 'A coffee plant is like a gold mine,' Basilides said.

Tiny jungle houses made of vertical bamboo poles lashed together with bark and protected with a thatched roof lurked on the edge of these burned fields. The jungle people were pale in comparison with those higher up. We asked for directions from a young pregnant woman with a small baby strapped to her back. We hoped to reach Nueva Esperanza, which means 'new hope', by nightfall. The woman carried a black cooking pot and her bare, bitten legs were black from the charcoal fields. She looked wretched. Her directions sounded dubious. Maybe she had never even heard of Nueva Esperanza; it was just a few huts, no more.

This route was new to us both, and although I knew vaguely which way we should be heading, finding a path was another thing. Faced with a choice, Basilides looked to see which path had been used most recently. We had been walking for eight hours in the steaming heat, sucking boiled sweets and drinking quantities of clear water at every stream we came to. Basilides also used it to dissolve great chunks of *chanchaka,* a home-made jungle sugar, which he drank to boost his energy levels. Dehydration is more debilitating than hunger. We struggled on, crossing on hands and knees a bridge over a tumbling gorge made from two great trees. But it soon became apparent we were 'temporarily misplaced'. Huge jungle ants walked over my boots and up my trouser legs as soon as I stopped walking. So we kept on moving; another bridge, then across a recent landslide that shifted alarmingly with each footstep. We had no idea where we were.

The sun was sinking fast as the brief golden evening light flooded the valley. Steep jungle-covered mountains rose on all sides. Hundreds of vivid green parakeets screeched low over the trees to their evening roost.

When at last we spotted three men working in a blackened field, still aflame, we knew we were nearing Nueva Esperanza. A woman emerged from a bamboo hut. She shook my hand warmly and told Basilides she remembered me. Basilides explained that I was going to Osambre, where the Bergs had lived, and hoped to meet my parents and sister, who was a Berg, on the way down from Accobamba and Lucmahuayco. Often in South America people so want to please you that they tell you what you want to hear. This woman was the first person to explain that the path from Lucmahuayco to Osambre was now impassable. My heart sank as I realised that Mum, Dad and Isso would be returning the way they had come and I knew they would be worrying about me.

It was dark when we reached the family I remembered at Nueva Esperanza. They worked the land as a cocoa plantation. The tiny Campa Indian mother, originally from deep jungle, came rushing forward with four huge bananas to revive me. I smiled and thanked her. As I rested on a log, I could hear Basilides' gentle voice talking to the woman in Campa. I remembered her well from my last visit: she had been married to Atonio and Antonia's sturdy only son, who had recently died of poisoning. She stood in the doorway peeping at me, the small children twisted round her legs curious to see their first *gringa*.

A powerfully built young man and a tiny old Campa woman appeared through the trees. The man smiled broadly as he came to greet me. I was stunned. This was my sister Isso's half-brother, Filberto Berg Lopez, now twenty-three years old. He had trained as a mechanic in Lima, where Dad and I had found him, briefly, in 1989, but had decided to come back to reclaim his inheritance, the ruins of his murdered father's farm.

Over a supper of boiled bananas, yucca and a little fish, we talked, in Spanish, of our sister Isso. And Filberto told me what he remembered of the bounty of Osambre before he had been taken away, aged twelve, from the advancing terrorist war to be educated in a poor part of Lima. Isso had been living just up the valley in Lucmahuayco. Elvin, his father, had been murdered within a few months of Filberto's departure. He told me of his hopes and dreams of rebuilding Osambre again from the one remaining hut. He and the old Campa lady were slowly clearing land. He had planted some maize, but until it grew, he had to return to Nueva Esperanza each week for food. He told me there was no way the Three Rs could get through from Lucmahuayco to Osambre since the terrorists had deliberately let the path become overgrown with impenetrable secondary jungle. Already two weeks late, we had to get back to Lucma hastily. Basilides, Filberto and I spent the night on a woven mat, each caught in the web of our dreams.

Next morning we began the long walk back to Lucma, climbing out of the steaming jungle and up onto the cold Altiplano. When we finally met up, Isso and I would have so much to tell each other. Two nights later we were back with Antonia and Antonio, who were surprised at the distance we had covered. Realising that I was exhausted, the old man kindly shone my torch to help me find all my clothes for bed, chuckling to himself at the *gringa's* strange kit. I climbed into my bivvy bag, which they had placed on top of the bamboo potato-sorting rack, and said goodnight. Then Antonio spread two gritty ponchos over me and gently tucked them in, murmuring something comforting to me in Quechua.

The next day we reached Lucma. The three Rs arrived shortly afterwards, and we were all thrilled to meet up again. Isso, full of her visit to her family, never stopped chattering.

16

Into Patagonia

JOHN

Dozing through two days and nights aboard buses all the way back down the narrow 1,500-mile strip of Chile, from Arica in the northern desert to the dairy country of Valdivia, I was turning over in my mind the jumbled events of the year since we had left Scotland. How had I performed? Lolloping along in a fancy yacht in the tropics, I had let myself go, over-eating and taking little exercise. I had become little more than a slob. At fifty-six, I had only a few more years of active life, so I knew I had better get a grip and make the most of them. Peru had restored my self-esteem; I was running and exercising again in the early mornings, and my brain was functioning well enough, though I noticed that distant objects still flickered rather alarmingly whenever I was tired.

On our team-building courses at home, we used a book called *Not Bosses But Leaders* by John Adair, who had been on the academic staff when I was at Sandhurst. And as the leader, I had not measured up too well to his three interlocking circles: Task, Team and Individual. Will's departure was evidence of my inability to balance them. But I was returning to *English Rose* leaner and fitter, and the old enthusiasm was bubbling up again, to everyone's relief.

The honeymoon period was over now. And all that drifting about among enchanted islands in the sun. How would I perform in the harsher environment of Patagonia and Antarctica?

We found Valdivia quite changed with the spring. Gone was the beleaguered air of Eastern Europe in winter. The bus station looked brighter and the taxi ride to the yacht club, through streets bright with blossom, much more cheery. Fresh green trees lined the riverbanks as the Austral University rowing eights raced by, and hot chocolate was no longer quite such an obsession among the family.

'The best there is – and the best there ever will be!' I laughed, reaching to shake J.W.'s hand as we came down the companionway into the cosy warmth of the saloon. Jon Williams, who had arrived from Preston to join us for the rest of the trip, had already been aboard for a couple of weeks and was busy working away on preparations for the navigation. Nearly three years had passed since the end of our successful Cape Horn canoeing expedition. After a season as an instructor at Ardmore, J.W. had read geography at Durham University before returning as chief instructor and Yacht Skipper. He had made a considerable impact on the John Ridgway School of Adventure, and Marie Christine and I were very fond of him. Intensely individualistic, he was intelligent, caring, innovative and energetic. His bits and bobs were all over the place at Ardmore and on *English Rose*. The top dropboard on the main hatch passed, not through a metal plate in the teak, but through a hole drilled in one of J.W.'s 10p pieces.

Now aged thirty, J.W. was feeling rather frustrated with his work in Manchester, helping university students with their computer problems, and finding promotion prospects in a recession bleak. He had always hoped to do a Phd on the Antarctic Convergence, and so the chance to sail south aboard *English Rose* had proved irresistible.

Our second new crew member, Bruce Gardiner, aged twenty-three, was what I would call a 'good man'. And from my angle he had two very strong points: the ability to listen and freedom from seasickness. Squarely built, with heavy forearms, he was keen to learn by trying everything and had no hang-ups. After his father had come on a couple of St Kilda cruises on *English Rose*, Bruce had spent a year as an instructor at Ardmore before going on to study engineering at Newcastle University, and now, with a good degree in his pocket, he was keen to see the Antarctic before embarking on a career in the motor or aviation industry.

It was especially good to see Andy's broad grin once again. He was in high spirits, even after the two long, dark and incredibly wet months he had spent working to get the boat ready for the Antarctic, with only the mischievous Tiki for company. And we were all thrilled to be reunited with our ship's cat. Much bigger now, she was no less vicious with tooth and claw in expressing her affection.

We spent a couple more weeks in Valdivia working up *English Rose*. If we were to be home in Scotland in early April 1995, we had to leave Cape Horn for Antarctica before the New Year.

REBECCA

I felt like half a person once I got back to the boat. In this familiar setting, our desperately close team was missing one of its original players. And the absent player was the one closest to me, the one to whom I threw and from whom I caught. Maybe this was a genuine strengthening experience, but perhaps it was just my upbringing that led me to believe that things that hurt or were uncomfortable helped me to stretch and grow. 'Doing nothing is doing wrong' was part of our family culture. I cannot remember one moment of my childhood when my parents were not busy. From March until October, each day was frenzied, and they dropped into bed exhausted. Weekends were no different from weekdays, except that on Saturdays, one course would leave and another would arrive. During the winter, once everything was battened down against the wind, there was some daring trip or other. At a place like Ardmore, there was always so much to do just to keep up, let alone to introduce new schemes and building. There was no electricity: light came from the reassuring hiss of paraffin tilley lamps; heat from the open peat fire or Rayburn. Cooking required heavy calor-gas bottles that had to be carried up the hill from the loch shore. Ardmore is a place on the edge of civilisation. Time remains at a premium, and maybe this is why we found the 'relaxed' cruising life hard to get used to. We were not accustomed to having hours to spare to amuse ourselves.

The long list of jobs which needed to be done to keep the boat running and up to the mark took my mind off things. Dad was never happy unless we were all working. The years he'd spent trying to keep a team all pulling in the same direction, putting 110 per cent of their effort into the task in hand, were not going to be brushed aside just because we were 'on holiday'.

Although I missed Will terribly, I was determined to fill my days and make the most of where I was: there would have been no point to it all otherwise. At sea I just did not feel right. I was always a bit sick, and I did not have the same urge to get on with things as I had on land, but now that the climate was similar to our own and the boat was in still waters, we all felt quite invigorated. In Valdivia there was a mass of cleaning to do, as this had not been Andy and J.W.'s top priority, and Tiki had taken to peeing in the forepeak and aft cabin at times.

I got on with reorganising the stowage and clearing out lockers to check our actual stock against the record in the stowage book. Some items which had been stored away at the back of the aft cabin after our first leg, for example Batchelor's dehydrated meals, Cup-a-soups and Thornton's fudge, were brought out as it got colder. We had been saving this valuable food for the cold and rough Antarctic weather.

From here on, settlements would become more and more remote, and prices could only go up. And with at least eight people on board, food was a large consideration. We hoped that the money we raised from writing articles would cover food bills, and any left over would go towards diesel.

So we stocked up on provisions in Valdivia, probably the last big place to buy food, at a supermarket whose very Germanic manager had a small boat at the yacht club. He spoke good English, which he had learned at college in America. He was in charge of the army reserves in the Valdivia region, and rumour had it that he had a portrait of Hitler in his house, though none of us ever saw it. On Wednesdays there was a 5 per cent discount at the supermarket, and minions in white coats were sent off to gather case after case of essentials while we spent three and a half hours sipping coffee in the manager's office, talking about sailing and how grateful the Chilean people were that we had fought and beaten their arch-enemies the Argentinians over the Falkland Islands – they had believed Chile was about to be invaded.

Another of my responsibilities was fuels, which included diesel for the 150-gallon fuel tank as well as buying plastic jerrycans to fill the main cockpit and almost double our capacity. Then there were oils for the engine and lubrication of the gearbox, which we made sure were the right viscosity for Antarctic waters. Anti-freeze had been brought all the way from home, along with distilled water for the 24-volt lorry batteries. We needed petrol and two-stroke oil for the Seagull outboard, which might eventually be used, although so far Dad had insisted on us rowing everywhere; paraffin and methylated spirits or alcohol for the galley cooker and batteries for the ship's large torches. We had to work out carefully how many gallons of each of these essentials we'd require.

Our duvet covers were getting threadbare. Each time I washed mine,

I wondered if I would ever get it back on. Duvet covers did not seem to exist in Chile, so after supper one evening, I got out the old Reed's sail-mending machine, veteran of two round-the-world trips on *English Rose*, and, with Andy helping to feed the material through, I whipped up a cover with pink convolvulus on one side and blue on the other. We bought the material as remnants from one of the great second-hand clothes shops common in Valdivia. J.W. had almost kitted himself out completely from these.

After Tiki's shore leave, and now that she was over six months old, Dad insisted on having her spayed. The strawberry blonde Tahitian tabby was too much for the dark strutting Chilean toms to resist, and she had taken a Latin lover in our absence. We would have liked Tiki to have had at least one batch of kittens, but there were threats that they would go over the side mid-ocean, and I suppose it was not really practical in such a confined space.

When we went to collect the still-drugged Tiki after her operation, we heard a strange, deep miaow coming from the surgery. The vet appeared to tell us that Tiki was just coming round, and took us to see what was making the noise. In a cage, kept warm with its own fan heater, lay a bundle of dark fur. It cried and cried. The vet opened a hatch and leaned into the cage, picking up the bundle. Immediately, it was quiet. He passed it to me: a huge-footed baby puma, found abandoned or lost out in the country, which appeared to be blind. It nuzzled in close and felt so soft. Mum and I found it hard to resist the temptation to take it back to the boat along with Tiki.

Our cat was wobbling around her cage, blinking as she came out of the anaesthetic. Her whole stomach had been cut vertically and the vet insisted on showing us five tiny kittens that he had removed. Tiki had been robbed.

JOHN

The great scare came when an earthquake hit Kobe in Japan, setting a *tsunami*, or tidal wave, racing across the Pacific towards us. The police advised one of two options: either put to sea and keep off the continental shelf, beyond the point where the long, low wave would rear up on its arrival in shallower water; or leave *English Rose* alongside the yacht club and camp inland on higher ground. Two wrecked ocean-going steamers lying in the river were testament to the power of a Pacific tidal wave, and anxious boat owners were racing to the yacht club from all over town. We decided to delay our departure until the *tsunami* reached Hawaii, where its potential could be measured. We slept lightly, trapped a dozen miles up river, wondering if we should have gone to sea. At dawn I walked to the gate to ask the sentry for news. 'No problema!' he grinned sleepily. The *tsunami* had diminished by the time it passed Hawaii. We could all relax.

Flurries of snow and a short, jubbly sea at the mouth of the Valdivia River in mid-October soon had most of us sick under grey skies, and Tiki yowled for the boyfriend she'd left behind. Bruce and Isso were the only two not to suffer. After a grim night, the trip to Puerto Montt dragged on all day. At last, *English Rose* docked – in a marina for the first time in her nineteen years. And very good it was. Hot showers made sleety morning runs almost enjoyable, and better still, the concrete wall and big tide at the new Marina del Sur allowed us to do our anti-fouling properly at last. Small tides and weak lifts had foiled our every attempt to paint the bottom of the boat all the way from the Panama Canal.

The very few boats and crews we met now had all been through the mill, and we listened closely for advice.

REBECCA

After all sorts of South American red-tape delays at the port captain's office, from which we had to 'clear out' giving our route and next port of call, we finally got away. To cries of 'Good luck!' from other sailors and yacht club friends, we finally hauled in our three anchors, set out in the river to keep us off the rickety wooden quay, and headed off downstream to the open sea once again.

Mum made some lovely salad sandwiches with a little thinly sliced onion in each one for lunch, which we ate while still in the river, but by the time we reached the mouth at Coral, most of us tasted the onion again. Three months on land had done little for our sea legs. J.W. and I shared a watch now, and he was sick shortly before me.

We were all pleased to reach Puerto Montt the next afternoon and to tie up safely in the excellent new marina. Next door to us lay the luxury yacht *Beagle*, which belonged to a Chilean banker. Jim, her Scottish skipper, invited us on board for very welcome mulled wine, and we returned later for supper cooked by Rachel, the cook and crew.

As well as painting a new coat of anti-fouling on the bottom of *English Rose*, we needed to check that the hull was in good order before heading south into the ice. At high tide we rested the yacht against the huge wall built to contain the 5m spring tides, painting the boot topping and cleaning the hull as the tide went out. Once she was dry, Andy greased and checked all the sea cocks. Then the rain began. We spent the night against the wall, hoping that the boat would not fall over, sideways or forwards, or sink too far into the mud beneath us. None of these fates befell us, but by the next day the rain was still falling steadily. We had to get the anti-fouling finished – it was really too much of a risk to chance another night against the wall if the wind picked up – so with the help of long, plastic sheets attached to the toerail, lots of drying rags and the highly dangerous use of electric fan heaters and hairdriers borrowed from *Beagle*, we attempted to dry the hull. We got it done, and though it was not the best job ever, *English Rose* looked pretty good for all her thousands of miles at sea.

The spirit of Chile was really alive in Puerto Montt, capital of the lake district. J.W. and I went to have lunch at Angelmo, the small fishing port famous for its fish restaurants. Tiny ramshackle booths showed off their specialities in the alleyways and loud *señoras* bade us enter their dens and try their *picoroco al vapor*, a giant barnacle whose flesh looked and tasted like crab, locally farmed 'salmon', *congrio*, a delicious white-fleshed fish, or the regional dish, *curanto*. We had been recommended the *curanto* at Juanita's along with *te frio blanco* – cold white wine served in teacups because they were not legally allowed to sell it. Inside, we found two columns of very small tables, jammed close against each other. Behind us, a couple of suited men were concentrating fiercely on their raw horse mussels. Over by the window sat a gaggle of ten middle-aged women, all dolled up for a party and very glamorous. They were eating all sorts of different dishes, screeching away at each other throughout.

After many toasts from different parties, our *curanto* arrived, large and bubbling: mussels, clams, sausage, chicken, pork, potatoes and a kind of flat dumpling in thick gravy. It was very filling, just the sort of lunch you would need if you were off to work in the fields.

An old squint-eyed fisherman with a butterscotch bobble hat pulled firmly down to his eyebrows came in and began playing patriotic songs on his squeezebox. The ladies needed no encouragement and burst into song, their dark eyes filled with passion as they let rip with their strong voices. They'd lived through some bad times, and I couldn't help but remember seeing very similar faces on the television years ago, standing in silent protest holding pictures of missing family.

MARIE CHRISTINE

I had not been nurturing a great desire to return to Patagonia. Twenty years before Bec's epic canoeing trip round Cape Horn with her dad, he and I had spent three months with two friends in what I thought was the bleakest corner of the world. We had travelled mostly in our two rubber dinghies to reach and make the first crossing of the Gran Campo Nevado ice cap. We didn't see a soul through almost three months of rain, snow and storm, and I had been cold, wet and frightened for much of the time.

With *English Rose* as ready as we could make her, we left Puerto Montt at the end of October, bound for the Chilean channels and the greater test, Antarctica. Strapped to the deck we had two long stout poles to push our way through the ice, and we had a good supply of food and spares for all equipment. Any extra space was taken up with Gato Negro, a wonderful Chilean red wine. Now, with J.W. and Bruce aboard, we were set for anything. I was lucky enough to have found a second-hand pair of Sorel blizzard boots – the kind Canadian professionals wear in cold conditions – and I hoped my feet would never be cold again. I was dreading what was to come. I have always suffered from chilblains, and one winter before the advent of electricity at Ardmore I got trench foot from the Caithness slate floor in our kitchen.

'Don't worry, Marie Christine. You needn't go out at all,' John would reassure me in his softer moments. But being 'her indoors' was the last thing I wanted. We both remembered the Southern Ocean on the Whitbread Race, when it was so cold below that condensation turned to ice, and even John was becoming keener on a certain level of comfort: plans were going ahead for two cabin heaters below decks. This time we were not racing, so a few pounds' extra weight was not going to be critical.

Bec had bought herself a huge jumper at one of the artisan stalls in Puerto Montt, knitted from a fleece. It seemed to grow longer each time she wore it. And Isso managed to find a wonderful blanket-type coat which she just had to have. John purchased the biggest available Patagonian knitted slippers and even Tiki was provided for: I found her a fleecy balaclava helmet at the market. I could tell the stallholder doubted my Spanish when I explained that it was for our cat, to keep her warm in the Antarctic. Never keen on confinement, Tiki didn't care for it much, nor for the smart blue quilted lamb's coat that Bruce's father had sent out. But she did, in extreme conditions, snuggle into the hat, for even though she grew fur between the pink pads on her feet, she was a short-haired cat, adapted to the sun. Poor Tiki; poor all of us.

Tiki and I were going through rather a rough patch. Returning to Valdivia after two months in Peru, I was dismayed to find that she had been creeping into our cabin and using the end of my bunk, tucked under a locker, as her lavatory. Cat litter was not available in Chile, so we had improvised with rolled-up bits of newspaper. She became a very well-read cat. I suspected that if her sheets weren't changed daily, being a fastidious creature, she would search for some other suitable spot – the dark recesses of my bunk.

Washing and drying anything in a wet, cold climate is difficult, but a foam mattress and cover on a boat with limited fresh water was a nightmare. The battle raged on. I tried everything – pepper, chilli powder, disinfectant, and spread newspaper permanently over the mattress as a precaution. I encased the mattress in an orange survival bag, which she scratched holes in, and installed an extra litter box in the form of a red washing-up bowl. I tried to improvise a curtain from a bivvy bag to block off my bunk. I did everything I could think of: prayed to God, invoked the Devil. But occasionally, if the door was left open, she would sneak in and I would be in despair.

'Rub her nose in it.' 'Throw her over the side.' Advice came from all quarters, particularly from Andy, who thought I was too soft on her. Pathetically, I felt sorry for her: it was hardly her fault that she had been 'saved' by us and expected to cope with this difficult life. It was a problem she and I would have to work out together. We needed her – she was a friend to all of us. We all loved and laughed over her antics. Andy had spent hours making a monkey's fist, which he hung on to a grabrail in the saloon so that Tiki could bat it back and forth.

As well as the main Antarctic crew of John, Bec, Isso, Andy, J.W., Bruce, Tiki and me, we took our friends Nick Asheshov and his wife Maria del Carmen out to their home among the islands off the east coast of Chile. Nick's son Igor was due to join us later for the ride to Antarctica and back to Brazil.

Also with us for six weeks was sweet, generous Val Greenhalgh, feisty veteran of many of the women's courses, neat and always elegant. Her earthy humour and grit was to add much to the fun and success of the time she was with us. She confided in me after the first few days that what she had been most concerned about was not the hazards of the tortuous Chilean channels, but that alcohol might not be allowed. A quick tour of the lockers would put anybody's mind at rest, and at the end of the day, once we were safely tied up in a web of ropes, John didn't object too strongly to me making high-octane Pisco sours for those of us too weak-willed to resist. Once she established that drinking was not quite forbidden, at any stop where there was a shop, Val would return with clinking bags, adding generously to the boat's supplies.

John was getting feverishly excited about the fishing. Not the gaudy muppets and line off the back of the boat now, but a tempting fly on his springy old Hardy split-cane rod, carefully transported from Ardmore. We were entering an area of almost virgin fresh water, and he had been dreaming of this moment all his life. 'Imagine, Marie Christine,' he had said as we planned the voyage, his blue eyes crinkled with excitement. 'All those inaccessible bays with rivers that we can visit. Maybe places very few people have ever fished. The secret is having the boat!' He had spent much time in the fishing-tackle shops of Valdivia and Puerto Montt, getting information and flies. But, squashed between the hurricane season in Polynesia and summertime in Antarctica, we were a bit early for the best fishing.

On one glorious day he caught a couple of silver salmon which I fried in butter and served with wild celery and a bottle of Chilean chardonnay we had cooled by hanging it off the boat's stern. Far from anywhere, while we fished, the others soaked in hot thermal springs, baths carved out of soft rock by long-gone Indians. We cooked doughnuts in a pot of hot fat over a fire by the water's edge and gazed at the snow-capped peaks of the Andes way above, beyond miles of thick tangled forest.

The Golfo de Ancud was sleeping as we gently sailed west, towards the scattering of islands in the lee of the larger Chiloé. The Jesuits had played a dominant role in these islands, and some fantastic churches had been built. We saw a particularly fine one on Quehue, but it was all locked up.

Our tight schedule – to include the fishing – allowed us barely two days at Castro on Chiloé, where we wanted to top up on fuel and water. On the first day Isso and I were sick: what had we guzzled that the others had not? For me it was fairly catastrophic, for the covered market was the last chance for Christmas shopping. I had bought my presents early in an attempt to avoid the usual last-minute panic – in August up in La Paz – parcelled them up and sent them ahead to the yacht club in Valdivia. The package never arrived.

We charged up and down the steep, narrow streets and found many of the old wooden houses, decoratively shingled on the outer surfaces with alerce, a tough, virtually waterproof wood which has enabled so many historic buildings to survive in spite of the wet climate. The alerce is among the world's oldest living trees, some of them over 3,000 years old. Vast tracts of them have been felled and now the few remaining ones are protected. The town was dominated by the large church in the main square up on the hill. We wondered who had made the decision to paint it lilac and orange.

Near the church we met up with Val, who had been enjoying the company of a charming Chilote gentleman who had taken her to the post office. Val ended up in a bar buying him a whisky by way of thanks. They had had a jolly time, and she looked brilliant, but now was maybe not the time to attempt to clamber down the 18ft slippery vertical timber pilings which supported the pier with all our parcels. The tide in Castro was huge, and the boat, still afloat was now far below us. Seeing our predicament, some fishermen offered us a lift in their boat and saved the day. We kept quiet about our saviours, and when the boys arrived back and made the descent themselves, not without difficulty, they must have wondered how we Amazons had managed.

That evening we headed down the coast to Quellón, a fishing port with a naval presence. The weather was worsening, and in the night our anchor dragged so we took turns to sit anchor watch, drawing straws for the order. A large ferry moved out slowly and fishing boats came in and out, requiring the watcher to be extra vigilant and careful not to confuse stationary and moving lights.

JOHN

In 1956, while a cadet in the merchant navy, I landed in Avonmouth after a painfully slow voyage back from Africa. I was only seventeen then, and the Somerset countryside in early summer left a lasting impression of England and home. Among the small green fields and woods on Quehue, with the dogs and geese and bent old ladies digging for cockles on the beach, I had a strange feeling I was once more in the Somerset of far-off days.

The fishermen waved with more enthusiasm here than anywhere we'd been so far; they laughed, making great wave motions with their arms and pointing ahead, towards the fearsome Gulf of Corcorvado. Andy was sick straight away but said he didn't feel too bad. We kept the engine running all the way across the open gulf, managing 9 or 10 knots with a squally westerly wind under leaden skies. Bruce never felt sick, but his salami and cheese on water biscuits soon ensnared the rest of us. Staring at the flickering yellow radar up in the doghouse, and still feeling queasy, I glanced up towards the land. Shrouded in rain and denuded of their forest, the low windswept grey Guaitecas Islands looked every bit as miserable as I felt. It was early afternoon by the time we came to anchor in the tiny port of Melinka, lying snugly at the northern tip of a mass of largely unvisited islands. A Lithuanian immigrant called Westhoff had settled in Melinka in 1859, naming the place after his wife. He'd set about felling all the cypress trees, and with the proceeds he came to own 200 boats. The islands were a fitting memorial: Westhoff had certainly not left the place better than he found it.

Melinka life centred on the sea. The young men dived for clams among the kelp in the icy waters of the Humbolt current sweeping up from the Antarctic. Dressed in tatty wetsuits, they breathed through long yellow pipes linked to erratic rusty compressors in the boats above them. They were scouring the seabed just as Westhoff had scoured the land before them. I didn't see any old divers.

In the morning we motored up a winding channel past a few lonely log huts bleached silver by the storms. It was a lovely day, so we anchored for a while and I took the chance to go for a run, alone, along the clean pebble beach. The flightless steamer ducks, oyster-catchers and hawks in this wild, empty sunlit place cheered me no end. The others, suffering from a sort of gastric flu, chose to walk instead, along a narrow path through the bush, across a narrow isthmus to the open Pacific.

This was the life: going where we pleased, wandering south through the archipelago. The densely forested islands were the tips of submerged rocky mountains. With a thousand anchorages to choose from, we picked the south-east corner of Isla Valverde for the night. It was low tide as we strode across the muddy beach at the mouth of a small stream. Dark tangled trees grew right down to the shoreline. I could see no sign of fish in the pools, but I did spot little squirts of clear water jetting up near our footfalls, which reminded me of the razorfish at home. Andy and Isso paddled back to *English Rose* for a couple of buckets while Val led the hunt for the white-shelled clams. Cooked in garlic butter and washed down with white Chilean wine, they made for a fine evening as the rain battered our decks.

Running before a westerly gale next morning, we dashed across the broad Canal Morelada and found shelter behind Isla Magdalena. Entranced by the whole area, I was finding myself visiting places with a rather more permanent view in mind.

MARIE CHRISTINE

As we travelled south, the weather worsened. It was becoming Patagonia as I remembered it. But at least being in a yacht with a cabin was a lot easier than those months in rubber dinghies and tents.

In 1972 we had all but lived off mussels; now everyone was strongly advised not to eat them. Stories abounded – the Frenchman who ignored the warnings and died in agony only a few hours after enjoying his *moules* – and apparently in the Chilean navy eating mussels was a court-martial offence. One theory was that the toxin had come across the Pacific in water ballast from Japan in the ships coming to load the mountains of wood chips we'd seen in Valdivia and Puerto Montt.

We could have spent months, years even, exploring so many islands, but it was already early November and we had a long way to go before stepping off the bottom of South America on our way to Antarctica after Christmas. And anyway, John wanted to get back to the mainland to fish some of the bigger rivers. It was calm for much of the time, and we were using the engine to keep up to schedule, knowing that we could still buy fuel along the way. It was a far cry from the Whitbread race, when we had been allowed to use the engine, out of gear, only for battery-charging.

A stiff northerly breeze soon had us across Canal Moraleda and into the narrow sheltered Canal Jacaf, with Isla Magdalena to starboard and the mainland to port, a mysterious world of convoluted fjords, thundering waterfalls and steep, tree-smothered slopes breaking out into snowy peaks and tumbling glaciers. Above and beyond, lay the eternal motionless blue distance. 'Wagner country,' John said to no one in particular. We all agreed. Very occasionally, we would see a wisp of woodsmoke and, rounding a bend, spot a homesteader, his boat – his only means of transport – pulled high above the beach.

Dense temperate rainforest, thick with bamboo, grew right down to the water's edge. The giant-leafed Gunnera Magellanica, shaped like a huge rhubarb, bright purple and cerise fuchsia and escallonia all fought for light. There were masses of a type of blackcurrant bush, Ribes Magellanicum, which was in flower, and looked as though it would bear quantities of fruit. Nobody I asked could answer me on this – all they ever talked of was the abundance of strawberries and apples which would ripen in the hot, short summer when we would be in Antarctica. And of course, there was *calafate* – Berberis – everywhere, with its thorny branches and brilliant yellow orange flowers. Twenty years ago our friend Francisco had told us, 'If you eat the berry of the *calafate*, you will return.' We did and we had.

'If only we were younger,' John said wistfully to me – I had never heard him mention age as a deterrent before – 'what a life it would be. It would be like going back thirty years to the time when we first lived in our leaky croft house on the Ardmore peninsula.' Yes, I thought to myself, three miles from the road and no running water or electricity. But the idea tugged away; the territory here was virgin, untouched. Without pollution or interference from humans, flowers, birds, and fish were so abundant. So was the rain – over 10ft fell every year.

It was getting dark when we finally dropped anchor and got tied up for the night in Bahia Dorita, a sheltered bay off Seno Ventisqeuros. To our amazement, a semi-naked man popped up from somewhere in the undergrowth of ferns on the shore and shouted something in alarm. It sounded like 'Omigod,' and then: 'Are you all right?' in Spanish. As we went astern, digging in the bow anchor, the man and his glamorous lady friend jumped out of their previously secluded thermal pool, and, covering themselves in towels, left for higher ground, fearing that we were going to crash into the shore. We were in one of our usual mooring commotions, shouting and revving and reversing.

Once secure, we looked further into the bay in the gathering darkness trying to guess what we had come upon. Something was happening here, all right. Lights illuminated a pier and alongside was a huge sleek white and blue hydrofoil resembling a spaceship. Timber buildings hugged the shoreline, one standing three storeys high and boasting twin towers. We'd heard that an American had built a fishing lodge somewhere near here in 1970, reaching the inaccessible lakes by seaplane.

Well before lunch next day, as we sipped Pisco sours from frosted glasses, Hugo, the urbane hotel manager, told us something of this development, surrounded by forest, jungle and water. 'The American couldn't make money here. If the weather wasn't right, the seaplane couldn't take off and people couldn't fish. They could be stuck here. It wasn't good for business. In fact it was almost a ruin when Herr Kossman bought it in 1985. He could see the potential and rebuilt the place.'

Outside in the rain, on a wooden post by the pier, sat a kingfisher: grey, white and russet. It sat so still I wondered if it was real. It was early in the season. The couple whose cavortings in the pool we had disturbed the night before had come on a package trip from Puerto Montt, landing at a small airfield a few hours away and joining the 30-knot Patagonia Express, an ultra-luxurious hydrofoil. The itinerary included a brief stop at the lodge, to enjoy 'walks in the rainforest and hot mineral water pools on the edge of the sea'. The tourists, mostly elderly Americans and Germans, then went on to visit Chile's spectacular San Rafael glacier. It was a grand concept.

Apparently, the naval architect owner had snorkelled to freedom from East Germany in 1961, coming ashore with only what he stood up in. Friends helped him get to Chile, where he'd made millions in shipbuilding. This hotel was a gift to his only daughter.

After a tour of the magnificent suites, we scuttled back to *English Rose* knowing how pleased our team would be to hear of Hugo's kind invitation to use the thermal pools when the guests were out.

Next morning, the Patagonian Express roared off leaving the hotel empty, and Hugo and his assistant Carmen came aboard for 'cocktails' before inviting us to the staff *asado*, or barbecue. Everyone welcomed us to the open-sided timber hut where the lamb was cooking, tantalisingly slowly, over a wood fire. Chilean red wine flowed, and in between the struggle to make conversation we laughed and sang and danced. And J.W. gazed, entranced, at Carmen.

Warm, steamy water ran down the pebble beach, close off the stern of *English Rose*. It was faintly sulphurous, but fresh, and nearly perfect for washing clothes. Val, Isso and I paddled ashore with soap powder, buckets and our dirty duds, where we were surprised by a couple wandering along the shore. I jumped up guiltily and engaged them in lively conversation, hoping they hadn't seen our dhobi, of which I was sure the hotel would never understand and certainly not approve. Jorge and

Nelly came out to see the boat and invited John and me to dinner in the hotel. We played at being real people, not the drop-outs we had become, remembering not to lick our plates to save the washing up. In our poor Spanish we discussed Jorge's business problems while I winked at the waiter I had danced with in the firelight of the *asado*.

As the hotel was more or less empty, Carmen asked if we would like to watch a video. She rattled through a list of English-speaking films, until Bec and I halted her with a shriek 'The Piano! We'd love to see *The Piano*!' John would have preferred something about sport or war, but he loved us all being together, so, as if making up for past occasions when we hadn't had the time to do things as a family, he would endure *The Piano* if that was what the majority wanted. Bec and I had missed the film because we were away, and Isso loved anything romantic with kissing. The boys and Val wanted to get on with writing letters, so the four family members trooped along to watch the movie.

The video-recorder was playing up, but nevertheless the story had Bec and me sitting on the edge of our seats. Being slightly deaf, John couldn't really hear; Isso didn't know what was going on and kept asking questions. Bec and I were far too transported to go into lengthy explanations, rattily retorting, 'Sshh. Just listen.' Plodding back to the boat in the pitch darkness, the rain escalated a family discussion into a full row. 'Bloody stupid . . . Woman's film . . . What was the point . . .? All those bare bottoms,' grumbled John. Wisely, Bec withdrew from the argument, going on ahead with Isso. I was getting more and more cross. I felt John's criticisms were levelled less at the film than at me for having enjoyed it. Briefly, I had escaped into another world, and now I was furious at having the magic destroyed by this silly argument.

Bruce, who came to pick us up in the dinghy, must have wondered at the shouting on the shore. He hadn't been on the boat very long and didn't know us that well. 'Did you enjoy the film?' he asked politely, signalling the start of the second round of the argument. I hopped into the boat and as John stepped on to join us I just saw red. In a terrible overpowering rage, I flung myself at my tormentor, pushing him over the side; screaming abuse, I picked up the paddle and whacked him as he struggled to get back on board. 'Oh dear! Oh dear!' I heard Bruce muttering, not knowing quite what to do. Isso was giggling, enjoying the drama hugely. Bec took charge. 'Come on, Dad,' she said sharply, and the two daughters helped their dripping father back into the dinghy. Bec levelled her blue-grey eyes at us both. 'Now just stop it, you two,' she said fiercely. 'Don't talk about the film any more.'

We were a sorry sight as we stepped back up on to *English Rose*. John, who does not get cross easily, was furious, and sat in a dripping rage. I was mortified at having lost my temper, and I had got all his kit wet. How would we ever get it all rinsed in fresh water and dry by morning, particularly his favourite short green Nokia wellies. And what about his trousers? They were his only pair. I was well and truly in the doghouse that night as John turned his back on me in the confines of our narrow bed.

But he doesn't harbour grudges, and next morning he had a new bee buzzing in his bonnet. 'Why don't we find a little spot down here in the south of Chile?'

Further north, around Puerto Montt, at the turn of the century, immigrants from Europe had been given 75 hectares of land plus 12 for each child, a pair of oxen, a cow with a calf, 500 boards, 100lb of nails, a certificate of ownership and free medical attention and medicine, which probably didn't amount to much. In return they had to build a house, clear 2 hectares of trees and fence it off. So keen was Chile to encourage settlement in this remote region that, we understood, the land was still being given away – or at least sold very cheaply. One third of Chile lies south of Puerto Montt and within that area lives barely 3 per cent of the population. 'You should come and live in a place like this, John,' friends had said.

'We'll migrate to Patagonia each autumn and escape the Scottish winter. It'll be eternal summer.' But there was a catch. 'You'd love living on an island off Tierra del Fuego, wouldn't you, Marie Christine? Think of the fishing.' My pioneering spirit was wearing a bit thin, and building a hut hundreds of miles further south from windblown trees which grew horizontally was not for me.

'Maybe somewhere not quite so extreme?' I suggested tentatively, aware that nicer places you have to pay for. I could not deny that the country had great allure. Isso wanted somewhere where she could have a horse and Rebecca merely muttered vaguely about coming to visit. But for me, I overwhelmingly wanted a sheltered plot where I could plant and nurture a garden in the best growing climate in the world. I wanted somewhere remote, by the sea, with a river; a place that had been lived in and abandoned, I yearned for an orchard with apple-trees with twisted boughs, bent under many seasons of fruit. Somewhere I could sink my fingers into the soil and plant, and where I could look up into the snowfields on the mountains. Had I been at sea for too long? John's priorities were a good anchorage for the yacht, and fishing, fishing, fishing. So it had to be between latitudes 40 and 45S, on a coastal fjord with abundant rainfall. This was not a problem in Chile's Region 10, where plenty of rain falls on the cold, mountainous jungle each year. We asked Hugo if he knew of anywhere that would suit us. He pointed us towards Aldunate, half a day away by boat.

We sailed out below the hanging glacier of Quelat in search of a dream at the end of a winding fjord leading nowhere. In a sheltered bay sat three timber houses. I felt a surge of wild excitement. Normally it's disappointing to see houses in remote bays, but somehow, out here in this frontier land, they had the opposite effect.

I could only gaze at my beautiful surroundings. The Aldunate property runs up a large, grassy valley with snow-capped mountains on three sides. On the fourth it is bordered by the bay into which two rivers run and where our boat was anchored. A young man galloped up on a horse, wearing a battered hat and sitting on a sheepskin saddle. He called out sharply to me, 'Permisso!' I quickly realised that he was the caretaker, and how impolite we had been not to have come to see him first. I apologised and his manner softened. José lived in a wooden hut near the shore with his wife and two children and looked after the enormous property for the Chilean owner, who spent most of his time in Cisnes, a little port some six hours away by boat.

José showed us round. The place had been neglected. The first wooden cottage was almost a ruin. Its roof was falling in and the bathroom floor had rotted away to the open air. But as you stepped outside into the hot sun, the air buzzed, there was honeysuckle, and dotted about the green field were eight cherry and eight apple trees, bright and sweet with blossom.

The main house, in a slightly better state of repair, stood on a hill, closer to the rivers. It commanded stunning views into the savage mountains. I had never seen such splendour. We wandered around, scrutinising the rotting timber foundation posts and the roof's wooden shingles and rusty corrugated iron, badly in need of attention. What would it be like sitting here in front of a big log fire? Hydrangeas circled the house, and a lawn spiked with rushes fell away to trees below. Much work needed to be done, and soon, to save it all.

At the back was a small kitchen garden which José's wife tended.

There were neat rows of peas, beans, onions; a huge blueish artichoke filled one corner, alongside some rhubarb, the first I had seen in South America. There were rows of raspberry canes, and the strawberries were full of white flowers. Pink roses and honeysuckle tangled in the fence and in the rickety greenhouse were rows of lettuce.

As we sat eating our picnic lunch of tinned sardines and biscuits, we talked about the possibilities of living in such a place. It had obviously been a big farm once. Across the river there was an enormous cattle shed, 100m long.

'What about you and Will coming to farm here, Bec?' John suggested. She thought long and hard before cautiously answering, 'I think it might be just too remote for us, Dad. And all that rain, I don't think we'd like it.' It was at least a six-hour trip from the nearest doctor, or shop, or school. It would be tough on a young couple. But it was a chance to farm, which was Will's great passion.

'You don't even know if it's for sale,' Val commented sagely. I had already got the garden planted out in my mind.

'Everything's for sale,' John retorted, dreaming of the two rivers and the perfect anchorage for his boat. I wondered if this was going to turn into one of John's missions.

'You must go and talk to Klaus Hopperdietzel in Puyuhuapi. He's your man. He'll know who owns the Aldunate property,' Hugo told us when we returned to our old mooring in Bahia Dorita for one last soak in the thermal springs.

A bitter wind rattled down from the glaciers that early morning. The village at the end of the fjord was mostly a collection of quaint old-style shingle cottages, dominated by three large imposing Germanic houses with sloping roofs designed to shed the alpine snows.

Back in 1935 four young German settlers had arrived by sea with a dream to set up a German colony run on Nazi community principles of equal effort and sharing. These men were to have been the forerunners of a larger group, but the outbreak of the Second World War four years later, made it impossible for any more Germans to leave their homeland.

Cut off from the outside world, the four pioneers and their families developed the land into a prosperous farming community. The settlement was virtually cut off from the outside world until a few years ago, when the Austral road, which travels south into Argentina, was extended to take in the village and brought summer visitors to Puyuhuapi.

Having grown up on war stories, John and I were intrigued. Were we back in a Nazi stronghold? There were wild rumours: a war criminal was said to be living alone at the end of the fjord to the north and one of the village elders might have been Hitler's chauffeur.

Klaus, a rather dishevelled man of about thirty-five, invited us into the German-style kitchen. I glanced around the neglected room. On one wall hung a framed photograph taken from the shore. It was Puyuhaupi, Klaus explained, a few weeks after the four young men had arrived. Smoke was rising from a crude hut on the shore, completely surrounded by huge trees. Three figures stood stoutly upright. I wondered if this house was where that hut had stood. It would take four of the Master Race to turn this jungle swamp into fertile farmland and build a village. Opposite stood a jammed bookshelf. John and I glanced conspiratorialy at each other. We had both seen the swastika on the spine of one book about Hitler, near it another on Adenauer and yet another on Jesus Christ.

John explained our interest in Aldunate. 'Maybe God has sent you,' Klaus said suddenly. We had the feeling that this lonely man was the last one of his kind left. I could tell he was intrigued and drawn to John. If we came to live here they would be friends.

Walther, Klaus's eighty-four-year-old father, blue-eyed and frail, joined us for lunch. Klaus's maid helped him to his upright seat at the table with a clear view down the long fjord. Walther was the last survivor of the original four. Klaus introduced us, explaining in German who we were. The old man's face brightened. We talked of the cold wind and the forthcoming summer, and Walther's health, the subject which seemed to interest him most. Practising my best German to fill a silence, I asked him if he took much exercise. He replied that he made his own suppositories and asked what I recommended for constipation. Somewhat taken aback, I suggested grated apple. Immediately he clapped his hands and imperiously ordered the maid to find some apples and grate them for him.

In 1950 Walther, who had trained as a textile engineer in the Sudetenland before coming out to Chile, had built a factory for his father, a professional carpet-maker. When his parents were at last free to leave war-devastated Germany they joined Walther in Chile. The business was a success, and in spite of, or maybe because of, the location, it became famous. Beautiful high-quality carpets, fit to grace any German home, were sold throughout Chile and beyond. We had seen some examples at the hotel.

Walther's younger brother had also come to Chile after the war. His time as a radio operator in the Luftwaffe, on the Russian front, had left him a nervous wreck. He stuttered and threw himself to the ground if ever he heard a shot. In the end he killed himself. The Hopperdietzel Bridge, which we had crossed, had been built by his family as a memorial to him.

The dream of a sharing community had long since fallen apart. Those of the four original founders who had more children required more funds to send them away to the German school in far-off Santiago, and this caused resentment. When the communists came into power in 1971, their land was appropriated and divided into plots, and most of the second generation left.

We sensed that Walther had expected much of Klaus. The burden of that expectation had left his son cautious, and he confided that he would rather keep his money in the bank than pursue further developments. But he said he was keen for us to come: I think he imagined John and himself going off on challenging expeditions.

After much talk, Klaus decided he would come with us as far as Puerto Natales on *English Rose*. He would take us to meet the man at Cisnes who was selling Aldunate. And maybe, if he had, it would all have turned out differently. But, at the last minute, after we had waited all that long afternoon, he told us that he couldn't come. Perhaps his reticence was the reason why Klaus was the last of the second generation still living in Puyuhaupi. Whatever it was, we will not struggle to live out our days in splendid isolation at Aldunate. But we will never forget cruising through the channels of this almost empty archipelago, and how we happened upon a place that utterly enchanted us and almost ensnared us in its beguiling web. How dangerous sailing is.

JOHN

We began our move back west across Canal Moraleda, motoring in a silky, flat calm towards the maze of channels leading south-west, through countless uninhabited outer islands, to Bahía Anna Pink, from where we planned to enter the Pacific on our way across the notorious Golfo de Penas. The gulf was the great divide separating the temperate forests of the north with their hummingbirds, from the harsher southern climate, where ice caps and glaciers dictated the temperature as the continent dwindled towards Antarctica.

'Hard to starboard!' Bruce screamed from his perch in the mizen crosstrees. *English Rose* heeled sharply to port, as I spun the wheel at 8 knots, cutting the revs with the other hand. Dead ahead, the bare rock lay hardly 2ft beneath calm, clear water. We all fell silent, each imagining hitting a jagged rock at full speed in liquid ice, far from help. With no ocean swell to mark the hazards, unsounded fjords are perilous. We must remember that not all rocks are covered with floating kelp.

17

Glaciers

JOHN

On our first approach to the open Pacific, a sharp gale drove us back into the channels and we spent an uneasy night sheltering behind an island near Bahía Anna Pink, fretting about the fearsome reputation of Golfo de Penas. But next morning fortune smiled and the sun shone as we ventured out on to a long ocean swell with a free wind which took us across the gulf in just under twenty-four hours. Entering the shelter of the bleak islands surrounding Canal Mesier, we felt as if we had just crossed the Pacific.

The glacier tongues came licking right down to the sea now, and the much colder climate had us well wrapped up. But the treeline was considerably lower, and this would give us much easier access to the mountains.

Beneath the ice caps, in tiny Puerto Eden, among the deep shadows of the steep-sided fjords which prevented any access other than by sea, we found one of only nine remaining Alacalufe Indians. In 1972, Marie Christine and I had stayed on their tiny dog-infested island, Unicornio, hundreds of miles further south, on our way to make the first crossing of the Gran Campo Nevado ice cap. The Alacalufe were a nomadic near-naked tribe who had roamed the channels in their dugout canoes for thousands of years. Now installed in a simple silver aluminium hut above a rain-swept bay, forty-year-old Veronica sat shyly by the black wood-burning stove in the centre of her blue-walled kitchen. At first she was wringing her hands with anxiety, but her face lit up at our mention of her family and soon she was grinning hugely over our old photographs of her Aunt Fresia and Uncle Alexandro.

This was a wild region, and our friends, dead now, had not died peacefully. Eduardo had been shot dead by a soldier who ran amok, Calisto killed in a shepherds' knife fight and Francisco eaten by his dog in his lonely woodcutter's cabin. Only Alexandro had made it to the hospital in Punta Arenas.

The strain of navigating by night through narrow channels with only lightning to illuminate the cruel peaks was beginning to show, and as usual small personal habits caused friction. In his conscientious efforts to get clear weatherfax print-outs, J.W. spent many hours in the aft cabin fiddling with the HF set, which reacted with all sorts of terrible irritating noises. He in turn hated the CD pop music served up by Isso, the music officer. 'J.W.'s either playing with his boodgie down back, or moanin' about the music!' is the way Andy summed it up. Personally, I'd never been happier. I was tremendously relieved at the happy outcome of our Peruvian journey; the prickly heat was a distant nightmare and there was no seasickness in the shelter of the channels. And in this majestic place we seldom saw any sign of mankind's destruction. Yet it was in terms of man's consumer society that some of us viewed this rare world of pure nature. 'It's soap-powder blue, is that glacier,' Andy snorted on his twenty-eighth birthday in Estero Peel, where we encountered masses of loose ice drifting before 35-knot winds.

Pressing on south, we spent a couple of days stormbound in Estero de las Montañas, a long, narrow fjord lined with steep glaciers falling from magical mountains. While I sympathised with J.W.'s wish to disappear into the mountains alone away from the CDs, I felt it was too dangerous. I could never quite free myself from the adventure school and my responsibility to parents. So we split into two teams: J.W., Andy and Bruce climbed in the morning and then the Ridgways and Val sallied forth in the afternoon.

Down by the sea everything was sprouting back into life with the spring. We fought our way through the wonders of the 'cold jungle' with its vivid green nothofagus trees, festooned with pale green moss and haunted by swooping black and red Magellanic woodpeckers. The pools underfoot were filled with clicking frogs and huge tadpoles, and river crossings with Isso never lacked drama. Once above the trees, we scrambled up precipitous chimneys of wet rock, to the sound of creaking glaciers. As we emerged on to the lip of a colossal cliff, falling directly on to the glacier grumbling far below, our fears attracted circling condors who looked on us as a meal about to be served.

In this inspiring setting, we felt alive. Marie Christine and I finally decided that the John Ridgway School of Adventure would, after all, open for its twenty-sixth season in May 1995. We were encouraged, too, by Bruce and Rita, in touch through the INMARSAT link. Spring for us was autumn for them, but high above that dear northern loch of home, where gales were already whirling the salt spray up on to their windows, they were nevertheless keen as mustard that the school should continue.

MARIE CHRISTINE

In the meantime we headed slowly towards Puerto Williams, the world's most southerly settlement, for Christmas. The huge-leaved Gunnera Magellanica and the walls of purple and red fuchsia that had hugged the shore gave way now to bare rock and scrub as glaciers became more numerous. At night we tied ourselves into a web of ropes to hold us fast in the notorious winds of this region. And one night, a 20-ton chunk of ice bumped against our stern and tangled in our lines. The time was 4.13 am. John (naked) and I (in my white nightie) perched on the stern, puzzling over this huge problem. After a bit of shivering, we crept back to our makeshift bed in the doghouse and slept fitfully while the monster growled and creaked. By morning it had left.

REBECCA

As we came sailing east through the Andes, my grandfather, informed of our position in our nightly faxes to his house on Lake Road in Wimbledon, was following our every move in his 1947, ninth-edition Bartholemew Atlas of the World.

This new countryside was especially bleak. Leaving behind the spectacular mountains and glaciers, we entered a land of undulating hills and convoluted wind-scoured waters where skeins of geese flew by, stretching into the distance towards the plains of Argentina and the Atlantic. Bundling along on the usual afternoon gale, we saw Puerto Natales at first as a little whitish dot in a vast landscape of sweeping empty spaces, the very end of nowhere. But at over 8 knots, this dot, once the largest refrigeration plant in the world, grew steadily into a spreading scatter of low tin buildings.

It was already late afternoon by the time we came up to the town, but in the southern summer there was no danger of darkness until nearly midnight. Painted in bright pastels of blue, white, red and green, the ancient frontier-post bungalows appeared to be hugging the ground in their efforts to avoid the endless winds which threatened to send them rolling like tumbleweed across the plains.

Puerto Natales wasn't the brightest of prospects, there was no mention this time of Mum and Dad buying a house. And poor Val, due to fly home to Manchester for Christmas, begged not to be put off immediately in this godforsaken place. Two grey navy patrol boats took up the end and one side of the pier, where people were signalling for us to come alongside. Thinking they knew best, Dad promptly ploughed a groove in the mud in his attempt to reach the free side.

'I don't think she'll come off this time!' he cursed, revving the engine hard astern and planning despairingly to get a rope to the nearest boat, moored further out in the channel.

Thinking quickly, J.W. cried: 'Everyone back to the stern!' And under the interested gaze of the locals, the bow lifted, just a bit. Ever so slowly, we slid gently back off the mud. 'Just burning the excess diesel off the injectors,' grinned Andy, nodding at the blue smoke coming from the exhaust. 'Not the best way to arrive,' said Dad, as he clambered into the dinghy with the ship's papers. 'Ah, well . . .'

I had had a splitting headache all afternoon and a slight tiff with Dad on deck. I sat in the doghouse away from the mêlée and noise below, crossly, watching him paddle in. I noticed two burly men on the pier who were also watching him as he came towards them. They wore heavy jackets, hands firmly in their pockets. The evening air was chilling.

'Yon Reedgway!' A guttural bellow boomed out as Dad reached the top of the iron steps and a great black bearded bear of a man embraced him. 'I thought it was you!' He roared with laughter, kissing both my father's cheeks. 'It was the way you tried to come alongside the pier.'

Conrado Alvarez had been the skipper of *Compass Rose*, the 50ft steel yacht which had supported us on our kayaking expedition round Cape Horn in 1992, and which had provided the inspiration for our own doghouse. Conrado had handled *Compass Rose* well in some pretty tight spots, and Dad and he had had great discussions about sailing in the channels famous for their ferocious weather and williwaws. I suppose I knew then that Dad hoped to come back with our own boat.

Conrado soon had the ship's papers cleared and three huge men wobbled back in the little dinghy with Dad and began hauling themselves up our frail wooden steps. Conrado enveloped me in a great bear hug and, lowering me to the deck at last, turned to the rail and introduced me to a huge silent man with a thick mop of black hair and a Kitchener moustache. 'This is the brother of my wife, Roberto MacLeod,' he rumbled. 'He is the best mechanic in Puerto Natales.' Roberto and I shook hands. It was like clasping a bundle of marlin spikes. The third man was Conrado's Uncle Victor, who offered us his mooring out in the channel for the night.

The beaming Conrado was overjoyed that we had come and we were delighted to meet our old friend again. The reunion turned into a major event. We shared our dehydrated curry and lots of Chilean red wine with our honoured visitors and tapes of the Pogues and Runrig enlivened the party considerably.

It was late, and after kisses all round, the three visitors climbed shakily over the side of the yacht into their open wooden boat, *Pato Donald* (Donald Duck), and wobbled home. '*Asado! Si!* We will have *asado* tomorrow night at my house!' Conrado boomed exuberantly over the misty water. It was nearly midnight and barely dark – time to go below and welcome in Bruce's birthday.

There are few things as enchanting as an early-morning run on a perfect summer's day in high latitudes. We groaned out of bed for exercises on the pier and a run at six the next morning, and, tottering back along the deserted seafront, we heard a whistle and saw Uncle Victor waving for us to join him for a cup of coffee at his home. The wood-burning stove in the kitchen had been converted to run on cheap local natural gas. Next to it we found Bruce, already tucking into a birthday plateful of bread and *manja*, a sort of spread made from boiled condensed milk. Then we met up with Roberto, who had a good long look over the engine. 'Mercedes OM314. *Muy bueno!*' he pronounced over the noise of the motor, holding one of his massive fingers lightly against a mounting bolt to test the vibration. Dad was jotting down everything he said, and this was music to his ears.

Outwardly, Puerto Natales and its small shingled tin houses did not appear all that thrilling, but its inhabitants were charming. Little shops sprang up in people's front rooms selling all sorts of junk: plastic toys, pink knitted table mats and baby clothes. These provided an unexpected extra opportunity for Christmas shopping. There were a lot of Chilean peculiarities which made unusual stocking-fillers: Indian lettuce hand cream in a small tin; sealed plastic bags of pickled onions and gherkins; *aji* a hot sauce made from chilli peppers, dried figs and apricots; popcorn; locally dried herbs; powdered fruit drinks; foil packs of black cherry jam; Nestlé chocolate; dried seaweed for soups and stews. And, of course, there were more familiar goods, which all seemed much more exciting and useful now: toothpaste and new toothbrush, and brand-new white knickers, even if not quite the style you usually wore. It was hard to go anywhere without having a long conversation. Perhaps my Spanish was improving, or maybe it was interesting for the locals to have someone to talk to. In any event, they were really friendly and fascinated by us living on a boat. And they warmed to us as a family, and especially to Isso.

Most time arrangements in South America are a little loose, to say the least, the *asado* at Conrado's house was no exception. We typical British had all been in a panic to get ready on the boat. Titi, Conrado's sixteen-year-old daughter, came to collect us from the pier at about 7.30 pm and we walked slowly to the house, arriving by 8 pm, by which time we were fairly hungry. Trooping through the small tin house into the alley at the back, we were a little dismayed to see that the lamb's carcass had only just been cut in two down the spine and speared on to the giant barbecuing stake, stuck in the ground at an acute angle over the gently burning embers. It was going to be a few hours yet before we got a bite to eat.

But the wine flowed and we began to chat. Titi's three-legged cat and her five black and white kittens wandered into peril under everyone's feet. The boys jumped over the fence into the long grass in the field next door and engaged in some shot-putting with one of Conrado's sons, who was a local champion. There were numerous jokes and photographs taken. The focal point of the evening, the cooking meat, was finally pronounced ready by Conrado and ceremoniously rushed into the kitchen by his wife, Annie, where it could be carved quickly. We left the dying embers and went inside, drawn like moths to the electric light. We helped ourselves from vast dishes groaning with meat, new potatoes and salad. Annie's home-made *aji* added spice to everything it touched and was far more tasty than the stuff from the shops, which was good, but pure fire. No sooner had we made some space on our plates than they were filled again. The mood was high and there were many '*saluds*'. Bruce could never have imagined before he left home that he would spend his birthday like this.

Full of fun, Mum said she would like to return their hospitality and cook a typically British dinner for the Alvarez family in their own kitchen. They accepted. When we returned next evening, we found Mrs MacLeod, Conrado's mother-in-law, already seated at the kitchen table. Although well into her eighties, she was still strong, like her children, Annie and Roberto. She had white hair and ice-blue eyes and a rather stern face. 'Will you take a scone with your tea?' she asked. It was more of a command than a question. There was something odd about this scene, like déjà vu, and suddenly I realised what it was. I could have been sitting in any Highland kitchen: Mrs MacLeod spoke perfect English with an Inverness accent. Her parents, both from the Black Isle, just north of Inverness, had come out to Patagonia as newlyweds. As a child, she had spoken only English at home, and it was not until she started school at the age of seven, that she began to learn to speak Spanish. Her mother never did speak it fluently, she said.

The birth of freezers had completely altered the structure of sheep-farming. Her father had come here as a wool expert, but, as happened in New Zealand, meat became a commercial proposition as well and eventually overtook the wool industry, which declined with over-production. A huge freezer unit was built on the seashore, and freezer ships came and went to England from here. Large landowners and strict regimes meant cheap labour, but when the 'people' took over in the 1972 revolution it all went to pot and ceased to function. Once Britain joined the EC, Patagonia's main market for frozen lamb disappeared.

Mrs MacLeod's current concern was an invasion of minks which had escaped from a fur farm further north. 'They eat the cows' titties. We'd shoot them, but Pinochet took all our rifles and we never got them back. What can we do?'

We persuaded Mrs MacLeod to join us and enjoy some food from the country of her parents' birth, which she had never seen. Mum had bought a massive piece of beef which would never have fitted in our oven on the boat, but was not out of place in Annie's kitchen. With me as the home-trained galley slave, we peeled piles of the potatoes and carrots we'd lugged through the streets, staggering under their weight. We were not quite sure how many we were cooking for. Sometimes in Chile more people turned up than you expected.

The Yorkshire pudding batter was made and the main course was sorted out. Pudding was to be the Scottish touch, Atholl brose, made from browned oatmeal and whipped cream with honey to sweeten it and whisky for flavour and warmth. Being from Scotland, we always carried whisky for special occasions and medicinal purposes.

I loved that afternoon. It was like stepping back in time, fifty years or more. Mothers and their daughters prepared the food with time to chat. Sometimes today we seem to be in too much of a hurry to enjoy things. Does television kill family life and interaction? Was this not just what Americans like to call 'quality time'? I hoped I would remember this as I grew older and had my own family. The Chilean contingent were amazed by the Yorkshire pudding, never having experienced anything quite like it before. The beef, of course, was delicious, and the Atholl brose slipped down well too.

Sadly, this was to be our farewell party. With the help of Conrado's sons and their jeep, we had filled up our jerrycans with diesel and found some more oil filters; topped up on food with another vanload that Mum had selected from the largest store in town – with plenty of fruit and vegetables, including three sacks of the precious potatoes we had missed so much on our long Pacific Leg. We also collected post and sent post home. We had also been on a wild-goose chase round people's houses for paraffin – they sold it from their own 45-gallon drums. Unfortunately, the town was dry.

Now Val had to leave us to get home in time for Christmas and we had to head on south as summer approached. On a grey morning we hugged her goodbye on the deck, dropped the mooring and motored out past the pier. Val waved her large white hanky in the way Dad often does. She was also trying to mop her eyes without us seeing. Conrado appeared on the end of the pier, lifting his jumper to reveal the *English Rose* polo shirt we had sent ashore for him with Val. I very much hope that one day I will return to Puerto Natales.

JOHN

We felt we'd abandoned Val. How would she manage without Spanish? She had been such an example of self-reliance to us all, and a special friend to Isso. I think we were all worried about her that Sunday morning as we disappeared back into the mountains. It was something to do with the huge windy loneliness of the place, which made us feel we needed to stick together.

Our progress was now synchronised to a rendezvous with Igor Asheshov in Port Famine, which lies just 25 miles to the north-east of

Cabo Froward, the most southerly point on the mainland of South America. A decade of these RVs with Igor in various parts of South America had taught me that it was never an easy exercise, and Igor made this one more difficult by changing dates and locations and failing to reply to faxes. Compared with the rest of us, Igor, who had brought Isso out of the jungle in 1986 and flown with her to Ardmore, was rather exotic and I wondered how the rest of the crew would cope with him as number eight in the plastic tube for a couple of months of bad weather. He knew nothing about sailing except that he suffered from seasickness. But he had won Rita's prize for the Fax of the Year from Miami:

Dear John,

We're about to be hit by Hurricane Gordon. Saw a car broadsided by a flying palm tree a couple of hours ago. I plan to open the storm shutters of my close friend Drusilla's flat in Bickell Harbour and walk out in my new Musto jacket and Henri-Lloyd pants, Nikon polarized sunglasses and Teva River Guide running sandals, clip a harness onto the balcony railings (we're on the 9th floor) and fly myself like a kite to impress the neighbours.

Following your brief instructions on kit, I have spent several million dolares (as in dolores, or pain in Spanish) at the Paragon Sporting Goods Co. on 18th and Broadway, in Manhattan. Before going into the store I took an anti-depressant pill given me by my close friend Gemma at her Park Avenue flat; she has experience of stress shopping. I bought Patagonia Capilene underwear, pneumatic jacket and windproof recycled Synchilla cardigan; North Face bib Polarfleece trousers; Railriders Supplex and Cordura Weather Pants, Jibes Shorts, and abrasion resistant Waterproof Sailing Shorts; Mont-Bel Goretex expedition climbing gloves; Timex Indiglow watch with rotating compass bezel; SpyderCo flip knife; Accupressure anti-seasickness wristbands; Nikon waterproof binoculars; Canon Sureshot waterproof camera; and more; then a stiff double Jameson Irish whiskey at Joe Mayo's Bar on 26th and Park.

I've got a 12v adaptor for my Power Book and I'm working on a regulator to allow it to take 24v. My portable CD-ROM drive will let me play music CDs as well as run what they call interactive games. I was offered some interactive sex games but I did not think the cramped conditions aboard would lead to anything good.

I'll see you in Pto Famine on 1 Dec. I understand the intensity on meeting you there, but there is a possibility that business may detain me in Lima/Santiago.

Looking forward to jiving with BOSE DJ Queen Isso super pronto. Hasta la vista, babies. Igor.

Compared to Igor, I'm a dull old stick. This rendezvous saved us going all the way to the exposed pier at Punta Arenas and then having to beat all the way back against the prevailing westerly winds. In the early morning a few battered wooden fishing boats occupied most of the tiny creek below the deserted Chilean navy settlement, miles from anywhere. Port Famine was where we had boarded Conrado's yacht, the *Compass Rose*, nearly three years before to head off for the start of our expedition to canoe round Cape Horn. The beach was all fossils. We lay at anchor, just waiting, though there was plenty of maintenance to do. Tooling along the empty road towards Punta Arenas on my early-morning run, I felt in no hurry. The sun slanted through the short, stout nothofagus trees with their small glossy leaves, catching the dew-wet grass at just the right angle. Oh wow! Paradiso!

A friend brought Igor by car late one evening, with enough luggage for a year or two and profuse apologies for being two days late. He had a grip full of CDs, as well as tapestry-kit gifts for Isso from his mother in Lima.

We sailed for Tierra del Fuego on a perfect morning. It was all so beautiful it made me want to cry. I found myself humming 'The Ride of the Valkyries', the Parachute Regiment march, which used to come so easily to mind in planes taking off for parachuting. Igor was at the helm and leaping sea lions stitched the still waters as we entered Canal Magdalena, all the splendours of Mount Sarmiento lying before us under the bluest sky. We adjusted the watches. A Watch was once again Marie Christine, Isso and me; B Watch, J.W., Rebecca and Igor; C Watch, Andy and Bruce. Igor's influence soon had B Watch renamed Bay Watch.

And I hoped bad weather would not come before Igor had a chance to settle in. We had a strong team of my most favourite people. The past and future didn't exist – the present was everything.

18

Tierra del Fuego

REBECCA

By early evening we had tied up and anchored in our now familiar spider's web. We hoped to stay in Caleta Olla for a few days and camp ashore. An enormous glacier emptied into the bay and snowy mountains rose straight up above our heads, cutting off our satellite communication with the outside world. J.W. was itching to get his crampons on and climb up into the snow and ice. Bruce was fairly keen to join him, but he had not done any ice-climbing before. We all wanted to go to the snout of the glacier and fit our crampons, but maybe this was not the best place to set off on a big trip. The safer snowfields lay far above the thousands of crevasses and the ice falls were creaking and groaning with the coming of spring.

Sitting round the table after supper, warming our hands on coffee mugs, we discussed the 'family camping trip in Tierra del Fuego' which had been such a key feature of our planning at home. After fourteen months and various crew changes, Dad felt he should draw some strands together and return to the original aim of the voyage. 'Maybe, at the end of the day, when all the trumpeting's done, the family outings will seem to have been the most worthwhile things in life,' he muttered, and Mum squeezed his arm with approval. 'Well, we four Ridgways will stick together and see where we get to.' Happily, Andy and Igor were willing to stay on the boat, giving J.W. and Bruce a clear run at seeing how far up they could get.

And so began the turmoil of packing rucksacks and rations, crampons and ice axes. 'Mama, are you taking your tapestry?' Isso called, to much laughter, from the dark recesses of her bottom bunk at the foot of the main mast.

'Yes!' came Mum's firm response, and the laughter stopped.

That night the rain drummed on the decks and the dropboards in the doghouse hatch rattled like loose teeth. The old boat swayed like an ageing boxer trying to ride the heavy blows from squalls which came bashing down through the trees. Our four o'clock start came and went. It was getting on for eight when J.W.'s hand stretched towards my bunk, holding a welcome cup of tea. Dad announced a twenty-four-hour postponement. The boat was knee deep in climbing gear, and some of the team got a bit tetchy with the waiting.

We rose at 4 am next morning. The bad weather had passed and the sky all around looked clear. We four were dropped off on the beach among tall trees by the glacier melt river and waved J.W. and Bruce off ahead of us. And I noticed Dad looking longingly after them, wishing he was going with them.

We walked along the narrow beach looking for some way through the seemingly impenetrable southern beech forest that grew in a great low knot from the edge of the beach to the green waters of the lake at the foot of the glacier. Struggling through this scratching, tangling undergrowth with heavy rucksacks tested our senses of humour, and Dad's failed. Second in line behind him, Isso giggled like mad every time he tripped. She was much more concerned with whether she had chosen the right colour of headband than about where we were going. And bringing up the rear, Mum and I kept stopping to look at the flowers. At least there were no insects biting us like there had been in other jungles we had walked.

After a couple of hours we reached a small alpine meadow on the crest of a spur leading up towards the jagged main ridge far above us. The snowy mountain peaks came out of the mists looking like gods. We pitched the red Quasar mountain tent on a good flat site next to a bundle of twisted nothofagus, tough little trees which had managed to grow only to about 10ft. In such a windy, wet and harsh place, I was amazed by the abundance of spring flowers and blooming notro, known as the 'fire bush' by the Yahgan Indians for its brilliant red flowers.

We lay down on a carpet of Patagonian moss, all colours from brilliant green, dense and spiky, dotted with tiny white star-shaped flowers, deep maroony-red sticky fly-catchers and the brilliant orange and yellows of the spongy spagnum that stood proud in large cushions, interspersed by the wispy grey and sand colours of brittle lichen.

Dad stalked off on his own to see if he could spot J.W. and Bruce up ahead. Reaching a hilltop, he looked up the full course of the glacier far below. Squinting through his little Zeiss monocular at the ice-scoured gully between the shrinking glacier and the mountainside, he became convinced this was the way to the snowfield above. Although the route meant descending 1,000ft or more and overcoming a few boulder problems on the way up, there was a convenient rocky spine leading clear up the side of the ice fall at the head of the glacier. Unfortunately, J.W. and Bruce were heading along the spine of the ridge, which from Dad's viewpoint looked dangerous.

He retraced his steps with a slight feeling of unease, returning less than pleased to find his three fellow campers sound asleep. But then the rain began to patter down and, as we soon discovered, four does go into a two-man tent. We had sardines and Chilean Mackay's biscuits for lunch and returned for more sleep during the frequent heavy showers, wondering how the boys were getting on on the ridge. By teatime we had all set out back up the ridge to Dad's hilltop look-out, hoping for a glimpse of the climbers. It was easier going without our packs. Nearing the summit, we rounded a corner and crept along a ledge to sit and look down on the glacier. A drumming sound had us crouching down. 'That's the biggest bird I ever saw!' cried Isso, as the first of a pair of condors swooped down on us, waggling their bald necks to get a better look at this potential carrion.

At last we were having our long-talked-of family camping holiday, and Mama was loving it. We walked and slept and talked, doing all the things you imagine a family doing together, but the things we never did do without an aim or reason. Much later, back at the tent once more, we cooked supper in the late summer light under the nothofagus tree that guarded us as a rowan does a croft house. Dad lay back, his mind on 'the bigger picture', watching Mum and I scampering about getting the meal organised. Isso looked off into the distance, hoping she wouldn't be noticed until the food was ready.

At last the cold drove us into our sleeping bags. Stiff old Dad found it difficult to undress and climb into his bag; Mum was quickly in, rubbing cream into her face, while Isso carefully folded her clothes and slithered into her bag next to Mum's. We all lay with our heads at the same end, and in the yellowy light permeating the tent, I read aloud some episodes of Shackleton's amazing voyage after his ship was crushed and sunk by the ice. The other three slipped into their own dreams of the adventures to come in the great and terrifying continent of Antarctica.

We were relieved for J.W. and Bruce when we woke early to find clear weather again. All morning we scanned the landscape for two small dots, seeing nothing until almost midday, when a minute moving form appeared on the edge of the snowfield, followed by a second. It had to be them. Through Dad's monocular and with the naked eye, we followed their progress diagonally up to a black outcrop of jagged rocks, then back on to the snow, one behind the other. Eventually they reached the top of the pyramid-shaped peak. We were thrilled, cheering and clapping, but they still had to get down again. They must have started their descent via another route, because we did not see them again.

We packed up and headed down to the beach, surprising a family of ashy-headed geese as they practised for bigger waters in a shallow peaty pool. From above, we could see an obvious path to the sea, so our return trip was much quicker. We passed through thick clumps of Cyttaria Darwinii, Darwin's fungus. Bacteria from these round yellowy-orange apricot-like balls induce the nothofagus to form a knot from which the fungus grows. The Yahgan ate the fungi that grew on trees, but none that grew on the ground, so it is known as Indian bread. The Yahgan dried it on sticks and it kept them going through the winter and early spring. Indian bread might look quite interesting, but I was glad we didn't have to live on it. It didn't have much of a flavour, and it had a jelly-like texture with a crusty outside, which none of us took to.

Isso and I went on back to the boat to collect some food while Mum and Dad found a good place to pitch the tent and got a fire going to cook our supper. As we climbed back into the dinghy, Tiki miaowed on the side of the boat and jumped down on to Isso's knee, so we took her along, calling to Andy that she was with us and hadn't gone overboard. Tiki had been ashore many times like this over the previous month. Always curious, she liked to walk around the outer edge of the Avon, never staying still for a moment, and jumping ashore almost before the dinghy touched the rocks, sometimes slithering and getting the odd boot wet. She then prowled across the rocks, miaowing all the while, but usually staying pretty close, nose and whiskers twitching continuously.

On our way back to Mum and Dad, Isso and I paddled past several ducks, preening themselves on the beach by the glacier-melt river. Tiki's pink nose twitched and she paced faster round the dinghy and over the oars. On the beach, Isso and I carried the dinghy well up into a sheltered grassy dip filled with large margueritas and tied it with both painters to separate bushes – we never took any chances with the weather. We collected some firewood as we walked through the forest. Supper was well on the way, and though our baked potatoes got slightly charred, they were still good with fried eggs and the nicely warmed Gato Negro tasted special from white enamel mugs. Tiki disappeared into the bushes but we could tell where she was by the incessant chirping of terrified little birds who had never seen a cat before. Tree-climbing was a skill she had not yet had the chance to hone, so the birds were in no danger unless they had heart attacks.

Sitting together on the bleached log beside our cheery driftwood fire, we watched a handful of terns circling above a tide rip off the point out at the end of the gently curving sandy beach. Beneath a lowering mussel-shell sky, snowy peaks lining the main channel gave out their own luminous light in the late evening, leading the eye in the direction of the faraway places from which we'd come. Across a couple of hundred yards of gravel flats and a milky strip of glacier-melt water, a colony of white-chested cormorants and black-back gulls huddled on a low whale-back reef of black rock surrounded by streamers of yellowy-brown kelp. And beyond the reef the black sea swirled with the turning tide, fretting white under the matted nothofagus forest clinging to the near-vertical walls of the island on the far side of the line, where striations of rock led up into the snow. We were a long way from home, yet it seemed very similar.

After supper, we walked along the beach to its furthest point, and as usual I was last, filling my pockets with shells. Here were drifts of tiny, delicate sea urchins less than 2cm across, entangled in dry grass and feathers all along the high-tide mark. And by a large rock were some huge pinky limpets with holes in their tops. I had made a necklace from lots of similar but smaller limpets found at Peninsula Valdez in Argentina, so I had all sorts of ideas for these giants.

After the rather squashed night before, we decided to sleep head to toe and see if that was any more comfortable. Tiki loved the tent. Not being inside it – she loved jumping up on top of it, rushing around, then sliding off it again. Dad was not amused.

'This tent cost a fortune. I won't have it wrecked by that bloody cat sticking its claws through the material . . . Just do something about it We can't have this all night.'

Unfortunately, all we could do was laugh, which made Dad even crosser. Sometimes we thought Tiki had gone, but then there would be a thud and she would appear on the roof again, like a gecko inside a lampshade, with only the dark lumps of feet visible. We tried to encourage her to come in, but she was having far too much fun to want to sleep.

'What if something big comes during the night and eats her?' I asked quietly.

'Sod that. Nothing will come and eat the bloody cat – just do something about the tent!' retorted my animal-loving father.

Mum got out and tried to encourage Tiki in again. She held on to her tight, but Tiki struggled free and was gone again. We left the tent open at one end so that she could come in if she wanted.

I awoke in the morning to find Tiki curled up on my carrymat next to me and Mum already up. The weather was clear again, for the third day in a row.

We packed up and went back to the boat, Tiki, tent and all. J.W. and Bruce returned in triumph shortly after us.

JOHN

It was already a midsummer evening as we reached the little Chilean navy base of Puerto Williams on Navarino Island. An old Second World War destroyer served as headquarters, with smaller warships huddled round it, armed to the teeth and ready to respond to the slightest move from 'macho' Argentina on Tierra del Fuego, barely 3 miles across the Beagle Channel. Though I didn't know it, I was about to buy a church for the last two remaining Yahgan Indians on God's earth.

With the setting sun in my eyes, I reversed *English Rose* up the narrow creek in a flat calm. Even though there were only three yachts moored there, the muddy backwater looked crowded. A large old wooden schooner lay first in line alongside a rusting grey hulk of an ancient channel steamer called the *Micalvi*, which was the yacht club. Rumour had it that the manager had come to Puerto Williams to open a brothel, but on finding the population below the regulation number for such an institution, he'd settled for a yacht club instead. He may have been uncertain of the difference.

'Keep looking into the water. The first thing to hit the bottom would be the rudder!' I muttered over my shoulder at Bruce, standing on the stern. As *English Rose* glided backwards, true as an arrow, I couldn't resist the old cry, 'Look, Mum – no hands!' By reversing the rudder and cutting the motor into neutral, I could remove the turning effect of the revolving screw.

Igor had run along the shore ahead of us and was now calling berthing directions from the tilted decks of the *Micalvi*. Marvelling at my fingertip control, I stopped *English Rose* dead, halfway along the broad, varnished schooner. To keep yachts away from him, the owner had left a small fibreglass speedboat alongside her, forcing us out to the absolute limit of the narrow channel.

'Pass further down,' called Igor, pointing at a smart red and white centreboarder. 'We must lie alongside *Kotic*.'

Slipping the gear handle back, I nudged the boat astern. Over the months, several people had told us there was insufficient water in this creek for a deep-keel boat like *English Rose*, and that we'd never get into it. Eight pairs of eyes peered into the murky water to see whether this theory would prove correct.

'Watch out for the spar!' bellowed a bear-like figure from the main hatchway on the schooner.

Crack!

I was looking up now, but it was too late – the eight pairs of eyes had strained downwards when the peril lay in the air.

Time stopped. Gazing up at the end of the schooner's long varnished yardarm, I still couldn't see the problem. I could jink round that spar, no bother. The way I was seeing the ball, a second was as long as an hour. But then I saw the other – broken – half of the spar, hanging dejectedly down, parallel with the mast.

'You better have a lotta money to pay for that!' blustered its American owner, trembling with rage in his hatchway.

'I'm very sorry . . .' was all I could stutter. All puff gone out of me, I slipped out and motored gently astern towards the unhappy-looking French couple who owned the smart aluminium *Kotic II*. We tied up in a hostile silence.

'He's a difficult man,' murmured Marcel, a friendly Belgian, as Marie Christine and I clambered miserably over the *Micalvi*'s rail on our way to the schooner. 'He's laid on the mud here for four years now, and he puts that spar out to prevent people coming alongside. It's been broken before.' Marie Christine and I bundled forlornly along the *Micalvi*'s rusty decks and dropped on to the heavy old trader built up in Puerto Montt a good few years before.

Scrambling down the companionway, we found Rick, square and fiftyish, looking old and tired, slumped in front of a television in a stuffy timber cabin furnished with a scarred table and bench seats covered with worn white leather cushions. Coloured lights on a tiny Christmas tree fluttered on and off.

'I'm sorry I blew up,' he said, with a broad grin.

'Well . . . I'm very sorry,' I replied lamely.

We perched uncomfortably on the stained white leather and breathed in the stuffiness while Rick flicked channels from *Pulp Fiction* to the news and back to *Pulp Fiction*. Then he outlined the story of his life, one long chapter of woes. Now a Christian missionary, he'd once owned a much bigger boat, but she'd been stolen and sunk by natives from Easter Island while he lay in hospital after a diving accident which had left him crippled. Pausing only to mention that the spar would cost US$2,000 or US$3,000 to replace, he flicked channels again and suggested we discussed the accident in the morning.

'Thanks for the visit,' he called after us in missionary speak as we crept unhappily back up the hatchway.

We spent a glum night in the doghouse and at breakfast a messenger brought news that Rick was ready to receive us. This time the Christmas tree was gone and Rick was settled in a rickety folding metal chair, peering distractedly into the colour screen on his Apple Macintosh Quadra and calling long-distance on his grey plastic phone. He motioned us to sit on the tattered floral coverlet of the bunk barely a couple of feet from him. Seemingly unconcerned at the cost of the call, Rick ignored Marie Christine and me and left us to chat with his aged mother, who was lying semi-conscious in a wheelchair by the table. I sensed that this lack of courtesy wasn't going down too well with my wife's Irish temper.

We squirmed for ten minutes and I cursed myself again for ever getting into this situation. Eventually Rick gave a sigh, put down the receiver and leaned towards me, reducing the distance between us to no more than a foot.

'Jaahn, are you a Christian?' he drawled, looking deep into my soul.

'Loosely . . .' I shrank under the blast of moral firepower.

'You know, I came down here, not knowing what to do,' he went on righteously. 'Then I read about Alan Gardner, the missionary, and I knew just what I must do. He died of hunger and cold in a cave near here, back in the 1850s. His dying wish was to build a church for the

Yaghan Indians Well, I'm building that church. Mind you, there are only two of them left now. They were both alcoholics when I found them.'

I smiled weakly at Marie Christine. She was fuming quietly. If it hadn't been for the missionaries, there would still be plenty of Yaghans and Alacalufes, and Onas, too. They'd been here for 4,000 years until the missionaries arrived. But I knew this was no time for her to air her own view of history.

'Here, take a look at the plans for the church,' Rick went on, flicking buttons on his AppleMac. I leaned forward and there they were, in glorious colour. A 6m by 10m timber doll's church for two, complete with Sunday school. I couldn't believe it. 'Would you like to make a contribution – say two thousand three hundred dollars – and we'll call it quits?'

'I'd rather see the receipts for the last time the yardarm was broken and make good the damage,' I said. 'We've no insurance and I must settle this properly.'

'Oh well, if you want to go down that route, I'll have to go and see the port captain and submit a report. And you won't get away from here in under three weeks,' he replied huffily.

'That's a bit like blackmail, isn't it, Rick? Others here say the yard has been broken before and that you put it out to keep boats from lying alongside you. That yardarm should have been led fore and aft. It's a hazard in a very narrow channel. When we were here a couple of years ago, you were lying inside the *Micalvi*, out of the way, where you should be now.'

The temperature was rising. 'That's the Devil speaking. That's how he operates, putting words into the mouths of others.'

'Blimey,' I swallowed.

'I can get upset. Even though I'm a Christian, I can get very upset,' Rick threatened.

'Or is that because you are a Christian?' I regretted it even as I spoke.

'I'm a poor missionary. You're rich.'

I'd fallen into a nutter's nest. We squabbled on for another half-hour before Marie Christine and I stomped out, saying that we'd try and get a quote for a new yardarm.

With Igor's help I managed to persuade the port captain to arbitrate the dispute. Rick, the damaged diver, hobbled in on his two sticks and we sat together on the dark leather sofa in the bay window of the spacious office. Rick asked for $1,750. The port captain thought for a moment, sighed, and suggested that this was fair.

Feeling I was not entirely to blame, I offered $1,000. The port captain turned to Rick bewildered. 'But I thought you'd asked for seven hundred and fifty dollars?' He'd misheard.

'I'll split the difference,' Rick replied, a little too hastily.

'OK,' I said, leaning across to shake his hand, knowing I'd lost the battle to win the war.

A couple of hours later I went back aboard the schooner with fourteen 100-dollar bills. Rick was on the blower again. He gestured at us to take a seat. The receipt, neatly typed out and ready for the port captain, was already lying on the table: our ticket to the Antarctic.

After a while Rick put down the phone and thumbed through the dollars. 'I'm bust,' he said. 'I'll have to go out and get some change. I'll give you the twenty-five dollars in the morning . . .'

Clambering back up the hatchway, I found the wily skipper of *Kotic* already on deck, speculatively turning the broken spar in his hands.

'I'm taking it with me,' I told him ruefully. 'It's the most expensive piece of wood I ever bought.'

'Combien?'

'Thirteen hundred and seventy-five dollars.'

'Non! Eet is a joke. You could get thees for a couple of hundred bucks!'

'Thanksalotty,' I grinned.

I took the right change round to the schooner myself – I didn't want Rick hobbling about on those sticks. He was still on the phone, his back to me. 'I'll tell you later how God brought us this money . . .'

We shook hands and his huge toothy salesman's smile reminded me of where we'd met before. The Granada, Slough: Burt Lancaster playing the evangelist Elmer Gantry.

We set about recovering the expensive timber from the broken yardarm. I was determined to strap the two 15ft lengths of varnished alerce pine to our decks and take them home, via the Antarctic. They would serve as both roof supports in Marie Christine's newly designed kitchen and a suitable memorial to my folly. And now I saw the full extent of that folly. Far from being pristine 1,000-year-old alerce, dragged from the mountainside by slavering bullock teams, as I had been assured, this tatty old stick was riddled with knots; in places it had even had extra pieces scarfed in. Rick and I grinned at one another. There's one born every minute.

Clearing our ship's papers to leave Chile within the hour, we sailed 30 miles back up the Beagle Channel, crossed over to the northern shore and entered Argentinian waters for Christmas.

REBECCA

During my childhood, Christmas had often been a time of worry and despair. All wild creatures became hungry as midwinter approached, and invariably the salmon we farmed in the sea were attacked by flocks of evil black shags which flew in like night riders from the *Lord of the Rings* and slashed our silvery beauties with their hooked beaks. We took it in turns to go out with the .22 rifle to repel these sleek black war jets. Worse were the crafty seals, who committed massacres on a grand scale. They worked in pairs in silence apart from their fishy exhalations. One would push up the net from the centre of the cage floor. In a panic the fish would dive, jamming into the corners, ready for the other seal, who swam up and bit the net with dog-like jaws, sucking the liver from the salmon. They were far more difficult to stop than the shags, and they had massive appetites. Once a pair had got a taste for it, they returned night after night for more feasting, and we lost hundreds and hundreds of fish. Fish oil rose to the surface, turning the air heavy and putrid. All we could do was remove the worthless rotting carcasses.

I remember once overhearing my parents in the kitchen, discussing how they could not afford to keep me at school much longer if this continued. I did not like school much, but I did understand that they were giving me the best they possibly could. Luckily, Dad invented a predator net which kept the seals at bay. But the gravity of this statement seemed enormous at the time. And it all happened just before Christmas.

After crossing the Beagle Channel and anchoring in the far-too-exposed bay in Ushuaia, Argentina, one thing after another went wrong. On the day before Christmas Eve, we replaced one of our eight 6-volt truck batteries, which would not hold its charge. All seemed well, and Mum went off to order a turkey and bought a small green fold-up Christmas tree while Isso and I went ashore to look at the expensive, glittery duty-free shops. Ushuaia, its 32,000 inhabitants housed in modern concrete buildings, contrasted sharply with the tacked-together weatherboard shacks of the small naval base of Puerto Williams, population 1,500. But both these settlements at the end of the world kept fully armed flotillas of camouflaged torpedo boats, which glared at each other across the Beagle Channel.

Isso and I were goggle-eyed at Ushuaia's main street, where all the famous international brand names were advertised – and the inflated prices to go with them. I was relieved I'd done most of my Christmas shopping in the second-hand clothes shops of Puerto Natales.

As we strolled back to the boat, an icy wind swept down from the Cordillera Darwin and our expensive ice-creams did not seem quite so appealing when our lips froze. We weaved through the glamorous shoppers, who, I imagined, were all wealthy *estancia* owners who came into town only occasionally, flying the eight hours to Buenos Aires more often. Stepping carefully over gaps in the planking on the old jetty, we passed *Kotic II*, the massive French yacht we'd met in Puerto Williams. It was already blowing a gale, and as I practised ferry-gliding with the dinghy, I saw Sophie on deck watching to make sure that we reached our home safely.

The air was filled with snow as we came alongside and there was action on our decks, too: a bolt broke inside the windlass while Bruce and Andy were paying out more chain to reduce the chance of our dragging the anchor.

Now we were stuck. In Antarctica, where 120mph winds were commonplace, the windlass would be vital. In spite of the Christmas decorations, the mood in the cabin was gloomy. To make matters worse, Igor was out on a binge with an old friend from his boarding-school days in Buenos Aires, probably the only person who might be able to get the windlass part fixed for us on Christmas Eve, but this friend happened to own one of the most glamorous clothes shops in the city, and Christmas Eve was his biggest shopping day of the year. We were counting on leaving on Boxing Day, but with the South American *mañana* as well as Christmas to contend with, our chances were looking slim. It was not the sort of thing Dad liked at all.

And then, to our horror, the dial above the chart table indicated that the power had dropped into the red. Another battery had crashed. We could not risk this happening in the Antarctic – navigation instruments and communications would be essential there, and there would be no batteries for sale on South Georgia or Tristan da Cunha – so we had to find three more. We managed it, but on Christmas Eve in the most southerly town in the world, it was not easy, or cheap.

Outside it was grey and grim. The gale had abated but the snow was down to the tree-line. It was a cold and frightening place. Unexpectedly, Igor reappeared. He had a new short, short hair cut and a smart new pair of jeans his friend had given him. He had also bought himself a pillow, pillowcase and sheet to make his bunk more homely, as well as numerous other gadgets, all on his Gold American Express card.

Unlike we frantic Brits, Igor was quite calm about the dramas that had befallen us. His half-Peruvian blood stopped him from getting too worked up about anything, and besides he did not have to worry about getting back to Britain by April. He was fairly confident he could get this sorted out; his friend would know where to go and who to speak to to replace the broken pin. But would anyone be doing this kind of work on Christmas Eve in South America?

Twelve chocolate Father Christmases, each wrapped in foil, hung from the little tree. Mum would not let us try even one, but Tiki found them great batting practice. Mum, Isso and I collected the Brazilian turkey from the supermarket while Dad stalked off to buy his Christmas presents, weighed down with all the windlass woes. Most of the shoppers were buying lamb: the favourite *asado* was more popular than turkey in Tierra del Fuego.

We were invited for a drink on *Kotic II* by the extraordinary Russian–Welsh–French couple whose only home she was. Oleg had designed and built the boat 120 miles inland in Brazil, employing local steel-workers who had never seen the sea. The boat had a retractable centreboard, so she could go into very shallow water and even sit on the bottom if necessary. The inside was like an open-plan house, the cabins like real bedrooms – quite different from our old 'prison ship', but not nearly as beautiful. Their floor was packed with food like ours. Just as fishermen talk about 'the one that got away', or their largest catches, sailors swap horror stories about close shaves or disasters they have had and give each other invaluable tips. Sophie told us in Ushuaia we could buy vacuum-packed beef which had not been frozen, and that this could be stored in our bilges for up to six weeks in these cold climes. This little piece of advice was to transform our standard of living in the days to come.

Igor returned with the fantastic news that he had got the piece for the windlass. Immediately, Christmas took on a brighter, more light-hearted atmosphere. We were on course again.

With every Leg, even every day, we had been on the threshold of something new and exciting. And now we all felt privileged to be on the springboard to dangerous, beautiful, untamed Antarctica. We would be on our own: there would be no one to answer distress signals; we could not afford to hit bergy bits, or even much brash, and if we got caught in the pack ice, we would be crushed.

By the time darkness fell, everything was back in order. Christmas carols filled the boat. The dimly lit cabin was alive with tinsel and streamers, lights and cards from home. The music officer was playing an American sort of pop tape of 'White Christmas' and the like. Tiki scratched my face and dashed around like a mad thing, wondering where all the new dangling bits of coloured paper had come from.

I still missed Will terribly, especially in particularly high or low times. I wanted to know all the minute details of his Christmas and his days at home. I tried to visualise his face, to imagine his expressions, jokes and the way he said things. I knew he would be having fun with his family. His first term at the agricultural college in Cirencester was over now. I wondered how he would feel when he opened the present I'd sent back with Val. It was a tapestry cushion, covered with entwined grapes, apples and leaves sewn in fresh greens, pale peach, deep reds and dark indigo, which I'd made during the evenings in the Chilean Channels. I also enclosed my copy of *Eva Luna* by Isabel Allende, to remind him of South America and me. 'Will – Enjoy this rich tapestry. I miss you and love you. Bec, Christmas '94, Patagonia.' There were still four months to go before we would see each other again, and from now on there would be few telephones or opportunities to post anything.

Mum was wrapping the presents for her extended family, her four new 'sons' as well as her husband and daughters. Just as if we were at home, she disappeared behind the closed doors of her cabin to the tantalising sound of rustling paper and the scream of Sellotape being pulled from its misshapen roll, which had sagged in the heat of the tropics. Newspaper or old magazines had been my favoured wrapping for some time. You could choose relevant pictures or articles for each person's present. Now we were dependent on newspaper for all manner of things: Tiki's litter bowl and tray, engine-oil changes, lining the galley cupboards and serious mop-ups. It would be in short supply for the next few months. We had, of course, saved the wrapping paper from the previous Christmas in the Antilles and birthdays during the year. We had discussions before anything that might be of future use was thrown out. If nothing else, living at sea had made us even more resourceful than we had to be at home, where we were a boat trip or a 30-minute walk to the car and then 100 miles by road from the well-stocked shops of Inverness.

Late in the evening, I opened the plastic drum of fortified orange wine which Mum had made from the recipe given to us at the yacht club in Valdivia. It consisted of litres of Gato Negro, orange peel, sugar and brandy. We had been dying to try it. At last it was ready, and Christmas was a good enough excuse. It smelled rich and heavy, but when I took a sip, it was horrible – the bitter, bitter taste of orange zest was overwhelming. Maybe it would taste better with more sugar, but I think the spoon would have to stand up in the glass to make it drinkable. Perhaps we had opened it too soon.

Isso was very excited. She got out her stocking and made sure it was visible on her jumbled bunk. Together we squeezed intriguing wrapped parcels and danced around the saloon. As midnight struck, police sirens, car and ship horns, bangers, fireworks and flares went off all around the town and harbour in wildest South America. In the half-light of mid-summer, I dashed out on deck with our battered old brass foghorn and blew it with all my might. Tiki pranced sideways on deck, her tail and back fluffed up, ears pinned back and eyes even wider than usual. Christmas was well and truly here. I dashed below crying, 'Merry Christmas, everybody,' then crashed into deep slumber on my seat on the port side while Tiki wrestled with my feet.

'Beek, look! Father Christmas has been.' Isso shook my shoulder.

'Are J.W. and Bruce back yet?' I replied sleepily.

'Yes. Bruce has been sleep-talking again,' my little sister chuckled. I wondered if she had been to sleep at all, what with all the worry about whether Father Christmas would actually find us this year. We were so far from home and so far from where we had been last year. He had a jolly long way to come.

'It's only five-forty-five! I think we should sleep a little bit more, darling,' I whispered.

'Okey-dokey,' Isso sighed in her sing-song, disappointed tone. 'I wake you later, OK, Beek?' She stomped off to bed again.

I glanced across the saloon to the long seat on the other side of the table where J.W. slept. There he lay, curled up in his sleeping bag, glasses askew on the floor. How bad would his hangover be? I lay and gloated for a few seconds then drifted off to sleep again.

It seemed only a minute later that Is woke me again, but it was 7.30 am. I picked up the two stockings I had put together for Mum and

Dad, as well as my own, left by 'Father Christmas', and followed her through the galley, up the ladder and into the doghouse. There, under the duvets and heavy rough woven blanket from Chiloe, with their hats on, slept Mum and Dad. There was a flurry of excitement as Isso and I tucked in at their feet. Then the unwrapping began and soon the bed was covered in a blanket of paper. Isso and I tied red cotton Levi's scarves around our heads and started to guzzle the sweets which made up most of our stockings. They were supposed to be saved for cold and hungry times in Antarctica.

At 8.30 am a drunken Igor got a lift back to the boat and scrambled his way aboard. There was a great deal of garbled chat and good cheer from inside and outside the doghouse before he slithered his way along the deck and crashed down to his bunk below. It seemed unlikely that he'd recover in time to open his presents and eat the turkey.

After porridge with real milk and bread with *dulce de leche*, came the present-opening. In one corner, Andy was coming to the end of the pile his Mum had sent him off with over a year earlier. Each gift had a label giving the date on which it should be opened. As before, they were all reference books relating to the area we had told her we'd be in at that particular time. They were brilliant presents, and we all looked forward to them.

There were piles of gifts from home, some from the women who had come on our ladies' course year after year. We were amazed at how well thought-out they were, especially those left by Val, which included individually wrapped cat biscuits and treats for Tiki. I gave the boys hand-knitted woollen socks from Chiloe to keep their toes warm as we headed further south; Mum gave them *maté* gourds and bottles of Pisco to remind them of their time in the channels and from Isso they got bags of sweets for night watches. From Mum I had a beautiful traditional Mapuche Indian-style necklace of rough silver with two llama-like creatures, nose to nose, linked to a flat engraved rectangle with four suns hanging below, and earrings to match. Dad gave me his slightly shrunken green Patagonia fleece jacket, and there was a *maté* gourd and straw from Isso. Igor came to towards the end of the presents, propping himself up against the sleeping-compartment doorway. He gave Mum, Isso and I flowery cotton handkerchiefs of different colours, and let the men choose their own from a selection of spotted ones.

My dear gran had sent us another parcel, with woollen gloves and Estée Lauder's Time Zone Moisture Recharging Complex for our faces.

She was terribly worried that her daughter and two granddaughters would arrive home looking like shrivelled old prunes after battling against the elements for so long. It was a real luxury to hold the cool, heavy frosted glass pot in your hardened hands, but not so nice to see the misshapen reflection of yourself on the gold lid. I kept mine in its pale green box until that fell apart, and turned its nightly application into something of a ritual. Rubbing the cool cream into my face and neck before I went to sleep helped to compensate for our rather squalid living conditions.

Not without difficulty, Dad, Isso and I had kept Mum's present a secret from her since Valdivia. Way back in July, when we had first arrived in Chile after crossing the Pacific, she had much admired a hand-knitted cardigan in the blues of the oceans, plummy purples and emerald greens of varying thickness and types of yarns. I liked it, too, and we had both been into the shop and tried it on a number of times, but as we were travelling, not earning, neither of us felt we could justify the cost. Just before we started south, I bought the cardigan for Dad to give to Mum. I tried to explain the plot to the lady in the shop so that she wouldn't give the game away if Mum came in again.

We had to hide the cardigan in Dad's kit, which was usually organised by Mum, so it nearly went wrong several times. Mum was absolutely amazed when she opened it and could not believe how we had managed to keep it secret, particularly as Isso was sometimes inclined to get over-excited and tell. Once I had bought two white ducks for Mum for Christmas from a farmer near Loch Ness. I managed to get them home in a large box, carrying them along the track in the dark with Dad, and hiding them for the few remaining days in Lance's spare hen house. Isso had not been with us for very long then, and one day when she had been up through the wood, Mum asked what she had seen. Isso replied, 'Two big white ducks.' I nearly screamed, but Mum, not suspecting anything, said, 'No, Isso. Those were hens.' We managed to get to Christmas Day without Mum finding out or the ducks escaping.

We had no Christmas crackers this year, but in the short interlude between presents and turkey, I decided that we should definitely wear paper hats. From the remains of crêpe wrappings, I made us all unique, brilliantly coloured crowns, the design dictated by the shape of paper available and my alcohol-propelled scissors.

The tropical turkey from Brazil was not quite as tasty as those at home, but delicious none the less. We ate as if there was no tomorrow, justifying this by the fact that we would need all the energy we could get from now on and would not feel like eating much when we broke out of the sheltered channels and into the dreaded 350-mile-wide Drake Passage between Cape Horn and Antarctica.

After our 1993 plum pudding, we lay back with glazed expressions clasping our stomachs, thinking of home and loved ones. Christmases at home, with Lance and Ada; cosy croft houses with fires pumping out heat from the peat we cut across the loch each spring; feeding the salmon and walking up over the hill or through the wood to see Lance and Ada for hot soup, brawn, sherry and mince pies; the Queen's speech; the short hours of daylight; listening to the cruel winter weather beating on the dark window panes.

Mum and I decided to paddle ashore to telephone Gran and Mum's two sisters and families, who were all together near Edinburgh for Christmas. I phoned Will, too. It was strange, because you never really know what to say – it is just hearing the voice at the other end which makes it worthwhile. You just want to know that he is safe and well and still loves you. The Argentinian telephone service was more expensive, but the line was clear and there was no delay.

First thing on Boxing Day, Mum and I rushed ashore to buy meat. The butcher's assistants in their white hats and coats were quite puzzled by the two Englishwomen who emptied their purses on the counter and explained that they would like all of that in meat, please. We chose some cuts that Sophie had recommended, though we did not know how they corresponded to British cuts. For US$150 we got twenty-five joints of good-looking vacuum-packed beef. Mum had brought her small day-pack with her, but that held less than a third of it. The man at the cash desk put the rest into two cardboard boxes for us and we staggered off down the street, legs bowed, with reams of cash-till paper flowing behind. I bet it was their best sale of the day.

We stashed the vacuum packs inside good old black bin-bags in the bilges under the galley floor, noting in the stowage book, under curious Spanish names, the quantities we had of each cut. Here the meat would be in contact with the hull and would be kept as cold as the seawater outside.

I looked forward with awe and great respect to seeing Cape Horn again.

John

The paperwork required to clear in and out of Argentina and Chile takes about half a day per visit. In Ushuaia the various agencies were dispersed around the city and expensive taxis raised the blood temperature. But the weather in the Drake Passage, between Cape Horn and the northern tip of the Antarctic, is so serious that it is worth returning to Chilean waters in order to retain the shelter of their islands while gaining as much westing as possible, thus leaving the confused seas on the continental shelf at the earliest opportunity.

As spring ripened into summer, opening the door to the Antarctic, ordinary people seemed to assume heroic proportions. There was a heady frontier atmosphere of exuberance and vitality. These were not grey days at the office.

Motoring very cautiously up the creek towards the *Micalvi* once again, we noticed the unusual deck profile of the exploration sloop *Pelagic* lying alongside Rick's schooner. Marie Christine and I had first met Skip Novak, her American owner–skipper, on the 1977–8 Whitbread Race, and he'd later visited Ardmore aboard Warren Brown's *War Baby* on his way to the Arctic. And in 1992, Skip had arrived in Puerto Williams with *Pelagic* as we were preparing to kayak round Cape Horn. I could tell from the wicked grin on those raffish, narrow features that I was in for a bit of a ribbing about Rick's broken yardarm.

'Say, John!' his American accent rang out from *Pelagic*. 'You wanna bring the missus along to the bar for a drink?'

The yacht club bar was in a large cabin on the *Micalvi*, probably the old dining room, directly beneath the bridge. The whole ship appeared to be listing a bit to starboard. 'I'm tellin' ya, I won't get tied to my boat, John,' Skip said as we clutched our glasses and lurched towards a motley group sat in the far corner.

'I'm more into mountaineering, than sailing, these days,' he confided, introducing me to a tall, broad-shouldered fellow with pebble glasses, white hair and thick, broken hands. 'Have you met Doug Scott, the Himalayan mountaineer?'

'Oh, wow! My hero!' I laughed, absolutely thrilled.

'I saw the TV film about your school. Very interesting,' Doug said.

'Oh, not so wow.' I shook my head.

'I liked the place where you live,' he went on, shaking Marie Christine's hand. 'I bet you have Enya on all day long.'

'Well, *you're* not much of a judge, then,' my wife smiled, sweetly.

Skip was on his way back from a successful three-week expedition to climb Sarmiento. The aluminium *Pelagic*, with her centreboard keel, had been able to penetrate spots other yachts could not.

We invited the whole crew of eight aboard *English Rose* and Marie Christine came up with a miracle supper. I was looking for inspiration, keen to hear Doug's views.

'A day in the mountains produces the direct opposite of the feeling a person has at the end of an evening watching television. How are your joints?' asked this frisky youth, a good four years younger than myself.

'A bit creaky. The knees are going, I think,' I replied ruefully.

'I try to raise a sweat every day – even if it's just chopping wood,' he went on, taking off his knee-length Wild Country socks. 'Here, these are to keep you warm in the Antarctic. Never give up!'

It was the greatest single act of resurrection in my life. It was time to come limping back.

19

The Most Southerly Yacht in the World

JOHN

Alone in the saloon, I found myself wondering why the British had such a fascination for the brief heroic phase of Antarctic discovery. I thought back to 1966, and those ninety-three days when I rowed across the North Atlantic with Chay Blyth; the simplicity of life then, stripped of career and family worries; the jokes, the sympathy and the glimpses of grace under the pressure from the simply overwhelming force of nature. Man is at his best with his back against the wall. Affluence undermines him. Chay and I had both been in our twenties then, and there had been some bad times, too. We had hoped to remember three things from our ordeal: to be humbler, more tolerant and more appreciative of the gift of life.

The Drake Passage, between Cape Horn and Antarctica, has a dreadful reputation. We set off from Puerto Williams a couple of days after Christmas with the main boom strapped down on deck and our trisail hanked on and bagged at the foot of the mast, ready for action as soon as the wind piped up. We called in for a night at Puerto Toro, another, much smaller, Chilean naval base among the trees on the east coast of Navarino Island. In the early morning, just as we were about to leave, a sinister black torpedo boat flying the skull and crossbones and bearing the chilling motto *Vencer o Morir*, came roaring into the rotting pier.

The crew were all dressed in black. When J.W. suggested asking them for one last weather forecast, I thought it advisable not to bother them. I slipped the old Mercedes into slow ahead. *Che sarà sarà* better summed up our approach as we slipped quietly out of the bay, hoisted our sails and headed nervously towards Antarctica.

By eight that evening, Cape Horn lay like a crouching lion some 25 miles out on our starboard beam. Surrounded by whirling clouds of grey-white ice birds and mottled Cape pigeons, each of us was lost in our own thoughts. Tiki, far from Tahiti, wowled inconsolably as we raced through wet, grey mist and Marie Christine just managed to grab a trailing ginger leg as its owner tried to bolt through the hatch on to the slippery deck. All too soon, there was that sour smell of vomit on my red Henri Lloyd collar as the grey seas and skies took their toll of all but Bruce and Isso. There was little wind at first, and we travelled slowly under cautiously reduced sail.

Three days of seasickness passed before poor Andy spoke for the first time since we left South America. J.W. made a fundamental GPS error, punching in latitude for longitude and vice versa as the waypoint. I'm sure I could have made the same mistake in such rotten conditions. By the time he discovered it, we were 50 miles from where we thought we were and it was nine o'clock in the evening. The distance to go suddenly shot up from 80 miles to 130. Having brought the boat from Ardmore to Valdivia myself, I had worried about someone else doing the navigation. From this point, we adopted a more open system, whereby all waypoints were written in the margin of the chart and consecutive watch leaders checked each one on the chart, and in the trusty Lowrance Global Navigator, and with the back-up from the INMARSAT GPS. The fanciest kit is still only an aid to navigation.

On watch in the doghouse, Isso continued to improve her powers of expression, reading aloud from a book given to her by her fellow pupils when she left school for the trip. She loved these gloomy yarns from *Scottish Hauntings*, written by a retired Scottish policeman, and her captive audience was in the right setting for tales of the supernatural. We peered groggily into the fog, searching for the ever-increasing number of icebergs, silent and ghostly.

The essence of the Antarctic Treaty recognises that 'it is in the interests of all mankind that Antarctica shall continue forever to be used exclusively for peaceful purposes and shall not become the scene or object of international discord'. It was profoundly colder now we had crossed the Antarctic Convergence, that variable physical boundary where the cold north-going Antarctic surface water sinks beneath the warmer sub-Antarctic water. These food-rich seas brought clouds of ice birds whirling about us, thick as snowflakes; fur seals frolicked and whales spouted around us.

On the afternoon of New Year's Eve, the cloud and mist lifted and we came out into fierce sun and blue skies, astonished to see the icebergs dotted all around. The sea fell calm as we sighted the 7,000ft summit of Smith Island from over 40 miles out. Barren ice cliffs warned us that we could expect no quarter if we made mistakes. 'Don't risk our lives!' warned Marie Christine when I took *English Rose* in too close to examine the blueness of a small berg. Seven position requests came in over the INMARSAT. As always, parents and family held me responsible for this recklessness. How many lives does a cat have?

After five long days, with snowflakes falling in the midnight dusk, 14 miles short of grim-looking Deception Island, we toasted in the New Year with Bec's miniature bottle of whisky. The mist rolled in and the luminous grounded bergs assumed nightmare proportions as Marie Christine and I conned the ship through broken ice, using radar and GPS. Shrouded in mist again, we passed close under Sail Rock, groping towards Pete's Pillar, a solitary needle of rock.

Intense excitement took over as snow began to fall in a sharp northeast wind and the forbidding half-light was yellowed by my ski goggles. From Pete's Pillar, we crept towards Neptune's Bellows, a narrow break in the steep, icy walls of the 5-mile-wide flooded crater which is the centre of Deception Island. In the early part of the century, the seawater in this crater had sometimes been hot enough to blister the paint on the whaling ships lying at anchor in Whalers' Bay.

'Twenty metres, eighteen, sixteen, twenty, twenty-two,' called Isso, relaying the echo-sounder readings from her starboard corner of the doghouse.

'Two-zero, one-eight, one-six, two-zero, two-two – thanks, Dolly!' I replied from the wheel. We were through.

As daylight returned on that grim grey morning, we anchored in a tiny lagoon formed by cinders from an eruption barely twenty-five years before. Eerie mists, rising from thermal springs to meet the lowering skies, gave the place the look of a nuclear battlefield. We washed down our porridge with a bottle of New Year Isla Malt. 'You know, the seabed is still rising here,' said J.W. as we peered out over dirty lava flats and snow-bound hills streaked with dust, which looked for all the world like iron filings on a sheet of paper in the physics lab at school long ago. Under a lowering leaden grey sky, a few elephant seals grunted in the shallows and the occasional penguin waddled on the beach.

I was exhausted. The accumulated trauma of recent days washed over me: breaking the schooner's yardarm in Puerto Williams; racing to get the broken windlass fixed and replace dud batteries in the rush of Christmas; having to get used to the idea of someone else navigating; six hours at the wheel as we approached Deception Island through the bergs: running aground on the still-rising volcanic floor of this bay; the responsibility of having the family aboard . . . but of course I was thrilled by it all.

Marie Christine

After a rest day in Telefon Bay, we wondered about visiting the Argentinian base. The chameleon Igor, Peruvian–Russian British passport-holder, really earned his stripes now. As he picked up the hand-held radio I hissed at him, 'Try not to say the *English* before *Rose* too loudly.' I needn't have worried. Igor's velvety voice was answered by a deep gravelly one and a long conversation ensued. 'They're very keen for us to come over. They're offering us baths and a meal.' That decided matters.

Steam was rising from the grey ash beach as we crept past Pendulum Cove, and patchy mist swirled on the surface of the water, created by the warm springs. 'Who's for a swim, then?' cried J.W. We weren't keen. It was an eerie spot. In 1829, Commander Foster of *HMS Chanticleer* established a pendulum station here, for carrying out experiments to determine the force of gravity. In those days, there had been a considerable inlet capable of affording anchorage for six vessels. Seventy-six years later, a Mr Mossman observed: 'Whether this is due to general elevation of land or to a filling up of the basin by volcanic emanations is a matter of conjecture.' And now it was completely gone.

A large red-suited figure strode down the beach to greet us as we bobbed ashore in the dinghy on a gentle grey swell at the Argentinian naval base. Roberto Cozzani, second in command, shook our hands warmly and led us up the broad concrete path to the orange-painted base. 'Mama, it's James Pond!' Isso whispered, pointing at the craggy Sean Connery lookalike. He had the same suave manner, too. Our party of seven (Bruce remained aboard for safety), followed in a procession through large white doors into a hangar-like hut containing all the supplies the Argentinians needed for the duration of the summer, and much more besides. We walked through stacks of building supplies and bits of machinery, skirting a ping-pong table at which a fierce competition was in progress. At the far end I could see a veritable Aladdin's cave of food. Stacked on shelves were sacks of onions, oranges, flagons of oil and ranks of tins, and hanging from the wall like truncheons were rows of pale, wrinkled salami, legs of cured ham and bundles of garlic strings.

Taking off our outside boots, we walked into the warmth of the main base. To our left were a number of tables and a hatch into the kitchen, where some men were eating an early lunch. The noise was loud and cheerful. To our right were low wooden armchairs, a television and video and a full bookshelf. The window looked out on to a lake which had once been an open bay where seaplanes landed. It had silted up during the big volcanic eruption of 1967, when the three bases, British, Argentinian and Spanish, had been rapidly evacuated. Now only the Argentinians remained on Deception, with half a dozen Spaniards in an orange hut just along the shore.

'The pilots stayed in the main hut, which we are renovating. This was just a store.' 007 waved his arms expansively. It looked pretty good to us. 'They would change over here, before flying on to our bases further south.' Time seemed to have gone backwards. But now the Argentinian navy were back, re-establishing themselves and renovating the buildings.

007 understood our needs, and took us without delay to the end of the building for a shower. J.W. got his shower next door going first, which left just a trickle of warm water coming out of ours. But it was enough to wash us and our hair, and when Bec, Isso and I returned to the mess room, clean and new again, we were complimented in true Latin fashion. I was glad I had put on my earrings and lipstick and was surrounded by such gallantry. I was quite happy to play the stereotypical female role. The base commander, Ricardo Oyarbide, of the gravelly voice, welcomed us officially. He was tall and blond and utterly charming. He poured us the best Argentinian coffee and quantities of Coca-Cola for Isso.

We were overwhelmed by their welcome. It was quite the reverse of what I had expected. It was war down here, but we were all on the same side. 'We are all united here. Only the cold and ice is the enemy. But, you know, there is much mutual respect between the British and Argentinian navy,' Ricardo explained later. The Falklands were just a little further to the north, and we all avoided talk of the conflict. Both Ricardo and Roberto had seen action, and Ricardo sported a livid scar the length of his arm. In our halting Spanish, we talked of other battles and of the much-feared Drake Passage. They told us of winds in excess of 85 knots recorded during the last two days in December, which, mercifully, had just missed us. It was luck and good judgement, but mostly luck.

Scientist Gabriella bounced in and we introduced ourselves. Slight, with a tumble of curly, auburn hair and a firm disposition, she was the only woman on this rather macho base. She and a colleague were the two token scientists among the thirty-strong naval presence. 'Come, we will show you where we work.' Their hut looked like a school chemistry classroom, but it housed all the necessary gadgetry: VDUs, computer print-outs, sheets of tracking graphs and calculations. They were monitoring the sulphur content in the gas emitted along the shoreline, and they also kept a close watch on seismic tremors. It was obviously an exciting posting, perched on the edge of a volcano which could erupt at any time, but we rather felt that, with all this technology, such work could have been done remotely by screen-watchers in Buenos Aires.

The whole detachment was there only for the short Antarctic summer, and they were rather inconclusive about Argentina's intentions on the island. They took us to see the old timber-built base, established in 1948, where a great clear-out was in progress. Sounds of hammering, whistling and singing filled the air; everybody was busy and spirits were high as they renovated this old abandoned building. Snow from many winters had forced entry in places, but the carpenters were fixing it all at high speed. 'Take some soap if you want,' 007 laughed. Huge boxes of green bars with 'Armada' stamped on them lay out in the bright sun on the frozen cinder ground. And, of course, we accepted the invitation.

'You will have lunch.' It was more of a command than a question, but we were happy to comply. We enjoyed the best Argentinian steak, with more for anybody who wanted it, washed down with red wine and the sweetest pudding of peaches and caramelised sweetened condensed milk. It was all wonderful.

Sharp orders in Spanish dispatched a team to get their inflatable to take us back to *English Rose*. As I had long wellies, I went to carry the front of the dinghy into the water, but I hadn't bargained on the gallant Argentinians: not only did they stop me picking up the dinghy, but once it was in the water, they scooped me up and carried me out to it, and the same for Gabriella, who was coming along to see the yacht. While I was shocked but rather pleased I hadn't had to struggle with the boat, I could tell she was used to this chivalry. She seemed to have the best of both worlds.

The Argentinians may have been strong on chivalry, but they were less so at getting some life out of their engine. Nothing would induce it to go, so they resorted to the paddles. The wind and tide were not in our favour. John, the Atlantic rower, was dying to take command, but the home team clearly weren't keen. By now many of the ratings had left their work and were watching from the shore as we slowly crabbed our way out to the yacht. Andy, who had returned earlier to relieve Bruce, let out a long warp which we eventually picked up, pulling ourselves along and upwind to the boat. A loud cheer went up from the shore. Laughing at themselves was not a strong point with our new friends, either. They were cheered up by some Scotch malt whisky and a large piece of Christmas cake, but dismay returned when they heard that we had decided to take advantage of the brief window in the weather and go on south. 'Please come back and see us on your return.' I very much hoped we would be able to do so.

JOHN

It was already 6 pm when we motored carefully past the rusted round fuel tanks of the long-abandoned British base on the opposite side of the crater from the Argentinians. These were the tanks, Ricardo had told us, in which the Germans had stored the fuel for their submarine fleet in the First World War.

Passing out through Neptune's Bellows, we found fog on the open sea, but the weather kept calm and, motoring south through the half-light of night, we were very grateful for the diesel the Argentinians had given us.

In the morning, away over to our left, soaring through breaks in the fog, where the sun kissed them, were the grandest mountains I'd ever seen. Dazzling white beacons above the greyness of the fog, marking the spine of the Antarctic Peninsula. At last the Ridgways had truly reached Antarctica.

The whole place had such romance; perhaps it was because even the wild creatures seemed to know they were safe, that this place was not owned by any country. It was open to all who dared. The whales, the creamy yellow seals and the parading penguins all seemed quite fearless.

It was as if we alone were present in a huge fenceless, frozen world of nature, where all living things shared our sense of freedom.

While the others paddled ashore to examine the bleached planks of the old British Survey hut on Danco Island, the family basked on deck in the sun and enjoyed one of Marie Christine's famous picnic lunches, with bottles of Beck's beer and little biscuits with olive pâté. Surrounded by grounded bergs, we lay to a kedge anchor in a fast-running tide. Under a sky of the deepest blue, thousands of gentoo penguins went about their solemn colony business on the slopes behind the hut. The air was so clear that it was difficult to judge distances, but the mountains rose sheer from the sea, as if coated in icing sugar, perfectly clean in every way. It was all such a contrast with our grubby human world. This was absolutely *it*. And I felt certain that if I was unable to appreciate this wonderful moment I would never find happiness anywhere.

After a few hours of threading our way through the ice, we nosed into Waterboat Point and tied up for the night, ropes to wire slings, four square in a tiny creek. It was all so dramatic; across Paradise Bay lay the Argentinian hut where, only a few years previously, a lone scientist had radioed for help, telling the world he was going mad. To speed relief he had set fire to the hut, burning it to the ground. And Waterboat Point was where Bagshawe and Lester had overwintered in an upturned boat in 1921–2. Set on a low finger of black rock, the few abandoned red huts of the little Chilean base sheltered us from the open water, serving as home for the thousands of gentoo penguins and their nests of piled stones. It was pretty chilly, but Igor's vodka martinis warmed us for Marie Christine's splendid roast beef and Yorkshire puddings.

After weeks of alarums and excursions we needed to lie up for a couple of days. A big depression was passing through the Drake Passage and this was our opportunity.

I was afraid of bad weather and very much aware that we were dashing from one secure anchorage to another, in between storms. And a gale buffeted *English Rose* that night. She rocked and lurched as the wind tore at her masts and shrieked through her rigging. Huddled together in the doghouse, Marie Christine and I found it hard to sleep. Our eyes were constantly drawn to the wind-speed needle which flickered around the dial above our heads. With all the dropboards in, we kept fairly warm on our planks, with layers of down sleeping bags, two duvets and the heavy wool blanket we'd bought in Chile. To conserve diesel, I'd persuaded everyone to do without the cabin heater so far.

Next morning, over steaming porridge and fresh bread, with icebergs sailing down the channel like galleons, we decided to stay put for another day. Parties hauled the dinghy along the 24mm rope warps and scrambled ashore to join the smelly squirting gentoos and scavenging sheathbills.

English Rose got away early next morning, albeit making slow progress. All around us, gentle whales came sighing up out of the depths to blow in the leads between the floes. This was as far south as we had expected to get, but with the help of the long poles we'd had specially made in Puerto Montt, we managed to push our way through the thick ice clogging the narrow Lemaire Channel. Two thousand feet above us, huge overhanging ice cliffs clung to the vertical mountainsides, just waiting for a thaw. It was heavy going and, overcome with hunger, we devoured Isso's drop scones and rhubarb jam faster than she could pass them up the hatch.

'Look out!' screamed Igor, choking on a scone and flinging his arm to starboard. Clinging to the wheel, I glimpsed three black fins, tall as fence posts, slicing through the gin-clear water, hurtling straight towards me. There was a broad blur of mottled black and white patches beneath the surface as the killer whales raced to kill. My nightmare was coming true: they couldn't miss the hull. But suddenly they were gone, slipping beneath the keel and rudder and shooting on towards the golden crab-eater seals crouched low on the floes. All around, gentoo penguins popped out of the water like black corks and flailed their terrified way up on to the ice, while the floes rocked in the wash of the monsters' charge.

'They must have been stalking us under the ice,' muttered J.W. No one could argue. We were leading a fragile existence.

It was already late in the afternoon when we inched through the Meek Channel and sighted a cluster of radio aerials outlined against the blinding ice. Beneath them we could make out the cactus-green buildings of BAS Faraday.

'You're the first yacht down here since last March,' called one of the lonely scientists, rather half-heartedly, over the VHF as we nudged aside the bergy bits. 'That'll make us the furthest south yacht in the world, at this moment,' I murmured, grinning happily at this surprise bonus.

MARIE CHRISTINE

Nothing could take away the intense excitement and elation I think we all felt on arriving at Faraday, at 65 degrees 15 minutes south, 64 degrees 16 minutes west. We had had a tough ride, and the strain and tension was showing all round in our scratchiness with each other. I felt so proud of the British base's Union Jack, which fluttered in the brilliant sunlight – even if it was sharing the flagpole with another. This was our first sight of British territory for fifteen long months. The conservation green of the base didn't quite match the bright red 'thumbs-up' thumb painted on a wall for the very few visitors who came.

The flat voice of the radio-operator who answered our call soon had us arguing vehemently. I didn't expect this rather half-hearted 'Hi, expect we'll see you ashore some time' greeting. We, and especially Latin Igor, couldn't help but compare this welcome with that of the Argentinians on Deception. 'It's all a question of morale,' John pointed out, and I had to agree. 'The Argentinians are moving in again and rebuilding, while from what we can gather, this is the last season for the British in Faraday.' We had heard rumours back in Puerto Williams that the new nation of Ukraine was about to take over this patch of British territory.

'Even so,' Bec interrupted, 'you'd think they would try to sound a bit more cheerful – after all, we are British too.' We had raised our spiffing new Red Ensign, much bigger and brighter than our old worn-out apology for a flag that had taken us as far as South America. Our new brave colours contrasted with the brilliant blue white of the ice and sun and sky.

I rashly added: 'I bet if it was run on service lines they would have had someone with a bit more zip on the radio.' Now the debate turned into a free-for-all, with J.W. absolutely on the side of the scientists and the casual approach, and Bec furious at his sloppiness. As if it mattered. But we felt we had come through hell to get here.

Pushing aside the bergy bits jamming the entrance to Stella Creek, the expert mooring team soon scrambled ashore with ropes to tie us four square to the rocks. We would be safe enough here, where in 1935–6 J.R. Rymill's British Graham Land expedition had wintered in their boat *Penola*. Their three-year journey provided conclusive evidence that the Antarctic Peninsula was part of the Antarctic mainland, and not a large island, as had been hitherto assumed.

Andy jumped about in the deep snow, avoiding attack by an angry skua. How good it felt to be safe. Whatever happened here, we were near help, something we hadn't felt for a week or two. After supper we went ashore. The unending snowy landscape was tinged rose by evening

Antarctic sun. Huge blocks of floating ice had now completely locked in *English Rose*. 'It'll probably go out with the tide,' Andy pronounced. Igor, assisted by Tiki, was on boat duty; the rest of us squeezed into the rubber dinghy and wobbled off, threading our way through the miniature icebergs towards the base.

We made our way carefully up freshly dug steps through a tall alley of packed snow to be greeted by Andy, a cheery, boyish-looking physicist, who had recently arrived on the *James Clark Ross*, a new survey ship, on its first visit of the summer. He led us into the large, square, green building. The heat was terrific. Looking at us through round glasses, his gaze lingering longest on Bec, he offered to show us round. Gratefully, we followed him up and down the shiny-floored corridors, peering into a small gym, a surgery equipped to deal with most emergencies, a laundry, stores and many laboratories with the latest computers and printers. Everything was here. It was a spaceship fixed in the fastness of a hostile environment. The operators, scientists with shorn heads, lived out their postings absorbed in their work. Intruding outsiders could disrupt the careful balance. While the Argentinian navy detachment had only come down for the summer, some of the fellows we were meeting had spent the long, dark winter here and even longer. Each of the twenty inmates had their space, crowded with piles of CDs and photos of girlfriends, penguins and seals tacked to the walls. 'It's a good place to save some cash, a time to buy the best audio, camera and ski equipment,' said Andy. It all seemed ominously like the film *Alien*, but out here the monster was the loneliness, the boredom, the bloke you didn't like. And health and safety regulations had altered the lives of these bravehearts as fewer and fewer outings were considered acceptable. In the past, they would have set off with dog teams on missions but now there were no dogs, and strict rules controlled all movement.

Duncan, the base commander, joined us. He was a huge man whose spring skinhead haircut was growing into an acceptable crew-cut, accentuating his big nose and deep-set eyes. 'Come and have a drink.' We followed his big stride up the stairs flanked by framed black and white group photos of previous years, stretching back to 1947, when Base F, West Coast Graham Land, as it was originally known, was established as a geophysical observatory.

I got the feeling that Christmas and New Year celebrations were still in full swing. Duncan positioned himself behind the curved wooden counter surrounded by every conceivable bottle, and the party began. John Shanklin, 'Mr Ozone', was introduced. On his narrow head, the base haircut made him look more Martian than human. He enthralled us with descriptions of his work and findings. It was here in the Antarctic that the thinning of the ozone layer had first been detected. John had probably told the story a thousand times, but we were riveted as he explained how critical ozone is in filtering out ultraviolet radiation, which is harmful and potentially lethal to all living organisms. The news was broken to the public and CFCs had to be reduced. Ozone depletion has occurred in the past with volcanic eruptions, but now the effects are exacerbated by chlorine gas from industrial pollution, and the graphs predict that by the year 2004 there could be a complete hole over the Antarctic which might not repair. John spent half the year back in Britain, trying to educate the public and appearing on everything from *Blue Peter* to science programmes. And I noticed that no one at this base went outside without sunglasses and barrier cream.

Those who had wintered over, like us, had been cooped up for a long time together, and I think they enjoyed having some fresh blood around. 'It may be a good way to save some cash, but it plays hell with your love life,' said Duncan with wry humour. It is hard to keep a relationship going from the other end of the world on messages anyone can read, relayed through INMARSAT via Cambridge, supplemented with a doubtful investment in Interflora. 'Good thing I kept my Christmas cards from last year – I think they've forgotten me back home,' he laughed rather sadly. There were no women on the Faraday Base, but propped up behind the bar was a raunchy photo of the women personnel on a distant American base. It might make life more interesting but undoubtedly it would distract. There was no escape here. Beyond the bar, and the ladies' underwear draping over the photograph, was a view that stretched for ever, a white horizon of sea and ice and mountains.

Thanks to modern technology, much of the work being carried out at Faraday can now be monitored remotely at the BAS headquarters in Cambridge as well as from the new survey ship. So from both a scientific and a financial standpoint, Faraday Base can no longer be justified. Both John and Duncan viewed the probable handover of the Base for ten years to the Ukrainians with regret.

We stayed snug in our creek for another two days, exploring the snowfields around us, four specks in a snowscape. Isso took huge strides to keep in Bec's footsteps as the Ridgway family struggled slowly through drifted snow to reach the Wordie Hut, an old black timber building kept in reserve in case of fire in the modern headquarters. The place had the smell of a Highland bothy and we found thirty-year-old copies of the *Scots* magazine lying around.

This was the furthest south we would be going. Stepping out into the snow, we turned for Home.

The weather remained peerless. The second night Duncan and John came for supper, and I think Duncan, in particular, enjoyed a night off from the base. We had one of our usual chunks of roast beef from Argentina, which was boringly delicious. How that meat transformed this Leg! It wouldn't have been half as nice or as comforting to tuck into pasta or our dehydrated alternatives.

The next day we invited the four stalwart Ukrainians for tea. They arrived dressed in smart grey suits, white shirts and dark ties. John immediately got on well with Jurij Oskret, the deputy director of the National Ukrainian Academy of Science. In spite of impossible language difficulties, sitting together they talked and laughed. Sixty-year-old Jurij exuded a tremendous enthusiasm and vitality. 'Capitalism may be bad, but you cannot know what we have suffered. You must not know!' We ate the chocolate cake I had baked specially, and drank Russian vodka and tea. The other three were Gennadi, a slick party official whose eyes flickered about shiftily; Sasha, a gentle radio-operator with soft brown eyes, and Volodia, called Bob by the scientists, who was tall, thin and courteous, and my favourite. The racket of conversation in the boat was deafening. There was so much we all wanted to find out about each other.

The following morning the foolhardies – Bec, Bruce, Igor, John and me – set off in the rubber dinghy, cracking the surface ice with our paddles, to meet the Ukrainians for a swim. I wondered if I would die. The base doctor had got up to be with us and the Ukrainians. It was into our cozzies, Bec looking lovely in her red one. She and I went first, running down the cement slipway taking care not to cut our feet on the sharp shells. The water was shockingly cold. A few strokes, a quick turn-round, and we were out. 'It only counts if you put your head under,' tough Bec taunted. I hadn't, and I certainly wasn't going in again.

Over breakfast at the base, Ukrainian Bob turned to me, 'Here there is so much! In Kiev we have no butter, cheese or bacon, and it is hard to get bread sometimes.' And when the empty coffee jar was chucked in the bin he remarked, 'I would treasure what they throw away.' He should have seen the aft cabin on *English Rose*, stuffed with empty bottles, jars and containers. We never threw anything out, in case it came in useful.

Later, in his tiny office, Jurij formally invited our family on an official visit aboard our yacht to Kiev. 'You can meet my wife then, Marie Christine.' He showed me a photograph of a very beautiful dark-eyed woman who looked like Scarlett O'Hara, her dark hair wrapped in a Russian scarf. 'We met when I was studying in St Petersburg. And my daughter . . .' He produced another snap. She was almost as beautiful as her mother, and I wasn't surprised when Jurij told me, 'She is a ballerina in Kiev.'

JOHN

The twenty-four-hour daylight enabled us to sail at any time, but it also brought overtiredness, which frayed tempers. It was after midday by the time Faraday received the very latest weather forecast from Rothera. Clutching the bulletin, we crept carefully out through the pancake ice, passing a large flock of blue-eyed cormorants, and headed back up the Meek Channel towards the soaring snowy peaks of the peninsula. Behind us hundreds of grounded bergs dotted the horizon like so many frozen islands. Our new British and Ukrainian friends waved forlornly from the shore and the rooftops. The base had the air of the frontier. Confronted by the irresistible elements, the face of a superior force, man is touched with heroism.

Some 8,000 miles lay between us at 65 south and Ardmore at 58 north. The sun shone fiercely from a clear blue sky and whales, seals and penguins were everywhere. At the wheel I didn't want to lose one precious minute, but at the wheel the glare was too much and my eyes felt gritty. I put on my sunglasses, which turned everything yellow, but I'd left it too late. I suffered mild snow-blindness for several days.

Trouble found us in the narrow steep-sided Le Maire Channel. In 40–50-knot gusts on the nose, we had some difficulty finding a way through the fast-drifting bergs. At last, six hours after leaving Faraday, we gained the shelter of Port Lockroy on Wiencke Island. Everyone was pretty well shot and nerves were jangling a bit as we struggled to anchor in high wind.

After an anxious night, under leaden morning skies, we set about a spell of make and mend while various parties took it in turn to go ashore. The scattered whale skeletons and a smelly penguin colony did nothing to dispel the air of chaotic decay in this abandoned British base. The collapsed roofs, burst ration packs and vandalised generators lent the place the air of a rubbish tip. It was not much of an example to other nations sharing the Antarctic continent.

In early evening, through lightly falling snow, we took advantage of improved weather and sailed for the Melchior Islands. In high winds, fog and ice, J.W., our navigator, the Mercedes OM314 and the Furuno radar really earned their stripes. Passing a strange copper-green mountain in the winding channel, we emerged into the open sea around midnight. A ship-shaped berg, over a mile long, complete with bows and sagging decks, was among the obstacles in our path. The radar brought us into a sheltered bay on Omega Island, but with the dawn we realised that the overhanging ice cliff opposite us was much too shaky. The creaking ice concentrated our minds on weighing anchor, hauling in the heavy warps and motoring the few miles to the red buildings of a long-deserted Argentinian base at Gallows Point on Gamma Island.

Unless there was a tidal wave, we were safe enough here, tied up four square in a narrow creek with a web of 24mm warps running to wire slings round boulders on the shore. It was grey and miserable, but hilarious tobogganing on plastic sheets; zooming down out of the mist on near-vertical slopes helped ease the tension of our situation.

The barometer plummeted from 1020 to 986 and we braced ourselves against 50-knot squalls, while convoys of bergs came sailing down the channel. Scrabble tournaments replaced tobogganing. It was pretty cold, but we were still reluctant to use any of our precious diesel fuel for the cabin heater. Instead we dressed to the maximum – I had to undo five zips to have a pee. At least the Argentinian beef made a treat of every meal.

One stormy morning Tiki went missing. The previous night, fed up with her wowling, J.W. had put her out in the main cockpit. This revelation did not go down well with the ladies. Everyone but J.W. came on deck and a tearful Bec paddled off in the Avon, calling Tiki's name hopelessly into the mist. With deep snow rising vertically from the banks of the ice-filled creek, we were on the point of giving up when suddenly Marie Christine shrieked with joy. 'There she is!' And there was our lesser god from Tahiti, a thin ginger stripe on top of a snow-filled ruined hut. 'Make no mistake, that is one tough cat!' laughed Igor.

With Tiki safely aboard once more, we went below and warmed ourselves with bowls of steaming porridge, wrapping our chilled hands round mugs of hot coffee. J.W. had prevailed upon us each to have our own named pot of marmalade on the table, but it was noticeable that while we dipped into ours, J.W. kept his in his locker and devoured all the available jam.

'Things *have* got bad!' pronounced Andy, moustache bristling, bouncing up and down in indignation. He resented this interference with the relaxed feeding pattern established many months before J.W. joined the boat.

Petty grievances quickly become enlarged on long trips in confined spaces, and, like office gossip, they might be intriguing at first but over time they become increasingly less so. I had noticed that J.W. always wanted to walk alone on trips ashore and although this was perfectly reasonable I was concerned about the possibility of a split developing between himself and the rest of the crew. On his arrival in Valdivia, full of fresh enthusiasm, J.W. had more or less taken over the navigation, easing the burden on me and allowing me to organise other things. But I did feel twinges of anxiety about the slight loosening of my control. I sympathised with J.W.'s desire to be the skipper on his own boat, but this was not the way it was now. He needed to share information more.

It would be wrong to exaggerate these petty quibbles, because I could not have wished for a better team. But they are an inevitable part of long voyages, and maintaining the balance is not always easy. Someone whose attitude may be exceptional one year can be quite different the next. The reason is quite simple: people change. They grow older, and pressures in their private and business lives alter them. And in the pressure-cooker environment of expeditions, these changes soon become apparent. Sometimes it feels as if you have lived a whole lifetime in just a few weeks. On occasions I have become so caught up with the intensity of a situation that on returning home, I have found I had forgotten large sections of my previous life. Fortunately, I have kept a diary every day since 1958, though now I am coming round to the view that an ability to forget things is important, and a selective memory very useful.

When the glass steadied once more, we sailed out through the murk and bergs heading for Deception Island. The 112 miles took fifteen queasy hours.

MARIE CHRISTINE

This time we had no qualms about the kind of welcome we'd be given on Deception. Our only worry was that bad weather might stop us from getting through the narrow pass aptly named Neptune's Bellows. We endured a sickening cross-swell, and only Bruce and Isso felt on top form. Frequent snow showers shrank our world, making us even more watchful of the many huge icebergs and accompanying downwind brash. Storm petrels fluttered and albatrosses wheeled their figures of eight in graceful arcs around the boat. Along the steep black cliffs of Deception we spotted three pairs of humpback whales, blowing a welcome into the grey, chill air. Just after 6 am we moored off the sleeping Argentinian base and grabbed an hour of sleep after a weary breakfast of porridge and bread. We awoke to hear Ricardo's deep, friendly voice. '*Eenglish Rose, Eenglish Rose*. Que pasa?' Igor took over and much talk ensued. 'Bring your towels. And does the señora wish to bring some *ropa por lavar*?' She most certainly did. Each of us had a big bag of dirty clothes and we probably wouldn't get another chance to do any washing until we reached Brazil, thousands of miles further north.

Again, the Argentinians gave us an overwhelmingly kind reception: hot showers and their tiny cabins, with poignant framed photos of wives and children propped on chests of drawers, to change in. As well as the washing, which was whirring around in unusual machines at the back of the building, where they emptied straight down into what looked like a permafrost soakaway, I had brought ashore a basket of some rather pitiful presents. I had baked a couple of cakes when we were stormbound at the abandoned base Port Lockroy, one lemon and one chocolate. Also along the way, among the ice, I had made some tart English marmalade which I thought they would enjoy with the crusty loaves Bec and I had struggled to bake during the lumpy journey the day before. Ricardo accepted our gifts as though they were the crown jewels.

The day ashore passed blissfully, and we finally returned to the boat at 2 am. We had under three months to get home and we were still at the end of the globe.

The next day an expedition was mounted to the gentoo penguin rookery, which was being monitored by scientists from the nearby Spanish base. John and I elected to stay behind while the rest of the team departed, bristling with cameras. We had seen a great number of different penguins, but none being bashed to death in the water by leopard seals. These sharp-toothed hunters lurk in the breaking surf where the penguins hop in and out of the water and are at their most vulnerable. Our bunch waited patiently all day in the bitter cold with their cameras poised, but happily for the penguins, it turned out to be a bad day for leopard seals and photographers. Eventually the crew returned, cold and very hungry.

To go with my green bar of navy soap, I was given another souvenir by the Argentinians. In the old hut there were a number of red-painted wooden racks, each containing three hand-blown glass water bombs, which served as rather decorative fire-extinguishers. I coveted these, but hadn't liked to ask if I might have a set. Unbeknown to me, Igor had mentioned this, and I was presented with a rack of bombs, with best wishes from the base. I hoped I would have more luck getting these fragile items home than I'd had with an ostrich egg which had shattered between Africa and Ardmore on a previous sailing trip.

We were sad at leaving these friends we wouldn't see again. We sailed early next morning, heading towards South Georgia, and away from the splendour of Antarctica.

20

Outposts of Empire

MARIE CHRISTINE

Spared by the perils of the Antarctic, we were now on our way in search of two very special friends. Tim and Pauline Carr had come sailing into our lives on a wild autumn day in 1989, dropping anchor in the loch at the foot of the croft. They had battled across the North Atlantic from Iceland, and needed somewhere sheltered to repair their boat before heading south to find work for the winter. John admired their self-reliance and skill. How grand it would be if they could stay, and maybe do some work on *English Rose*, he suggested. Tim and Pauline were acutely sensitive to their surroundings, and it was several days before they made a decision – it would have to suit them both, and *Curlew*, they said. They had bought *Curlew* – a 28ft gaff-rigged Falmouth quay punt almost a hundred years old – in 1968, lovingly restored her and lived aboard in spartan simplicity, and they always referred to themselves as a family of three. *Curlew* had neither engine nor radio transmitter, but sailed for more than twenty years all around the world, from the Arctic Circle to the Antarctic Peninsula. That winter, with *Curlew* moored safely in Loch a'Chadh-fi, Tim had lined much of *English Rose* with pine and teak while Pauline painstakingly applied nine coats of varnish to every wooden surface, and our trusty boat glowed with the attention. Since sailing away from Ardmore in the spring of 1990, they had been awarded the Blue Water Medal by the Cruising Club of America.

I think it was the simplicity of their lives, devoid of accumulated possessions, and their sense of purpose that impressed us most. Some people, however far away they may be, remain for ever in your thoughts, and Tim and Pauline Carr were two such people, the only permanent residents on South Georgia.

REBECCA

Our trip across the Scotia Sea to South Georgia took a cold and bumpy week. Once we rounded Cape Melville and cleared the South Shetland Islands, clustered around the northern tip of the Antarctic Peninsula, we ran into a strong northerly wind and the full weight of the Southern Ocean swell soon had us groggy. With grey seas melting into grey mist and grey skies, visibility was really dreadful and there were icebergs everywhere. Dad decided to push on north into the heavy seas for several hours to make sure we cleared Elephant Island, somewhere out to our east.

'These chilblains are driving me mad,' I cursed, tottering off watch in the Antarctic night. Mum came crawling past me, clipped herself on to the jackstays and disappeared into the blackness of the aft cockpit. I crept below, shedding sopping red waterproofs, boots, gloves and layers of hats, my ears still buzzing from icy spray and hailstones rattling on my hood like flung pebbles.

Grabbing a mug of hot lemon and ignoring Tiki's caterwauling, I hauled myself forward to my bunk, flopped down and began scratching madly through two pairs of thick socks, feeling like an overweight Michelin woman struggling on a rocking tube train in rush hour. There wasn't a lot of high fashion in my life.

My father, the fax exile, sat hunched over the chart table, tap-tap-tapping away at his laptop. As if by magic, his usual 'I gave my yesterday so you could have your today' deafness seemed to have vanished. 'Stop whingeing, Rebecca,' he barked, eyes still glued to the screen. 'With eight bodies each producing one kilowatt of warmth, we have no need for the cabin heater.' Our family motto ought to be 'Nobody said it would be easy'.

Tiki didn't think much of the cold. She grudgingly wore a padded lamb's coat, but her manners didn't match the Sloanie look. Although she made a welcome hot-water bottle in my bunk, she savaged me whenever I tried to move. She found Igor quite exotic and delicious, and her amorous overtures slightly ruffled even his cool.

JOHN

Success is so much a matter of grinding attention to detail, and there was a danger of the basics being disregarded. It wasn't long before I was writing stern notes in the log, urging watch leaders to watch out for chafe, tighten guys and secure winch handles in their pockets. Cape pigeons, storm petrels, ice birds and albatrosses swirled around us. The log showed sightings of blue whales, but I don't think we were really experienced enough to be reliable interpreters of the various whale spouts we observed.

Bad news came from Rita. Lance Bell had had a stroke, and had been helicoptered to hospital from his croft on the other side of the wood at home. Ada was back in Teesside, and he was incarcerated in an old folks' home. He wouldn't be returning to his beloved Ardmore. He'd kept me on a level path over the wild years, and together we'd hauled many a lobster creel on fine summer mornings. 'There's nobody indispensable, save Adam!' he'd snort but now I was so sad I had to stop everything. For the truth was that I knew this to be the time of my life. It wouldn't be long now before they were wheeling me into the institution as well. Self-indulgent twit.

At last we were able to bear away from the north-west wind and lay a course to take us to a notional point 100 miles west of South Georgia. Briefing a green-faced Andy on the watch change that the Yankee must be poled out to port was like delivering a death sentence. But he and Bruce set to on the foredeck with a will while I stayed at the wheel. Once the diminished trade-wind rig was set up the motion eased a bit and though we were still a long way south, life settled into the familiar, grim, swaying twenty-four-hour ocean routine. 'It's just like Leg 2 with Bruce and Rita,' chuckled Andy, 'except now we have to eat beef every day. Bruce would have loved this – no pasta.' The race was on to finish all the Argentinian beef before we crossed the Antarctic Convergence. We knew that once the sea temperature increased, it would very quickly go bad.

The team was working well and there was a fair bit of banter. 'Igor's been perfuming himself in the heads for the last hour, and now he's just helped himself to more meat,' grinned Andy. Igor was certainly adjusting to the life. He had much more to learn about sailing than the others, but his carefree approach and his Peruvian cooking added another dimension to our existence.

Marie Christine's birthday, 18 January, dawned rough and cold and we saw our last iceberg at 55/46 south. Everyone appreciated the contribution Marie Christine had made to the voyage, so we all made a big event of it. Bruce and Rita faxed greetings from Ardmore, and Bec decorated the saloon with the well-worn 'Happy Birthday' banners from Bruce's party on the Atlantic on Leg 2. I had bought a handsome oyster-shell hairpin box from the Gambier Islands for the occasion and Isso came up with a collection of combs and thimbles from goodness knows where, as well as her own funny card for 'Mamalita'. The glass had been rising all day and we had to change the rig as the wind went round from north-east to south-east. By teatime it was too rough for the cake and Chilean champagne, and when A Watch came on at midnight it was pretty cold and bumpy. Half a dozen hourglass dolphins raced along beside us, guiding us to South Georgia.

Fog came with the rain, and small fur seals began to dance around us. Then a wind piped up from the south-west, blowing us on. At last the sun came out, and there was South Georgia. We had a few hours to get into Grytviken before it got dark.

My first impression was surprise that the island was so high and so remote. Covered with snow, its 9,000ft mountains sent huge glaciers tumbling down to the sea. It wasn't part of Antarctica, yet it was quite different from South America – unique, in fact.

MARIE CHRISTINE

We had escaped the Antarctic with only a few scratches from the ice, but here we were again, two weeks later, in just as hazardous a situation. With 40 knots of wind on the nose in the pitch dark, we were fearful of loose ice in the black water. Williwaws swooped down from the snow-covered mountains on either side, keeping us battling to hold the course as we steered up the narrow fjord, with the old whaling harbour of Grytviken somewhere out to starboard. Everyone came up on look-out, and John tried calling into the night on our hand-held radio. It hardly seemed possible that anyone could be living in this hostile place. Then, to our relief, an immensely reassuring English voice crackled out of the blackness: 'Hello *English Rose*, we were expecting you . . . Roger, Roger. Yes, it's quite safe for you to tie up at the wharf.' Sarah, the harbourmaster's wife, had saved our bacon.

Rounding King Edward Point, we spotted *Pelagic*, the veteran sloop we'd met in Chile, all lit up to guide us in. We could just make out two other yachts moored alongside the broken-down whaling station snugly tucked in at the end of the fjord: *Kotic*, with French Sophie and her physicist husband Oleg, whom we'd met at Puerto Williams and again at Usuahia, and bright red *Damien II* and the Poncets. These three boats and their owners were legendary. They spent their lives working in the most hostile of waters, sailing among the ice in their frail craft. But where were Tim and Pauline Carr?

'Come aboard and have a whiskey.' We didn't need a second invitation from the crew of *Pelagic*. Bec and I sat with our hats firmly on our heads in spite of the heat in the cosy cabin below. We hadn't been able to wash our hair for two weeks, and the same went for our clothes. I just hoped we didn't smell. That evening in Grytviken only three of the team were on board: Mike, a young American boatbuilder, and ultra-British Frank and Hamish. They told us that Tim and Pauline were sailing 'somewhere round the island'. My heart sank, but I suppose we were not surprised: I suspected that three boats in the harbour was just too many for them. Searching around such a dangerous coastline, would we ever find them? But our spirits soon rose with some good glugs of Irish whiskey and news of the rest of the *Pelagic*'s party, who were currently struggling to get up Mount Paget, the highest point of the British Empire. Changing the subject, Mike turned to me: 'What a pity you missed our barbecue yesterday. We even had a lovely fresh daffodil salad.'

The next day John and I and Isso (reluctantly), set off round the bay, passing dozing female elephant seals resting, scratching and hurrumphing in the tussock grass. A group of moulting king penguins gazed haughtily at us, pecking and preening their fine orange, black and white plumage. In the tiny cemetery where Sir Ernest Shackleton is buried, we picked heaps of crisp dandelion leaves from around the graves – in spite of the whiskey, I was sure Mike couldn't have meant daffodils. This would be our first fresh green salad in weeks.

After leaving Deception, John, Isso and I had taken it in turns on watch to read out loud from Shackleton's *Valiant Voyage*. The story came alive for us, for once past Elephant Island, we had followed almost the same route as his 22ft open lifeboat, the *James Caird*. Eighty years earlier, Shackleton and his five men, weak from months of struggle, reached South Georgia across the Scotia Sea, a bitter, stormy distance of 650 nautical miles, which John considered the greatest voyage ever recorded.

Now Shackleton was buried in this lonely graveyard on the hill over-looking King Edward Cove. The whales and whalers were gone, and the whaling station Grytviken – 'pot bay' – abandoned. At its height, 6,000 people had been employed here. There had been a bakery, a cinema and a neat, white Norwegian church. The station was still in working order when the final caretaker left, in tears, in the early sixties, but now the ruthless weather had rendered it a rusted tangle, a fitting memorial to the thousands of gentle giant whales that had been butchered here.

South Georgia is within the icy Antarctic Convergence zone on a route to nowhere, and precious few visit the island. Apparently we were only the fortieth yacht ever to have stopped there. Captain Cook, our old friend from Polynesian days, came upon South Georgia in 1775. He describes it as follows.

> a huge Mass of Snow and ice of vast extent . . . the inner parts of the Country were not less savage and horrible: the Wild rocks raised their lofty summits until they were lost in the clouds and the Vallies laid buried in everlasting snow. Not a tree or a shrub was to be seen, no, not even enough to make a tooth-pick.

Since the Falklands War, the British had strengthened their presence, and all told there was a garrison of about forty Royal Fusiliers, a har-bourmaster-cum-magistrate and half a dozen ornithologists and scientists, many of whom left with the onset of winter. The redoubtable Tim and Pauline had become the first couple to live there all year round since the whalers left. Working with their artistic skills to create the South Georgia Whaling Museum and living aboard *Curlew*, tied up alongside an abandoned sealer, they were held fast in the southern winter ice.

The following day we left Grytviken wondering if we would ever find Tim and Pauline. On the second day of our search, after a night anchored in a dismal canyon, the sun at last pierced the band of thick mist which encircled the island and, scanning the coastline with binoc-ulars, we spotted at last *Curlew*'s hibiscus mast, tucked away in a neat rock-girded lagoon.

Tim rowed out, grinning broadly, and we held our breath as John fol-lowed his white pram dinghy through the kelp in tune with Isso's mantra-like readings from the echo-sounder. Among the rocks and swirling kelp on either side of our narrow slalom course, noisy families of playful seals and countless penguins dipped in and out of the clear water.

Pauline and Tim jumped on board, and we hugged each other. 'How long can you stay – a month?' Pauline asked, bright-eyed. We celebrated our reunion with a bottle of champagne brought from Ardmore and my birthday cake, saved for this moment. It was so good to see them again.

When Tim and Pauline went ashore in the late afternoon, I paddled over and left a shiny red box tied with a matching ribbon in *Curlew*'s cockpit. It was for Pauline, something I had brought from Ardmore. I hoped Tim would allow her to keep it. I had once lent her a favourite long blue silk skirt , and it had looked lovely on her, the different shades of blue matching her eyes. She wore it that evening to have supper with us on *English Rose*, and her face was radiant. We had come a long way to deliver it.

We spent two magical days tucked away in the remotest cove on the planet. The sun shone and the whole place throbbed with life in high Antarctic summer. Along the shore, king penguins posed in groups or shuffled in their fine orange and white shirts; gentoos and chinstraps popped in and out of the gentle surf; noisy, boisterous fur seals pushed each other about, their young screaming out for food whenever an adult returned from the ocean. We observed slumbering moulting harems of vast elephant seals, their mates, a little way off, like giant sumo wrestlers half-heartedly rearing up and bashing one another.

'Danny, don't go any closer,' Isso implored. But John was bravely advancing towards a group of the biggest bull elephant seals flopped on the shoreline. 'I want to see their snotters,' he called back, waving his 'podger', a broken Choco Indian canoe paddle, at us. If aggravated, an elephant seal will roar and belch air, pumping up his proboscis in the process.

'So this is how our glorious eighteen-month sea journey will end,' I wailed. 'With John squashed by an elephant seal!'

We recognised friends from Antarctica everywhere. On the summit of a hill we stepped among macaroni penguins, their punk orange hairdos waving above the tussock grass; further up were nests with light-mantled sooty-eyed albatrosses, delicate terns and skuas. We had never, ever seen anything to compare with this day.

On the second evening Pauline cooked us a splendid supper aboard *Curlew*. Everything was home-made and wonderful: lentil soup and brown bread, sweet and sour pork with tussock grass-shoot salad, and a choice of chocolate or custard pie. What a feast she had prepared for us in such a tiny space, ingeniously making full use of only two paraffin rings and a pressure cooker.

We paddled back to *English Rose* at midnight, to the sound of penguins and seals. Fearful of a huge low moving towards South Georgia, we knew we had to leave next morning.

We were up at 5 am, and soon had the three warps in. In their pram dinghy, Tim and Pauline led us through the kelp and rocks out into clear water. With tears in our eyes, we waved goodbye to our two gallant friends, and disappeared into the fog.

JOHN

We left South Georgia motoring in a calm and worrying about diesel consumption for the 4,000-mile dogleg sail up the Atlantic to Natal on the north-east coast of Brazil, via Tristan da Cunha, where we could not expect to find fuel. With our main tank full, augmented by the red jerrycans we had stowed on deck in the main cockpit for Antarctica, we had a total of 240 gallons of diesel. And now we had a deadline: to reach Ardmore in time to run our month-long instructors' course before the start of our twenty-sixth season in early May. Motoring through calms like the Doldrums would be necessary.

Once the sun set over the 9,600ft Mount Paget, we had a calm, dark night of hand-steering, with much luminous plankton and squid in our prop wash. We decided to hoist the sails to save fuel, and then we all got a little tetchy with the frustration of covering only 49 miles in twenty-four hours.

The south-east wind arrived at last, and soon we were making 7 knots on beam reach in a rising sea. Shortly after 9 pm, Andy, vomiting over the side in pitch darkness, thought he saw an iceberg at 200m fine on the port bow. He screamed a warning to Bruce at the helm. Then the 'iceberg' breached, jumping clear out of the water. It was a whale. Cascading white phosphorescence, it crashed back into the sea with colossal force and shot straight at the boat, passing right under the bows. 'I thought it was going to hit us – it was so close!' Andy gasped. The whale jumped again, close in on the port side, but then it disappeared. I remembered Jerome Poncet telling me in Grytviken that he'd been sunk by a whale while skippering the Italian yacht *Guia*, a good way to the north of our present position. It had been calm, but the boat went down in seconds, amid a lot of confusion. The Italians were rather excitable in the liferaft, and luckily a ship had come along within a few hours.

The distances we covered were increasingly daily, widening the gap between us and the Antarctic, and by noon on 1 February we were only 40 miles south of the Antarctic Convergence. Everyone was dreaming of the sun and as the anxieties of the Antarctic receded, J.W. relaxed and began writing his inspiring poems in the log once more:

> *How many shades of grey*
> *Can there be in a day?*
> *'Tis very difficult to say.*

My own entries were a little more prosaic. 'Could each individual put fifteen minutes each day into leaving the boat better than you found her. Please.'

Igor searched some old *Cosmopolitan* and *She* magazines we were given on South Georgia for recipes. He produced some Adobo, a Mexican seasoning for old meat, which demolished the last of the fast-failing Argentinian beef and used up most of Marie Christine's failed orange wine. Then he declared Friday a Cosmo Day, and outlined the fashions to be worn: 'Racy red overcoat with nifty peaked hood; long leggings, with a choice of red, green or blue; randy rubber galoshes, calf-length, in blue or white; special-order loud luminous flashes in green; underclothes to suit particular tastes.'

A storm put an end to all this jollity. Lying on my bunk, facing forward on the port-side seat of the saloon, I gazed queasily up through the port-forward window. Breaking waves sluiced across it and I worried lest the crazing of the perspex was as bad as Tim Carr had warned. Up there on deck, by the shrouds, a tail of rope streamed rigid in the wind like a pink elephant's trunk. Tentacles of salt water stretched across the teak lining boards on the inside of the main bulkhead, greening Isso's effort with the Brasso on the well-travelled brass clock, whose second hand ticked my life away. I worried about the rivets at the spreader roots on the mast, where I'd hit the schooner's spar in Puerto Williams, and about the way the self-steering lines kept breaking. The going was getting rough.

By midnight mountainous seas were raking the decks as J.W., Bec, Marie Christine and I tried various manoeuvres to ease our situation in the shrieking wind and driving rain. The demented wind seized on the heavy number 2 Yankee furled round the forestay, shaking the whole boat. Our searchlight was shorting, and while Marie Christine aimed the beam up into the sails, the fillings in her teeth reacted with one another, making the raindrops fizz on her cheeks and giving her the taste of old pennies in her mouth. Blimey. At the wheel, I decided that steering 080 was too hard on the boat, so we tacked to 310 degrees and headed in the wrong direction. It wasn't until we got home that we found that the rigging screw at the foot of the forestay had been stretched by a load in excess of 5 tons. Soaked through after an hour of battling with sheets and furling lines, we gybed on to the trisail alone and jilled along at 2 to 3 knots. This was the first time I had stopped *English Rose* in her twenty-year life.

By the time A Watch came on again at 6 am, the wind had dropped to 25 knots and backed north-west. We were on our way again, and thought we were through the worst, but at 9 am, 670 miles south-west of Tristan, the glass bottomed at 1,000 and began shooting up. The wind raced to 50 knots and the sea became a sheet of foam as we roared along under a scrap of staysail and the trisail. It was the stuff of dreams.

Within a couple of days the wind dropped, and we had sun and light breezes on a sea of delicious milky blue with endless horizons. Once again it was like the South Pacific. Storms sharpen the mind, and morale soared: cheerful faxes from Rita brought arrangements for the instructors' course and bookings for the coming season. We were on our toes again and difficulties became challenges.

'We're north of the Roaring Forties,' Igor announced, waking A Watch on 8 February with a traditional Amazonian Ucayali riverboat breakfast of special eggy bread. Still half-asleep, Isso tripped on the way to the doghouse and hers shot into the oilskin locker. Then Marie Christine stumbled and spilt a kettle of boiling water over the sleeve of her red Henri Lloyd jacket.

Riding a huge swell under clear skies, we slipped between Inaccessible and Nightingale Islands and watched Tristan da Cunha come bulging green out of the sea, gently curving up to its 6,760ft volcanic cone. Rita faxed advice from J.W.'s dentist, via his mum in Preston, which had him biting on cloves and hoping to find a doctor when he got ashore. We urgently needed a bit of shelter for some running repairs: the crack in our main boom was widening.

A couple of fellows lifting crawfish creels from a small yellow boat waved enthusiastically, pointing towards the north-west corner of the island. Ashore we could see people at work in their potato patches. There was no anchorage to speak of, though thick kelp beds extending several hundred yards out from the coast along the north shoreline indicated an apron of shallows. We found only a rocky bottom without real holding ground and the swaying kelp confused the echo-sounder, so we tried a stint with the lead line before committing too much chain. 'Head more to the heast!' the harbourmaster's steady voice advised us over the VHF. He was keen for us to anchor in 11 fathoms, but I felt we had to find shallower water. In fact we were lucky to be able to stop at all: we had arrived on one of only sixty or seventy days in each year when it is calm enough for the fishing boats to put to sea.

Once we were securely anchored, the island medical officer came on the radio, a young South African doctor on contract. He needed to know if we had any coughs or flu, because the islanders suffered badly from asthma. He was relieved to hear we had come from the freezing sterility of Antarctica and were completely clear of viral complaints, and sent out the harbour boat. 'D'you get many yachts in here?' I asked Joe. 'Hohh, yess!' replied the sturdy boatman slowly, his square brown face cracking into a brilliant smile. 'Sometimes we get three; heven five, some years.' With aitches preceding many words in the old-fashioned tongue, he reminded me of those other brave island boatmen on faraway Pitcairn.

Across the saloon table, Sergeant Conrad Glass, smart in his black and white British police uniform, went about his business in a thorough manner. He was a swarthy descendant of Corporal Glass of Kelso and the Royal Artillery garrison which was sent to the island in 1816 to prevent the French from invading St Helena and rescuing Napoleon. Sergeant Glass asked politely if we would wipe our shoes before going ashore, just in case any residue of the frozen wastes of South Georgia should contaminate the 47 per cent of Tristan da Cunha given over to conservation. As part of their research into pollution by chemicals like DDT, HCB and PCB, the universities of Milan and Sienna had recently examined leaves, mosses and lichens from twenty-six parts of the globe and concluded that Tristan has the lowest level of contamination in the world.

Poorly anchored on a small ledge on a jagged volcanic cliff, we rolled heavily on the swell, uncomfortably aware of our vulnerability. The cliff was in fact the mouth of a solidified river of black lava which, thirty years before, had poured down from the erupting volcano only a few hundred yards from the village. In the heavy rolling, our tin teapot slid off the table, somehow splashing the white deckhead as it fell. Behind us, the tiny settlement of Edinburgh crouched in the wind on the north-west corner of the volcano. It was by far the most spick-and-span place we'd seen since leaving home. Backed by mighty cliffs soaring way up into the clouds, this was a dangerous place for boats. Iron rule had it that all the stubby crawfishing boats must ride the surf into the little harbour by 5.30 every evening at the latest so that the crane could lift them clear of the hungry sea before dark. The scatter of low, white-washed stone buildings, with their roofs of red, green or blue, pointed their massive lava block gables at the prevailing westerly storms.

As Joe took us ashore, I complimented him on the comforting note of his engine. 'Yess, eighty-horse Ford. Come hoff a wrecked yacht,' he chuckled.

Once up the iron ladder and on the stone quay, we paused, legs wobbling on the still, black volcanic rock. We were out of the wind for the first time in what seemed an age. A couple of locals mending crawfish pots stared at us, their strong-featured faces gazing shyly as if we were visitors from another planet. But the sunlit silence and unaccustomed warmth of that sheltered spot brought a surge of life back to our limbs. It was springtime after a long, dark winter.

Leaving poor J.W. to discuss his toothache with the doctor, I took the family to meet the Administrator. We were ushered into a large room at the far end of the government building, through whose windows the clear blue horizon appeared to show the curve of the earth. The Administrator was surrounded by banks of computer screens and a plankful of switches, stretching wall to wall. Levering himself up from behind his large corner desk, he strode across the room to greet us, bristling with that almost-forgotten British reserve so untypical of the other countries we'd visited. He was a fine upstanding fellow of about my own age, immaculately clad. I felt the smartly pressed tweed jacket aged him a little, though the staid appearance was relieved somewhat by the thin gold ring in his left ear. As we exchanged pleasantries, I felt a fresh spring in my legs, the joints felt looser and the knees flexed. Coming out from the anxieties of the Antarctic, my hopes for a little flourish in the back straight of life were beginning to lift. Once a boxer, I had the feeling I might have the Administrator's knees awobbling if I could just catch him with my right hand over his straight left; pivoting from the hips, I might still come up with a right cross like the one which had dropped the army champion thirty years before. Perhaps I had kept a little back after all. I was moving forward again.

A demure young woman in grey twin set and glasses changed a few dollars for us in the island's bank room, and we set off to buy eagerly awaited fresh vegetables from the store. She was far too polite, or shy, to ask us for the £3 landing fee, so I had to return later and offer the money.

'Any more chickens caught in the mission garden will be destroyed,' read the notice in the shop window. At the counter, Marie Christine asked an elderly man with a tanned and kindly face about prices, but he smiled with embarrassment and waved her towards the produce. Sergeant Glass told us later that many of the older folk don't hold with money, still preferring the potato currency, the traditional way of bartering with the few visiting ships.

Friends at home had given us the names of some people to look up for them. All the little houses on Tristan lie together, so Evelyn Hagan was easy to find. Her cottage, sheltered by a stout hedge of New Zealand flax, lay up a path between narrow green lawns bordered with delphiniums, geraniums and fuchsia. A short, dark-haired woman of middle age in a smart yellow lace blouse, Evelyn stood, tanned and capable, at her front door. She was expecting us: with only eight families on the island making up the 300 souls, everyone knows everything on Tristan. Piers, her husband, was a descendant of Captain Andrew Hagan, the American whaler who'd married one of Corporal Glass's daughters in 1849. But Evelyn was a Swain before she married, and this was a Swain family home. Over the generations, bits had been built on to either end for other branches of the family.

Politely nibbling oatmeal biscuits to make them last, and sipping tea from real cups and saucers, we were stunned into silence by the unaccustomed total stillness of the sunlit cottage. It was as if we were already home, on a bright spring morning on the west coast of Scotland. Conversation is not an art much practised on Tristan as visitors are so rare, and I found myself thinking of Thomas Swain from Hastings, who'd settled here in 1826 after serving under Admiral Nelson aboard HMS *Victory*. One of five lonely bachelors on the island, Thomas was desperate for a wife. As a ship bearing five volunteer women from St Helena approached, he swore he'd marry the first lady to step ashore. True to his vow, he married Sarah Jacobs, a coloured woman who was already the mother of several children.

We got talking about the eruption of 1961. 'Hoh yes, I was heighteen then,' Evelyn remembered, her dark eyes brightening at the mention of it. 'Hof course, we didn't know what it was. The rumblin's began in

June. We never himagined it would ever come to hanything.'

'It must have been absolutely terrifying,' said Marie Christine.

'No, not really. Heverythin' that age is hexcitin'. Then one mornin' in Hoctober, we looked hacross the green field at the back here, and it just split open. An' then we saw the sheep fallin' in, and smoke come pourin' out. The Hadministrator sent word to go to the potato patches a mile or two down the coast. So we just hup an' left, leavin' heverythin'. We were hevacuated to England, a camp near Southampton. And we didn't come back for two years.'

We asked if she had really wanted to come home to Tristan after that. 'Hoh, we wanted to come home, hall right!' Evelyn insisted. 'We didn't like the robbin' and the murdrin'. It did us good, mind – we hislanders learned to stick hup for hourselves!'

Elaine Repetto, nursing in Glasgow, had asked us to look up her mother Margaret, a descendant of shipwrecked Italian sailors. We found her spinning wool with half a dozen friends, strong, no-nonsense women full of character working swiftly with cones and looms. Their harsh, asthmatic coughs were just a part of the price they'd had to pay for living on this remote island without outside blood. 'Don't be shy, don't be shy!' They chuckled at our embarrassment, treating us to delicious hot tea, steambrass pie and home-made cakes. This joint effort to spin wool was typical of the islanders' way of tackling annual tasks, like 'rattin'' or gathering sheep, just as it had been in the crofting communities at home.

We noticed that the wind was getting up on the bay far below and so we scuttled back to the shop to finish getting the groceries. 'Well, me dears, what you be wantin'?' chunky Vera smiled over the counter. As Conrad the policeman had already promised us some of his new crop of 'taters', Marie Christine bought a sack of 'turnups', a box of long, green-topped onions and some tight, crisp cabbages, all home-grown. Vera promised us carrots and rhubarb – 'Makes lovely crumble' – if we could collect them next day from the communal island garden, but it wasn't to be.

'How does that compare with the boat you rowed across the Hatlantic with Chay Blyth, then?' asked Conrad as we paused on our way to the boat to look over the last of the canvas-covered whalers. He pointed to the whaler. 'She won the sail down to Nightingale Island for the guano in March this year. The wind was light and she was hempty. But I won the race back, heavy laden, in my new fibreglass whaler,' he told us proudly.

Though I'd never met him, I recognised the widower the moment he turned on to the road, still a hundred yards off. The powerful champion grower of onions and turnips, tanned and square, was bowed with grief. He came up the hill aimlessly, and Sergeant Glass introduced us as he passed. He shook our hands with his bear-like paws. 'Tell them my missus passed haway,' he muttered, averting his tear-filled eyes. Our friends at home had warned us of his grief, and I thought again of Lance and Ada and the empty Blue House on Ardmore, the tragic inevitability of it all. How short is life. 'Yes, of course . . . I'm very sorry,' I replied. To cover his distress I changed the subject. 'White horses in the bay.'

'Yes, from the north-west. Come hup real quick from there,' he said more briskly. 'You'd best be going while you can.'

'Yes, we must.' He shook our hands again and shuffled on his way.

We all bundled into Conrad's Land Rover and rattled down to the quay. The harbour boat was waiting. We had to be clear of the harbour by 5 pm so as not to hold up the craning out of the returning fishing boats.

The deck was surging up and down the wall. Just as we were about to fend off, a white cardboard box full of vegetables and fish was handed down to us. The rough inscription read: 'To the Ridgway family with love from the Hagan family.'

At sunset, a broad reach took us streaming away from Tristan. Behind us a cluster of streetlights pricked the darkness at the foot of the vast black volcano. Did they really need streetlighting? Surely they couldn't be 'hafeared o' muggin'' on Tristan da Cunha?

21

Homeward

JOHN

Before us lay the 2,500 miles to Brazil, where Igor would be leaving us. To begin with we needed to head north through the variables for 500 miles or so, searching for the south-east tradewinds, then we needed to hitch a ride on that broad band of steady wind blowing north-west up the Atlantic from South Africa to north-east Brazil.

We had a fair wind for the first couple of days. J.W.'s toothache was gone and repairs to the main boom looked solid. Bruce was lost in his lonely job of cleaning and greasing all the winches, and with his salami blowing free in the rigging, Igor opened his season of 'super-elegant' meals with fresh crawfish tails and rice. Maybe the sunburn was affecting his modesty, but none the less people appreciated the difference between the cuisine of Peru and Preston.

But then it fell glassy calm. With barely two months left to get home we had to motor, and the old worries about running out of fuel returned to haunt me. J.W. summed it up in the log:

> *Steering in the light of the silvery moon*
> *Not much wind, but lemon cake and merry tune.*

Valentine messages came fluttering down into the INMARSAT from outer space as we crawled towards the magic tradewinds. Tiki growled with delight as she caught her first Atlantic flying fish, which crash-landed in the scuppers on a perfect dawn, and Bec sighted a lone white-tailed tropic bird, the first of these ethereal visitors we'd seen since leaving the South Pacific eight months before. Some eight hundred miles out of Tristan, we narrowly missed a 60ft tree, complete with roots, which must have drifted all the way across the Atlantic from South America. It was only just afloat, the best-disguised hazard we had encountered in our 501 days.

We were catching plenty of dorado and tuna now, and Igor treated us to his authentic Peruvian *cebiche*, cutting the raw fillets into small cubes or strips and marinading them in fresh lemon juice with a little salt and pepper, garlic and some finely sliced onion. If he felt we were tiring of this delicacy, he might add soy sauce, freshly grated ginger or coconut milk. But it seemed you could overdo the *cebiche*: first Andy and Bec felt sick and achy, then Marie Christine and I succumbed. The odd thing about this was that we were the four who had eaten raw fish in the Caribbean and Pacific. The other three, who had joined *English Rose* in cold waters, seemed unaffected. In the Pacific and the Caribbean we had been warned to steer clear of big fish to avoid ciguatera, a poison which builds up in large fish feeding on small contaminated fish. We wondered if we still retained traces of this poison within us and whether our illness had been triggered off by further contaminated fish.

It was getting hot now, and the cupboards were searched for the last of the Polynesian coconut suntan oil. Isso gasped whenever she saw Bruce in his shades. 'Mama! Tom Cruise! Like *Top Gun*!' We were still going so slowly that Tiki was able to spend her days peering down at a couple of striped pilot fish riding the shade under our bows. After sin-glehandedly dealing with seventy spiders in the forward heads, J.W. lost himself in his quest for weather faxes, asking to be woken any time the radio made a noise like 'a snail eating lettuce'.

In preparation for the beaches of Brazil, Igor took to developing his pecs, and even Isso joined him, pumping iron on the trembling foredeck to the beat of 'Pump It Up' and 'I Have the Power'. After my own guest appearance, we discussed 'enthusiasm', Henry Ford's vital ingredient for success. It was not something which had ruffled the waters of Igor's pond too often. 'What is it, Igor, that lifts a man above himself, just once or twice in his lifetime?' I asked.

He thought for a moment, then the famous high cheekbones lit up with a huge grin. 'Well, it's never affected me. I think it must be some kind of madness!'

At last we reached the tradewinds and we did indeed ride the fabulous gravy train we'd discussed so often since leaving Polynesia eight months before. All hands peered skyward, comparing the set of our sails with photographs and diagrams in pamphlets and books scattered about the doghouse. Even Rebecca was seen with a book entitled *More Sail Trimming*. I was impressed. Perhaps we were getting somewhere at last. But closer examination revealed that it was unread, although it did contain a few pressed flowers.

Bowling down the avenues of fluffy tradewind cloud, we settled down to eleven steady days and nights of hand-steering under the patriotic colours of our spinnaker balloon. J.W. summed up the drill:

> *Marie Christine in the morning*
> *Comes up from the doghouse, still yawning*
> *With a nice cup of tea*
> *And brief pleasantry*
> *Says: 'Right, let's put up the awning!'*

How valuable were those sunny days when family and friends who knew each other so well could glimpse a state of grace, a peace of mind earned over 500 days of paradox. I felt that my own mind had been opened during the long, quiet days and nights, grappling with the essential truths of a brief human existence. Whatever happened now, the family would be at the centre of my life. In the end I would not have to say, 'I misjudged it all,' and I asked for nothing more from the trip.

Brian Cunningham from Leg 1 raised his thought-provoking weekly fax to new heights:

Perhaps the brain has the equivalent of a laminar flow region (like water from a tap), where all the ordered information and processes are well catalogued and indexed. This is our acquired and inherited knowledge, conscious and subconscious.

Outside this region there is the equivalent of chaos, masses of unstructured, uncongealed elements of data and half-formed thoughts: a swirling mass of unstructured and unintelligible information derived from the incalculable quantities of sensory input the brain receives every second; a region of wild turbulence and disorder. Chaos.

We are only vaguely conscious of this chaotic region. Here lurk the demons of madness. Yet isn't genius on the edge of madness? What is actually happening at the boundary – at the edge of chaos? If the analogy of our example of the water flowing from the tap holds true, then at the edge of chaos there is an erratic stream of tiny whorls of disordered thought which come spinning out of chaos to penetrate the laminar region.

Are these tiny whorls the seeds of creative thought? Does inspiration heighten our awareness of them and allow us to crystalise the occasional one into a brilliant idea? For so much of our brief time on earth, we are content to exist in the secure and predictable laminar world. However, when we face the demons at the edge of chaos we can sense these tiny whorls of creative thought as they come spinning out of the blue . . .'

On Day 504, out there on the empty ocean, I had the time to read and turn this over in my mind. It seemed strangely familiar. It seemed to me that I needed to step outside myself to encounter that fourth dimension in which my own 'original ideas' were spawned. The monotonous rhythm on those 4,000 long lonely cross-country runs at Ardmore had created the chemical reaction in my brain from which ideas for the school of adventure, as well as for expeditions and books, had flowed.

Each one of us was now coming to terms with the realities of life under that artificial dome of neurotic, computerised chaos which is modern Europe, with its licences and permits, shameful surpluses and dreary unemployment; the out-of-touch, bumbling, grossly inefficient bureaucracy run by pompous, floundering professional-schoolboy politicians whose being centred on the exercise of power.

And yet . . . Rita's messages over the INMARSAT C brought the challenge of beginning the twenty-sixth year of the John Ridgway School of Adventure right on to the chart table, and with the old eagerness seeping back into my veins, I found myself looking forward to arriving home and getting to grips with the future. What interested me most was leadership. I began to think about how I could best get the idea of this across when we began the school again in May. I remembered the long years of team-building courses, with the visits to teams in coal mines, on oil rigs, in railway yards, television, computer and telecommunications companies – even the MoD and BBC TV graphics unit in London.

I'd had long discussions with J.W. on a range of subjects and a popular theme became an article from *The Times* about 'Generation X': the first to have used computers as children, and the first to have been able to take for granted the opportunity to travel abroad. They had, however, lost their trust in the things that had seemed so reliable to my own generation: marriage, education, religion, personal relationships, a career. Now, it seemed, parents couldn't be trusted to stay together; education appeared to lead nowhere. And with such a choice of warring religions, it was illogical to believe that only one could be right and the rest false. Openness about sexual abuse and date rape made it hard to trust personal relationships. Employers preferred machines to people – they neither took holidays nor went sick. Careers were no longer on offer. 'How do you educate children against cocaine when they believe in nothing?' asked Igor.

But I'd worked with many people from Generation X, both instructors at Ardmore and course students. They seemed more intelligent, healthier and more self-confident than I remember being at their age. And life goes on: leaders will always be needed.

I was returning to Ardmore, where I belonged, and where no one else had wanted to be when we first arrived. The log fires of winter would soon be over; spring would be turning to summer, unwrapping day by day like a longed-for birthday present. The house next door had been empty for fifteen years, ever since Granny Ross had died; quite soon we would be gone, too. I had to make the years count.

Experiences fall like leaves in a rainstorm, a very few sticking to the passer-by. What I had experienced over the years were glimpses of the human spirit, and I could try to pass them on. I had looked into myself and been appalled: I didn't add up to much, a lightweight, really. I had nothing to offer but that bit of spirit; the times when I had spun a second into an hour and everything had seemed possible. Ever since rowing the North Atlantic in 1966, when the two men in the other boat had died, I had known how little time there was.

We were averaging close to 150 miles each day now, and I noticed that with my more relaxed frame of mind, there was no return of the dreadful prickly heat. And I was able to exercise daily with Bruce. Based on his rowing and rugby at Newcastle University, he organised daily circuit training on the foredeck. His three sets of nine exercises used my faithful set of Heavy Hands weights and concentrated on the stomach muscles. Those fierce half-hour work-outs chased away Brian's demons of chaos and caught some of those tiny whorls of creativity as they came spinning out of a very blue sky.

Since joining us in Valdivia, Bruce had played a blinder. We were lucky to have him as chief instructor. He revelled in hard work – nothing had proved too much for him. Secretly I had wondered if the purple patch might end, if it was setting standards he might be unable to maintain. But he never faltered.

Natal featured small on our 1977 chart of Brazil. Home to a cosmopolitan mix of almost 400,000 people, its cluster of tall white skyscrapers gleamed like a space-rocket launching base against a backdrop of monotonous dull green jungle on a featureless flat coastline. We had a little trouble negotiating the reef which ran about 3 miles off the coast, but it was nothing compared with crossing the bar of the Potengi River. Fortunately, Igor was pretty handy with Portuguese and managed to persuade the skipper of a small fishing boat to help us through the rocks and into the racing brown river. Dugout canoes with single triangular sails plied the fierce current with a nonchalance that emphasised the clumsiness of our own efforts. We motored upstream, past a white hexagonal fort on a low peninsula, and anchored off a sleepy little yacht club on the outskirts of town. Then we paddled ashore to the fifth-largest country in the world. It was hard to relate Brazil to the frozen continent from which we had come.

Natal was steamy hot, but at least the south-east trades kept the air moving. The yacht club was clean and friendly but rather more social than boating, really. Igor, nearing the end of his own journey, had found Natal in the sixty-ninth edition of the *South American Handbook*, and for days he had been sending extravagant faxes to a place called the Oasis Hotel, demanding a room with a poolside view. For his part, Raul, the portly half-Swiss, half-Bolivian proprietor, had been replying with exuberant claims of luxury, always closing his own satellite communications with the greeting, 'Ship ahoy'. He met us with 'Rommel', his battered microbus, and, waving aside all question of Customs clearance, he whisked Igor and his Gold Card through the back streets to a room, which, though small, was decidedly larger than the blue pool alongside it. 'Brazil is wait, wait, wait,' cried Raul, sipping an exotic drink facilitated by the Gold Card, 'The bank was closed for four months. If you get an appointment with manager, you wait three days.'

We had come out of our way to Brazil simply to drop off Igor. We Ridgways needed diesel and a little food, but more than anything we needed to be on our way. J.W., too, was pining for home. He embarked

on a convoluted campaign to buy aquamarines for his girlfriend. I knew
Igor's Gold Card was out of date, but he would not be denied his return
to playboyhood. And for their all-night carousals, he and Raul found a
more-than-willing accomplice in quiet, steady, decent young Bruce, who
looked more dishevelled with each dawn. Canny Andy, as ever, heard
all, saw all and said nowt. Two days was long enough.

Luckily for Igor, he was delayed in Natal when we sailed for
Noronha. It was a bumpy trip: we were swimming in sweat and bucking the south-east trades for a couple of hundred miles offshore until we
found a rolly anchorage amid pale brown turtles in the lee of the island.
Igor was waiting for us, fresh off the plane and ready to party, complete
with new Gold Card, good wishes from Raul, wines and tropical fruits,
fresh CDs and a thousand photographs of Antarctica. Already he had
befriended the local police lieutenant, who put a jeep at our disposal.
Fernando do Noronha is a steamy green paradise island with golden
beaches and a startling 1,000ft-high, smooth grey volcanic plug. It is
famous for its clearwater scuba diving, but there was a strange lack of
hotels. Cruel frigate birds patrolled the bay and boobies plummeted
into the water all around as local fishermen cast ring nets over dense
shoals of small fish. Once a pirate stronghold, the lonely island lay on
the direct sailing route from South Africa to the Caribbean. But everything was run down and it had a big drug problem. Second World War
guns pointed drunkenly at the sky and the prices were the highest we
had encountered since leaving home in October 1993. As Raul had
warned, coffee was cheaper in Switzerland.

After a single day we were more than ready to go. We weighed
anchor and motored slowly in towards Igor, a solitary figure on the
breakwater. Waving sadly, we turned and headed north. Isso collapsed
in a storm of tears. Glancing back, I could see Igor standing there alone
until we passed out of sight round a headland, and I felt my old friend
knew that this was probably the end of the long South American chapter of my life.

We now had three weeks to cover the 2,500 miles across the equator
and up the middle of the Atlantic to the Azores. Leaving the south-east
trades, we struggled north through doldrum calms, squalls and thun-
derheads, all the while plagued with 'Raul's Revenge', which claimed
each of us over the following ten days or so. For a while I cut the
watches to one person so that the sick could get a good night's sleep for
the first time since we'd left South Georgia six weeks earlier. This also

provided solitude. I counted the shooting stars under a velvet tropical sky, and wondered.

From Noronha, it took us three days to reach the equator. We caught a 30lb tuna for lunch on a big red and brown muppet. Crossing into the northern hemisphere again, we toasted all those brave souls who had sailed with us over the past seventeen months. Although we missed Igor, we were all excited about going home.

REBECCA

With Igor gone, B Watch consisted of J.W. and his G-string, and me in my bootlace bikini from Barbados. We'd had fun with Igor, whose perspective on life was somewhat different from our more wary British approach. Igor dreamed big – and he had the guts, bullshit and charisma to carry it off. I'd become fond of him after our dramatic trips in Peru and his reassuring, laid-back jokes when we'd kayaked round Cape Horn three years before. And I knew he'd have died laughing if he could have seen J.W. now, clad in a small corner of the mauve and tangerine pillow case he had bought in Ushuaia.

We had been spoiled for sunbathing in the Pacific, but Bruce and J.W. had missed the tropical bit. I tried to keep out of the sun under my battered mouldy straw hat or sometimes an umbrella, while J.W., who had always covered up in the sun, even crossing to the shady side of the street to avoid it, now followed a strict regime of timed, contorted poses to get the perfect tan. He'd already burned his bum sitting for too long on the bow. To complete his new look he shaved off his beard for the first time since he was eighteen, and the rest of the crew encouraged him to pass through this gruesome metamorphosis alone, strictly out of sight, behind a sail. Our watches slipped by with discussions of design ideas, colours and fabrics and J.W.'s plan to go into production with an old sewing machine that might clunk into action in his patient girlfriend's flat. I hoped the tan would be appreciated after all his hard work.

I just could not wait to get back and see Will. I had received chocolate, a bundle of letters, Valentine cards, even a copy of *Woman's Journal* magazine – which I thought very sensible for Will until, some days later, I discovered *Muscle and Fitness* inside it. He had tried this trick before, slipping a copy into my bag as I entered a terrifyingly trendy hairdresser in Inverness to have my hair chopped before we left. I longed for these pranks and to be with him again. I just knew it would be all right.

I enjoyed the gypsy lifestyle, the wonders of the sea, the drifts of Portuguese men o'war, the stunning shades of colour on sea and sky in the moments around sunrise and sunset. Man could never produce such beauty, yet nature seemed able to do it with ease. I tried to capture the shades of colour with my camera for future inspirations in silk – maybe I could turn them into hats? But I still yearned for the land, and now I yearned for home. To sleep in a still bed, with clean white sheets; to have three showers a day if I wanted, clean hair and plenty of water to rinse away the soap; to step inside my house, with its familiar smells; to touch delicate petals. To find a cat curled up in a ball on my bed. Not to be continually worried about how much food, water, diesel, paraffin and meths was left, or to be woken at 4 am every day to go on watch.

Life as we knew it now was about to change dramatically and a new chapter would begin. People had said, 'You'll never settle down after this.' I wondered. Who wants to settle down, anyway? Isn't there always something new over the next horizon to be experienced? This journey had broadened all our worlds and shown us a way of life we'd never imagined. Perhaps our eighteen months afloat would have changed me.

Although we had seen so many extraordinary places and met fascinating people, on water I had only really felt at home in the swell-free Chilean channels, where the lurking seasickness had gone completely. The rest of the time I just did not feel quite right. I think this was the hardest thing to deal with at sea. It was as though everyday something ate away part of my enthusiasm and will to carry out even small jobs. I was dying to wake up each morning raring to go.

Isso seemed well suited to our temporary life. There was no chance of strangers turning up in her world in the middle of the ocean. She knew all of us, and fitted into the order of things. And Mum had been as gritty as ever, a tough act to follow. But I knew she longed for the land and to get digging.

Dad had done a sterling job in his organisation of the whole trip, as ever, even if I found him impossible some of the time. What father is not occasionally impossible in his child's eyes? He was more suited to life-and-death situations than to cruising along. He should have spent his life involved with war. Come to think of it, our life at home is as close as anything I've seen to battle stations.

JOHN

Close to Africa, the Southern Cross sank low in the night sky and the Plough and Pole Star commanded centre stage. The desert dawn gave a yellow light, and thin, wispy cloud bearing red dust from the Sahara transformed the rising sun into a huge red balloon which had difficulty coming unstuck from the horizon. Early on one such morning, we met the *Megabuck*, a red Norwegian tanker, coming at right angles to us, fully laden with oil from Bonny in Nigeria. Altering course to pass astern of us, the Indian officer of the watch told us she was bound for Philadelphia, but he had no time to give us a weather forecast.

On the sea, there were more and more traces of man, in the form of oil slicks and lumps of black coagulated tar, plastic and glass containers and floating garbage. But there were still turtles, dolphins, man o'war jellyfish and plenty of flying fish for Tiki to crunch on my bunk whenever she came down from her perch on the mizen boom. And one afternoon, Andy saw a huge whale jump clear of the water. The occasional lonely white-tailed tropic bird fluttered around us for a while and a brown noddy landed on Bec's head.

Our thirty-first wedding anniversary gave Marie Christine and me the chance to contemplate. Perhaps, as I had already wondered, these eighteen months of truly being with the family would turn out to be the most rewarding thing of all for me. The four of us having meals together in the doghouse, and going ashore together in exciting places. Isso and I racing through her multiplication tables – 'Better to get it over and done with, anyway, Danny,' she'd smile tolerantly as we came on watch. Her Quechua culture gave her a different slant on life from ours. 'Where's your wristwatch?' asked her mother. 'Oh, I don't know. I think it's hiding,' she'd say vaguely. The way she spoke the spirited little orphan's words when reading *Anne of Green Gables* suggested she genuinely saw herself as Anne. Marie Christine was thrilled. 'If you really learn to enjoy reading books, this whole voyage will have been worthwhile for me,' she said. But I wondered how Marie Christine and Bec really felt about the voyage. Would they rather have spent these eighteen months at home?

Would I recommend other families to undertake such a voyage as ours? The question people must ask themselves, before leaving their jobs and setting off across the far horizon in a small boat, is: is it all going to be worth it? After this trip, maybe I had some answers.

For one thing, and rather sadly in some ways, modern communications have shrunk the world, and GPS on yachts, enabling them to navigate much more easily, will soon shrink it a good deal more. There has, I feel, to be something more to it than a simple desire to see the famous places so glowingly described in old sailing books. In the 1990s, we had seen them, in the Caribbean and Polynesia, and almost without exception, they were little more than threadbare tourist traps. Local pilots and tourist guides were useful: the places they recommended were rapidly becoming the places to avoid. So it was not so much Tahiti and Bora Bora, both plumb on the annual American migratory route, that lingered in the soul, but harbours and islands well off the beaten track and far from international airports, places still accessible only by small boat, in Panama, the Tuamotus and Mangaréva.

And in the more romantic instance of an escaping couple, it's likely that one partner will believe in the dream rather more keenly than the other. The many boats we had seen for sale were evidence of the strain the commitment to sail away imposes on any relationship – graphic illustrations of wrecked dreams in the Caribbean, Panama and Polynesia.

The dash for gas continued. We never did find the north-east trades, and before long we were faxing Mercedes to see if, in an emergency, we could run the diesel engine on paraffin and 3 per cent lubricating oil. We'd used this mix for the whole of the 1977–8 Whitbread race, but that had been with a 15hp Lister engine. Mercedes' German efficiency surfaced again: 'We wish to advise that the most suitable mix would be 10 gallons of diesel with 10 gallons of paraffin . . . A marginal loss of power may be experienced, with a slight increase in exhaust smoke emitted.' What a splendid engine it was.

Ardmore was now closer than Natal. Still 600 miles short of the Azores, I wrote another dreary parable in the Log:

> More soldiers are killed on patrols to enemy lines on the way back than are ever killed on the way out. We're probably all a bit jaded from sailing without much of a break since Christmas . . . We are now approaching the difficult bit: the last 2,000 miles to home. Can we all concentrate on the three principles. All do something for the boat each day.

It got very bumpy and we all went quiet. When the seas calmed, J.W. issued a Cosmo Style Day report:

Shorts and T-shirts disappearing fast, with trousers and jumpers
taking their place.
Pareus still in evidence for the hardy few.
Jackets and waterproofs starting to be worn, while wardrobes are
searched for those winter woolies.
Bunches are in profusion, sprouting fountains of colour.
Footwear for cold tootsies: fur for those so inclined.

Then he spotted Pico, looming 7,613ft above the mist on the island of
Horta in the Azores. Everyone came on deck, eyeing the steep little
islands longingly: we all knew what the north of Scotland was like in
March, and this would be our last chance to relax for a few days in
decent weather before tackling the cold North Atlantic.

Horta didn't let us down. The sprawling old white buildings of Faial,
and its narrow cobbled streets, provided just the solid European reassurance we needed. In early spring the port was quiet and balmy, more
or less deserted. Everyone seemed to have time to speak to us. The grub
was good, and our main concern became whether we dared leave without painting our boat's name on the sea wall – legend has it that those
who don't bother soon meet with an accident. Marie Christine and Bec
bought little pots of red, white and green paint and left their own
'English Rose', in a rectangular frame on the lava blocks, just for good
luck. J.W. managed to drop his six Natal megadeal aquamarines in the
harbour, but using the scuba gear, he succeeded in recovering three of
them – only to find a letter from his girlfriend telling him the romance
was over. Oh, blimey.

In Peter Alvedo's Café Sport, overlooking the sleepy harbour, we just
sat still and let the warm feeling of security soak into our bones.

Overlooking derelict docks in far-off London, way up in the tallest
building in Europe, busy people were fanning their cards through security locks and taking their places before an armada of grey screens in the
vast open-plan office. A decision was taken: on Saturday 15 April, the
Ridgway family would be on the front cover of the *Daily Telegraph*
'Weekend' section. A photographer was tasked to trek north and snap
the moment when our dinghy crunched gravel on the Ardmore beach, no
later than Monday 10 April. Journalist Trevor Fishlock, a redoubtable
mariner and raconteur, collected his ticket and rode the smooth jet to
Faial via Lisbon. Marie Christine and I met him as he came through
Customs, a tall, curly-haired fellow, athletic but slightly rumpled, in

blue shirt and cords, clutching his own Brownie camera. We hadn't seen him since he'd covered our departure from Ardmore for the *Telegraph* eighteen months before. Gaunt from a bout of midnight oil-burning, he looked as if a spell before the mast might straighten his backbone. 'John Ridgway, as I live and breathe!' he beamed, in imitation of his mentor, John Arlott. We both liked Trevor. The same age as me, he'd been around, too: three years as the *Times* correspondent in New York, another three in Delhi and three more for the *Telegraph* in Moscow.

Coming out of the harbour, we hoisted a little sail and turned north into the chop, beam on to a stiff evening breeze. Trevor joined A Watch, making his bunk on the starboard seat in the saloon.

MARIE CHRISTINE

Now that we had Trevor with us, the pattern of our days altered, and we behaved differently towards each other. How crucial the ingredients in the mix are. The permanent team made much more of an effort. Perhaps the fact that Trevor was going to write about us made us all try that bit harder. John went into excited overdrive. He and Trevor talked non-stop for days. I felt rather sour, and Isso and I pulled faces at each other on watch while the two men jawed on. But once the initial excitement had worn off and we could all join in, it turned out to be good fun.

It was like ticking off the days before the school holidays. The degrees north were entered lovingly on the remarks page in the log. We were creeping up two or more a day, depending on wind direction and strength.

Rita's fax confirmed that Tiki would have to go into six months' quarantine. We'd expected this, but we were shocked to discover that it was going to cost £1,500. Bec and I kept a watchful eye out for her safety, but I knew John in his heart felt like us: she was part of the team, she had shown great courage and could not be abandoned now. Late one night the sneaky North Atlantic, up to its old tricks, produced a rogue wave that washed her right across the aft cockpit. Bec just managed to grab her as she was going over the side; then she carefully dried her and wrapped her up in a towel, settling her down in the doghouse. By way of thanks, Tiki, true to form, sunk her teeth into Bec's nose and there was blood everywhere. We tried to keep the cat below, but it was impossible. She especially liked it when we were up on the foredeck, and she would find a way out through the barriers of netting and canvas and join in. Not all of us were as committed to her protection. Someone wrote in the log at 4 am on 3 April: 'Storm petrel released after being caught between liferafts and galley window. Tiki very excited and tormenting SP.' Well, she was guarding us, wasn't she?

I so wanted her to reach Ardmore. I wanted her to feel the freedom she had never known in her short life, even if it was to be postponed for a further six months. She just had to survive the next few stormy days.

As indeed did we all. This area had nearly been our undoing on the outward haul, and with ferocious spring gales never far away, John was extra careful. Among the shipping lanes once more, we kept the radar on for much of the time, with foghorn and flares on the chart table. I hardly dared think of Ardmore – it seemed dangerous to tempt fate.

Coming off watch on the morning of 5 April, Day 549, I wrote excitedly: '800 miles to Ardmore.' After the distances we'd covered, it seemed like nothing. With a following wind of 5 to 6 knots, we were making a respectable 170 miles a day. In a week's time we would surely be home. It was all rain and fog now as we rolled along on grey seas piled high by a vigorous southerly airstream. About us now were the familiar birds of home – fulmars, kittiwakes, shearwaters and the parrot-faced puffins – and Atlantic white-sided dolphins barrelled along beside us.

Down below it seemed inconceivable that the life to which we had become so accustomed was shortly to end. It felt strange not having to conserve our food: unlike in Polynesia or Antarctica, wherever we fetched up now we would be able to buy basics. Nor did we need to ration our precious fresh water. Meals were more lavish than they had been for a long time. Bruce excelled with spaghetti carbonara using Azorean bacon, eggs and cheese, and J.W. battled away daily to produce the perfect sponge. I had been giving him lessons since the Antarctic and he was getting close.

Whenever there was a spare moment, Bec, Isso and I sat in a row and worked on our tapestries. Bec giggled, and called us 'the knitting Nancies'. She was frantically trying to finish a spectacle case for Rita as a small thank you. I knew I would never again have the luxury of so much free time. In the Chilean channels, as an act of faith as much as anything else, I had started on an intricate tapestry of a parrot, which I planned to make into a cushion for my mum. I had stitched through storms and calm, tropics and ice. It just had to be completed by the time we picked up the mooring in Loch a'Chadh-fi. Our instructors would be arriving at Ardmore shortly after us, and the time for sitting and waiting was all but over.

In a game of cat and mouse, the wind blew from all around the compass before it disappeared. We calculated to the last pint of diesel how long we would be able to keep the engine running. J.W.'s pencilled notes in the log worked out what time we would arrive if we maintained 5, 6 or 7 knots. Sometimes I felt so excited I could hardly breathe; the next moment I'd feel sad that this magnificent voyage was nearly finished. It had been as hard as I'd expected, sometimes harder. 'Who would greatly gain must deeply venture' – we had surely greatly gained. Together we had seen the earth, from Panama to Polynesia to Peru; the chilling brilliance of Antarctica with its wealth of wildlife. We had shared excitement and laughter; lived through fear and overcome discomfort. Compassion for each other had strengthened our family bonds. Precious Isso had triumphed. With a wisdom beyond her years, she had accepted what she had seen of her family in Peru; had understood, without bitterness, their sacrifice for her good. She was happy with us.

But it was John to whom we owed so much. He had been the architect of this adventure; he had seen us right. I thought about the lines from Tennyson's 'Ulysses', which could have been written for John – 'How dull it is to make an end. To rust unburnished, not to shine in use – and wondered how long it would be before he became restless again.

Every hour brought us nearer our goal. We rolled into the Sea of the Hebrides, with force 10 winds only a day behind us. Eagle-eyed John was first to see land, the misty island of Barra. We sped on, excitedly spotting familiar landmarks – Neish, Vaternish, Trodda – and in gathering darkness we picked up the lights of Lochinver, Stornaway and Stoer Point. The bulk of Handa Island loomed out of the night. John had sailed more than 750 times around this island, so there shouldn't be any more surprises.

I had not dared allow myself to think of this moment until it was actually happening. Shafts of watery sun pierced the chill grey April dawn as we sailed into the loch. It was 554 days and nights since we had set off, and our odyssey, with its many snares to test our watchfulness, skill, and, above all, patience, was complete. I could finally surrender to the soft, safe embrace of this gentle and most beautiful of places – home.

I hopped down the narrow hatch, grabbing at a few of my personal items – toothbrush, camera, shampoo. But nothing was vital now. The moment of arriving had changed the status of all my possessions. The meagre hoarded treats – a half-bottle of whisky stuffed under the spare jumpers that doubled as a pillow; the hidden squares of chocolate; the few faded clean clothes – lost their value at a stroke. Once I stepped ashore, faithless as a fickle lover, I would turn my back on the boat. It might be all of another seventeen years before I committed myself again; before I was prepared to take the vows required for this special order of yachtperson, forsaking privacy, comfort, space and accepting a constant undercurrent of dread.

>   *And so the story ends, the circle is complete,*
>   *Farewell to ocean waves, I have ground beneath my feet.*

JOHN

With so many plans racing through my head, I couldn't sleep. Approaching Loch Laxford just before first light, we dropped the sails for the last time, keeping a sharp eye out for the Whaleback Rock in the darkness. Once we were in the loch, I went below to pack a few things. Out of the swell it felt strangely smooth. I was touched to see that someone had cut the 'Happy' out of Bruce Reynolds' old birthday banner and stuck it between the clock and the barometer. Not a bad verdict after 554 days together.

I spun the wheel to port at 4.20 am, halfway down Laxford, with everyone on deck and Ben Stack outlined in the first pale flush of dawn. The cold water welled up from the rudder, chuckling in our wake as we curved happily into Loch a'Chadh-fi. 'Home, sweet home!' cried Isso, gazing longingly up at her bedroom window in the white croft house high on the hillside above the loch. 'All my clothesies!' Down by the shore, I saw figures framed in the light from the doorway of the bunkhouse. The wooden buildings could do with a coat of creosote, but otherwise there seemed to be no damage.

We picked up our mooring under the wood at the first attempt and I sent one final fax to Bruce and Rita in the croft house above the trees: 'Floating subunit to Base Camp: the eagle has landed. Thanksalotty.'

As we lugged our stuff up the beach, Bec said suddenly: 'Dad was right. He always is.' I'd never heard her say a thing like that before. I was rather pleased. I think it meant she enjoyed the trip. And she was thrilled that Will was arriving at any minute. Isso went racing up the hill and disappeared up to her room to have a shower, rifle through all her precious 'clothesies' and unpack all those plastic bags. Marie Christine and I walked off together to see how the giant wellingtonia trees were coming on. They were eighteen months old now – they should be fully grown in another couple of thousand years. Pinching a dark green branch, I smelled the delicious tang of rising spring sap.

In the house we took off our red ocean suits and perched on the sofas in the sitting room, the silly grins on our faces expressing a mingled sense of disbelief and triumph. 'It's only a couple of days to Norway,' someone said. 'Nothing in a giant's stride.'

Marie Christine disappeared to dig up the brooch she'd buried in the hillside in 1993. And Bec was thrilled when Will arrived for supper.

Postscript

The track that stops there is a final one.
So absolute its ending that it seems
Whatever other tracks are lesser copies of
– Paradigm of them all. The sea, the sun
Are the next stage, with nothing in between.
A quick place this to know your journey's done.

The journey, not the direction. It goes on
Beyond the wild rose and the barking dog
With a bird's rush to soar out into space:
It shows the lie the journey is, undergone,
It seems, for the direction's sake and not
The croft it sets its endless love upon.

The sea rips in between two claws of stone
Or races out, as meaning does with words.
– So, here's a statement at its seeming end.
Only who makes it knows that it has flown
Into a space where dogs need never bark
Or roses in their thorns be overblown.

'Ardmore', Norman MacCaig

JOHN, April 1996

As I sit here in the tower, exactly a year after our return, spring is coming once more. The greylag geese have returned to nest on the croft, a mother otter is playing with her young down by the shore and three red deer, like brown giraffes, come to munch the grass on the inbye land each evening. After their own adventures while we were away, out in the big wide world of Kinlochbervie, our two tabby cats, Fuega Basket and her mother, Ginger, are back in the house. Indoors they live on windowsills, fearful of Tiki from Tahiti, who arrived home from quarantine to assume the role of Blake's tyger. But, against all the odds, the blue tits are creeping into Isso's plywood nest box by the window.

Looking across the sea loch over the tumbling grey foothills leading towards the snowy Foinaven Ridge, I feel I'm stuck to the very edge of the world, so far from everywhere we've been together. This little island, which calls itself Great Britain, containing less than 1 per cent of the earth's population, seems caught in a neurotic frenzy. Yet this is where I belong.

And I ask myself again what we achieved by our journey. Was it worth the risk?

I have been getting up at three in the morning to write this story. Others have told me it's not the sort of lifestyle they'd want, but I prefer to keep along the edge.

Bec and Will are back from a winter on a sheep station near Invercargill in New Zealand. Lance and Ada never returned to live on Ardmore, and Bec and Will bought the Blue House to become the crofters at number 80 Ardmore, where our own story here began in 1964, the year we were married. They have painted the old tin house inside and out, and it looks completely different. But the memories of our own days there come flooding back whenever we visit the other side of the wood.

Our trip affected me physically and mentally. At the age of fifty-seven, it has taken me a year to recover from the lack of exercise. The running is only now returning properly, but I feel good in myself. Bruce Gardiner's circuit training has been continued on at least four days a week, and upper-body strength has steadied the weight at 15st 5lbs. The quality of fingernails and toenails is still down – we should have taken multivitamin tablets throughout the voyage. Whether tooth enamel recovers completely from the citrus fruits of Polynesia is uncertain. Mentally, I seem more concerned with dotty eternal truths now.

And I do fling open the windows on good days, and play that magnificent Polynesian music.

Precious friends we met write from far away, asking when we will step on to the magic carpet once more and sail beyond the far horizon. Arun Bose and Andy have spent the winter on *English Rose*, rebuilding the steerage, realigning the engine and fitting a new exhaust system. Proctors have built a new main boom. Norseman found that both rigging screws fitted to the foot of the forestay had indeed been stretched by the Profurl furling gear, and four of the nineteen strands of wire which make up the inner forestay were found to have broken under the wrapstop. It looks as if we should have been advised to increase the strength of both wire and rigging screws when fitting headsail furling gear. It's a good thing it didn't come tumbling down in Antarctica.

For the past thirty years my summer hobby has been the cutting of bracken, nettles, rushes and thistles, generally improving the few acres of grass which lie here among the bare rocks of the surrounding hills, in the shelter of the most northerly wood on the west coast of Britain. What began with weeks of scything has slowly progressed to pin-point work with long-handled shears on the steep pasture. Tons of lime and basic slag, fertiliser and seed have made it look 'something like' to the ragged skeins of greylag geese honking their way north, persuading them to divert and nest at Ardmore instead of continuing their long flight on to Iceland.

And now that only 1 per cent of ancient Scottish natural woodland remains, we have set about protecting the Ardmore wood from the new colonies of roe and red deer which invaded while we were away. And badgers leave Bruce and Rita's garden looking like a ploughed field and snuffle around the hundred or more trees which Marie Christine and I have planted on our croft. They are mostly giant redwoods, wellingtonia and coastal redwood, but there is a fair showing of oak, lime, chestnut and beech, as well as apples and pears, together with a few cherry and plum trees. And a few nothofagus friends from Chile. It's something we should have done thirty years ago.

> *I think I will never see,*
> *A poem lovely as a tree.*
> *Poems are written by fools like me,*
> *But only God can make a tree.*

My sneaky wife is trying to get some chickens, too, but the old magic carpet still looks inviting to me. Maybe we should sail off again . . .

And after it all, maybe the triumph is to be going into our twenty-seventh season at the adventure school with the same team who set out together on *English Rose* in October 1993.

But of course this is no fairytale. I am trying to do my usual balancing act, and worrying that Marie Christine will fall ill from working too hard: doing all the cooking, accounts and office work involved in running the business. Worrying that the money will run out and I will end up letting the others down: Bec and Will, with their sheep, goats and chickens, struggling to make a life on the other side of the wood; and Andy, who's been a good old stick over the long haul. I want to see them right.

But then, the lucky thing is to find a struggle. As Borrow put it in 'Lavengro': 'Follow your calling . . . Bound along if you can; if not, on hands and knees follow it, perish in it, if needful. But ye need not fear that . . .'

Ardmore has certainly been that calling.

Thanks

Our voyage was made possible by the goodwill and encouragement of very many people in many places and we would like to thank them:

Bruce and Rita Reynolds at Ardmore and on the Atlantic;

Andy Adamson, Will Burchnall, Jon Williams, Bruce Gardiner and Igor Asheshov;

Brian Cunningham and Richard Robinson on Leg 1, Reginald Ridgway in the Canaries, Paul Ridgway in the Caribbean, Richard and Jink Morris-Adams in the Caribbean, Val Greenhalgh in Patagonia;

Arun Bose, John Chapman, James D'Albiac, Nigel-Hunter Gordon, Heather Kirk, Tim Pilkington, Jim and Cathy Ross, James and Jackie Ross, Ian Smith;

Will Elsworth-Jones and Trevor Fishlock at the *Daily Telegraph*; Philippa Harrison and Andrew Wille at Little, Brown; Elaine Thompson at *Yachting World*;

Keith Clarke, Chris Wheddon and Vaughan Young at BT, Derek Bloom at (Batchelors) Brooke Bond Foods Ltd, David Walls at Bose (UK) Ltd, Duncan Bradshaw at Van den Berg Food Service Ltd, Brian Cunningham and Howard Ford at IBM, Andrew Pound at (Bovril and Marmite) CPC (UK) Ltd, R.H. Underwood at Micro-Mesh Engineering Ltd, John McConnell at Pentagram Ltd, Chris Jones at Norfab Products Ltd, Vincent Margiotta at Princes Foods Ltd, Kevin Lawton at Quaker Oats Ltd, James Robertson at Robertsons (Orkney) Ltd, Roy and Moira Morley at RM Electronics in Southampton, John Hunt at Rolex in London, Murray Macintyre at Simpson Lawrence Ltd, Pat Melville at (Stockans) Tod Holdings Ltd, Joseph Avilla at Sybron Chemicals Inc, Michael Thornton at Thorntons plc, Tony Dwerryhouse at John West Foods Ltd.